THE LIFE AND WORK OF HENRY ROBERTS (1803-76), ARCHITECT

The Evangelical Conscience and the Campaign for Model Housing and Healthy Nations

BY THE SAME AUTHOR

European Cities and Society. The Influence of Political Climate on Town Design. (London, 1970 and 1972)

The Victorian Celebration of Death. (Newton Abbot, 1972)

City of London Pubs. A Practical and Historical Guide. Co-author Timothy M. Richards. (Newton Abbot, 1973)

Victorian Architecture: its Practical Aspects. (Newton Abbot, 1973)

The Erosion of Oxford. (Oxford, 1977)

English Architecture: an illustrated Glossary. (Newton Abbot, 1977)

Nunhead Cemetery, London. A History of the Planning, Architecture, Landscaping and Fortunes of a Great Nineteenth-Century Cemetery. (1977)

Mausolea in Ulster. (Belfast, 1978)

Moneymore and Draperstown. The Architecture and Planning of the Ulster estates of the Drapers' Company. (Belfast, 1979)

A Celebration of Death. An introduction to some of the buildings, monuments, and settings of funerary architecture in the Western European Tradition. (London 1980)

Classical Churches in Ulster. (Belfast, 1980)

The History, Architecture, and Planning of the Estates of the Fishmongers' Company in Ulster. (Belfast, 1981)

The Egyptian Revival. An Introductory Study of a Recurring Theme in the History of Taste. (London, 1982)

Henry Roberts, aged 25. A pencil-and-wash drawing by Daniel Maclise, dated 1828. (*Collection of Mrs. J. C. Cuningham*)

The Life and Work of
HENRY ROBERTS
1803-1876

**The Evangelical Conscience and the Campaign
for Model Housing and Healthy Nations**

James Stevens Curl

PHILLIMORE

1983

Published by
PHILLIMORE & CO. LTD.
Shopwyke Hall, Chichester, Sussex

ISBN 0 85033 446 2

Printed in Great Britain by
BIDDLES LTD.
Guildford, Surrey

and bound by
THE NEWDIGATE PRESS LTD.
Dorking, Surrey

ABSTRACT

The architect Henry Roberts (1803-76) obtained his early education in the offices of Fowler and of Smirke, and at the Royal Academy Schools. In 1831 he entered the competition to design the new Fishmongers' Hall in London, which he won in the following year. He established his own successful practice, and his commissions were varied.

From 1835 he became involved in the design of buildings to house the poor, and from 1844 he was intimately connected with the Society for Improving the Condition of the Labouring Classes, a body that enjoyed the support of the Prince Consort and of Lord Shaftesbury. Roberts' designs were exemplars for a generation to follow, while his model houses for the Great Exhibition of 1851 became world-famous, and inspired changes in many countries.

Roberts was a prolific writer and a tireless advocate of housing reform. His many publications and his designs for improved dwellings were distributed throughout Europe and America, and influenced pioneers in the field of housing the poor. He was responsible for the successful campaign to abolish taxes on windows and on bricks, and was a promoter of structural innovation, patenting some ideas himself. Several of his suggested reforms became part of the machinery of public housing in Britain and in other countries.

The study describes the life and work of a talented and underestimated architect who influenced changes in attitudes to housing. It discusses the practice and connections of a successful Victorian professional man, stressing the significance of a network of influential clients, and providing detailed evidence of patronage. The relevance of the work in the historical context is to shed light on a career that was very closely bound up with real reform and with the eminent Evangelical philanthropists of the day.

CONTENTS

LIST OF PLATES
(between pages 104 and 105)

Frontispiece: Henry Roberts. A pencil-and-wash drawing by Daniel Maclise, 1828

Sources of each plate are given with the captions printed with the illustrations. Where no source is given, the photograph is by the Author or is from his collection

LIST OF TEXT FIGURES

ACKNOWLEDGEMENTS

Many people have contributed to the making of this study, which grew from post-graduate research I carried out at University College, London. First of all, I owe an immense debt of gratitude to Professor N. F. Watson and Dr. A. M. Foyle for their help, advice, constructive criticism, and encouragement. Dr. Foyle was responsible for interesting me in Henry Roberts initially, and I acknowledge with admiration his pioneering work on a neglected architect. I am also extremely grateful to Dr. Foyle for so generously making some of his notes and papers available to me for study. I must here pay tribute also to all those members of staff at the Bartlett School of Architecture, University College, London, who helped me when working on this study, especially Miss Marie Davies and Miss Madge Bridge.

I have been greatly helped by Mr. Peter Bezodis of the Director-General's Department, Greater London Council, for information from the index material of *The Survey of London.* Mr. John Sambrook very kindly helped me with Census, Death Certificates, and other matters. Father Aquinas, of St. Paul's Vicarage, Dock Street, permitted me to inspect and photograph both the church and vicarage.

Mr. James D. Galbraith, Mr. Ian Grant and Mr. George P. Mackenzie of the Scottish Record Office, H. M. General Register House, Edinburgh, have gone to extraordinary lengths to help me with the material relating to Roberts in Scotland, and I am very grateful to them for all their trouble. Miss Kitty Cruft, of the National Monuments Record in Edinburgh, has also been most kind, as have Mr. David Walker of the Historic Buildings Council in Edinburgh, and Miss Anne Riches of the Scottish Development Department. I have had courteous and prompt assistance with material in the Surrey County Record Office from Dr. D. B. Robinson, the County Archivist, from Mrs. Angela Doughty, and from Mrs. Sheila Himsworth. Mrs. M. M. Rowe, Head of the Record Services, Devon County Record Office, has been a useful source of help regarding the Kennaway papers.

Miss Hermione Hobhouse has assisted with information, as have Mr. Howard Colvin, Mr. Ralph Hyde, and Mr. John Greenacombe. The Rt. Hon. the Earl of Gainsborough was kind enough to permit me to inspect his house, and Mrs. Sharratt of Exton Park was also instrumental in helping me. Mr. Robert Nicholls of the Exton Estate office gave much of his time for which I am grateful. I acknowledge information from Lord Kinnaird in connexion with Roberts' friendship with his family. Mr. Geoffrey Steeley supported and encouraged me at the outset of the work. Professor Ben Farmer and Dr. John Warren very kindly gave every possible help, and I am extremely grateful to them for their understanding, efficiency, and great assistance. Dr. J. Mordaunt Crook supplied me with copies of his card-index for study. Mr. Robert McKinstry provided a revised and enlarged edition of Roberts' works including most of the material relating to the housing for the labouring classes.

Mr. Alan Turner, who has worked with me on several projects, very kindly came out of retirement to assist with photography, while Mr. Rodney C. Roach efficiently processed my own pictures, and copied many of the plans with speed and with skill. Mr. Harold Leach kindly helped with photographs, as did Mr. D. Russell Craig.

Mr. and Mrs. Andrew Stewart of Cumloden, Newton Stewart, were most kind, as were Mr. and Mrs. Edward Strutt of Garlieston. Dr. W. V. Wadsworth of Toft Hall Psychiatric Centre was most helpful over Roberts' work at Toft, and Mr. E. G. M. Leycester-Roxby also kindly passed on information. Mr. Charles Stewart of New Abbey was his usual kindly and hospitable self. I am also grateful to Mr. James Hunter-Blair, to Mr. R. H. Johnston-Stewart, and to Miss Helen Drew for help with the Scottish connection. Mr. G. L. E. Lindow of the Athenaeum also rendered assistance.

Mr. Thomas Hearn, Director of the Peabody Trust, kindly made the Minutes of the Society for Improving the Condition of the Labouring Classes available for study. Miss Glenise A. Matheson, Keeper of Manuscripts of the John Rylands University Library of Manchester, rendered considerable assistance, as did the Archivist of Lincolnshire County Council, the Librarian (Mr. E. G. W. Bill) of Lambeth Palace Library, and the staff of Somerset House. I am also indebted to Mr. H. L. Schollick and to Mrs. Penelope Jessel for help with Augustus Hare; to Miss Jean Kennedy, the Norfolk County Archivist; to the Rev. John Miller Scott of the Church of Scotland in Covent Garden; to Mr. Peter A. Clayton; and to Miss Dorothy Ritchie of the Local Studies Library, Nottinghamshire County Council.

I am grateful to the staff of the British Library; to the staff of the R.I.B.A. British Architectural Library; to the staff of the Guildhall Library, City of London; to Mr. P. A. Woodhead of Leicester University; to the staff of the Leicester Polytechnic Kimberlin Library; and to the staff of the Hertfordshire County Libraries and Record Office. Mrs. M. O'Docherty of the Hertford County Libraries was indefatigable in her search for material, and has my warmest thanks.

I acknowledge the Gracious Permission of Her Majesty the Queen to study documents. The assistance and kindness of Sir Robin Mackworth-Young and of the staff of the Royal Archives, Windsor Castle, in making material available for study, rendered my task most agreeable. Mr. W. K. Macfarlane, Secretary of the Diocese of Guildford, has also rendered assistance. Mr. Arthur E. Barker, Archivist and Librarian of The Society for Promoting Christian Knowledge, has been most helpful. I am also grateful to the Rev. Walter Barker, of the Church's Ministry among the Jews. Mr. Sinclair Gauldie, Miss Joan Auld, of Dundee, and Miss Trudy Prescott, of the Humanities Research Center, The University of Texas, also helped. Mr. C. A. H. James, Secretary of the Royal Commission for the Exhibition of 1851, most courteously arranged for me to see documents relating to the Model Dwellings at the Great Exhibition.

Mr. Ralph Hyde and his staff at the Guildhall Library Prints and Maps Department exceeded the requirements of duty by giving me an immense amount of time, and by making a constant flow of material relating to the Fishmongers' Company available for study. Mrs. A. Haines of The Missions to Seamen, St. Michael, Paternoster Royal, was most helpful. Mr. E. S. Earl, Clerk to the Worshipful Company of Fishmongers, kindly gave of his valuable time to show me round the Fishmongers' Hall, and I acknowledge the generous permission of the Company to quote from Dr. Priscilla Metcalf's *The Halls of the Fishmongers' Company. An Architectural History of a Riverside Site* (London and Chichester, 1977). I am also grateful to Dr. Metcalf for granting her permission.

The Librarian and Curator of the Freemasons' Hall, Mr. Haunch, has given me much help. I am also grateful to Miss Constance-Ann Parker of the Royal Academy of Arts, and to Mr. F. H. Thompson and to Mr. John Hopkins of the Society of Antiquaries of London for valuable information. Mr. J. S. Skidmore of the Royal Society of Arts has also been extremely helpful. I acknowledge the generous assistance given by Miss L. M. A. Rose of Huntingdon County Record Office, and the courtesy and help of Col. David Smith, Bursar of Kimbolton School. Mr. Peter St. B. Green and Mr. Peter Fisher have also been most kind. Mr. N. E. Turner of Messrs. Clayton, Leach, Sims & Co. endeavoured to put me in touch with survivors of the families who benefited from the Wills of Roberts and his daughter. Mrs. S. Joyce Soutter very kindly sent me information relating to the late Frederick Albert Roberts and his family in response to my advertisement in *The Daily Telegraph*. I am also grateful to the Rev. Geoffrey Curtis, Vicar of Grayswood in Surrey, to Mrs. Cornwall, and to Miss Stella Frend, for information and for giving up so much time to aid me. It was Miss Frend who was responsible for putting me in touch with Mrs. J. C. Cuningham, F. A. Roberts' great-niece. Mrs. Cuningham most kindly allowed me to see the family possessions, among them the portraits and other mementoes. I am also grateful to the Rev. J. C. Cuningham, to Mr. M. C. Cuningham, and to Mr. and Mrs. J. Cuningham.

Mr. S. G. Harlock provided me with information about the schools in Sidmouth. Mrs. Hilary Chambers of Cheshire Record Office kindly helped with information about Toft Hall. My thanks also go to Mrs. Margaret De Motte, Sub-Librarian, Local History Library, Central Library, Manchester; to the County Archivist, Kent County Council; and to Mr. C. E. Busson, Librarian of the Ramsgate Public Library. I also acknowledge the help given to me in connexion with the Norbiton Parsonage and Schools by the Vicar of St. Peter's Church, Norbiton, and by Mr. C. G. Walmsley.

Many others have influenced me, helped to shape the project, stimulated ideas, or given leads in one way or another. I must pay tribute to my former teachers, Mr. William Murray and Mr. Ferguson Sprott, who did so much to shape my thoughts in the early days of my studies. I owe an especial debt to Mr. James Warwick, who initially helped me practically in my youthful architectural studies, and who remained an ally and friend through several years. Herr Arthur Korn was one of the first to interest me in working-class housing when he was my tutor between 1963 and 1965, while Mr. Patrick Shiel and Mr. John Minett also stimulated my interest some years ago. Heer Jan Tanghe, Professor Peter Breitling, and Professor John Nelson Tarn all discussed 19th-century housing with me, while the late Mr. James Lomax-Simpson (who designed much of Port Sunlight) was most informative on the political and artistic climate of the 19th century. The late Professor H. J. Dyos also discussed the historical background with me, and I very much regret that his untimely death prevented his commenting further as my work proceeded. Dr. Helen Rosenau was generous and informative about Utopian visions. Professor John Nelson Tarn very kindly lent me one of his photographic negatives, and permitted me to quote from his own work, for which I am very grateful.

I owe a very considerable debt of gratitude to Madame E. Eschbach, Bibliothécaire of the Société Industrielle de Mulhouse, who arranged for many documents to be photographed and photocopied. Madame Eschbach was also extremely helpful when I visited the library in Mulhouse, and assisted me with sources, documents, and books. Her courtesy, efficiency and efforts went far to help me, and my study has been considerably enriched by the material she put at my disposal. My thanks are also due to Miss Judith Allan, Reference Librarian at the Australian High Commission, London. I am also grateful to Mr. Ward J. Childs, Archivist III of the Department of Records, City of Philadelphia. Mr. J. H. Love, Principal Archivist of the State Library of South Australia, also provided useful information with great courtesy. Thanks are also due to Mr. P. L. Kennedy, Parish Archivist of the Parish of St. Giles, Camberwell, for assistance. The Archivist of Mill Hill School went to considerable trouble to seek out information for me.

There have been others, too numerous to name, who have helped in one way or another, and I hope that a general note of my appreciation will suffice. However, I would like to mention in particular the assistance I have had from Mr. Stephen Heywood, Mr. John Pollock, Miss E. Plincke, the Rev. F. A. Skinner, Mrs. K. P. Woodgate, Miss J. Mauldon, Mr. Richard Brown, and Mr. P. J. Hollingsworth. My late father, Mr. George Stevens Curl, told me much about London housing in the first decades of this century. I very much regret that he did not live to see my work on the subject take shape. My mother very kindly provided hospitality, and accompanied me when I was searching for traces of Roberts' work on the Duke of Manchester's estates in Ireland. I am also grateful to Mr. Stanley Carter, of the *Colet Arms* in Stepney, who kindly put me in touch with a number of people living in philanthropic dwellings in that rich and fascinating part of London's East End.

I am extremely grateful to Mrs. Marguerite Johnston, who typed the work from an unseemly manuscript, and who heroically went over all the ground again when I had altered the typescripts and made many additions and changes. The final version of the text was typed by J. J. Neal of Leicester. My daughters, the Misses Astrid and Ingrid Curl, my wife, Dr. Eileen E. Blackstock, and Mr. Jonathan Taylor helped me to check and correct the proofs, and gave up many hours of their time to do so: I am indebted to them, and to all others who so generously assisted me.

JAMES STEVENS CURL
Leicester, London, Mulhouse,
Oxford and Winchester, 1978-83

The blessings bestowed on us by the Almighty can only be realised in proportion to the help which we are prepared to render to each other

Albert, Prince Consort
Quoted by Henry Roberts in his
On the Essential of a Healthy Dwelling,
given at the Institute of British
Architects on 20 January 1862

INTRODUCTION

A moment's reflection must show that the highest achievements of architecture are accomplished through the instrumentality of the working classes, whose skill and persevering industry conduce as much to the fame of the Architect as the steady valour of the soldier does to weave the crown of victory around the brow of his triumphant General.

Henry Roberts: *On the Dwellings of the Labouring Classes*. London, 1867, p.1.

THE LITERATURE that deals with the events, ideas, and personalities of the nineteenth century grows each year. The astonishing achievements of the period have aroused both the hostility and the admiration of commentators. Unlike previous centuries, the Victorian age was documented officially, well, and comprehensively, and offers an enormous quarry from which historians may fashion their studies.

The nineteenth century was an age of unparalleled expansion. It brought in its wake problems on a scale with which society found great difficulty in coping. Change and reform were effected all too often in response to disasters such as epidemics, or by fear of contagion from the unknown. The tremendous social problems caused by the Agrarian and Industrial Revolutions have stimulated many studies, and there have been specialised and thorough examinations of Victorian philanthropy. The growth of working-class housing in England has been admirably chronicled by Professor John Nelson Tarn in his *Five Per Cent Philanthropy. An account of housing in urban areas between 1840 and 1914*,[1] and there have been studies of urban growth and of the phenomenon of the Victorian city.[2] There are also several studies of individual nineteenth-century architects and engineers,[3] and no doubt many more books dealing with the lives and works of those responsible for the design and construction of the fabric of Victorian cities will be written.

Great reformers, such as the Prince Consort, Wilberforce, Lord Shaftesbury, Chadwick, and many others, have attracted their champions.[4] It is odd that a man who was in the forefront of the design and development of philanthropic housing, and who was himself a great reformer, a prolific writer, a much sought-after lecturer, an associate of Shaftesbury, of the Prince Consort, and of other illustrious Victorians, a successful architect with several distinguished buildings to his credit, and a large aristocratic *clientèle*, has so far not attracted the attention he deserves,[5] and is not mentioned in standard biographies of those eminent Victorians. Even in recent works by historians of the nineteenth century, Henry Roberts receives scant attention, although he was intimately involved with many organisations that involved Shaftesbury, the Prince, and many other great personages. Roberts was an architect, a professional to his fingertips, who worked tirelessly for the reform of housing for the masses, despite having a constitution that was not particularly strong, and despite

1

having a character that was sensitive and somewhat susceptible when adversely criticised. Henry Roberts was unquestionably a talented, inventive, imaginative, innovative, and even brilliant architect. He was favoured by his pecuniary circumstances, and by a disposition that seems to have been very much in tune with his times. He was fortunate in that he had been a pupil of two of the most able architects of the previous generation, Fowler and Smirke, and had an encouraging start as a student. He was able to undertake a lengthy tour of Europe, during which he not only became familiar with the great works of architecture, but saw early experiments in Italy to alleviate the lot of the poor.

Fortune did not desert the young architect on his return to London, for he set up his own practice, and won the first premium in the competition for the best designs for one of the most important buildings in the City of London, the new Hall for the Worshipful Company of Fishmongers, when he was still in his twenties. Soon afterwards, Roberts designed the first of his buildings for the poor, the Destitute Sailors' Asylum in Whitechapel, and became actively interested in the plight of the less fortunate members of society.

When Roberts was starting out in his career, many towns were growing, and problems grew with them. No observant, intelligent man could fail to notice that there were too many people in towns who had no access to the basic requirements of space, light, clean air, pure water, privacy, and good drainage. Roberts was certainly keenly aware that all was not well with the urban multitudes, and, unlike the vast majority of his professional contemporaries, was deeply concerned about the magnitude of the problem. There is no doubt that the complacency and lack of interest shown by the architectural profession was also true of society as a whole, for that society was rigidly stratified, and one layer was scarcely aware of the conditions of the layer above or below. That complacency was only fractured by disasters, such as the epidemics of cholera, typhus, and typhoid, that broke out with great ferocity in the 1830s. Although the unsavoury poor districts suffered most from cholera and from the other diseases, the epidemics were not contained within the ghettoes. Cholera especially did not respect boundaries, and the middle classes suffered too. Prince Albert himself was to die in 1861[6] partly as a result of the bad sanitation in the royal residences, and it began to be seen that the breeding-grounds for disease could export their contagion to the homes of the better-off. The death-tolls from cholera were such that action became necessary, and the first moves to cleanse the cities tentatively began.

The main problem with the fabric of towns was that often property intended for one family had to accommodate many lodgers. The manufacturing centres demanded labour, and thus well-defined ghettoes of workers were created in evil-smelling courts, in big houses that had been deserted by their middle-class owners, and in houses that were conveniently placed near the factories. Classical notions of the town as an agreeable, civilised place were no longer true, for the manufacturing districts were squalid and ugly, unhealthy and hideous, mean and uncultured. It was little wonder that the Englishman's dream of the house in the country began to take shape, despite the fact that most of the town-dwellers in the 1830s and 40s were countrymen who were escaping from the insanitary hovels in rural districts.[7] By the 1840s many towns were places where poverty, ill-health, disease, filth, squalor, poor drainage, inadequate

water supplies, and hopelessness were common. Human spirits and bodies became
undernourished and stunted, and death came soon to the inhabitants.[8] The problems
caused by large numbers of people settling in towns and in districts intended for a
much smaller population were great. When cholera and other epidemics took their toll
in the 1830s, at a time when political reform and the fear of revolution were very much
in the air, the realisation that action was necessary to improve the conditions of the
labouring classes first dawned on society. The stirrings of a feeling of guilt about the
treatment of the working classes began to be felt, not only because of fears of
Chartism or of revolt, but because of the rise of an Evangelical Christianity that
encouraged the first effective signs of concern for the welfare of the poor.

The wealthy and the upper-middle classes managed to segregate themselves further
from the masses and from the squalor by moving out to the new and healthy suburbs.
An idyllic residential area was available to those who could afford it. Yet much literature of the period savagely attacked the squalor and degradation in which the poorer
members of society lived, and the horror of so much poverty, as revealed by Dickens,
undoubtedly helped to change the climate of opinion in the country in favour of some
positive action to improve matters. Yet it was generally true that architects and their
clients failed to perceive the problems or to attempt to grapple with solutions. Eclectic
and romantic villas in the latest styles were all very well, but aesthetics and good design
were denied the multitudes. One of the first professionals to understand this was
Henry Roberts, and it was his skill and imagination that were to create the first outstanding examples of modern design and planning for the working classes. There was
an insatiable demand for a lot of accommodation on a minimum of land near the
places of work, but the price the working classes could afford to pay was pitiably
small. Roberts realised this, and designed a block of flats on an urban site that was
noble, dignified, and superbly planned. His working-class housing in country districts
was architecturally excellent, and, where land values were low, exploited the possibilities of good design and of refined detail.

All of Roberts' designs for working-class housing were produced in the period after
Edwin Chadwick had been appointed Secretary to the Poor Law Board in 1834. This
appointment was probably the most important event in the history of nineteenth-
century sanitary reform, apart from its direct cause, the cholera epidemics. The latter
were so serious that the Poor Law Board was approached to study the conditions in
towns following the epidemics of 1837 and 1838. In the 1830s and 1840s, public
health became a great political issue, and Chadwick and his Board began investigations
that had no precedent in scope or in scale.

The appearance of the findings of the Poor Law Board's *Report*[9] was a milestone in
the history of urban sanitation. Not only was it a comprehensive and thorough document, based on information provided by the Boards of Guardians all over the country,
but, by its very thoroughness and impeccably researched facts, it told of a state of
things in Britain that was profoundly shocking. It proved what enlightened persons had
been saying about conditions. The *Report* described the foul air, the poor drainage,
and the lack of wholesome water, and was critical of the piecemeal planning and poor
architecture of so many working-class districts. Even where tenements had been built
by building clubs, they were 'frequently the subject of complaint as being the least

substantial and the most destitute of proper accommodation'.[10] The *Report* emphasised the importance of some system of philanthropic housing, organised on a communal basis, and derived from exemplars, as providing the best possibilities for improvements in health and in social conditions. Significantly, Edwin Chadwick had been greatly influenced by Jeremy Bentham and by other radical thinkers of the day in the first decades of the century.[11] Bentham, with his ideas for a Panopticon, and other schemes, was not uninfluenced by some of the Utopian theorists of France,[12] while Chadwick noted that certain experiments in the provision of model housing had already taken place in Scotland, at the Owenite foundation of New Lanark, at Cupar in Fife, and at Catrine in Ayrshire.[13]

The subject of nineteenth-century theories and experiments in working-class housing is enormous, and is beyond the scope of this study. However, Henry Roberts was fully aware of most of those theories and experiments. He knew most of the important figures in the movement to improve the dwellings of the labouring classes; he was influenced by some of the early theorists, and influenced many of the later practitioners; and he contributed enormously to the literature and to the architectural vocabulary of working-class housing. The architect Sydney Smirke (1797–1877), the younger brother of Sir Robert Smirke (1780–1867), Roberts' mentor, was a friend of Henry Roberts. Sydney Smirke proposed the radical idea that model dwellings should be built in the suburbs, with fifty or sixty rooms, all well ventilated and heated, fireproof, well drained, and supplied with good water.[14] The great Thomas Cubitt contributed to the *Report* by suggesting that legislation should ensure that speculative dwellings were not built outside towns where the buildings would be of little use, as the working classes needed to be near their places of work. Chadwick recommended in his *Report* that builders should be obliged to submit their plans to local authorities for approval in order to ensure that coherent schemes and policies would result. In other words, he was trying to achieve something nearly like modern town-planning legislation. The *Report* emphasised the necessity of setting up administrative machinery to ensure that drainage, water supply, reasonable standards, and good planning replaced the anarchy prevalent at the time. The benefits of a scientific approach and of rational constructional solutions were stressed. The influence of the ideas of Bentham was very real in this epoch-making *Report*.

Although 1842 saw the publication of the *Report*, the year is generally remembered historically for massive unemployment, for economic recession, and for general shortages caused by poor harvests. The Chartists were active in demanding better conditions, notably in housing, under Feargus O'Connor,[15] and certain enactments were passed to improve conditions in the mines and factories, largely through the efforts of Lord Ashley, a leading Evangelical Church of England Tory who was to play an important *rôle* in the history of housing reform and in the life of Henry Roberts.

The great *Report* by Chadwick and his colleagues was viewed by many members of the Establishment as biased and dangerous, but it was filled with such an overwhelming weight of documented evidence that it could hardly be shelved. The state of affairs it revealed was so shocking that a Royal Commission on the Health of Towns was established in 1843 in order to examine the findings of the *Report*. This Commission was very thorough in its researches, and it probed the evidence of the medical profession and of building surveyors. No doubt to the discomfiture of many, the Commission, far from being critical of the *Report*, not only corroborated what Chadwick had already found, but added further evidence to suggest that conditions were truly dreadful. Public administration was incompetent; legal requirements to provide drains and water supply had not been complied with; and overcrowding and filth were endemic. The final *Report* of the Royal Commission appeared in 1845, and contained recommendations to control the widths of streets, the amounts of open space required, building standards, and building regulations generally. The Commission suggested that local authorities should be enabled to raise funds to buy property for improvement, but it was more concerned with the enforcement and stiffening of the existing administrative machinery than with more radical reforms. It avoided, for example, an outright denunciation of back-to-back housing, or of cellar-dwellings, because any attempts to close cellars or back-to-backs would have made the problems of overcrowding elsewhere even worse. However, both Chadwick's *Report* and that of the Royal Commission revealed officially that all was not well. The system of *laissez-faire* had not created conditions that were humane, and indeed had ensured the poor lived in revolting circumstances that were a threat to the health of towns as a whole. Furthermore, both *Reports* indicated that radical public-health measures were imperative in order that everyone should not suffer from the threat of contagion.

Henry Roberts had seen urban poverty in Naples and in other places while on his Continental tour in 1829,[16] and he noted the attempts which were being made to improve matters. In England he was acutely aware of urban and rural poverty, and he was deeply involved in a growing concern for the welfare of the masses that became notable in the 1830s and 1840s. The Evangelical Conscience (that developed as a reaction to eighteenth-century spiritual sloth and hatred for 'Enthusiasm', and in spite of the climate of *laissez-faire*) began to stir men of good will to positive action, and the first individual attempts were made to come to the aid of the masses of men, women, and children whose deplorable conditions were so vividly described in the *Reports* of the Poor Law Board and of the Royal Commission on the Health of Towns. Roberts had concerned himself with the alleviation of acute poverty early in his career while designing the Destitute Sailors' Asylum in Whitechapel in 1835, and he became associated with the Evangelical Christian bodies that were involved in bringing gleams of humanity to the deprived poor of the cities. Many of these bodies had a solid aristocratic backing of Evangelical Christians in the van of whom was Lord Ashley.

As reference will be made throughout this study to the Evangelical movement, some clarification of the term seems appropriate here. The Anglican Communion is defined in standard encyclopaedic works as a fellowship within the One Holy Catholic and Apostolic Church of those constituted Dioceses, Provinces, or Regional Churches in communion with the See of Canterbury. The Anglo-Catholics within the Church of England insist upon the 'Catholic' character of the Anglican Church, and regard the Church of England as being in full continuity with the pre-Reformation Church *in* England, with no historical or apostolic break. There was a High-Church Party in England in the seventeenth century that included many notable divines, including Laud himself and Curl of Winchester,[17] and this Party did much to restore the dignity of the liturgy before the Civil War virtually eliminated all ancient practices with the victory of puritanism. The Oxford Movement, in the early years of the reign of King William IV, set out to revive the almost lost belief in that historic continuity of the institutions and liturgy of the Church of England. Secularism and religious expediency were well advanced when, in 1833, ten Church of Ireland (the Anglican Established Church in the Sister Kingdom) bishoprics were suppressed,[18] and, as a result, John Keble began his campaign against what he called 'National Apostasy'. In the same year the first of the *Tracts for the Times* was published. These *Tracts* consisted of a series of arguments that dealt with the historic bases of ecclesiastical doctrine, principle, and practices within the national Church. The distinguished authors of the *Tracts* were chiefly John Henry Newman, Keble himself, E. B. Pusey, Isaac Williams, and R. H. Froude. Newman's famous *Tract 90* was unacceptable to the Evangelical or 'Low-Church' branch of the Church of England, and so great were the animosities within the Church that there were several secessions to the Roman Catholic Church in 1845. Many divines found that the historic break with Rome under Henry Tudor savoured more of political expediency than of ecclesiastical purification. The Evangelicals, or Low-Church Party, regarded the Tractarians, as they became known, as 'Romanists', or certainly as suspiciously near the 'Papist' position, and were reinforced in their suspicions when so many went over to Rome as a result of examining their logical position and that of the national Church. The Evangelicals eschewed ritual, and even the symbol of the Cross was viewed with distaste as 'Papist', a state of affairs that will be familiar to those who know the Church of Ireland today, where crosses on altars are rare and crucifixes are virtually unknown. Matters were exacerbated further when more secessions to Rome occurred in 1850 as a result of the judgement in the infamous Gorham case. George Cornelius Gorham (1787–1857)[19] was an Anglican divine whose Evangelical views caused him to be examined in 1847–8 by Bishop Phillpotts of Exeter (a High Churchman) on the difficult doctrine of Holy Baptism. The Bishop decided that Gorham's doctrinal position was suspect, if not unsound, and refused to institute him to the benefice of Bramford Speke, a living that had been presented to Gorham by Cottenham. Gorham appealed to the Arches Court of Canterbury, where judgement went against him in 1849. In 1850, however, Gorham (clearly well advised in political matters) appealed again to the Judicial Committee of the Privy Council, which decided in the same year that his view that in 'no case is regeneration in baptism unconditional' was tenable within the Church of England. This judgement, and the arguments from 1847 to 1850, caused great anguish among the members of the High-Church, Ritualist, Anglo-Catholic, Tractarian Party, and many High Churchmen went over to Rome, while several Evangelicals (equally disgusted with what appeared to be a secular judgement in ecclesiastical affairs) also left the Church, but became Dissenters.

The Oxford Movement, comprised of persons otherwise known variously (and usually pejoratively) as the Puseyites, Tractarians, and Ritualists, emphasised the study of theology and of ecclesiastical history, and encouraged a full understanding and revival of the ancient liturgy. This, of course, would require an adequate architectural setting to be truly convincing, so the Cambridge Camden Society (founded in 1839 by J. M. Neale and Benjamin Webb) sought to carry the aims of the Tractarians into architecture by reforming church design and by reviving a ritual that would need a suitable architectural framework, with all fittings and furniture. The main object of the Society was to promote the study of 'Ecclesiastical Architecture and Antiquities' and to restore 'mutilated Architectural remains'. The Society began to publish its hugely influential monthly paper, *The Ecclesiologist*, in 1841, a journal that became the mouthpiece of the Gothic Revivalists, and the chief arbiter of taste in considerations of architectural correctness in churches. Very quickly it became apparent that woe betide any architect who failed to come up to scratch in the pages of *The Ecclesiologist*.

Architectural criticism in the paper became more and more shrill, and adverse notices in *The Ecclesiologist* became very damaging professionally, as Henry Roberts was to learn later.[20] If a church were not built in a 'correct manner', with all the approved trappings of Ecclesiology, then its designer was torn to shreds in the pages of the magazine. If a church were not 'arranged' for the full 'Catholick' ritual, then it was denounced with venom and violence.[21] Classical buildings, needless to say, were ignored in its pages. *The Ecclesiologist* became the guardian of Tractarian principles in church architecture, and ensured a triumph for the 'correct' architectural notions of church-building, as laid down by the Society. It was small wonder that churches built without chancels, or as mere preaching-boxes for congregations of the Evangelical persuasion, were damned absolutely and finally. Roberts himself was to suffer greatly from the criticisms in *The Ecclesiologist* of his churches of St Paul, Whitechapel, and St Matthew, Nottingham, and he was not by any means the only architect whose essays in the Gothic taste were so lambasted by the critics that no reputation could survive.

The Tractarian parochial clergy achieved great success in bringing Christianity, literacy, and morality to the slums of London and of the industrial towns, but, although they were evangelists in one sense, they were not Evangelicals in the usage of ecclesiastical history. Yet other forces besides those of Ritualism developed in the course of the nineteenth century to contribute to the civilising of urban man. In 1811 the National Society was founded, a body that perhaps did more for the education of the poor than all the other educational organisations put together until the State took over responsibility for teaching (a responsibility that we, in the closing decades of the twentieth century, might regard with some apprehension). In 1818 a *Church Building Act* was passed in order to bring religious instruction to a rapidly expanding population, and in 1836 the Ecclesiastical Commissioners were established, a body that became responsible for the management of church property.

A new spirit, Evangelical in nature, began to grow up before the rise of Tractarianism, and indeed continued to develop parallel to the growth of the High Church Party, although the latter held a monopoly as arbiters of taste in matters of ecclesiastical architecture. This renewed Evangelism was largely led by Charles Kingsley and by F. D. Maurice. The aim of the Evangelicals was the social teaching of the Gospel, and Ashley Cooper (later Lords Ashley and Shaftesbury), as an ardent Evangelical layman, was in the forefront of those groups that worked for the amelioration of the condition of the working classes as a direct result of their Evangelical faith. The Evangelicals could be described as the Protestants within the Anglican Church.

Spiritual torpor was *de rigueur* in eighteenth-century England until John and Charles Wesley and George Whitefield made their influence felt. Yet the Augustan sensibilities

of the Georgians were disturbed by the 'Enthusiasm' of the Wesleyites almost as much
as those of the Evangelicals were to be upset by the Ritualism of the following century.
The torpor could not co-exist with Wesleyite fervour, and so a separation from the
Anglican Church of the group known as Methodists became inevitable, to the sorrow
of the Wesleys, let it be said. *Within* the Church of England itself (as opposed to the
Methodists), the Evangelical Revival (where long sermons, Sabbatarianism, hymn-
singing, moral earnestness, a puritan outlook, and a Protestant approach to religion
were characteristics) depended more on Whitefield's Calvinism and Sabbatarianism
than on Wesley's Arminianism,[22] and so tended, oddly, to be more severe, Protestant,
and puritanical than Methodism. The Evangelicals were undoubtedly aided in their
success by xenophobia and by fear of Revolutionary excess (as practised in France
from 1789 until the end of the Terror, and again in 1830 and in 1848), and so teaching
by example, by temperance, by moderation, by observing 'The Sabbath' (meaning
Sunday), and by Good Works, was emphasised. The xenophobic aspects of the
Evangelical movement also encouraged insular attitudes, national inward-looking, and
unpleasant jingoism. Charles Simeon and Daniel Wilson led a campaign to improve
clerical piety, (doubtless necessary when considering the average Georgian parson),
and there can be no questioning of the colossal impact the Evangelicals had on the
tone of nineteenth-century society. However, the Evangelical movement lacked
coherence in upholding the historical ecclesiastical principles of the seventeenth-
century divines (such as Laud and Curl), and, like many of the Dissenting sects, it had
a serious flaw (to High Churchmen) in that it depended excessively on the personality
of charismatic preachers rather than on tradition, on the legitimacy of Apostolic
Succession, and on the catholicity of ritual. Nevertheless, the Evangelical Movement
within the Church of England, led initially at Cambridge by Simeon and Isaac Milner,
and at Clapham by the Venns, Thorntons, and Wilberforce, achieved a great deal in
the reform of abuses. It was in the vanguard of the promotion of Sunday Observance,
although this cause is unfashionable today. It did much to educate the masses, to lobby
opinion in favour of more humane laws: it was the prime force in the abolition of
slavery; in the setting up of legal frameworks for the control of conditions in factories,
mines, and prisons; and in the first attempts to ameliorate the physical condition of
the labouring classes. The Evangelicals were opposed to Ritualism and to Ecclesiology,
and at times their lack of historical awareness put them almost within the camp
of the growing number of Dissenting sects. Ashley himself was closely
associated with a number of influential Dissenting clergymen, including the
Milleniarists, and his views veered towards Nonconformity on many matters. The
Queen was of a distinctly Evangelical persuasion, as was her Consort, and was suspicious of the Tractarians, especially after the Gorham case, when many divines went
over to Rome.[23]

Benevolent paternalism may sound pejorative in the language of today, but had it
not been for the high-mindedness of an aristocracy and of an upper-middle class
(both of whom were predominantly of the Evangelical persuasion), conditions in
Victorian Britain might have been infinitely worse, and the social consequences been
more terrible than they were. The Evangelical Conscience probably did more to alter
the national consciousness of England than has been realised hitherto, and while

there are opinions current that would deplore what that Evangelical Conscience did to the nation, there can be no question that it was of immense importance.

It was in a climate of religious revival and of moral earnestness, and at a time when the horrific truth of the conditions of the poor was being officially admitted, that Henry Roberts began his work in the field of philanthropic housing. Various societies had been set up, including the Health of Towns Association of 1844, and the Association for Promoting Cleanliness among the Poor: the former to improve drains, water-supply, construction, ventilation, and illumination of dwellings; and the latter to establish public baths and wash-houses. *The Builder* magazine was founded in 1842, and in 1843 the architect George Godwin became editor. Under his crusading leadership, *The Builder* became a clearing-house for all sorts of information on urban and sanitary reforms, from housing to cemeteries.[24] *The Builder* constantly exposed horrific conditions and sanitary scandals, and publicised new ideas and advanced designs. Through Godwin, who knew Roberts, but who does not appear to have been a friend, as Godwin was more radical and less religiously inclined, the condition of the labouring classes was constantly before the readership, and for forty years *The Builder* was a great force for reform and an invaluable source of information.[25] This study has drawn heavily on the journal, where ideas were aired, horrors were revealed, and reforms were advocated.

Cholera, typhoid, famine, economic difficulties, and the revelation of the miserable conditions of a large part of the population could hardly fail to affect the outlook of a young, successful, religious man, who was educated, travelled, and, it seems, of independent means. Henry Roberts had designed and built one of the most distinguished buildings of the Greek Revival in the City of London at London Bridge in the first half of the 1830s. The Gothic Collegiate School at Camberwell followed in 1834, and in the next year Roberts became involved in the design of buildings associated with the Destitute Sailors' Asylum in Well Street, Whitechapel.[26] Various commissions followed, mostly for houses, for church alterations and for new churches, and for several works for aristocratic clients, all of whom were of the Evangelical persuasion. Roberts' next work was the joint terminus for the Croydon, Brighton, and South Eastern Railway Companies at London Bridge. In 1844, following a period as a successful architect, with a wide range of clients, Roberts became a founder-member and later Honorary Architect to one of the first of the exemplary housing societies that grew out of the climate of opinion created in the wake of the revelations of the great *Reports*: the Society for Improving the Condition of the Labouring Classes had acquired its driving force and dominant ideologue. This Society set out to show the possibilities for housing the poor, and, by publishing designs and by building Model Dwellings, provided examples for others to follow. The amount of built exemplars bore little relation to the enormous impact the Society had on subsequent developments all over Europe. The S.I.C.L.C. was a pioneer of a new type of housing: it showed the way towards a future where the poor would be decently and hygienically housed. All the original designs of the Society were produced by Henry Roberts, who was also the executive architect for all the built exemplars. Not only were Roberts' designs remarkably advanced, but they became models for generations of designs for working-class housing. The sheets of his designs published by the S.I.C.L.C.

were sold to developers all over the country and world (*see* Figures and Plates), and thus buildings by Roberts, or derived from designs by him, are found over a wide geographical area. He was responsible for the repeal of Window Tax and of the tax on bricks and on other materials. He was a tireless pamphleteer, lecturer, proselytiser, and propagandist. He carried his Evangelical zeal to practical conclusions. His ideas became disseminated over many countries and in many societies. His work was known throughout the civilised world, and his plans influenced architects wherever there were problems of housing the poor. His Model Houses for Families erected by H.R.H. Prince Albert at the Great Exhibition of 1851 became world-famous, and were the exemplars for countless experimental dwellings. As the author of many books and pamphlets Roberts had an immense influence, and many of his prophecies and ideas became enshrined in legislation long after his death.

Henry Roberts not only provided the exemplars for a new type of mass-housing. He was to a very large extent responsible for a change of attitude that might be described as a new climate of social awareness. Ultimately, that maturing of responsibility helped to create a new atmosphere so that State intervention in public housing became acceptable. This study will trace the career of Henry Roberts, will describe his works, both written and architectural, and will discuss his main influences on his own time and on subsequent periods.

Chapter 1

AN OUTLINE OF
THE CAREER OF HENRY ROBERTS

... the Victorian architect, if he were a man of any ability or enterprise, was well able to make a living without maintaining that connection with the building trade which had been the chief resource of so many of his Georgian predecessors. Churches, prisons, town halls, bridges, warehouses and factories were going up apace ..., while country houses and suburban villas continued to provide rich commissions for the domestic architect.

Howard Colvin, *A Biographical Dictionary of British Architects 1600–1840*, London, 1978, p.39.

HENRY ROBERTS (1803–76) was born a British subject in Philadelphia, Pennsylvania, in the United States of America,[1] on 16 April 1803.[2] According to the Royal Academy Schools Register, he was aged twenty-two on 28 November 1825 (when he entered the Schools on the recommendation of Robert Smirke), and, according to the 1851 Census, he was forty-seven on 30 March 1851.[3] His mother may have been an American, and there are what appear to be occasional Americanisms in some of Roberts' own prose. His father was Josiah Roberts, whose address was 4, Gould Square from 1806, but the *Directories* fail to indicate residence in London in 1802, so presumably the family was in the United States at that time. In 1819 Josiah Roberts' address was Fen Court, Fenchurch Street, and by 1822 he also had an address at 10, Camberwell Terrace, a house that the family appears to have occupied until 1847, and that is given as Henry Roberts' address in the Royal Academy Schools Register.

Josiah Roberts was born in 1773.[4] He appears to have had long business connections with the United States of America, for Frederick Albert Roberts' great-niece, Mrs. J. C. Cuningham (formerly Miss Ethel Mary Dixon), owned, in 1979, an invitation to Josiah Roberts to attend a Ball on 22 February 1798 'in honour of the Birth of George Washington'. As the invitation to Josiah Roberts was to him only, it would appear that he was not then married, and may have found his wife among Pennsylvania society. It does seem clear, however, that he spent quite some time residing in the United States in the closing years of the eighteenth and the early years of the nineteenth century.[5] According to information provided by the Department of Records, City of Philadelphia,[6] Josiah Roberts was a merchant with an address at 212, South Third Street, Philadelphia, in the year between 1802 and 1803, and it was presumably there that Henry Roberts, the second son of Josiah Roberts, was born.

Mr. and Mrs. Josiah Roberts and their children set out for England in 1804 or 1805, and seem to have remained there while the children grew up. In the second decade of the nineteenth century, probably around 1812, Josiah Roberts and his wife had

11

silhouettes made of themselves and their three sons, Charles, Henry (Plate 2), and Frederick.[7] In 1828 Daniel Maclise made exquisite pencil-and-wash individual drawings of Josiah, of Mrs. Roberts (Plate 1), of the boys Charles and Henry (Plate 3 and Frontispiece), and of the two daughters (Plate 4), one of whom was called Mary or Maria.[8] There may have been a drawing made of Frederick Roberts, but this does not appear to have survived. They were a handsome family: Josiah at forty-five was going bald, and was slender and finely made; Mrs. Roberts was a kindly-looking woman, with a humourous face; Charles was heavily built, and was a handsome young man with a pleasant, open face; the two girls were very pretty. Henry Roberts was very like his father in appearance, with refined, sensitive features. As a young man of twenty-five he was almost delicately beautiful, with a long nose turned up at the end, and a long, thoughtful, wistful face (Frontispiece). To judge from the surviving silhouettes, made when they were children, Henry seems to have been very like his brother Frederick in appearance, for Frederick had the same upturned nose, had a similar shape of head, and was of similar build.[9] The family seems to have been well-off, and appears to have been on friendly terms with the distinguished artist, Daniel Maclise, who was to produce a portrait in oils of Josiah Roberts in 1828 or 1829.[10]

According to Hodder,[11] Josiah Roberts succeeded George Fife Angas as a South Australian Colonisation Commissioner late in 1835. He was a Commissioner until 1840. The Commission was disbanded in 1842 when the functions were taken over by the South Australian Division of the Colonial Land and Emigration Board.[12] The Roberts family was closely connected with the colony from its foundation until the early years of the present century.[13]

Josiah Roberts died on 18 November 1846 at Camberwell Terrace, aged seventy-three. The cause of his death, according to the Death Certificate, was 'Natural decay and old age.'[14] A Maria Johnson (presumably one of Josiah's daughters) was present at the death. Some letters from Henry Roberts to his brother Frederick (who was at Frankfurt at the time) demonstrate a tender devotion and concern for his father in his last illness. In 1979 these letters survived in the possession of the family.[15] Josiah Roberts either disposed of most of his estate before his death, or had fallen on hard times, for the May 1847 Administrations at the Public Record Office reveal that on 8 May Administration of the Goods, Chattels, and Credits of 'Josiah Roberts late of Camberwell in the County of Surrey Gentleman & widower deceased was granted to Charles Roberts one of the natural and lawful Children having been first sworn duly to administer.' The sum mentioned was two hundred pounds.[16]

Henry Roberts' brother, Charles (later of St John's Wood, London), was a broker, dealing in spices, saltpetre, and drugs, and set up his office at 110, Fenchurch Street in 1826. Charles Roberts had various addresses in the City until 1860, and, when his brother won the Fishmongers' Hall Competition, his office was at Jefferys Square, St Mary Axe.[17] Charles Roberts was the father of Frederick Albert Roberts, of Grayswood, Haslemere, Surrey (born 23 May 1848, died 9 October 1938).[18] F. A. Roberts is mentioned as a beneficiary in the Wills of both Henry Roberts and of Henry's daughter, Theodora Amélie Roberts.[19] F. A. Roberts was a Director of the Equitable Reversionary Interest Society, and kept the Australian connections established by his grandfather alive, as he was an Auditor of the South Australia Chartered

Company.[20] Both Henry Roberts and his daughter, Theodora Amélie, had financial interests in the Equitable Reversionary Interest Society.[21] As will be mentioned later in this study, F. A. Roberts appears to have been the last surviving close relative of Henry Roberts, and he was to obtain several of the architect's personal possessions. Many family portraits and mementoes passed to F. A. Roberts' great-niece, Mrs. J. C. Cuningham, who has kindly made these available to the Author for study. Charles Roberts (Henry's brother and F. A. Roberts' father) lived in Hamilton Terrace, St John's Wood, adjacent to a house occupied by the Clayton family. The Claytons also had interests in the Equitable Reversionary Interest Society, were closely associated with developments in Australia, and were friends of Henry Roberts. Charles Roberts, like his brothers, was an inventor, and there are several medals won by him in the collection of the Cuningham family. All in all, the children of Josiah Roberts appear to have been attractive and accomplished.

It has not been possible to ascertain where Henry Roberts received his education, but in 1818, at the age of fifteen, he was articled to Charles Fowler, who had recently established his own architectural practice. Fowler was born in Cullompton, in Devon, in 1792. He served his apprenticeship with John Powning of Exeter, and paid off his articles in 1814. He set up in practice with David Laing, and took on Roberts and J. M. Allen as pupils. Fowler had a good grasp of structure, and undoubtedly had a formative influence on young Henry Roberts. From the 1820s Fowler had a sound reputation as an architect and as an expert in structural technique. He retired in 1852 and died at Marlow in 1867.[22] Roberts spent seven years with Fowler, who was a sensitive and talented architect.

While in Fowler's office, Roberts would have been familiar with the Courts of Bankruptcy, Basinghall Street, that were erected between 1818 and 1821 to Fowler's designs.[23] Other works produced in Fowler's office during Roberts' stay there included the new market at Gravesend in Kent of 1818-22;[24] Teffond Evias Church, Wiltshire, of 1824-6;[25] Totnes Bridge, Devon, of 1826-8;[26] St Paul's Church, Kilburn, of 1826;[27] and alterations at Syon House, Isleworth, for the third Duke of Northumberland of 1819-30.[28] Other schemes with which Roberts would have been acquainted were Covent Garden Market of 1828-30, and several designs for the west country, including No. 14, The Close, Exeter; the Corn Market at Tavistock; the Lower Market at Exeter; and further proposals. Roberts may have worked on the renovation of Syon House during 1819-25, although the conservatory (which, with Covent Garden Market, made Fowler's reputation), designed for the third Duke of Northumberland, dates from 1827-30. During Roberts' period in Fowler's office, the older man was preparing an entry for the London Bridge Competition, which would doubtless have familiarised young Roberts with the site of the Fishmongers' Hall. Fowler won first premium in the competition in 1822, but he did not build the structure, as his designs were set aside in favour of those by John Rennie, an experience that Roberts was to remember in later years when he himself won the first premium in connection with the competition to design the new Hall for the Fishmongers' Company.

Roberts must have been a quick and able pupil, and a draughtsman of some distinction, even in those early days, for in 1824 he won two medals in a competition organised by the Society of Arts.[29] One drawing was of a free re-interpretation of a

Corinthian capital, the rendering being in a sepia wash. The other drawing was of 'a bridge adapted to the purpose and site of London Bridge'. Roberts was awarded second prize in the competition and was given the Large Silver Medal of the Society. Unfortunately, these drawings have not survived. The bridge design was like a triumphal arch.[30]

Roberts also participated in the limited competition to design new buildings for Mill Hill School in 1824. From minutes in the Governors' Minute Book of May 1824, it appears that designs were invited from six architects. The six were William (later Sir William) Tite (1798-1873), J. Field, W. Brooke, J. Griffith (presumably John Griffith of Finsbury who designed the chapels and other buildings at the General Cemetery of All Souls at Kensal Green),[31] W. Ford, and Henry Roberts. At first glance it would seem surprising that a young man of twenty-one should be selected, but an acquaintance with the personalities associated with the School demonstrates that he was chosen through his Evangelical connections. The Protestant Dissenters' Grammar School at Mill Hill, Hendon, was founded in 1807 for the purposes of affording a first-rate liberal education to the sons of gentlemen who were debarred by the ecclesiastical arrangements of other large public schools from sending their children thither. The Roberts and Clayton families appear to have had intimate connections with this School, and no doubt a good word was put in for young Henry. In the event, Brooke failed to finish on time, and Tite's plans were awarded first prize in November 1824. Tite (who had been a pupil of David Laing) was appointed architect in February 1825, and the new buildings in the Greek Revival style were opened in June 1827.[32] The Rev. John Clayton, who occupied a high position in the Congregational body, and who had been a member of the Countess of Huntingdon's Connexion, was selected to give the inaugural address. John Clayton's son, the Rev. William Clayton, became Chaplain to the School and pastor of the village church on 16 May 1831. According to the Rev. Thomas W. Aveling, in his *Memorials of the Clayton Family*, published in London in 1867, the Claytons were closely involved with the London Missionary Society, and the Rev. John Clayton Junior was Joint Secretary of the Society, a body that maintained close links with affiliated Evangelical churches in St Petersburg. The Rev. John Clayton Senior was a member of the Eclectic Society, as was Baptist Noel, and had been minister of the King's Weighhouse Chapel, Eastcheap, where the Roberts family were members of the congregation. Old Clayton (1754-1843) was known to the Venns, to the Thorntons, and to Wilberforce at Clapham, and indeed Jacob Thornton persuaded him to preach to the convicts in the Woolwich Prison Hulks. The Claytons were closely associated with the Missions to Seamen. Apart from the influential links with the Countess of Huntingdon's Connexion and with the Clapham Sect, the Claytons were also known to the Giles family, who were friends of young Roberts. When the Rev. William Clayton was inaugurated at Mill Hill School, there was a strong Camberwell contingent in the audience. Like Baptist Noel and the Venns, the Claytons were closely associated with fashionable congregations of the day.

In 1825 Roberts joined the progressive office of Robert Smirke (1780-1867) who was to be knighted in 1832. Smirke was a powerful influence on Roberts, and the two men appear to have got on well.[33] During Roberts' stay with Smirke several works were carried out in the office, including alterations to Millbank Penitentiary of

1824-8;[34] alterations to the Inner Temple;[35] alterations to Somerset House;[36] the Royal College of Physicians, and the Union Club, Trafalgar Square (now Canada House);[37] the British Museum;[38] the General Post Office;[39] the Custom House;[40] the Equitable Assurance Company's office, Bridge Street, Blackfriars;[41] London Bridge approaches, including the street façades to King William Street and Borough High Street;[42] King's College, Strand;[43] the County Courts, Lincoln;[44] the Council House and shops, Bristol;[45] the Sessions House, Maidstone;[46] and the Infirmary at Shrewsbury.[47]

Thanks to the influence of Smirke, Roberts entered the Royal Academy Schools on 28 November 1825,[48] and thus, by the time the young man set off on his Continental tour, he was thoroughly familiar with new public buildings, with current architectural practice and taste, and with the leaders of the profession at the time. Roberts was certainly in Italy in 1829,[49] and may have started his travels in that year, or in 1828, in which he he sat for the pencil-and-wash drawing by Daniel Maclise (Frontispiece). He developed an enduring love for Italy, and was to be fortunate enough to live there after 1853. Perhaps his visit to Naples in 1829 was the most important part of his tour, for while there he became aware of the dreadful poverty and overcrowding, and he was especially impressed by the *Albergo di Poveri*, or *Reclusorio*, begun by King Charles III in 1751 from a design by Fuga. The building was designed to contain 2,600 inmates in six storeys, the upper floor being used as workshops for weaving, shoemaking, and tailoring. It was one of Roberts' first tastes of philanthropic housing,[50] and may have had a very great influence on his subsequent career, especially the concept of communal planning.

Roberts was back in England by 1830, and appears to have obtained several architectural commissions, none of which can now be identified. His first office was at 23, Suffolk Street, in the heart of a part of London that had been transformed by Nash, Wilkins, Smirke, and Burton. It was from the office in Suffolk Street that he was to submit his successful entry for the Fishmongers' Hall Competition at the end of 1831.

If there were any buildings of note by Roberts before the Fishmongers' Hall, they have proved elusive, although he himself mentions that he had under his direction 'Several practical works' in 1830. Roberts' great opportunity came with the winning of the competition to design the Fishmongers' Hall in 1832, and this enabled him to take on a young pupil, George (later Sir George) Gilbert Scott, in the same year. Scott described the older man as his 'very excellent friend, Mr. Henry Roberts, who had recently obtained by competition the appointment of architect to the new Fishmongers' Hall, at the foot of new London Bridge'.[51] Scott went on to say that 'Mr. Roberts had, subsequently to his original period of pupilage, been for a considerable time in the office of Sir Robert Smirke, whose tastes, habits, modes of construction, and the method of making working drawings, he had thoroughly imbibed. He had subsequently made the lengthy continental tour customary in those days, and had not, I think, very long been in practice since his return. He was of independent circumstances, and was a gentlemanly, religious, precise, and quiet man. I was the only clerk in the office at the time, though he subsequently took a pupil, so that I had the advantages of making all the working drawings of this considerable public building,[52] from the foundation to the finish; and of helping in measuring up the extras and omissions, as well as of constantly seeing the work during its progress.'[53]

Scott's engagement with Roberts lasted for two years, and though 'Beneficial' to the younger man, it 'seemed almost a blank' in his memory, 'from its even and uneventful character.'[54] During this period, Scott attended a course of Sir John Soane's lectures at the Royal Academy, which Roberts had also heard.

In 1834 Roberts gave Scott the job of Clerk of Works to 'a small work at Camberwell' (actually the Collegiate School at Camberwell), a Gothic building completed in 1835 that was demolished in 1867,[55] which Scott 'superintended throughout its erection.' The construction was 'very rapid, and was completed in the autumn of the same year.'[56] Scott's conscience told him that his work at Camberwell was 'more beneficial' to himself 'than to the building'. The Camberwell School at Camberwell Grove cost £3,600. It was constructed of the then fashionable white bricks with stone dressings, and its style was 'strictly collegiate'.[57] It was founded under the patronage of the Bishop of Winchester 'on the principles of the King's College'.[58] The cloistered entrance was one of the more agreeable features of the design. The building contained a large school-room, capable of subdivision into three compartments, a library, and three other classrooms. The school later went bankrupt, and was subsequently demolished.

Roberts was probably appointed architect of the school through his Camberwell connections,[59] and the headmaster, J. A. Giles, was clearly a friend, for he was one of Roberts' proposers for election as a Fellow of the Society of Antiquaries of London in 1838.[60] The School was a symmetrical composition that consisted of a tall element (in a somewhat thin Early English manner) that contained the school-room. There was a central bell-cote on the ridge of the roof. The tall central rectangular hall was illuminated by paired lancets at clerestorey level, and by single lancets at the back of a five-bay arcade (in the Perpendicular style) that formed the centrepiece of the design. The arcade was stopped at either end by symmetrically placed single-storey wings illuminated by three-light windows with flat hood-moulds (Plate 16).

In 1834 Roberts became the recipient of a bronze medal, the Soane Medallion, which is still in the possession of his heirs. In the following year, while still working on the Fishmongers' Hall, Roberts was producing drawings for the London and Croydon Railway Company.[61] In that year, he became honorary architect to the Destitute Sailors' Asylum in Well Street where a Sailors' Home that was to be the forerunner of many model lodging-houses had only just been opened.[62] Roberts' introduction to the Destitute Sailors' Asylum marked a turning-point in his career. He appears to have been introduced to the Asylum through the London City Mission, which was supported by his friend Baptist Wriothesley Noel (1798–1873). Roberts was a subscriber to the Mission, and doubtless became interested in the lot of the poor even further as a result of his contact with Noel, one of the most popular Evangelical preachers of his day.

Baptist Wriothesley Noel was born in Scotland, the sixteenth child and eleventh son of Sir Gerard Noel-Noel, Bart. He became minister of St John's Chapel, Bedford Row, in 1827, where the Thorntons, Wilberforce, and Zachary Macaulay were members of the congregation. They and other influential members of the Clapham Sect were impressed by Noel, who seems to have become acquainted with Roberts in or before 1835. Noel was a leader among Evangelical churchmen. In 1835 he addressed a letter to the Bishop of London on the spiritual condition of the metropolis. Both home and foreign missions enjoyed his aid, and in 1840 he carried out an inquiry into the condition of schools in towns. Like Roberts, whom he clearly greatly influenced, he was deeply concerned with both the physical and moral welfare of the poor. He was opposed to the Corn Laws, and gradually became more radical and dissenting in his views. In 1846 he helped to found the Evangelical Alliance. As a result of the Gorham case (explained in the Introduction), which drove some High Churchmen to Rome in 1847–50, Noel moved further in the Evangelical and opposite direction, and announced his conversion to the Baptist cause. As a Baptist minister, he attacked the union of Church and State, and became yet more outspoken in his opinions. In 1849 Noel was publicly re-baptised by immersion. He vigorously supported the North during the Civil War in America. He was the author of *A Plea for the Poor*.[63] His brother, Gerard Thomas Noel, was married to Susan, daughter of Sir John Kennaway, Bart, of Devon. Kennaway became a client of Henry Roberts. The eldest brother of Baptist Noel became first Earl of Gainsborough, was a friend of Wilberforce, and was a client of Roberts.[64]

Doubtless the memory of the *Albergo di Poveri* in Naples was still fresh when Roberts designed the Asylum, but the commission was important as a precedent. Here was a young, successful architect, with a major building being completed in the City, and with excellent connections, working on an obscure building in London's East End. The Asylum was to be the prototype of several lodging-houses he was to design in the next decade, and marked his first venture into the field of designing buildings for the poor. Roberts himself acknowledged the debt he owed to the plan of the Sailors' Home, also in Well Street, only a few yards to the north of the Asylum. According to a footnote in Roberts' *The Dwellings of the Labouring Classes*, revised edition, of 1867, the Sailors' Home 'must in some respects be considered the prototype of the improved lodging-houses. It was opened in 1835; and the cost of fitting up the last dormitory was defrayed at the sole expense of her lamented Majesty the Queen Dowager, a munificent patroness of the Labouring Classes' Improvement Society'. This 'admirable establishment' lodged 300 inmates, and was, with the Destitute Sailors' Asylum in the same street, 'a monument of the self-denying and devoted energy of the late Captain R. J. Elliott, R.N.' Roberts explained that as the Asylum offered an example of how to suggest 'arrangements suitable for a class below that of ordinary labourers, and not within the range of the designs carried out by the Society for Improving the Condition of the Labouring Classes, such as Ragged-school boys, or nightly lodgers, known as trampers', plans of it were reproduced in the Appendix of his book. He also noted that a second floor could be added to 'provide for the nightly separation of the sexes in a caravansary lodging-house, a description of building much needed in all our towns, and even in many villages', so great were the numbers of poor itinerant labourers abroad at the time.

The Destitute Sailors' Asylum is a two-storey building, seven windows wide, with a stucco front banded to resemble ashlar (Plate 17, Figure 1). There was a Mess-Room on the ground floor, with an office and kitchen, and the first floor contained a

ELEVATION.

PLAN OF DORMITORY FLOOR.

The open Roof extends over the Superintendent's Apartments, and is ventilated at each end.   With an additional Story this building would accommodate with berths 150 persons.

PLAN OF GROUND FLOOR.

The Yard contains arrangements for Washing, and a Stove for Drying and Purifying Clothes. with a Bath and other requisite conveniences.

Fig. 1.   The plans and elevation of the Asylum for Destitute Sailors, in Ensign Street, formerly Well Street, Whitechapel, London.

dormitory and a flat for the Superintendent. This lodging-house in a part of London that was unknown to fashionable society, marked a significant point in Roberts' career. He was to design more buildings contiguous to this site, apparently through his friend-ship with the Rev. Baptist Wriothesley Noel, who was rapidly making a name for himself as an Evangelical preacher within the Church of England, and through Captain R. J. Elliott, R.N., a friend of Noel. Captain R. J. Elliott, R.N., who died on 30 April 1849 aged 59, was closely involved with the Episcopal Floating Church Society. He was the chief benefactor of the Destitute Sailors' Asylum and of the Sailors' Home in the same street. He had the Commander's out-pension of Greenwich Hospital conferred on him. He had served with distinction in the Napoleonic Wars. *The Sailors' Magazine* for 1846 says of him that by 'his untiring exertions for a series of years he succeeded in awakening an interest in favour of seamen, and, undaunted by opposition, or cold indifference, or by the scoffing and ridicule with which he was frequently assailed, with a singleness of purpose unexampled, and by the incessant devotion of his time, talents, and purse, he at length established the Sailors' Home and Floating Chapel, and was mainly instrumental in setting on foot the building of the Seamens' Church'. In the event, the Asylum was opened on 23 December 1835.

This building, and his association with Noel, were to be of extraordinary importance in moulding the architectural career of Henry Roberts. Noel's work with the London City Mission was to bring Roberts' name before many influential people who were of the Evangelical persuasion. The design for the Fishmongers' Hall had established Roberts with members of the Company, and with Whig elements working for reform; and it had also rendered him acceptable to the Tory Establishment through Sir Robert Smirke. Now his friendship with Noel (who was to officiate at Roberts' marriage to Catherine de Swetschine on 15 April 1847)[65] was not only to bring him to the atten-tion of persons in whom the Evangelical Conscience was strong, but was to open all sorts of doors to aristocratic patronage. Baptist Noel himself was a member of the Noel family, Viscounts Campden, and Earls of Gainsborough.[66] 'Baptist' and 'Wriothesley' were names favoured by the Noel family, many of whom are buried in Chipping Campden in Gloucestershire, and in Exton in Rutland.[67]

By 1835 Roberts was well established. He became a founder-member of the Institute of British Architects in that year, by which time he had already been in occupation of his offices at 18, Adam Street, Adelphi for some three years. This address appears on his beautiful drawings for The Glebe House at Southborough, Kent, for which the contract was signed in May. The contract and drawings survive in the Drawings Collec-tion of the R.I.B.A. The design shows a house of two storeys over a basement, with accommodation in the roof-space. In the basement were the usual offices of kitchen, scullery, and store-rooms. The ground-floor accommodation consisted of a vestibule, a spacious hall and staircase, a library (with built-in bookcases), a drawing-room, and a dining-room. On the first floor were three large and one small bedrooms (all with fireplaces), a water-closet, and a store-room. The attic-floor had three rooms with fireplaces, a housekeeper's closet, and a store. The roof was covered with slates, with a lead flat in the centre (Plates 18–23).

The style of The Glebe House owed something to the Greek Revival, for the architraves were all slightly battered, like those of the Fishmongers' Hall and of the vicarage of St Paul, Dock Street, Whitechapel. The architraves were joined by a plinth at ground-floor level, and by a string-course at the first floor. Part of the entrance front projected forwards, so that the wide overhanging eaves was interrupted by a pediment in which was a semicircular-headed light. A similar projection with pediment was arranged on the garden front, with a three-sided canted bay at basement- and ground-floor levels. The composition was therefore asymmetrical. All windows were of the sash type, and the front door had four panels, with a rectangular fanlight over. Chimneys had modillioned cornices and Egyptian pots. The coach-house and stable block was severe and simple, with a loft.

The Glebe House does not appear to exist today. The drawings are signed by John Martin (a carpenter and joiner from Tunbridge Wells) and by Henry Barrett (a brick and tile maker also from Tunbridge Wells).[68] These appear to be contract drawings. The precise location of The Glebe House has also been lost, and there is no sign of the name on old Ordnance Survey maps. The directories of the last century have also been unfruitful regarding the location of the house.

The only connection it has been possible to establish between Roberts and Southborough is that in the neighbouring parish of Bidborough the Rector from 1829 until 1846 was the Rev. William Gay, a staunch Evangelical, who died in Camberwell on 11 November 1846 aged 53. Roberts' nephew was a Charles Gay Roberts, and the Gays (the family confirms) were closely related to Roberts as well as having connections with the Venns and with the Clapham Sect. One of the patrons of Bidborough was another Evangelical named Chippindale of Tonbridge, who was a brother-in-law of Gay. The latter, however was presented with the living of Bidborough by Charles Elliott, another Evangelical, and brother-in-law of one of the Thornton family of Clapham. It would therefore appear that Roberts had close family and religious ties with the Southborough area. The house known as 'Wyatts', Rectory Drive, Bidborough, designed by James Wyatt in 1790, was the Rectory for 167 years, and stands next to Glebe land. The old Rectory has gable windows and details identical to those on Roberts' drawings, so The Glebe House may have been intended for the Glebe lands at Bidborough.

According to information kindly provided by the Kent County Library and by the Rector of Bidborough, Henry Chippindale lived at Bidborough, and his name occurs in the 1841 and 1851 Census returns. From the order in the Census, Chippindale lived close to the Rectory. It was probably for Chippindale, therefore, that Roberts designed the Glebe House. From the details of the 'Wyatts', it would appear that Henry Roberts also carried out substantial alterations to the Rectory in a style matching that of the Glebe House.

In 1837 (the year in which he was elected a Fellow of the Institute of British Architects) Roberts added the north aisle and north chapel (Plates 24–25) to the church of St Peter at Yoxford in Suffolk[69] in the Gothic style. These additions were altered again later, by a different hand. It has not been possible to establish definitely why Roberts was appointed to design the works at Yoxford (although the Stradbroke family was influential in the affairs of the parish and was later to play an active part in the Society for Improving the Condition of the Labouring Classes), but it is reasonable to speculate that his friendship with the Rev. Baptist Wriothesley Noel, the well-connected and successful Anglican clergyman, was a probable source of his introduction to such work.

Much more likely than either of these speculations, however, is the possibility that Roberts got the commission immediately as a result of the institution of Samuel Thomas Roberts to the living of Yoxford (that had become vacant by the cession of Henry William Rous Birch) on the presentation of Sir John Forbes, Bart., on 23 February 1837. The precise relationship of Samuel Thomas Roberts to the architect has not been discovered, but it would appear that this was a commission through family connections. The north aisle of Yoxford Church contains mural monuments to the Clayton family, including James Clayton (*ob.* 1861). Francis Stephen Clayton was Roberts' solicitor, and Francis Hare Clayton was a beneficiary of the will of F. A. Roberts, Henry's nephew. The two families were close friends. In the same aisle is a mural tablet to the Davy family, including Eleazar Davy (*ob.* 1803), High Sheriff of the County of Suffolk, and David Elisha Davy (*ob.* 1851). Eleazar married Frances Anne, daughter of the Irish peer, Lord Carbery. Roberts' second daughter was baptised Lydia Anastasie Davy, so clearly there were strong family ties with the parish of Yoxford (a fact confirmed by Mrs. J. C. Cuningham to the Author in 1979). The Davy family was very Evangelical in persuasion, as the names would suggest. In a letter by S. T. Roberts to the Incorporated Society for Promoting the Enlargement, Building, and Repairing of Churches and Chapels, dated 3 April 1837, Henry Roberts is referred to as a 'first-rate Architect from London' whose services were acquired '*at the cost of a Friend*'.

In 1837 the church, constructed of brick, flint, freestone, and mortar, consisted of a nave, a south aisle and a chancel. There were galleries to the west and south. Roberts' new work was constructed of flint, with brick and stone dressings. There is a north door, and three two-light Perpendicular windows with bar tracery and four lights over. There is a three-light window to the west. The elegant piers are octagonal, and there is a low segmental arch between the north chapel and the north aisle.

Roberts appears to have reset the mural monuments, having carefully taken them down from the original north wall. Among these monuments is that to Robert Henry Cooper (*ob.* 1851) of Rust Hall, Tunbridge Wells, and Yoxford. The Coopers were related by marriage to Henry Roberts, and F. A. Roberts (Henry's nephew) left money in his Will to a Cooper.

In the following year Roberts exhibited a design for the Grosvenor Square Chapel in Manchester at the Royal Academy. The exact wording of the *Catalogue* for 1838 is 'No. 1195. Original design for Grosvenor Square Chapel, now erecting'. Roberts may have made his Manchester connections through Sir Robert Smirke, who had designed the church of St Philip at Salford in 1822, or possibly through Francis Goodwin (1784-1835) whose designs for the old Manchester Town Hall and Assembly Rooms of 1822-5 have certain stylistic similarities to Roberts' final entry for the Fishmongers' Hall competition, especially in the details of the east elevation.[70] However, the chapel does not appear to have stood for long, for it was replaced by Grosvenor Square Presbyterian Church, the foundation-stone of which was laid in 1849. The architects for this ungainly classical building were Starkey and Cuffley, of Manchester. The title of Roberts' building was apparently the Scotch Presbyterian Reformed (or

Covenanting) Church, Grosvenor Square, Chorlton-on-Medlock. It seems that Roberts had fairly close association with the Presbyterians, for he was to design the Scotch National Church at Covent Garden and Wigtown Church in Scotland. Once more, Evangelical fervour appears to have stood him in good stead with his clerical clients.

Between 1838 and 1840 Roberts had two important commissions through his Evangelical connections. There were Escot (or Escott) House, rebuilt for Sir John Kennaway, Bart, in 1838, and the Escot Church, of 1839–40, for the same client. The design drawings for Escot House (a foursquare structure in the classical style, of yellow brick with stucco dressings) survive in Devon County Record Office [71] (Plates 26–28). A drawing of 'Escott House, Devonshire for Sir John Kennaway, Bart.' was exhibited at the Royal Academy in 1838. The *Catalogue* for that year numbers Roberts' exhibit as 1222. The simple rectangular building (of two main storeys, a basement, and a roof-storey) stands on a podium. The main rooms are on the *piano nobile* level, and the entrance gives access to a formally planned central staircase. The house has several pronounced Greek Revival elements, and the proportions display a refinement reminiscent of the Fishmongers' Hall. The interiors have distinguished Grecian detailing, and the fireplace surrounds are identical to some of those in the Fishmongers' Hall (Plates 28–30).

Escot Church was built as the Chapel of SS Philip and James in the Parish of Ottery St Mary, Devon. It is within the grounds of the House. It is in the Early English style of architecture, and is constructed of coursed rubble with freestone dressings (Plate 31). It consists of an aisleless nave, a chancel, and a porch and vestry. There is a bell-cote at the west end, crowning the gable. The nave is four bays long, and is illuminated by lancets. Three lancets pierce the west end, and the chancel east window has two lights and a quatrefoil light over. The chancel has Decorated vaulting. The Gothic mural tablet to the Kennaways may have been designed by Roberts. SS Philip and James was consecrated on 1 May 1840.

The bell-cote at the west end was a solution arrived at after Sir John Kennaway had objected to the 'small campanile' which Roberts had originally proposed. Roberts was at a loss to know where to place the bell, and Kennaway did not want a tower.

As stated previously Kennaway was of the Evangelical persuasion, and had a son who was to become a leading philanthropist and supporter of Evangelism. Once more Roberts' introduction to his client was probably through Baptist Noel, although there may also have been Devonian connections through Charles Fowler, who had been Roberts' mentor, and who was himself from Cullompton. Fowler rebuilt Bickleigh Church for Sir Ralph Lopes, Bart, in 1838,[72] and designed two lodges for the same client at Maristow House, Devon.[73] It is not beyond the bounds of possibility that Fowler may have introduced his former pupil to Kennaway, or at least put in a good word for him among the Devon gentry.

However, the most likely connection with Kennaway was through the Noels. Baptist Noel's brother, Gerard Thomas Noel, took as his second wife in 1841, Susan, daughter of the first Sir John Kennaway. Charles Edward Kennaway, second son of Sir John, was vicar of Chipping Campden, and was married to Emma, daughter of the Hon. Gerard Noel. The Gainsboroughs were patrons of the living at Chipping Campden. Sir John Kennaway, the second Baronet (1797–1873), was Sheriff of Devon, and shared an enthusiasm for Evangelical Christianity, and for reform, with his son, with the Noels, and with Roberts. There was thus a strong family connection between these important people in Roberts' life.

It was probably through Kennaway, through Fowler, or possibly through his great friend Arthur Kinnaird, that Roberts was commissioned to design a house at Alphington, near Exeter, for Samuel Trehawke Kekewich, M.P. for South Devon from 1858, and Sheriff of Devon in 1834. Kekewich (1796–1873) died at Peamore, the house which Roberts had designed (Plate 37). The precise date of Peamore has proved elusive, and documentary evidence appears to have been destroyed. Peamore is a large house, gabled in the late-Jacobean or early-Carolean manner of the seventeenth century, with flat hood-moulds and classical Georgian sash-windows. Although it has been altered and converted into flats, it possesses one interior by Roberts: the library. This room, now divided, has exquisite classical decorations and a fine marble fire-surround similar to designs in the Fishmongers' Hall, at Escot, and at Toft Hall in Cheshire (Plate 53).

Titled clients seem to have flocked to Roberts, for in 1839–40 he produced designs for minor alterations at Claydon House, Buckinghamshire, for Sir Harry Verney, Bart. These drawings survive among many other papers at Claydon, but are only for insignificant changes. Again there was a connection with Baptist Noel, for Sir Harry Verney, Bart, M.P., married Georgiana, daughter of the eighth Baron Kinnaird whose family was closely connected with the Gainsboroughs. Arthur Fitzgerald Kinnaird was a friend of Roberts, and was to be best man at the architect's wedding in 1847.[74]

In 1840 Roberts joined the Athenaeum Club, and was to remain a member until his death. Doubtless he made many prominent contacts there. Between 1840 and 1841 Roberts produced designs for the rebuilding of Elvetham Church near Hartley Wintney, Hampshire, for the third Lord Calthorpe (Plate 32). Drawings by Roberts for this building, the Church of St Mary at Elvetham, were exhibited at the Royal Academy in 1841 (No. 1041 in the 1841 *Catalogue*, which refers to a 'Church in Elvitham [*sic*] Park, Hants.', and Roberts' address is given as 18, Adam Street, Adelphi). The *Catalogue* specifically mentioned the 'new tower and porch', so it would appear that Roberts certainly designed these elements, although it is not certain if the present Gothic spire, with its grotesque gargoyles, is by Roberts. It may be that the spire and the details are by S. S. Teulon, who designed Elvetham Hall for the fifth Lord Calthorpe in 1859–60. The church itself is in the Norman style, and is built of flint with freestone dressings. The nave and chancel are under one continuous roof, and the interior is plain, even dull, although Roberts did re-set earlier monuments. A certain sensitivity is found in Roberts' work where he incorporated earlier features in new buildings. The church is now redundant. The third Lord Calthorpe (1787–1851) was an Evangelical churchman, and had become acquainted with Roberts through Baptist Noel and the London City Mission. Calthorpe was later to become a Vice-patron of the Society for Improving the Condition of the Labouring Classes, and was known to Lord Ashley, to Lord Kinnaird, and to other eminent men with Evangelical consciences who also knew Roberts. Calthorpe owned the land at Bagnigge Wells on which Roberts' first scheme for the Society for Improving the Condition of the Labouring Classes would stand.

On 29 November 1838 Henry Roberts was elected a Fellow of the Society of Antiquaries of London, his proposers being Edmund Lodge, Sir Robert Smirke, Edward Dalton, and J. A. Giles, formerly headmaster of the Camberwell Collegiate School which Roberts had designed.[75] His address at that time was 18, Adam Street, Adelphi, from which he practised from 1832 until 1842.[76]

Roberts' most important buildings up to this time had been the Fishmongers' Hall, London Bridge, of 1831-5, in a stately Greek Revival reminiscent of the work of Sir Robert Smirke;[77] the Collegiate School, Camberwell, of 1834-5, in the Tudor Gothic style;[78] the Destitute Sailors' Asylum, Well Street (now Ensign Street), London Docks, of 1835;[79] The Glebe House, Southborough, Kent, 1836;[80] the north aisle of Yoxford Church, Suffolk, of 1837, in the Gothic style:[81] and a singularly important commission, Escot House, near Ottery St Mary, Devon, for Sir John Kennaway, Bart., of 1838.[82] He was also to design a house near Alphington, Devon, for Samuel Trehawke Kekewich.[83] Kennaway was a keen Evangelical Christian, whose son was to become a leading philanthropist and supporter of the Evangelical movement. Doubtless Roberts met him through his Evangelical connections, probably through Baptist Noel. Also in 1838 designs by Roberts for the Grosvenor Square Chapel, Manchester, were exhibited at the Royal Academy. From 1839-40 Roberts worked on Escot Church, Devon, for Sir John Kennaway, Bart., another essay in the Gothic style.[84]

Roberts made alterations at Claydon House, Buckinghamshire, for Sir Harry Verney, Bart., during 1839-40.[85] In 1840-1 he rebuilt St Mary's Church, Elvetham, near Hartley Wintney in Hampshire, for Lord Calthorpe, in the Norman style. The church is now (in 1980) redundant. The spire, gargoyles, and symbols of the Evangelists would seem not to be by Roberts, for they are in the Gothic style. Some commentators have suggested the spire and gargoyles are later additions, probably by S. S. Teulon, who designed Elvetham Hall for Lord Calthorpe in 1859-60.[86] In 1842-3 Roberts built Norton Manor for Charles Noel Welman in the Tudor Gothic style.[87]

During these years, Roberts had been consolidating his position. In 1835 he had become a founder-member of the Institute of British Architects (it was not to add the prefix 'Royal' until 1866).[88] His election as a Fellow followed in May 1837. He was elected to membership of the Athenaeum on 2 March 1840, having been proposed by Samuel Boddington and seconded by Edward Jacob. He was to use the Club as his London address long after he had retired.[89]

In the Royal Academy Summer Exhibition of 1838 there were no less than three drawings by Henry Roberts. These were of Escot House, Devon, of the chapel in Manchester, and of the Banqueting Hall of the Fishmongers' Company. Throughout the decade following the triumph of the Fishmongers' Hall, Roberts was busy with his practice, as the list of his works shows. There were considerable numbers of alterations to existing buildings. The north aisle and north chapel of St Peter's Church at Yoxford formed part of a general rebuilding and restoration in 1837, although Roberts' work has been partly obscured by still later alterations. In 1840 Roberts built a small house for J. A. Giles at Bagshot, but this has proved difficult to locate.[90]

Now we find a curious episode in Roberts' life. On 30 January 1835 he wrote to the London and Croydon Railway Company offering his services as an architect.[91] He had his connections, for his father was a shareholder, and his brother, Frederick

Roberts, was a director. Indeed, most of the Roberts family fortunes were to be tied up in guaranteed Railway Stock and in shares of the Equitable Reversionary Interest Society, as the Wills of Henry and Theodora Amélie Roberts show. On 23 September 1839 Roberts offered to study the problems at London Bridge, and in November 1839 he was appointed architect in which capacity he designed a public house on railway land at Glean Alley. He also prepared a layout for buildings on the site of Sydenham Reservoir, and was consulted by Chadwick on questions of drainage and health. At this time he also planned a new public house on the site of the *Old Green Man* Tavern.[92] Roberts converted and added to the stations at the *Jolly Sailor*, Anerly, *Dartmouth Arms*, and New Cross. Anerly had an 'entertainment house' for £800 added to it by Henry Roberts.

On 20 March 1840 a Joint Committee of the Croydon, Brighton, and South Eastern Railway Companies met to decide to build a joint terminus at London Bridge, and joined with a fourth company, the London and Greenwich, to accomplish this aim. John Urpeth Rastrick (1780–1856) was responsible for the elevated railway lines, and with William Cubitt, was consulted by the Joint Committee. Rastrick and Roberts were asked to produce plans for arched foundations. On 30 September 1840 Roberts was appointed architect for the new terminus, and Thomas Turner was appointed Clerk of Works. Rastrick appears to have designed a façade for the station, and it seems that both he and Roberts were jointly responsible for the finished design. Roberts only got paid £930 in fees for the job. The proportions of the new building were elegant, and it is regrettable that this second major work by Roberts in the classical idiom only survived until 1851 when it was demolished to make way for the later terminus.[93]

The style chosen was an Italianate manner much in vogue at the time (Plate 33). The building had a modillioned cornice and rusticated quoins, and had a tower like a campanile, with an upper stage pierced by three round-headed openings on each side. Flanking the two-storey office building of eleven windows width (divided into a central three-windowed pavilion, two three-window wings, and two side-pavilions of one-window width) were single-storey screen walls linking the building to triumphal arches with heavily rusticated voussoirs and quoins. The Italianate style was generally approved of by *The Illustrated London News*,[94] which credited the several parts of the new building to G. Smith, H. Roberts, Rastrick, and Thomas Turner. Smith (1783–1869) was District Surveyor of the Southern Division of the City of London from 1810, and Surveyor to the Mercer's Company from 1814, retaining both posts until his death. Smith was a Fellow of the Society of Antiquaries of London, a member of the Surveyors' Club from 1807, and a Fellow of the Institute of British Architects, of which he was Vice-President from 1844–5.[95] Here we find two successful architects (Roberts and Smith) who were well-known to two great London Companies that had a number of members devoted to the cause of providing better buildings as part of a general urban improvement.[96] Smith had laid out the beautiful Mercers' Estate in Stepney in the 1820s.[97] Roberts was a former pupil and a friend of the great Sir Robert Smirke, who was a leading figure in the field of metropolitan improvements of the 1830s and 1840s. Smirke was a Tory who enjoyed High Tory patronage. Lord Shaftesbury (or Lord Ashley, as he then was) was also a High Tory of Evangelical persuasion, and was later to be closely associated with Roberts and with the Prince Consort in philanthropic housing. Here were Roberts' main connections, with the vital one of the Evangelical movement in the Anglican Church.

In 1845 Smirke was presented by former pupils with a bust of himself by Thomas Campbell that is now at the R.I.B.A., and Roberts was associated with this tribute. The pupils were C. R. Cockerell (1788–1863), William Burn (1789–1870), and Henry Roberts.[98] Smirke, who was meticulous himself, appears to have liked and trusted Roberts, who seems to have got on with most people at this stage of his career. Roberts' gentlemanly habits and his devotion to Christianity of a somewhat Evangelical persuasion, together with his reliability as a professional, commended him to the eminent men who were forming the first philanthropic societies.

In 1843 Roberts exhibited a design at the Royal Academy for Norton Manor at Norton Fitzwarren in Somerset, an essay in the Tudor Gothic style, for Charles Noel Welman. The exhibit (No. 1210 in the *Catalogue*) refers to 'Norton Court, Somerset'. This also appears to have been a commission derived from the connections of Baptist Wriothesley Noel, who was to be instrumental in getting Roberts appointed as architect to the new church in Dock Street, Whitechapel, in 1846. Charles Noel Welman of Poundisford Park (1814–1907), who bought Norton Manor, was a son of Thomas Welman and the Hon. Charlotte Margaretta Noel, daughter of Sir Gerard Noel-Noel. There was a further connection in that Charles Noel, first Earl of Gainsborough and third Baron Barham, married Elizabeth, only daughter of Thomas Welman. It is quite clear, therefore, that Roberts' friendship with the Noels and with persons of Evangelical persuasion (particularly those with associations with the Clapham Sect) was of primary importance in obtaining his commissions.

Norton Manor is of brick with stone dressings(Plates 34–35). It is in the Jacobean style, and has some charming Gothick interiors (Plate 36). There is a fine dining-room with linenfold panelling and a built-in sideboard. The main living-room is large, with a Jacobean-style plaster ceiling, and a fireplace in the Gothick manner. The library-study has a built-in safe. The terraces, making use of contours, are exceedingly attractive. The house is now the officers' mess at Norton Manor Camp.

On 11 May 1844 the Society for Improving the Condition of the Labouring Classes was founded in Willis' Rooms, St James', and Roberts began his long association with the Society, an association that was to last for twelve years, and in fact that was never to be truly sundered. Roberts was a founder-member.[99] The Society was established under the patronage of the Queen, and Prince Albert was the first President. One of the principal objects of the Society was 'to arrange and execute plans as models for the improvement of dwellings of the labouring classes'. Roberts became a member of the committee, and was appointed Honorary Architect. From this period most of his output was concerned with the promotion of the Society's aims, either in tracts, booklets, or lectures, or in the production of designs for model housing. The Society and its work will be described subsequently.

In the beginning, the Society for Improving the Condition of the Labouring Classes published plans of model dwellings (Fig. 2), but eventually the Committee decided that the best way of making a dent in public opinion was to build actual examples. Money was raised by subscription and by loans. Roberts himself was a generous donor.

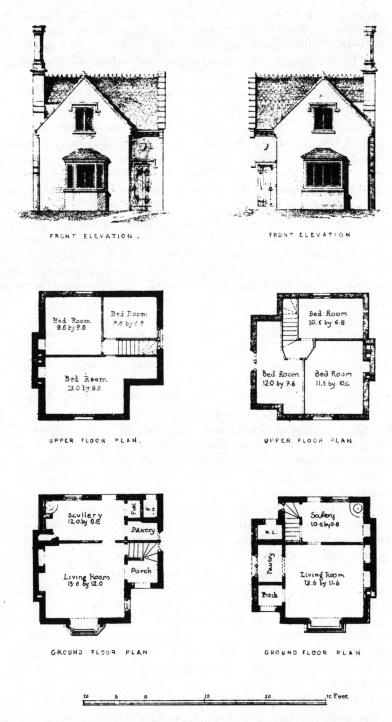

FRONT ELEVATION.   FRONT ELEVATION

UPPER FLOOR PLAN.   UPPER FLOOR PLAN

GROUND FLOOR PLAN   GROUND FLOOR PLAN

Fig. 2. Henry Roberts' designs for single cottages suitable for gate-lodges, lithographed by Day & Son. (See also Plate 57 and Plate 83)

With amazing speed, the first project was well advanced by the end of 1844. Henry Roberts had designed a set of model dwellings on a restricted site near the former Spa of Bagnigge Wells,[100] between Lower Road, Pentonville, and Gray's Inn Road. The site was purchased by the Society from Lord Calthorpe, a devoted Evangelical Anglican, who was also a Vice-Patron of the Society.[101]

The plans were published and working drawings were made in order to encourage improvements elsewhere in the country (Figures 3 and 4). The Society next turned its attention to the provision of a Model Lodging House for Working Men. There were many houses in London and in other cities where inexpensive accommodation could be found by the thousands of single workmen in search of employment. According to contemporary records many of these houses were unsavoury in the extreme. Not only was physical uncleanliness usual, but several houses seethed with criminals. Vice and degradation were common bedfellows.[102]

Roberts himself was to denounce typical Lodging-Houses of the period as 'a reproach to Christianity in England'. The Society purchased three houses in Charles Street off Drury Lane, and Roberts produced plans to convert these into a hostel for eighty-two working men (Figure 5). A Superintendent was appointed, and stringent rules were drawn up that were to form the basis of all regulations for the houses owned and managed by the Society.

The Model Lodging-House for one-hundred-and-four men in George Street, in Bloomsbury, followed in 1846 (Figures 6 and 7). The ground floor contained the offices and flat for the Superintendent, a library, and large common room. Above were four floors of dormitories with separate compartments. Heating was by warm air carried in ducts. The basement contained a wash-house, kitchens, locker-rooms, and stores. The Model Lodging-House was designed to improve health and comfort, while providing good moral tone and a certain amount of intellectual improvement in the form of books and newspapers. This house was opened in May 1848 by the Prince Consort who, in a speech at the Freemasons' Hall nearby after the ceremony, praised Roberts' designs. It appears that the cleanliness of the establishment paid off, for during the dreadful cholera epidemic of 1849 the inmates of the Model Lodging-House escaped unscathed.

At this time Roberts occupied offices at 13, Suffolk Street, so he seems to have preferred his original haunts to Adelphi. It had been several years since he had designed the Destitute Sailors' Asylum, but he was to be involved in the East End once more. From 1818–45 many London dockers and seamen worshipped in the *Brazen*, an old warship known as the Floating Church. It was founded by the Episcopal Floating Church Society. There were other floating churches. One of the leading lights among the floating churches was George Charles Smith (1782–1863) who founded the Home Missionary Society in 1819, a body that enjoyed the support of Baptist Noel. Smith (a Baptist) had opened the first Floating Chapel on the Thames in 1819, and founded the London City Mission Society in 1824, a body that also had the support of Noel. Smith also erected the Sailors' Home on the site of the old Brunswick Theatre, Wellclose Square, in 1828.

The Episcopal Floating Church Society had close associations with Smith, with the Sailors' Home, and with the Destitute Sailors' Asylum which Roberts had designed in

VIEW OF THE MODEL BUILDINGS NEAR BAGNIGGE WELLS,

Between the Lower Road, Pentonville, and Gray's-Inn Road.

Fig. 3.   A 'View of the Model Buildings near Bagnigge Wells, between the Lower Road, Pentonville, and Gray's Inn Road'. Henry Roberts' first scheme for the Society for Improving the Condition of the Labouring Classes, 1844.

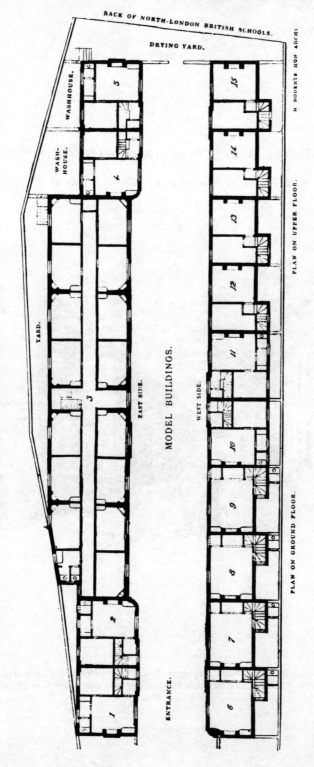

Fig. 4.   Plans of the Model Houses at Bagnigge Wells.

THE RENOVATED LODGING-HOUSE, CHARLES STREET, DRURY-LANE.

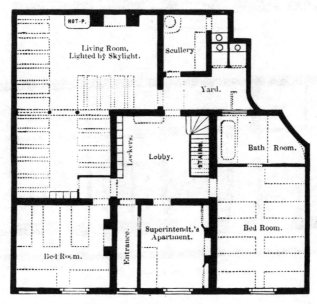

Ground-Floor Plan of the Renovated Lodging-House, Charles-street, Drury-lane.
to accommodate 82 Single Men.

NOTE—This House was formed out of three old Houses

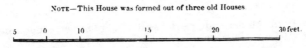

Fig. 5. The Renovated Lodging-House in Charles Street, Drury Lane. A prospect and a ground-floor plan.

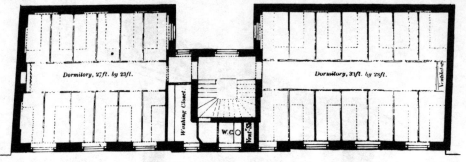

PLAN OF FOUR FLOORS OF DORMITORIES.

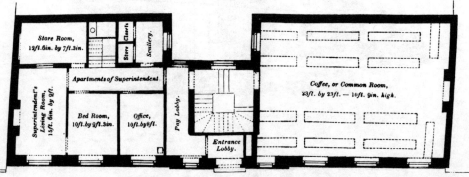

PLAN OF GROUND FLOOR.

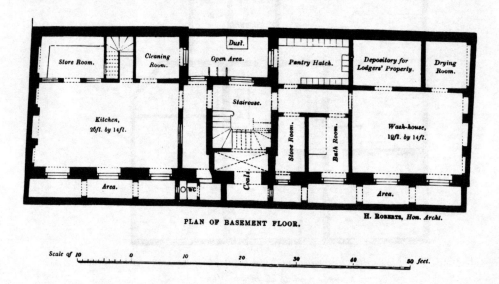

PLAN OF BASEMENT FLOOR.

Fig. 6.   Plans of the Model Lodging-House in George Street, Bloomsbury, to accommodate 104 working men.

1835, At the London Tavern, Bishopsgate, a meeting was held presided over by Thomas Hamilton, ninth Earl of Haddington (1780-1858), First Lord of the Admiralty from 1841 to 1846.[103] Also at the meeting was Captain Sir John Franklin, who was to lose his life so soon afterwards on the fateful expedition. The meeting resolved to build a new church on shore to replace the *Brazen*, and land was purchased at Dock Street adjacent to both the Sailors' Home and the Destitute Sailors' Asylum. It was decided to build a new church in the Early English style, and Roberts was appointed architect through the influence of Baptist Noel and of Captain Elliott. Construction started on 16 March 1846.

Prince Albert himself took a great interest in the project (Plate 42) and laid the foundation stone.[104] The silver trowel, mounted in an ivory handle, used by Prince Albert at the ceremony, still exists in the collection of the Cuningham family. It is inscribed

> 'The Foundation Stone of the Church for Seamen of the Port of London was laid with this Trowel on 11 May 1846'.

It also is embellished with the name of Henry Roberts, as architect.

Roberts' ecclesiastical buildings did not please the Ecclesiologists, alas! St Paul's Church for Seamen, Dock Street, Whitechapel of 1846-7 in the Gothic style, cost £9,000, and seated eight hundred people. It was built on part of the site of the Brunswick Theatre by William Cubitt and Company. It had galleries that were subsequently removed, and had free sittings. The criticisms of the architecture, however, were devastating. The design was considered to be 'extremely poor: a vulgar attempt at First-Pointed'. The fact that the church had only a vestigial chancel was criticised. Roberts' work was a 'commonplace design put together without harmony'. The critic said that there was 'not the least idea in the composition'. There was a crop at the top of the spire surmounted by a vane representing a ship, 'a singularly vulgar thought' (Plates 40-41). The church was, as a whole, 'stale and insipid'.[105]

The vicarage of St Paul's, beside the church, was built later, but it is yet a fine late-Georgian town-house by Henry Roberts (Plate 43). It is of stock brick with stucco dressings. The building consists of three storeys over a basement. The main façade is three windows wide, with a central door. The ground-floor windows have stucco architraves that are reminiscent of Greek Revival, and are similar to those of The Glebe House at Southborough in Kent. At the back of the church is the Destitute Sailors' Asylum of 1835, in Well Street, now Ensign Street, but the building is now a warehouse. There were thus three documented buildings by Henry Roberts virtually adjacent to each other.

Next came a Tudor-Gothic school, designed in 1846, and built between 1846 and 1848 adjacent to the Church of All Saints, Sidmouth, in Devon (Plates 38-39). This building was of rubble with freestone dressings, and was simple in the extreme. It had a school-house attached which has now been demolished, and the school building itself has also been altered. Roberts was appointed architect through the influence of Sir John Kennaway, Bart., who was the patron of All Saints Church and a trustee of the School. Only a few years before, Roberts had built Escot House and Church for Kennaway.[106]

Fig. 7a.   The Model Lodging-House in George Street.

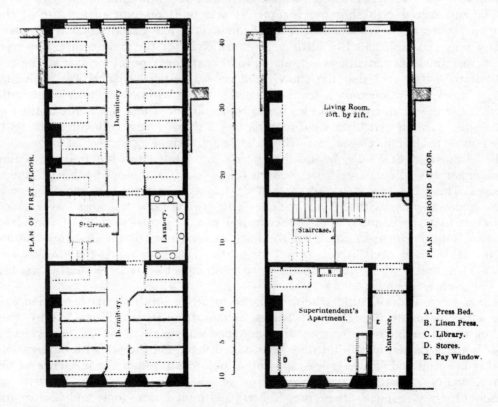

Fig. 7b.   Plans of the Model Lodging-House at 76 Hatton Garden, for 57 single women.

Tudor-Gothic was also the style chosen for St Peter's Parsonage, Norbiton, in Surrey, of 1846-7.[107] In fact, Roberts seems to have favoured a late-Gothic style in many of his domestic buildings. Some of the drawings of the Parsonage survive (Plates 44-45). The site of the Parsonage was on Glebe land belonging to the benefice of Norbiton, adjacent to the Parish Church of St Peter, Norbiton, at the rear of the *Liverpool Arms* public house. It was a handsome house, with a library, drawing-room, dining-room, and waiting-room grouped round a spacious hall with staircase. The kitchen, wash-house, and utility rooms were in a distinctly separate wing. On the first floor were six bedrooms, two dressing-rooms, and a water-closet. All rooms had fireplaces except the small dressing-room, closets and stores. Roberts' client was the first incumbent of St Peter's Church; the Rev. John Welstead Sharp Powell, of St Edmund Hall, Oxford. Powell knew Baptist Noel, and was himself of the Evangelical persuasion. He also had Devonian connections. The Parsonage, with its tall Tudor chimneys, no longer survives. It was constructed of brick with 'Patent Portland Cement' dressings. The specification survives in the Surrey Record Office. Demolition took place in the late 1950s. A manuscript note, evidently written by one of the incumbents of St Peter's Church, refers to the 'erection of the present parsonage, built after a design and plan of the incumbent with the aid of Mr. Thomas Tindal Walker, one of the churchwardens, and subsequently perfected by the skill of Henry Roberts Esq. of Suffolk Street, Pall Mall, the accomplished architect of Fishmongers' Hall'.[108]

Work at the National Scotch Church, Crown Court, Covent Garden, followed in 1848, with two school-buildings. Most of Roberts' work for the church has been demolished, and the church was largely rebuilt in 1905. Roberts had already carried out works for the Scottish Presbyterians at Manchester, and he was to build Wigtown Church later. Once more, Evangelical connections seem to have been the source of Roberts' introduction. The Scotch Church was in a somewhat coarse *Rundbogenstil* by R. Wallace (Plate 46). It was a fashionable church, with a celebrated minister, the Rev. John Cumming (1807-1881), who was a convinced Milleniarist, certain that the Second Coming and Apocalypse would occur between 1848 and 1867. Cumming was the guiding light behind the enlargement and rebuilding, commenced in 1847. The total cost was £5,000, and the work was completed in 1848 with 1,000 sittings. Income from pew rents was £1,500 per annum, but Cumming refused to accept more than £500 in order to pay off the debt. Cumming also raised funds by which the Schools in Little Russell Street were added in 1849, and the Ragged Schools in Brewers' Court were established in 1855. Cumming was an active philanthropist, and was extremist in his Evangelical views, to the point of obnoxious anti-Papist bigotry. In view of the Milleniarist fervour and the extreme fear and hatred of Roman Catholicism, the obvious connection between Roberts and Cumming would appear to be Lord Ashley, whose prejudices concurred with those of Cumming.[109]

There is no evidence that Roberts was a Milleniarist, that is, one who believed that Christ would return to establish a Kingdom on earth *before* the Day of Judgement. Shaftesbury certainly linked the return of the Jews to Palestine, and the establishment of a bishopric in Jerusalem (with which he, Prince Albert, and the Prussian diplomat Bunsen were so intimately concerned) with the Second Coming.[110] The first Anglican Bishop of Jerusalem was Michael Solomon Alexander (1799-1845), who was born of

Jewish parents in Schönlanke in the Grand Duchy of Posen. Alexander was ordained by Archbishop Magee in Dublin in 1827, and was closely associated with the London Society for Promoting Christianity among the Jews, and with the programme for Evangelising the Jews of West Prussia and Posen. In 1841 the King of Prussia commissioned the Chevalier (later Baron) Bunsen as an envoy to the British Government to obtain for Protestants the privileges enjoyed by the Latin, Greek, and Armenian Churches in the Ottoman Empire. Alexander was made Bishop of the United Churches of England and Ireland in Jerusalem. According to Mrs. J. C. Cuningham (Frederick Albert Roberts' great-niece), the Bishop's children were related by marriage to the family of Henry Roberts. When Alexander died suddenly outside Cairo in November 1845, his eight children and his widow were cared for by a Committee set up by Lord Ashley. F. A. Roberts frequently referred to the Alexanders as late as the 1930s, and kept up his contacts with the family. Bishop Alexander arrived in the Holy Land by sea. His coming was more like a military triumph than a churchman's entry. He travelled on a perhaps unfortunately named man-of-war, the *Devastation*, and was greeted with an artillery salute on his entry to Jerusalem. The Bishop was closely associated with the Victoria Emigration Society (with strong Australian connections as had the Roberts family), and with philanthropic organisations generally. The appointment of a Jewish Anglican with a strong Lutheran backing to the see of Jerusalem alienated many Anglican High Churchmen. According to *The Jewish Encyclopedia*, Alexander married in 1821 a Miss Levy, of Plymouth. He was baptised on 22 June 1825 in St Andrew's Church, Plymouth, and his wife was baptised at Exeter six months later. The surviving children of the Bishop and his wife were closely identified with Evangelical and philanthropic movements.

The position of Bishop of the United Church of England and Ireland in Jerusalem was established by an arrangement between the German, Lutheran, and Anglican Churches, and caused much embarrassment to the High Churchmen, who would not recognise Lutheran Orders. Indeed, the appointment of Alexander provoked opposition from many quarters, including the Roman Catholic Church, and it was one of the major causes of Newman's secession to Rome. Great importance was attached to the appointment of Alexander in Jerusalem, owing to his Jewish origins, and there were strong overtones among those Evangelicals who wished to see the strongest of religious, family, and political ties between Prussia and Great Britain. There is a very full biography of the Bishop by J. F. A. de le Roi, published in Gütersloh in 1897 under the title of *Michael Solomon Alexander, der erste evangelische Bischof in Jerusalem*.

Lord Ashley's intensification of his religious views took place around 1835,[111] at the same time as Roberts' involvement with the Destitute Sailors' Asylum and the growth of the Noel connection. Ashley became increasingly involved with official Evangelism, and by 1840 had emerged as the leading Evangelical layman and the leader of the party that was lacking in outstanding clergymen. At the centre of Evangelical life were the 'six societies': the Church Missionary Society, the Religious Tract Society, the Colonial and Continental Church Society, the London Society for Promoting Christianity among the Jews, the British and Foreign Bible Society, and the Church Pastoral Aid Society. Ashley became closely involved with all these Societies.[112] However, in the 1840s, the High Church party left the C.P.A.S., led by Gladstone, and Baptist Noel became a Dissenter. Other Churchmen went over to Rome, causing fear and trembling among the Evangelicals who hated 'Puseyites' and Tractarians perhaps as much as Popery itself. Animosities were strong. The Evangelicals began to hold Sunday evening services[113] at Exeter Hall (where the Society for Improving the Condition of the Labouring Classes had offices) to counteract Ritualism.

The strong sense of personal salvation that was so emphasised by the Evangelicals combined with conventional, even stifling, codes of behaviour and with Benthamite ideas of political economy. The result was that most Evangelicals were not able to see society as it appeared to the poor, and by the second half of the century many Evangelicals began to doubt their faith, partly due to the effects of Darwin's work on all those who took the Bible literally, and partly because of the desertion of their ranks by those who found Rome, Ritualism, or Dissent more congenial. The decline of Fundamentalism created a vacuum that was to be partially filled by a Socialistic belief in progress, in science, and in inevitable advancement. Original Sin, in many circles, was discarded, and assumptions were made about the Goodness of Man rather than on an insistence upon Redemption. The effects were far-reaching. Concern with sin was transmogrified into social reform, and Fabianism became the late-nineteenth-century equivalent of what the Clapham Sect had meant to reformers of the early 1800s.[114]

During the mid-1840s Henry Roberts was planning to marry. The lady of his choice was Catherine de Swetschine, the daughter of a Russian nobleman, Demetrius de Swetschine. Mademoiselle de Swetschine was twenty-seven when Roberts became her husband on 15 April 1847 at a ceremony in the Parish Church of Paddington. Henry Roberts was thus one day short of being forty-four when he entered into matrimony. It is not clear why he remained a bachelor for so long, for he was of 'independent circumstances'[115] even when young George Gilbert Scott was working for him in the 1830s. It seems that Roberts had his own fortune at a fairly early age, and he was undoubtedly successful as an architectural practitioner. His father had died in the previous November, but, as has already been made clear, he had not left a large estate. It is possible that Josiah Roberts had distributed his wealth among his children before he died, and that Henry Roberts had postponed his marriage until after his father's death. Mrs. Josiah Roberts had predeceased her husband, and her estate may have contributed to Henry's affluence at a comparatively early age. It is probable, too, that the etiquette of Victorian mourning customs postponed the marriage until a decent interval had elapsed since Josiah's death in 1846. From the Will of Henry Roberts, it seems that he settled some money on his bride at the time of the marriage, and that she was provided for by her father as well. The couple seem to have been very well off.

The Rev. Baptist Wriothesley Noel officiated at the marriage ceremony. Henry's brother, Charles Roberts, was there, as was James Foster from the London City Mission, and J. Coles Symes. The marriage was reported in *The Times*.[116] The best man was the Hon. Arthur Fitzgerald Kinnaird, who had been attached to the British Embassy at St Petersburg from 1835-7, and who had presumably known the de Swetschines while in Russia. Kinnaird became a Member of Parliament, became a Vice-President of the Society for Improving the Condition of the Labouring Classes, and eventually succeeded to the Barony.[117] The St Petersburg connection is clearly significant, for, as has already been noted, the London Missionary Society, with which the Claytons, Baptist Noel, and the Hon. Arthur Kinnaird had close links, was intimately affiliated with Evangelical churches in the Russian capital. It would seem that Catherine de Swetschine (like many old Baltic families) was of the Evangelical rather than Orthodox persuasion, and her religious beliefs would have brought her into contact with English Evangelicals, especially through the London Missionary Society. Again, there were close connections of an historical and family nature between the de Swetschines and the aristocracy of the ancient cities that lined the Baltic shores. Thus there were ties with illustrious families of Prussia as well.

Catherine Roberts, *née* de Swetschine, appears to have been a formidable lady. Even in 1979 surviving members of the family were able to recall stories of her eccentricities and of her single-mindedness. Frederick Albert Roberts, Henry's nephew, remembered her well, and used to tell his great-niece, Mrs. J. C. Cuningham, of Catherine's devotion to the Evangelical cause. Catherine Roberts made a habit of smuggling Bibles and Protestant tracts into Italy under her voluminous skirts. Mrs. Henry Roberts was not only completely sure of herself: she was convinced of the rightness of everything she did.

On 31 May 1848 Olivia Maria Pauline Roberts was born.[118] Two other daughters, Lydia Anastasie Davy Roberts (born 19 June 1851), and Theodora Amélie Roberts (born 8 June 1856), lived to survive their father.[119] The eldest girl appears to have died young,[120] but her precise date of death cannot be established. There do not seem to have been any other children.[121] Roberts was now reaching the peak of his career and fame. His achievements until 1853 were remarkable, and it is a tragedy that his success was to be so soured by events.

The next project by Roberts for the Society was the 'Model Houses for Families' in Streatham Street, Bloomsbury, generally regarded by most commentators as the architect's most important and advanced work in the *genre*.[122] In this distinguished design forty-eight families were accommodated in a three-sided block grouped round a central courtyard (Plates 62–63 and Figures 8–11). Access was arranged via balconies. Each flat was self-contained, had its own lobby, and consisted of a main room, two bedrooms, a kitchen, and a water-closet, a tremendous advance in terms of standards for the time. A communal bath- and wash-house was also provided. There was a resident Superintendent who was empowered to sell fuel and provisions to the tenants. The entire building was constructed to be as fireproof as possible, the floors and the roof being constructed of arches of hollow bricks, a technique Roberts had previously used in the Fishmongers' Hall,[123] derived from experiences he had gained while working with Sir Robert Smirke. Arches sprang from cast-iron shoes spaced by tie rods, and were covered and levelled with concrete, a material again pioneered by Smirke, and used by Roberts for the foundations of the Fishmongers' Hall. These Model Houses are now managed by the Peabody Estates, and have been renamed Parnell House.

There were other, minor schemes that will be mentioned in connection with the work of the Society. In the present chapter one other design by Roberts for Model Dwellings for a poorer class of family deserves mention. This was Thanksgiving Buildings, Portpool Lane, Gray's Inn Road, so called because a sum of over five thousand pounds was raised towards its construction in church collections on the

Fig. 8a. The south and west side of the internal quadrangle of the Model Houses in Streatham Street, Bloomsbury.

Fig. 8b. The exterior of the Model Houses for Families, Streatham Street, Bloomsbury.

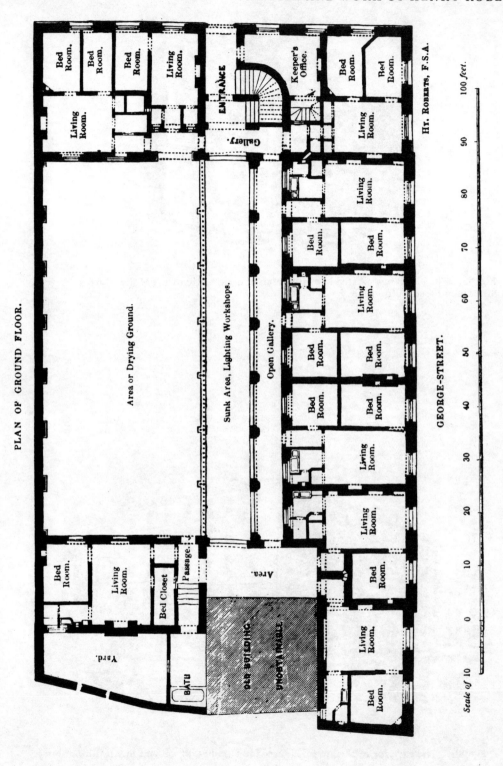

PLAN OF GROUND FLOOR.

Hr. Roberts, F.S.A.

Fig. 9.   Plan of the ground floor of the Model Houses for Families at Streatham Street.

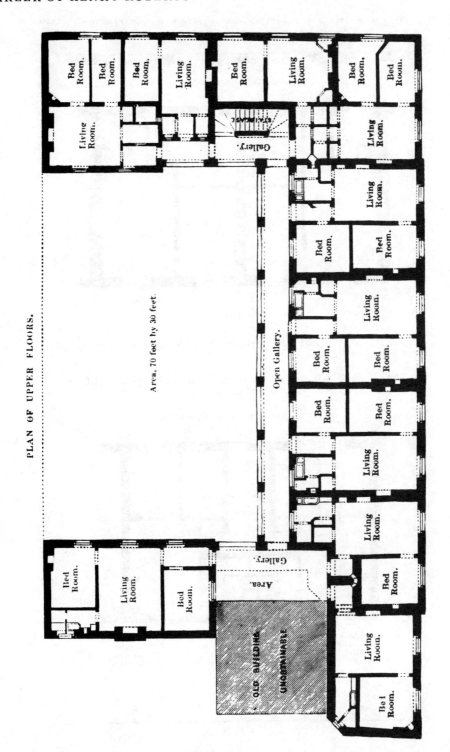

THE MODEL HOUSES FOR FAMILIES IN STREATHAM STREET, BLOOMSBURY,

TO ACCOMMODATE 48 FAMILIES, AND HAVING WORKSHOPS ON BASEMENT.

PLAN OF UPPER FLOORS.

Area, 70 feet by 30 feet.

Open Gallery.

Bed Room.

Living Room.

Bed Room.

Gallery.

Area.

OLD BUILDING UNOBTAINABLE

Fig. 10. Plan of the upper floors of the Model Houses for Families at Streatham Street.

BUILT BY THE SOCIETY FOR IMPROVING THE CONDITION OF THE LABOURING CLASSES.

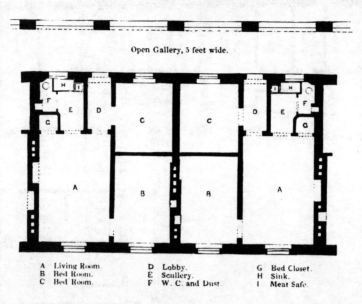

Open Gallery, 5 feet wide.

A	Living Room.	D	Lobby.	G	Bed Closet.
B	Bed Room.	E	Scullery.	H	Sink.
C	Bed Room.	F	W. C. and Dust.	I	Meat Safe.

Fig. 11a. Plan of two of the Tenements in the Streatham Street Model Houses for Families.

Fig. 11b. Plan of two of the Tenements in the Dwellings for Labourers at Birkenhead, showing the internal stair.

BUILT BY THE BIRKENHEAD DOCK COMPANY.

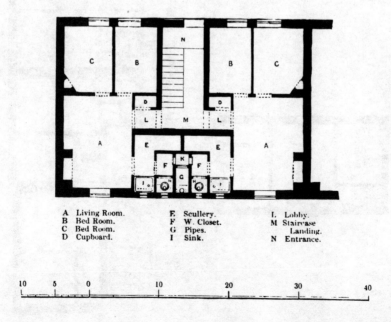

A	Living Room.	E	Scullery.	I	Lobby.
B	Bed Room.	F	W. Closet.	M	Staircase
C	Bed Room.	G	Pipes.		Landing.
D	Cupboard.	I	Sink.	N	Entrance.

10   5   0   10   20   30   40

Day of National Thanksgiving for the deliverance from the cholera epidemic of 1849 (Figures 12 and 13). It is intriguing to compare Victorian philanthropic housing as such a monument with say, the *Pestsäule* of Vienna (of over a century before), erected in thanksgiving for deliverance from the Plague. *Tempora mutantur, nos et mutamur in illis*. There was accommodation for twenty families in one- and two-room flats, and sixty-four rooms for some hundred and twenty-eight women. Similar to the arrangements at Streatham Street was the balcony access to the flats although the single rooms were approached via a corridor on all four floors. In a separate block was the communal laundry. Rents were only one shilling per week per person for the single rooms, a very reasonable sum compared with the 'fourpenny lodgings per night' common in the East End.

In 1849 Roberts patented an invention that was dear to his heart: the hollow bricks that provided cheap, light, well-insulated building components ideal for working-class housing (*see* Figure 23). The patent still survives in the collection of Mr. J. F. C. Cuningham. A steady stream of designs flowed from Roberts' office in the 1840s and 50s including the National School at Norbiton, Surrey, of 1851;[124] the rebuilding of part of Exton Hall, Rutland, for the Earl of Gainsborough, of 1851-2, in the Jacobean style;[125] additions to Toft Hall, Cheshire, for Ralph Leycester;[126] and additions to Kimbolton Castle, Huntingdonshire, for the Duke of Manchester.[127]

Apart from these substantial works, Roberts produced a number of designs for working-class housing, including the pioneering scheme for houses in Lower Road, Pentonville, of 1844, now demolished, for the Society for Improving the Condition of the Labouring Classes;[128] houses in George Street, Bloomsbury, of 1846-7, for the S.I.C.L.C.;[129] houses in Streatham Street, Bloomsbury, of 1849-50, for the same Society;[130] Thanksgiving Buildings, Portpool Lane, Gray's Inn Road, for the Society;[131] model houses exhibited at the Great Exhibition of 1851, subsequently re-erected in Kennington Park;[132] and houses at Windsor, Berkshire, for the Royal Windsor Society, of 1852.[133]

The beginning of the 1850s (a decade which was to see Roberts more deeply involved in philanthropic housing and in the publication of his ideas) produced the National Schools at Norbiton, Surrey, in 1851.[134] This building, again in a late-Gothic style, was built by the road from Malden to Kingston, and consisted of a single-storey school-house for girls and infants, to which was attached a two-storey house for the teachers (Plates 47-50). Accommodation in the dwelling-house consisted of a kitchen, a parlour, and a scullery with pantry on the ground floor, and three bedrooms with fireplaces above. There was a walled yard for the house, with a water-closet, a fuel-store, and an ash-store. Lavatories for girls and for infants were placed at the end of the building, beyond the yard. The materials were again stock brick with stone dressings. The Schools were established through the efforts of the Rev. J. W. S. Powell, who was also responsible for the appointment of Roberts as architect. Presumably Powell was so pleased with his new Parsonage that he had no hesitation in going to Roberts for further work. The Schools were enlarged in the same style during the nineteenth century, and a new entrance has been added. Much of Roberts' original design survives, however. The manuscript notes kindly made available by Mr. C. G. Walmsley include a later reference to Roberts in another hand. 'Mr Roberts, who

INCLUDING A PUBLIC WASHHOUSE. WITH A CELLAR BENEATH FOR HUCKSTERS' GOODS.

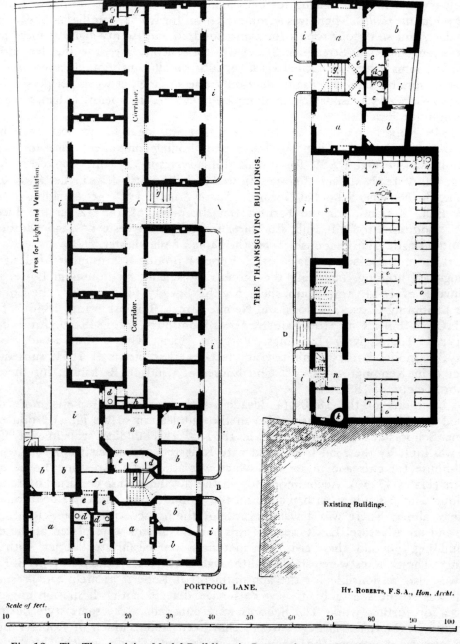

Fig. 12.   The Thanksgiving Model Buildings in Portpool Lane, Gray's Inn Lane, to accommodate 20 families and 128 single women. The plans by Roberts.

Fig. 13. The view of the east side of the Thanksgiving Model Buildings, Portpool Lane, Gray's Inn Lane.

had when the architect for the parsonage been requested to furnish a plan for two schools, one for 100 infants and one for 100 girls, besides proper accommodation for the teachers...' duly produced designs for the buildings that stand (somewhat altered) today.

The next commission took Roberts further afield. In 1850 the kirk session and heritors of the parish of Wigtown in Scotland were undecided as to whether the church should be repaired or rebuilt. In that year John McLure, master of works to the Earl of Galloway, president of the heritors, was directed to draw up plans for rebuilding. After he had submitted his report, the session decided to investigate the possibility of repair before being committed to expenditure, and engaged William McGowan, architect, of Dumfries to report. McGowan favoured repair, subject to the approval of the Presbytery. However, the latter body called in yet another architect, John Henderson of Edinburgh, who decided the church should be rebuilt. As a result, on 18 October 1850, the Presbytery directed the Earl of Galloway to procure plans, which he did on 5 December 1850, but no indication is given in surviving papers as to the basis on which he chose 'the architect who furnished' the plans. The heritors' minutes of 22 March 1851 record that the Earl had obtained working drawings from 'Mr. Roberts' who is also recorded as being the architect who supplied the plans in 1850. The meeting approved the plans, and Roberts was appointed architect. In a letter from Roberts to the Earl dated 19 July 1852, it was explained that, as the contractor for the supply of the heating system was unable to make delivery, he (Roberts) had engaged another company that had executed works at Galloway House and at some churches in which the Earl was interested. This suggests that Roberts may have had some acquaintance with certain of the Earl's projects on previous occasions.[135] Wigtown Church was completed by 24 March 1853 at a cost of £2,037. Roberts' fees came to £112 16s. 0d.[136]

The church is constructed of basalt with granite dressings, and is in a coarse version of First Pointed (Plate 55). The building is basically a rectangular preaching-box, seven bays long, with an aisle separated from the body of the building by a three-bay arcade with octagonal piers and responds. There are three lancets with a roundel piercing each gable end of the nave. The vestry, the porch, and the aisle all have roofs with ridges at right angles to the nave-roof. There is a short tower with a stumpy spire. All Henry Roberts' original drawings survive in the church. Roberts also designed the entrance-gates.

It is clear that Roberts was appointed through the influence of Randolph Stewart, ninth Earl of Galloway (1800–1873). The Earl had attended the Annual General Meeting of the Society for Improving the Condition of the Labouring Classes on 22 May 1846. Also present were Baptist Noel and Henry Roberts (who was first referred to as the 'Honorary Architect' at that meeting).[137] Obviously Lord Galloway met Roberts through the Society. Lord Ashley, later Lord Shaftesbury, stayed with the Galloways for six weeks at Cumloden, one of Lord Galloway's homes in Scotland, in 1847. There is another possible reason why Roberts may have been appointed architect for Wigtown Church. The architect William Burn (1789–1870) was a former pupil of Sir Robert Smirke, and had, with Roberts and Cockerell, presented a bust of the master to Smirke in 1845. Burn had carried out works at Galloway House for Lord

Galloway, and may have introduced Roberts' name to Galloway, who also made the acquaintance of Roberts at the Annual General Meetings of the Society. Lord Kinnaird also knew Lord Galloway, and Roberts had long been a friend of the Hon. Arthur Kinnaird, M.P. It will be remembered that Roberts had previously designed churches for the Scottish congregations in Manchester and at Covent Garden.

Roberts' friendship with Baptist Noel introduced him to the Earl of Gainsborough for whom he designed extensions at Exton House, Rutland, between 1851 and 1852;[138] The old Hall of the Noel family had been destroyed by fire in 1810, although the ruins still stand in Exton Park to the east of the church. The present Hall consists of a nucleus that forms the core of the whole composition (Plate 51). Three plain stone gables are visible to the north, and a gabled façade with three Venetian windows appears to the west. The first part of an extension seems to have been to the south, where a new dining-room was built very much in the manner of Roberts' classical style. There is a cast-iron fireplace of fine workmanship with a marble mantle, not unlike the fireplaces in the Fishmongers' Hall, and the plaster cornice displays Greek Revival anthemion motifs. Tall sash-windows and central French doors give access to the southern aspects of the Park in which the Old Hall and the church are features in the landscape. The only decorations are the cornice of the ceiling and an incised Soanesque pattern on the exterior of the timber mullions. The exterior of this part of the front has segmental arches of stone over the window openings, and simple string courses, but in the centre of the façade, over the doors to the dining-room, is a stone porch in a vaguely Tudorbethan style. This three-bay portion has a slight resemblance to the main elevation of Prince Albert's Model Lodge for the Great Exhibition of 1851. According to evidence[139] the rebuilding was of 'the centre', but unfortunately the drawings do not appear to have survived. The house has two massive additions in the Jacobean style (presumably contemporary with the south porch), one to the north-west, and the other to the south-west. The north-west extension is linked to the old house by a canted corridor, while that to the south-west is more intimately 'joined' to the older house and to the dining-room. The interiors of these two extensions are of a Jacobean revival style, and the cast-iron hopper-heads on the exterior of the south-west extension bear the date 1853. There are slight stylistic differences between the extensions to the north-west and that to the south-west. From these, the dates on the hopper-heads of the south-west part, the identification of Roberts' extension as being the 'centre' of 1851–2, and the splendid classical fireplace in the dining-room, it would appear to be reasonable to deduce that Roberts designed the south-western extension, the porch on the south front, and possibly the dining-room as well (because of its close stylistic affinities with the Fishmongers' Hall), although he is likely to have built this rather earlier, or perhaps redecorated it. The north-western extension would appear to be slightly later, and does not have dated hopper-heads. The chapel of St Thomas of Canterbury attached to the south-east of the house was built in 1868 to designs by Buckler after the conversion of the then Earl to Roman Catholicism. There are several details of the Jacobean-style extensions by Roberts that are accurately copied from the ruins of the old Hall. The chimneys, the gables, and the window details are scholarly copies by Roberts, presumably to give some degree of architectural continuity to his scheme. Indeed the south-west extension is very assured in terms of proportion, and is handled much more convincingly than the later work. The interiors of the 1851–3 extension have similar details and mouldings to those inside Norton Manor in Somerset, which Roberts had designed for C. Noel Welman in 1843. Lord Gainsborough, being related to Welman, could have decided that Roberts would be his architect having seen Norton Manor.

There are three lodges in Exton Park. The single lodge of 1867, dated on the heraldic devices over the door, is nearest the village, and was still occupied in 1979. Stylistically, it is similar to the north-west extension of the house, and may be by Buckler, who appears to have been retained as architect at this time. Many of the details, such as the hood-moulds, are poorly proportioned, and lack Roberts' assurance. The twin two-storey lodges, with gateposts capped by harts, and with inventively designed cast-iron gates, are quite different in style, however, and display a classical rigour that suggests Roberts at his best. These very pretty neo-Jacobean lodges, with curved gables and small windows with lead cames, were roofless and derelict in 1979, but were made good for habitation in 1980, with rebuilt chimneys. Although they are not dated, they are stylistically earlier than the single lodge, and their refinement suggests Roberts' hand.

Roberts also carried out additions to Toft Hall, Knutsford, Cheshire, for Ralph Leycester about this time (1851).[140] This is an odd house on an E-plan, with a central porch carried up as a tower. The E-plan front is thirteen bays wide. There is a second tower behind the main tower on the opposite side. The stucco front was not part of Roberts' additions.[141] Before the stucco front was added in c. 1819 (presumably by Cockerell senior, who carried out works for the then owner), the building was of brick with stone quoins, and had the appearance of a seventeenth-century building into which sash-windows had been inserted. Roberts added a handsome addition with gables in the Jacobean manner (Plate 52). The ground-floor survives as Roberts left it. It has a fine marble mantle and cast-iron fireplace not dissimilar to other fireplaces by him at Peamore, Alphington, at Escot, and at Fishmongers' Hall. The decorations include scagliola piers, fine plasterwork of a pronounced Greek Revival flavour, and exquisite painted plaster-strips (Plate 53). In fact, the interior is purely classical, while the exterior is Jacobean. Roberts' client, Ralph Gerard Leycester (1817–1851) of Toft did not live long to enjoy Roberts' extensions. Yet again there appears to have been a connection with the Noels, for the Leycester-Roxby family included Gainsborough names like Wriothesley and Gerard. Augustus J. C. Hare, the author, who was the son of Francis Hare and Anne Frances Paul, was adopted shortly after his birth by Maria Hare, the widow of the Evangelical clergyman, Augustus Hare. Maria Hare was a Leycester of Toft, and was deeply affected by the death of Ralph Leycester in 1851. Augustus J. C. Hare refers to 'Madame Swetchine' in his writings. This 'Madame Swetchine' (the spelling of the name in English seems to vary), was of course Sofiya Petrovna Swetchine (1782–1857), the Russian authoress, who ran a brilliant *salon* in Paris, and who became a celebrated convert to Roman Catholicism. Catherine, Roberts' wife, was a distant relative, by marriage, of the famous Madame Swetchine. Hare probably knew Roberts and his family in Florence. The Leycester-Roxbys were also slightly connected with Clapham. It is likely that Roberts was appointed at Toft through his Noel connections, although there is a further architectural link in that C. R. Cockerell, the son of the

Cockerell who had carried out alterations at Toft in 1819, knew Roberts, and had also been a pupil of Smirke. Burn, Cockerell, and Roberts had presented a bust to Smirke in 1845. There is yet another connection in that Sir John Dean Paul, Bart., the banker and chairman of the General Cemetery Company at Kensal Green, who was an active member, with his son, of the Society for Improving the Condition of the Labouring Classes, happened to be the maternal grandfather of Augustus J. C. Hare, and was related by marriage to the Leycesters of Toft. Paul sat on committees with Roberts, and it could well have been this well-known Baronet who introduced Roberts to Ralph Leycester and his family. Paul's bank in the Strand foundered in 1855, after Roberts had gone to Italy. According to Augustus J. C. Hare, in his autobiography, Sir John Dean Paul was 'rather mad. After he had done his best to ruin all his family, and had totally ruined hundreds of other people, he said very complacently, "This is the Lord's doing, and it is marvellous in our eyes" '. Paul seems to have had his fingers in many promotions during the 1830s, 40s, and 50s, and was a highly respected figure. There can be no doubt that the collapse of his bank did the S.I.C.L.C. no good at all.

Roberts' connections with the Gainsboroughs at Exton Park, and with the Society for Improving the Condition of the Labouring Classes, helped him to obtain the commission to carry out works at Kimbolton Castle for the sixth Duke of Manchester[142] who was a Vice-Patron of the Society in 1850.[143] At Kimbolton, in Huntingdonshire, Roberts bravely followed in the steps of Vanbrugh and Hawksmoor, who had remodelled Kimbolton in the eighteenth century. Furthermore, Alessandro Galilei had also contributed to the design. The dining-room ceiling has a panel treatment not unlike the pilaster-strips at Toft, and Roberts may have been responsible for this and for the reconstruction of the Parade Room or Saloon ceiling. An original design for model cottages by Roberts survives in the Huntingdon Record Office among the Manchester papers, dated 1848 (Plate 58). It seems that there was a spate of building of model cottages on the estates of the Duke and on the lands of Lady O. B. Sparrow. There is also a perspective drawing for a double-fronted house with a Gothic porch that is unsigned, but which appears to be in Roberts' hand (Plate 59).

Even more significant is a letter to Roberts at 10, Connaught Square about patent hollow bricks. There was a 'misunderstanding regarding the number of Patent Hollow Bricks' allowed by Roberts to be made by the Duke of Manchester without paying Roberts for the use of his Patent. Twenty thousand was the figure mentioned. Certainly, two lodges on the edge of Kimbolton are by Roberts (Plate 57), and are identical to designs published by the Society for Improving the Condition of the Labouring Classes (Fig. 2). In any case, a balance of £70 10s. 0d. was sent to Roberts c/o Plowden and Cholmeley, Rome, on 16 February 1855 for professional services to the Duke of Manchester.[144]

Roberts' early experiences of witnessing poverty in London and on the Continent clearly made a great impression on him. The reformist atmosphere among the members of the Fishmongers' Company must have impressed him as well, and indeed he may have made some useful contacts while working on the new Hall. Despite his considerable gifts as an architect of fine buildings exemplified in the Fishmongers' Hall, Roberts is undoubtedly of great importance as a pioneer of working-class housing. From the 1840s he spent most of his working career trying to improve the dreadful housing conditions prevalent among the urban poor, and after his sudden retirement in 1853, he continued to be active in the field, both as a lecturer and as a writer. As stated, he was a founder-member and later Honorary Architect to the Society for Improving the Condition of the Labouring Classes, with which Lord Shaftesbury was so intimately connected. In 1852 Roberts also became Honorary Architect to the Windsor Royal Society, which the Prince Consort had founded 'to promote and carry out the improvement of the dwellings of the working classes in Windsor', and designed the charming group known as Prince Consort Cottages, Alexandra Road, Windsor.

Roberts' output on the subject of dwellings for the working classes was considerable, although he tended to prolixity, like many of his contemporaries. His most celebrated works are *The Dwellings of the Labouring Classes, their arrangement and construction* (London, 1850, revised in 1867), of which a French edition was published by order of Louis Napoleon in the same year; *The Model Houses for Families built in connection with the Great Exhibition, 1851* (London, 1851); *Home Reform, or, What the working classes may do to improve their dwellings* (London, 1852); *The Improvement of the Dwellings of the Labouring Classes* (London, 1859); *Plans issued by the Society for Improving the Condition of the Labouring Classes* (London c. 1852); *The Progress and Present Aspect of the Movement for Improving the Dwellings of the Labouring Classes* (London, 1861); *The Essentials of a Healthy Dwelling, and the extension of its benefits to the Labouring Population* (London, 1862); *The Physical Condition of the Labouring Classes, resulting from the State of their Dwellings* (London, 1866); and *Efforts on the Continent for improving the Dwellings of the Labouring Classes* (Florence, 1874).[145]

The attribution to Roberts of a little pamphlet called *Proposed People's Palace and Gardens for the Northern and Midland Counties to Employ Factory Operatives* (London and Manchester, 1863) would appear to be unfounded on fact. Frederic Boase in *Modern English Biography* credits the architect with this publication, as does Howard Colvin in his *Biographical Dictionary of British Architects*. The British Museum *Catalogue* identifies Roberts as 'Henry Roberts F.S.A.' and indeed Roberts identifies himself with the letters of his Fellowship of the Society of Antiquaries of London on most of his title-pages. There is no designation of 'F.S.A.' on the title-page of *Proposed People's Palace*, and, apart from the fact that the author was a Henry Roberts of Manchester, there is not a shred of evidence to suggest that the subject of this study was responsible for this little tract. In the copious writings of Henry Roberts, F.S.A., a definitive style emerges: it was dry, factual, and hardly ever became polemical. *Proposed People's Palace* is littered with exclamation marks, capital letters, and all sorts of exaggerations that are quite foreign to the architect. In short, there is no resemblance whatsoever between the style of the known works of Henry Roberts, F.S.A., and that of the Henry Roberts who wrote *Proposed People's Palace*.

The Society for the Improvement of the Condition of the Labouring Classes had achieved much, but it was to get its greatest publicity through the good offices of the Prince Consort by exhibiting Model Houses at the Great Exhibition of 1851. The Committee of the Society approached the Commissioners of the Exhibition for a suitable site, but was initially rebuffed. The Prince intervened and obtained a site for the Society in the Cavalry Barrack Yard adjoining the Great Exhibition despite the opposition of the Duke of Wellington, who was convinced that the soldiers in the Barracks would compare their quarters unfavourably with the standards set by the Model Lodge, as it was called. In the event, the Duke, as usual, had accurate instincts, for most barracks throughout the country had to be modernised during the next decade.[146] The Prince Consort's Model Lodge, otherwise known as the 'Model Houses for Four Families', was 'Erected by Command of His Royal Highness Prince Albert, K.G., At the Exposition of the Works of Industry of All Nations, 1851'. It has almost become an article of faith that these houses were designed by the Prince Consort, since he showed a keen interest in, and suggested alterations to, an original plan previously published by the Society. He also paid for their construction. They were, however, unquestionably designed by Henry Roberts, and the building incorporated several ideas pioneered by the Society (Figures 18-21).

Early in 1852, Roberts had read a paper before the members of his Institute, with Earl Grey in the Chair. This paper was entitled 'On the Dwellings of the Labouring Classes', and it included an impassioned appeal to the profession for moral and practical support in the campaign to improve the housing conditions of the poor. Roberts' acquaintance with so many prominent members of society led him to be invited to join the Metropolitan Sanitary Association in 1850. This Association brought together a formidable array of influence, prestige, and talent in the persons of the Bishop of London, the Archbishop of Canterbury, Lords Normanby and Ashley, Charles Dickens, and Henry Roberts. In March 1851 Roberts went to Ramsgate to meet a body of men interested in promoting dwellings for the labouring classes. Indeed, according to *The Labourer's Friend* of 1852, some ten homes were erected on the basic plan of the Model Lodge of Ramsgate, and these will be discussed later.

In 1852 Roberts became Honorary Architect to the Windsor Royal Society. Among the objects of the Society was the improvement of the dwellings of the labouring classes in Windsor. Two terraces of houses were built on a site near the Long Walk for some forty families (Plates 71-73). The plan was similar to that of the Model Lodge at the Great Exhibition, and hollow brickwork was used, although this material was not used for any of the model houses based on the 'Prince Consort's Dwellings' in other areas. It seems that S. S. Teulon was responsible for some later buildings in Windsor Great Park, based on Roberts' original plans.[147] In 1852 several foreign delegations, impressed by the model dwellings at the Great Exhibition, visited the S.I.C.L.C. houses at Bagnigge Wells of 1844 that stood upon what is now open land behind the Mount Pleasant Hotel. French, Italian, and Belgian visitors greatly admired the work of the Society for Improving the Condition of the Labouring Classes. A Congress was duly held in Brussels to discuss public health and housing, attended by Lord Ebrington, Dr. Arnott, Henry Roberts, and Charles Cochrane. It seems Roberts made several influential friends at Brussels, for in March 1854 he was in Genoa writing on plans for workers' houses, and he mentioned plans in Turin for housing two hundred families. *The Builder* carried reports of flats being erected in Florence in a gratifyingly classical mode.[148]

Just before his departure for Italy, in 1853, Roberts had another commission to design a church, this time in Nottingham, which was expanding at the time. The church of St Matthew in Talbot Street, Nottingham, of 1853-4 fared little better than did

St Paul's at the hands of his critics. The foundation stone was laid on 2 July 1853. St Matthew's, like St Paul's, was 'First-Pointed, with clerestoried nave, and lean-to aisles' (Plate 54). It had pseudo-transepts, a chancel, and a tower in the angle between the north transept and the chancel. The tower was surmounted by a tall broach spire. The transept gable had a large and broad unequal triplet; the aisle walls had broad-hooded lancets; and the clerestorey windows were couplets. In the north-west angle of the nave was a small square turret surmounted by an octagonal cap. The west front had two very low turrets. There was 'little merit or power' in the design, and the 'arrangement' was 'unsatisfactory' to the Ecclesiological Society.[149] The church was consecrated by the Bishop of Lincoln on 15 January 1856, and a separate ecclesiastical district was assigned to it on 27 May 1856 out of the parish of St Mary. St Matthew's was closed on 31 July 1954 by an Order of Council, and the parish was united with that of Holy Trinity. The church is practically all demolished. The commission doubt-less came to Roberts through his connections with Evangelical Christianity, notably Baptist Noel and Charles Edward Kennaway, vicar of Chipping Campden.

The land for the new Church and for the parsonage was given voluntarily by George James Philip Smith of the Inner Temple, London. One of the main subscribers was the Rev. Joshua William Brooks, Vicar of St Mary's, Nottingham. Subscribers gave £1,000 in 3 per cent. Consols, £300 for the repair of the fabric, and £5,000 for the building and furnishing of the church.

The contractor was James E. Hall of Nottingham, and the building work was under the superintendence of R. Jalland, the architect, of Nottingham, who designed the contemporary St Mark's Church. The patrons of St Matthew's and St Mark's were H. Kingscote of Spring Gardens, London; E. H. Fitzherbert of Torrington Square, London; R. Ramsden, the Rev. C. W. Eyre, and the Rev. J. W. Brooks. Both churches together cost £9,000, and the endowment of St Matthew's was completed by the Rev. G. Dundas, the incumbent of the district. The Church Extension Society made a grant of £4,500, and among the subscribers were the Bishop of London, and John Bockett of Clapham.

It must be admitted that as an architect of churches, Roberts was not at his best. The work at Yoxford is reasonably self-effacing, but the church at Elvetham is in a somewhat mechanical Romanesque style that cannot be regarded as distinguished. His other churches tend to be meanly detailed, and clearly Roberts was not really at home in the Gothic style. The churches in Dock Street and in Nottingham were not in the first or even second ranks of exemplars of Gothic Revival. Nevertheless, the vitriolic criticism of *The Ecclesiologist* must have wounded Roberts, and may have had an adverse effect on his standing with the Society for Improving the Condition of the Labouring Classes. A parallel case of the destructive effects of ferocious criticism by ecclesiologically-minded writers can be seen in the career of Enoch Bassett Keeling, whose standing as an architect was severely weakened by those who wished to see Gothic treated in a more scholarly fashion.[150] Bad notices could quickly put com-mittees off, and it is more than likely that the power wielded by the Ecclesiologists was such that the S.I.C.L.C. was gravely concerned that their Honorary Architect was so out of favour. The impact of the exemplars of the Society would be severely jeopardised by the low esteem in which the Honorary Architect's designs were held by powerful critics. An architect whose ecclesiastical works were described as 'extremely poor', 'vulgar', 'commonplace', 'stale and insipid', and displaying 'not the least idea in the composition' would have his standing undermined at a time when *The Ecclesiologist* and the pro-Gothic camp had become the arbiters of respectable taste in Victorian England. No doubt H. Harward, Honorary Secretary of the Society for Improving the Condition of the Labouring Classes, and the Committee were understandably nervous when they wrote to Roberts on 15 December 1856 to 'enquire as to the state' of his health and to ask if he did not consider it 'more advisable for him to retire'. The Committee decided to abolish the office of Honorary Architect, and Roberts was asked to resign.[151] This he did, but, as he had been a singularly successful pamphleteer and propagandist for the Society, and had produced many distinguished designs for model dwellings for town and country, it was clearly not Harward alone who was anxious to get rid of Roberts. It is therefore quite possible that the denunciations of Roberts' ecclesiastical designs did his professional reputation great damage, even though his work for the Society could hardly come under the critical eye of *The Ecclesiologist*. His association with Sir John Dean Paul, who had connections with the Leycesters of Toft, and who probably introduced Roberts to Ralph Leycester, must also have undermined his credibility after Paul's bank had collapsed in 1855.

Henry Roberts continued his association with the Society for Improving the Condition of the Labouring Classes for several years. The minutes of the committee meetings demonstrate that he was zealous in his attendance. He also personally replied to the many enquiries received by the Society, especially those requesting model plans. He planned St George's Buildings, Bourdon Street, which were erected by John Newson in 1852-3. Newson built a further five model lodging-houses based on Roberts' plans. In May 1853 Roberts was presented with a service of plate in recognition of his services at a dinner in the Freemasons' Tavern.[152] Most of this plate survived in the collection of the Roberts family until at least the 1930s. The chest in which the plate was presented, however, still exists, and is in the collection of the Cuningham family. The Earl of Shaftesbury was in the Chair when Roberts received the presentation. The chest has a brass plate on which is engraved:

'Plate presented by several Noblemen and Gentlemen
to Henry Roberts, Esqr., F.S.A., A.D. 1853.'[153]

At this time, Roberts was undergoing a severe crisis in his personal life. Frederick Albert Roberts, Henry's nephew, told his great-niece in the 1930s that, between 1851 and 1853, his uncle Henry had enjoyed an indiscreet liaison with 'a member of the lower orders'. Mrs. J. C. Cuningham recalled the exact phrase in the presence of the Author in 1979. This affair not only appears to have caused great scandal among the Evangelical Christians of the S.I.C.L.C., but put Roberts' marriage in jeopardy, and lost him the honours for which he was destined. It is perhaps significant that the gift of the plate was inscribed as being from various gentlemen rather than from the Society. Recognition by individuals and friends would be possible, but, once the scandal of Henry Roberts' liaison became known, official recognition by the Society became inappropriate in the climate of the day. This service, the election as a

Vice-President of the Society, and the acclaim on the Continent were the only rewards Roberts received for his gratuitous efforts to ameliorate the condition of the labouring classes. Mrs. J. C. Cuningham remembered F. A. Roberts' telling her that after the success of the Great Exhibition houses, Henry Roberts was to be honoured in 1852. Unfortunately, his indiscreet affair with a lady of humble origins became public knowledge, and the reward that Henry Roberts had so richly deserved slipped from his grasp. Victorian morality would not acknowledge a known adulterer by rewarding him with an honour, especially as he had been so closely associated with the Prince Consort, whose views on such matters were strict.

Henry Roberts had one or two compensations, however. Apart from the gift of the plate, he was given a Coat of Arms in 1853. It is officially described as:

'on a Mount Vert a Holly Tree Proper, in front thereof a Goat Statant Armed and unguled Or gorged with a Collar gemel Sable and in the Mouth a Sprig of Holly also Proper'

for the Crest. The Arms are described as:

'Ermines a Goat Passant Argent horned and enguled and between three Annulets Or'.[154]

This was to be used by Henry Roberts and by other descendants of his father Josiah and of his uncles John and Richard Roberts.

Thereafter, as far as possible, Henry Roberts was paid remarkably little attention by the British Establishment. Yet such was the high regard in which he was held internationally, especially in Prussia, in France, and in Italy, that he did not cease to be important, and, as the years went by, his visits to Great Britain were reported conscientiously in the various *Proceedings* and *Journals* of learned societies and of philanthropic organisations.

It appears that Roberts had a breakdown in his health some time in 1853, and he went to Florence in November that year. He lived for a time at the *Villa Niccolini* outside Florence. In his publication of 1859, *The Improvement of the Dwellings of the Labouring Classes through the Operation of Government Measures by those of Public Bodies and Benevolent Associations, as well as Individual Efforts* Roberts states that his 'active participation in the management of the society . . . ceased in 1853, when the effects of over-exertion in its cause obliged [him] to go abroad'. It appears from the evidence of the Cuningham family, however, that the departure for Italy was not only connected with his overworking. It is possible, despite his own efforts in the cause of improving the condition of the labouring classes, and despite his own un-doubted Evangelical persuasion, that Roberts found his wife's fanatical Protestantism and her powerful personality overwhelming, and turned to a member of the class for which he had done so much. He probably found the admiration of a lady from humble origins difficult to resist when compared with the formidable Catherine. Whatever the reasons (and it is unlikely that the full details can ever emerge after so long), the love affair did him great harm personally, socially, and in terms of his career and his advancement. A breakdown at a time of great emotional stress, and when his work was again under particularly vicious fire from *The Ecclesiologist*, is hardly surprising under the circumstances.

The sequel leaves a sour taste, even today. The Society for Improving the Condition of the Labouring Classes, which owed nearly everything it had ever achieved to the efforts of Henry Roberts, having left the gift of plate to individuals in 1853, now behaved with a vindictiveness that suggests a calculated vendetta. The abolition of the post of Honorary Architect, the roundabout and somewhat hypocritical method of ousting Roberts from his position, and the distressing failure to recognise his very real contribution are disagreeable and unpleasant. It is difficult to draw any conclusion other than the abolition of the post was merely a ploy to force Roberts' ejection. Roberts did indeed resign, but felt deeply hurt by this treatment. He wrote to say that he felt that the Committee, by throwing away experienced professional advice, was making a mistake. After all Roberts had done for the Society it was hard to bear, and indeed his exertions for the Society had taxed his health to the point that he was obliged to go abroad in 1853. A letter (of 27 December 1856) from the S.I.C.L.C. stated that the 'future operations in the opinion of the Committee require that all plans for public works should be thrown open to free competition' in order 'to secure the advantage of a variety of talent'.[155] Roberts was invited to become a Vice-President of the Society, and at first refused, then relented. It is clear that his indiscretion, and possibly his industry in the field of reform, had put him beyond the pale even among the members of the Society he had served so well. It is quite possible that Roberts' expertise aroused jealousies among those less intellectually equipped than he. Whatever the reasons, there is no doubt that Roberts was no longer highly regarded in certain quarters. He had lost a career, honours, health, happiness, and even the honorary position from which he had contributed so much to the cause of the amelioration of the working classes.

Roberts states that he was responsible for most of the publications and plans of exemplars put out by the Society, and that he continued to 'revise and add to' the plans from his retreat in Italy. The receipt of Harward's letter of 27 December 1856 must have caused Roberts considerable pain and anguish. Depression may have contributed to a decision to leave England, for his Fishmongers' Hall was already extremely old-fashioned in appearance, and classicism was a language few people were supposed to speak any more, at least if the Goths and the Ecclesiologists had their way. The critics of *The Ecclesiologist* ignored all new classical buildings, and denounced all Gothic designs that did not meet their rigorous standards. As a designer of cottages that were vaguely Gothic in style, Roberts produced several agreeable sets of plans, but for grander Gothic works his skills failed him. He was too much of a classicist. Where Renaissance or Classical motifs were demanded, as at Exton, Claydon, or Escot, his expertise did not fail him: he was much more at home with classical designs.

Only a few more remarks are necessary concerning Roberts' aristocratic connections. Through Baptist Noel he had been introduced to ecclesiastical, Evangelical, and philanthropic societies, and also to families like the Noels, Lord Calthorpe (a close friend of Wilberforce),[156] the Kinnairds, the Kennaways, and others. His acquaintance with the Prince Consort, through the S.I.C.L.C. and the Great Exhibition of 1851, would have opened many doors to him, while the influential Lord Ashley, later Earl of Shaftesbury, who clearly held Roberts in high regard, cannot have been an unimportant figure in his professional career. Roberts was also a personal friend of Arthur Kinnaird, M.P. (who with a Nonconformist industrialist called Samuel Morley lent the impecunious Lord Shaftsbury £12,500 interest free).[157] Kinnaird had once been attached to the Embassy at St Petersburg, between 1835 and 1837, and had been best man at Roberts' marriage in 1847. As Roberts' wife came from a distinguished Russian family, it is likely that Kinnaird was the agent of their meeting. Arthur Fitzgerald Kinnaird was the third son of the eighth Baron Kinnaird. He was born in Perthshire in 1814 and died in 1887. He was a partner in the banking firm that became Ransom, Bouverie & Co. Pleydell Bouverie was a leading figure in the promotion of nineteenth-century reforms. Kinnaird himself was a leading Evangelical, and was considered the natural successor of Lord Shaftesbury as an influential philanthropist. He became the tenth Lord Kinnaird in 1878. His elder brother, the ninth Baron, introduced steam ploughs and reforms in mining and in farming to his estates. Arthur Fitzgerald Kinnaird's wife, Mary Jane (1816–1888) was associated with the sending of nurses to the Crimea, and with many Christian and charitable societies. She was a niece of the Earl of Gainsborough. Arthur Kinnaird's sister, Georgiana, was married to Sir Harry Verney, Bart., another of Roberts' clients (he was at Harrow with the future seventh Earl of Shaftesbury). As the Hon. Arthur Kinnaird, M.P., Roberts' friend was on the Committee of the National Association for the Promotion of Social Science, a body to which Roberts contributed several papers. Kinnaird was a Vice-President of the British and Foreign Sailors' Society and Sailors' Institute. The Patron of that Society was the Prince Consort. Old Lord Kinnaird was a Vice-Patron of the Society for Improving the Condition of the Labouring Classes, as were Lord Calthorpe, the Bishop of Peterborough, and the Duke of Manchester. As an influential member of the Society, Lord Kinnaird had been responsible for fitting out several model dwellings in Dundee and in Westminster.[158] Lord Kinnaird was a Knight of the Thistle, and a friend of Roberts through his son, the Hon Arthur Kinnaird. It was probably he, or Arthur, who introduced Roberts to the Earl of Galloway.

Through the Society, and through his philanthropic work, Roberts also knew Earl Spencer, the Earl of Ducie, Lord Teignmouth (a member of the Clapham Sect), Lord Henry Cholmondeley, the influential M.P. W. A. Mackinnon (who was a leading figure in sanitary reform, including the establishment of cemeteries),[159] the Dean of Carlisle, the Duke of Marlborough, and many others. Roberts was to travel widely, advising landowners on improved housing for their estates. He seems to have had a vast connection of aristocratic landowners and landed gentry. He was known to the Prussian Royal House, to Louis Napoleon, and to influential philanthropists in France, Germany, Switzerland, and Italy. When Queen Victoria met Roberts in the Model Dwellings he had designed for the Great Exhibition, she was 'graciously pleased to express her gratification of what she saw'.[160] During his years in Italy Roberts was friendly with many members of the Tuscan and Roman aristocracy, and his existence did not pass unnoticed by the House of Savoy.

From the mid-1850s Henry Roberts appears to have spent a great deal of time in Italy, but he did travel all over Western Europe, and argued the case for better working-class housing wherever he went. He approached the Grand Duke of Tuscany about the slums of Florence, and legislation was passed to ensure that a system of inspection of unseemly property was set up. Roberts visited the Exposition in Paris in 1855, and he saw the model houses there.

In 1856 Roberts was in Genoa, and philanthropic housing societies were formed there and in Turin. In October 1856 he visited Prussia, after he had attended the *Congrès de Bienfaisance* at Brussels that summer and proposed a resolution that 'it is of public utility that the Working Classes should be enlightened by all possible means with reference to the improvement and maintenance of their houses in good order'. He also argued for cleanliness of persons and dwellings, and for good ventilation, sound structures, and dryness. Many model dwellings were erected in Belgium, influenced by Roberts' published designs.

The National Association for the Promotion of Social Science invited Roberts to give a paper in Liverpool in October 1858. Roberts responded by writing *The Improvement of the Dwellings of the Labouring Classes*. He noted after his visits to Berlin, Munich, and Mulhouse that slightly higher rents were charged so that the inhabitants would eventually buy their houses. Roberts advocated that this system should be universally adopted to encourage pride of ownership.

He also visited a model village for workers at Mulhouse based on philanthropic principles. In 1858 he was inspecting the temporary lodgings of all those persons displaced by Baron Haussmann's plans for Paris. As a result he wrote a memorial to Napoleon about conditions, no doubt encouraged by the fact that his original paper to the Institute of Architects had been translated into French. Roberts also visited Marseilles and Genoa where other philanthropic schemes were being pioneered. He kept up a full correspondence with the S.I.C.L.C., despite his retirement as Honorary Architect in 1856, and his writing were published in *The Labourer's Friend*.

In 1862, on 20 January, he gave another paper to the Institute of British Architects entitled 'On the Essentials of a Healthy Dwelling and the Extension of its Benefits to the Labouring Population' which was published in that year. Aspects of housing, such as the site, water supply, construction, damp-proofing, ventilation, heating, drainage, and amenities were covered. There followed two evenings of discussion, and George Godwin, Editor of *The Builder*, contributed. In 1866 Roberts visited some model housing at Guise, which he mentioned in the 1867 edition of *The Dwellings of the Labouring Classes*, and was still contributing to *The Labourer's Friend*. Several of his pamphlets and books were translated into Italian through the offices of his friends in Florence. He contributed papers on the subject of model housing for the working classes to the British Association, to the National Association for the Promotion of Social Science[161] and to many other bodies.

Roberts gave a paper on the progress and present aspects of the movement for improving the dwellings of the labouring classes in 1860 in Glasgow.[162] He gave a review of measures passed since 1858, together with the activities of the S.I.C.L.C. He also referred to the Hertford Building Company for Building and Improving Dwellings for the Working Classes, established in 1858. He discussed efforts in Scotland to promote improved dwellings.

His influence was disseminated in Australia, the United States, India, Tuscany, Prussia, Sweden, Switzerland, and France. Most of the books published by the S.I.C.L.C. had been written by Roberts, and Roberts' plans became world-famous.

It appears that Roberts spent a great deal of time in England from 1858–64. No reports from abroad were published in *The Builder* during those years. Doubtless the struggle for the unification of Italy made living in that country less attractive. We know that Roberts spoke at the I.B.A. in 1862. At a London meeting reported in *Transactions* of the N.A.P.S.S. of 1862[163] Roberts spoke on 'Measures taken by Employers for promoting Habits of Prudence amongst Building and Engineering Workmen'. He also argued that the labouring classes should be instructed on sanitary matters.

Roberts was aware that it was not only good drains, sound construction, light, and air that could contribute to the improvement of the condition of the labouring classes, although he recognised that it was pointless to provide Bibles for people who lived in deplorable, insanitary, and overcrowded hovels. In order to give the working classes a suitable environment in which individuals could read and otherwise improve themselves, however, he was always insistent on the necessity to construct dwellings to model standards. Once the model dwellings had been built, however, it was necessary to pursue the improvement of the bodies and minds by providing decent food, by instilling cleanliness in general habits, and by encouraging education. Henry Roberts was enthusiastic about the efforts on the Continent to provide cheap but wholesome food for the inhabitants of the working-class settlements, and he was also interested in the attempts at Mulhouse, Guise, and other centres to build up cultural activities, libraries, and educational establishments. In this respect, Roberts was firmly following in the footsteps of the radical thinkers in France, and in 1862 he published a pamphlet entitled *The circulation of a pure and instructive literature, adapted to the capacities and means of the labouring population.* This was a reprint from the complete *Proceedings of the Congrès International de Bienfaisance* of 1862. In this, Roberts argued for cheap editions of wholesome and educational books to be made freely available, or even at a very small charge, in order to bring the world of the spirit and of the intellect to the deprived masses. Albertian high-mindedness is very much to the fore in this document.

The *Proposed People's Palace* by Henry Roberts also dates from this time, but, as already stated, it is by no means certain that the author was the architect, Henry Roberts, F.S.A. This pamphlet argued that the factory workers of the Manchester area, thrown out of work because of the American Civil War, could be employed to lay out a People's Palace and Gardens on the lines of the Crystal Palace, which would be more creative than putting them on relief. Such a palace, following the success of the Manchester Fine Art Exhibition, would become a regional exhibition centre as well as a cultural mecca that would educate the masses. Inventions, crafts, art, and all sorts of tools and machinery could be on show for the benefit of the producers and the purchasers. Music, literature, and art could flourish. This would be a centre where even humble artisans could exhibit their products, and prizes would be awarded for beneficial inventions and ideas. What is more, such a building could be constructed by levying a small amount in all the surrounding counties, but the result would eventually be self-financing.

If Henry Roberts did write this pamphlet, he changed his style very remarkably when doing so. The possibility cannot be ruled out, but there are considerable doubts.

Whatever the truth, Roberts returned to Italy in 1864 and lived at Nervi, near Genoa, where he introduced his ideas to the Marchese Carlo Torrigiani, who built one four-storey philanthropic block by 1865.

At Guise, Godin-Lemaire attracted attention with his *Familistère*. Roberts saw this development in 1866, and wrote a report for the S.I.C.L.C. about his visit. The 1867 Paris Exhibition had a section on model housing. Various European rulers followed the example of Prince Albert in their enthusiasm for philanthropic housing. Both Roberts and Chadwick saw the exhibition, but Chadwick thought the exhibits inferior to the houses Roberts had designed for the 1851 Exhibition in London. One curious incident occurred when Chadwick tried to suggest he was the genius behind the Model Lodge design, and Roberts had to put him firmly in his place. At Mulhouse, the Mayor, M. Jean Dollfus,[164] told Chadwick that the designs for model houses there were based on a study of the plans of H.R.H. the Prince Consort's Model Dwellings. The plans had been widely publicised by Roberts, so his designs were known all over Europe.

Henry Roberts visited London in 1873. He saw Scott and T. H. Wyatt for the last time. It must have given him great satisfaction to see how his friend Peabody was to develop his ideas of philanthropic housing. Model dwellings were going up all over the place, at Bisagno, Modena, and Parma as well. Copies of some of Roberts' papers were distributed in Roman schools through the influence of his aristocratic friends.

When Roberts lived at Nervi, near Genoa, in 1864, his ideas were brought before the Italian public by the Marchese Carlo Torrigiani, a senator in Turin, who argued for housing reform in the senate. Roberts was probably influenced to go to Genoa by F. L. Wollaston, the merchant-banker who was engaged in trade with Genoa, and who was a friend of Noel and who was an influential member of the Clapham Sect. In Florence, the ancestral home of the Marchese, Torrigiani promoted a Building Society which erected a large number of dwellings four storeys high, dispersed throughout the cities and suburbs. After 1865, when Torrigiani died, the work was carried on by the Marchese Guerzoni, another friend of Roberts. The Florentine dwellings were all of the tenement type, and owe little in appearance to Roberts' designs, although the planning is not uninfluenced by the Englishman's work. Roberts published Italian versions of *Home Reform, or Advice to the Labouring Classes*, and three hundred copies of this work were bought by the Syndic of Rome for distribution in schools. In Genoa, the Duchess of Galliera and her son, besides presenting the *Palazzo Rosso* to the city, gave two million francs for the construction of twenty houses at Bisagno. Modena and Parma followed suit. Clearly the aristocratic connection, gained through Roberts' English and Russian contacts, was important in Italy as well.[165] Through the *Accademia delle Belle Arti* in Florence (of which he was an Honorary Member) Roberts met many members of the Italian intellectual aristocracy, and he continued to contribute papers to learned societies in Britain until his death.

Roberts spent his last years at the *Villa Romana* (Plate 60), near San Gaggio, on the *Via Senese*, Florence, where he died on 9 March 1876. It is a charming villa in a secluded garden. There, Roberts passed his time in retirement, enjoying the Tuscan climate, and taking part in the activities of the *Accademia delle Belle Arti*. His death was reported to the R.I.B.A. Ordinary General Meeting by Charles Barry.[166] Barry mentioned the house Roberts had designed for Kekewich near Alphington, Devon, and some of Roberts' papers that had been published and distributed in Belgium and in Italy. His passing was noted by *The Labourer's Friend,* and in the *Transactions* of the Society of Antiquaries of London. The Minutes of the Society for Improving the Condition of the Labouring Classes of 5 April 1876 noted that the Committee had received with sincere regret the report of Roberts' death. Tribute was paid to his 'great services'. His Will was proved on 7 June 1876. He left an estate of about £25,000, divided between his wife, two daughters, and two nephews. His Will[167] is dated 1873, and specifically mentions the silver plate given to him in recognition of his work as Honorary Architect to the Society for Improving the Condition of the Labouring Classes.

Roberts was buried in the Protestant Cemetery in Florence, otherwise known as the *Cimitero degli Inglesi* (opened in 1828), near the graves of Mrs. E. B. Browning, of Walter Savage Landor, of Arthur Clough, and of Theodore Parker.[168] Also buried there was Southwood Smith (*ob.* 10 December 1861), the philanthropist and sanitary reformer, who knew Roberts in London and in Florence. The Register in the cemetery records that Roberts died on 9 March 1876 aged seventy-four, but this must mean 'in his seventy-fourth year'. His grave was numbered 1349.[169] The *Registro Alfabetico* also records the burial of another Roberts, 'Lidia *née* Schéhavtzoff', who was born in Russia and who died in Naples on 10 February 1877. She was buried in grave number 1382. A thorough search of the cemetery failed to reveal the graves, but an examination of the records of the *Cimitero Evangelico degli Allori* near Roberts' villa at San Gaggio revealed that Catherine Roberts was buried there in 1905. A visit to the grave was illuminating. In Section B VII 68–71 the whole of the family lay interred (Plate 61). In No. 68 the stone was inscribed 'In Memory of Henry Roberts Esq., F.S.A., late of London. Born 16 April 1803, Died 9 March 1876'. Next to him, in No. 69, lay Lydia A. D. de Schéhavtzoff, *née* Roberts,[170] who was born on 19 June 1851 in Russia and who died in Naples on 10 February 1877. Also buried in the grave was her baby daughter, Véra, Roberts' grand-daughter, who lived from 21 March 1876 until 20 May 1877. Véra, too, had been born in Russia, and had died in Florence. Her father was 'Pietro de Schéhavtzoff'. Next, in grave No. 70, is Catherine Roberts, *née* 'de Svétchine', who was born on 2 March 1820, who died on 20 November 1905, and was buried on 22 November. Lastly grave No. 71 was occupied by Theodora Amélie, 'daughter of Henry and Catherine Roberts', and 'Founder and for 35 years Directress of the Medical Mission'. She was born at Vevey in Switzerland on 8 June 1856 and died in Florence on 19 March 1916. It is therefore clear that when the *Cimitero Evangelico degli Allori* opened in 1878, Catherine Roberts chose a prime site for her family to be reunited in death. Henry, Lydia, and Véra were reburied there, and Catherine and Theodora Amélie joined them in 1905 and 1916 respectively. There they lie today, in a peaceful, beautiful cemetery on a hillside near Florence, only about a kilometre from their home, the house where Roberts died.

From the surviving pictures of the Roberts family, from letters, and from discussions with Mrs. J. C. Cuningham, a picture of Henry Roberts and his family has emerged from the nineteenth-century fog of obscurity. Henry Roberts comes out as a man of extraordinary gifts. He was sensitive to a degree, highly intelligent, deeply moralistic and concerned for the welfare of his fellow-creatures. From his letters to his brothers, he appears to have been warm and affectionate, and devoted to his father, old Josiah. The letters to Frederick Roberts at the time of his father's last illness are touching, informative and compassionate. His powerful advocacy of reform in order to provide decent housing, his professionalism, and his many talents would make him an interesting personality in any period.[171] His indiscretion with a working-class lady lost him the prizes that would have secured him an honoured place in the pantheon of great Victorians. He seems all the more human for his frailty, and the stern impressions of the strict Evangelical Christian, superb professional, and earnest reformer are softened by the knowledge of the great crisis in his life.

Chapter Two

THE REBUILDING OF THE HALL
OF THE FISHMONGERS' COMPANY

Most extraordinary does it ... appear to strangers, that having maintained, almost exclusively at your own expense, the burden of one of the longest and most expensive wars which Europe ever witnessed, you should at its termination find the means of erecting such numerous and costly piles of elegant architecture; nor can we, in beholding them, fail to reflect how incalculable are the resources of a free, enlightened, and united people.

'Marquis de Vermont and Sir Charles Darnley, Bart.'
London and Paris, or Comparative Sketches, London, 1823, pp.221-3.

THE YEARS following Waterloo were times of great metropolitan improvement. One of the most ambitious schemes was the building of a new London Bridge to designs by John Rennie. By 1827 it had become apparent that the venerable Fishmongers' Hall would have to be demolished to enable the works on the Bridge to be carried out, but some five years were to pass before a suitable design for new premises for the Fishmongers' Company would be selected. In 1830 the last vestiges of the old Hall were demolished, and the offices of the Company removed to Aldermanbury at the end of 1829. When King William IV opened London Bridge in 1831, the site of the Fishmongers' Hall was empty for only the second time since the Middle Ages.

A special Committee of wardens of the Company was set up, known from August 1832 as the Building Committee.[1] For a decade, the members of the Committee and the Clerk to the Company dealt with the Bridge Committee of the City, with the architect, and with the contractors. The most dominant member of the Committee was Matthew Wood, alderman, M.P., Lord Mayor, and later chairman of the House of Commons Committee on metropolitan improvements. Wood was a founder member and leading light of the Reform Club in 1834.[2] Other members of the Building Committee were John Towgood, William Sturch, Samuel Mills, Evan Edwards, and Joseph Wilson. The Clerk to the Company was John David Towse. All in all, the members were of a liberal disposition, firmly on the side of reform, of modernity, of progress, and of improvement. There were strong associations between the Company and University College, and indeed the Company was a shareholder in the College, founded in 1825 as the University of London.

A key figure in the rebuilding of the Fishmongers' Hall was the Company's Surveyor, Richard Suter (died 1 February 1883), who began his career as a pupil of D. A. Alexander, and who succeeded Alexander as Surveyor to both Trinity House Corporation and the Fishmongers' Company in 1822, remaining Surveyor until 1867. Richard

Suter was an assured and talented architect. He designed churches for the estates of the Fishmongers' Company at Banagher and at Ballykelly in County Londonderry, and exhibited both designs at the Royal Academy in 1827. He was also responsible for several other important buildings at Ballykelly. He designed St Peter's Hospital, Wandsworth, Surrey, in 1849–51 (exhibited at the Royal Academy in 1851), and the Old Schoolhouse, Gresham's School, Holt, in Norfolk.[3]

The Bridge Committee and the Building Committee of the Fishmongers' Company were in constant touch. It became clear that the design of a new Hall would need to take close account of the massive new Bridge, and both Committees were aware that any design would have to be 'proper'. Drawings defining the new frontage were prepared in Rennie's office, and details of a new embankment wall were prepared by Suter in consultation with Jolliffe & Banks.[4] Jolliffe & Banks of Beaufort Wharf, Strand, were well-known public-works contractors and engineers. They were entrusted with the building of the new Bridge to the designs of John Rennie. The firm had built Waterloo and Southwark Bridges, the Custom House Wharf, and a great many other major undertakings. Materials for the embankment wall were granite, brickwork, ragstone, planks, and piles. Early in 1828, when the embankment was being constructed, Jolliffe & Banks consulted Suter about the advisability of laying down foundations for a new terrace, and agreement was reached to take down the old terrace, excavate, and fill with gravel and stone well grouted. Nevertheless, old brickwork was used as hardcore, dressed over with cement, rather like the old terrace constructed between 1668–9. The ground below the terrace had been filled with old piles, and the contractors suggested these should remain. However, Suter was less sanguine, and with the disastrous sinking of the Custom House three years earlier somewhat to the fore in his mind, recommended removal of the old piles. The Building Committee took Jolliffe & Banks' advice, with unfortunate results, as Henry Roberts was later to determine.

Suter prepared plans to show how much of the site could be let, and went as far as to prepare sketch-plans to demonstrate how the Hall would relate in mass to the Bridge. No doubt the Surveyor was irritated by the number of queries about the future design of the Hall, for young architects with aspirations were anxious to submit plans. The Committee of the Company was clearly not too happy with Suter's proposals, and it was decided to offer 'premiums for the three best designs' in an architectural competition. One of the earliest attempts to interest the Company in a scheme was by J. A. Hansom and Edward Welch, who proposed a Corinthian temple on a high podium in 1828. That design later became the Birmingham Town Hall, which Hansom and Welch won in the competition of 1830. The drawing of an unlabelled Corinthian temple in Guildhall Library is probably that referred to by Welch in 1835: 'I thought a temple mounted on an elevated basement would be a fine design for the Fishmongers' Hall, and would rise above the Thames and Thames Street with a proud outline, and would command considerable admiration. Mr. Hansom then sketched out the design (he sketches better than I can), and soon afterwards gave his sketch to me. I put it into the hands of my friend Capt. Freeman for the purpose of introducing us to the Fishmongers' Company, when occasion might offer. That sketch is what Birmingham Town Hall now is.'[5] Hansom and Welch entered the competition for the Fishmongers' Hall in 1831, but their Roman temple on a high base was out of tune with the style of the new approaches to London Bridge. The Greek Revival had become established.

In August 1831 it was decided to proceed with the rebuilding of the Hall, and £50,000 was set aside for the purpose. The architectural competition was advertised in *The Times*, in *The Morning Chronicle*, and in *The Herald* in September. Designs were to be submitted by 13 December, but this condition was altered to 31 December. Premiums of £200, £150, and £100 were offered for the three best designs, all of which were to be submitted under anonymous mottoes. The wording of the competition is similar to that of the 1822 London Bridge competition, and site plans, copied from Suter's drawings, were available to competitors. The competition instructions were drawn up by Suter and Towse, and were not exactly clear in their intentions. The most significant architectural problems were to give the building important frontages both to the river and to the viaduct leading to the Bridge. The space between the wharf level and the level of the viaduct was to be occupied by a minimum of two storeys containing the cellars, warehouses, and offices, and the Hall kitchens. The basement was to produce 'the greatest possible Value or Rental'. The upper part of the building was to be faced with Bath or Portland stone, or with 'Compo' (a form of stucco). The lower part was to be faced with granite. There was no condition laying down the style, or insisting the design would be sympathetic to the details of the Bridge.

The competition details were sent out to two hundred and twenty-three architects, excluding copies handed out to would-be competitors by members of the Court of the Fishmongers' Company. There were eighty-three entries, most of which were classical in style, and which respected the character of the Bridge. One of the entrants (No. 47) was Charles Fowler, who had won the London Bridge competition, but whose design was set aside in favour of that by John Rennie. Two entries were Gothic in manner, and ten competitors submitted models of their schemes.

On 6 January 1832, the designs were inspected, and from 10–24 January they were exhibited at the Company's temporary accommodation in Aldermanbury. Various letters were received by the Company from competitors who were anxiously awaiting the outcome. Richard Suter wrote to say that other Halls were being rebuilt by the Company Surveyors, and it is clear that he was somewhat upset by the competition. He found himself in a 'peculiar position', for his reputation would be affected by any decision. In any case he exhibited a drawing of the Hall at the Royal Academy.[6]

A short-list of eight schemes was drawn up on 2 February. Two days later design No. 43, consisting of two portfolios and a model, with the motto *Mihi cura futuri* and the logo of a goat, was chosen for the first premium. The model, of wood, with a glass case, appears to have been made by Stephen Salter of Hammersmith, a celebrated architectural model-maker of the day. Correspondence at Guildhall Library suggests Salter was responsible for the model. The author of the winning scheme was Henry Roberts, of 23, Suffolk Street, Pall Mall. The second premium was won by John Davies, of 4, Devonshire Square, and the third premium went to Lewis Nockalls Cottingham, of 4, Basing Place, Waterloo Road. All three designs were classical. Roberts was the youngest of the three winners at twenty-eight, and was certainly the least experienced, although he had excellent offices behind him. It is interesting to note that the goat symbol appears on a gold seal ring that was formerly owned by Frederick Albert Roberts, and which, in 1979, was in the possession of Mrs. J. C. Cuningham. F. A. Roberts also owned a seal, mounted in ivory, for use with wax. This seal formerly was owned by Henry Roberts. The book-plate of Charles Roberts also featured a goat, part of the Roberts family crest. The goat also features in the Coat of Arms granted to Henry Roberts in 1853, and described in the previous chapter.

The design by Henry Roberts worked extremely well (Plates 5–15), although the siting of the kitchens two floors below the banqueting hall would appear to be inconvenient in today's terms. The block was to be rectangular, with north and south wings projecting to the west. The main entrance on the eastern side was linked by a flight of steps to the approach to the Bridge. The carriageway from Thames Street to the wharf was driven under the western projections of the wings. The arches over the carriageway and the arcade of the basement podium were to reflect the massive vaults of the viaduct. Roberts explained that the character of the 'Bridge is here preserved by a Terrace supported on a series of Arches, all the details of which exactly correspond with those of the Bridge, and thus the otherwise objectionable Pier at the foot of the Water Stairs becomes a connecting link'. Indeed the huge modillioned cornice proposed by Roberts exactly matched that of the Bridge and the pier, and lined up with the earlier cornices. The podium contained two storeys devoted to warehouse accommodation that were expressed behind the arcading. The kitchens were placed between the top warehouse-storey and the main entrance-floor of the Hall, lighted from east and from west. The Hall itself was of two apparently identical storeys, unlike in a Palladian arrangement where the top storey would be of lower height. Roberts' master-stroke, however, was to try to place the great Hall itself in a central position, and to carry it above his main entablature as an attic. The great Hall was placed centrally, five bays long, on the east front, with two projecting attic wings over the *antae*. It was less easy to place the Hall centrally on the river front, but he got over the problem by creating a mighty engaged hexastyle range of a Giant Order of Ionic columns supporting a pediment on the south. Thus the river front was suitably grand, while the façade to the west of the viaduct was also treated symmetrically, basically of two storeys on a podium, with a Giant Order of *antae* and two central engaged Ionic columns *in antis* supporting a crowning entablature and balustrade. The arms of the Company gave focus to the centre of the attic storey.

The plan is ingenious. Although the south front is hexastyle, the rooms are not arranged symmetrically behind the south façade. The Court Dining Room occupies the western four bays of the Giant engaged Order, so that a subsidiary axis is created that leads north to the grand staircase. There was a certain similarity to William Wilkins' new University Club, while Roberts' staircase resembled that in the Athenaeum, with its central flight, dividing left and right, then returning in flights against the walls of the staircase compartment. The difficulties of lighting on the west were overcome successfully by creating a light-well between the projecting wings on the west, over the carriageway, so that the frontages on the south and north could extend to the boundary.

There were elegant refinements in Roberts' design that can only be truly appreciated with intimate study of the building itself. The bases of the engaged columns on the south front are visible from the river, as the parapet of the terrace that stands proud of the south front is lower than the main *piano nobile* floor-level. The battered effect of the architraves is very subtle, and is barely discernible. In addition, Roberts introduced an extra cill within the frame of the lower windows, thus giving these lower windows a slightly enhanced importance in keeping with a remembered Palladian past.

If the exterior combines fine massing and proportions with refined detailing, the interior was even more subtle. The segment of an ellipse that formed the section of the ceiling of the Banqueting Hall owes something to the section of the arches of London Bridge itself, as Dr. Priscilla Metcalf has convincingly pointed out. This ellipsoidal section was very unusual for its date, and may be compared with the flat coffered ceilings and the segmental sections of other Halls.

It is not surprising that Roberts should have produced a building of such complexity and elegance. His office at 23, Suffolk Street, was in a fairly new building, not far from Trafalgar Square. Wilkins' University Club (later rebuilt to designs by Blomfield) was opposite; Decimus Burton's new shops had recently been completed in Pall Mall; while Smirke's Union Club and Royal College of Physicians were near at hand. It is clear that the influence of the great Smirke was uppermost in Roberts' mind as he produced his drawings. Indeed, in his letter of 31 December 1831 that accompanied his entry to the competition, Roberts stated that a 'reference to Mr. Smirke' would no doubt be perfectly satisfactory as to his 'professional qualifications, having studied under him during the erection of the New Post Office, the British Museum, the restoration of the Custom House', and many other buildings.

Perhaps even more significant was the fact that the approaches to the new Bridge had been under the supervision of Smirke since 1829, so Roberts was obviously conscious that his design should not offend the eye of the distinguished architect. The influence of Smirke is also discernible in Roberts' use of iron plates to create a fire-resistant barrier between the warehouses in the podium and the Hall above. Smirke had used similar techniques at the Royal Library of the British Museum and at the Custom House which Smirke had reconstructed after its collapse. Roberts also followed the practice of Smirke by providing a 'bed of grouted lime and gravel' as a secure foundation instead of piles. In other words, Roberts formed a raft of concrete to act as the foundation of the new Hall.[7]

It is also interesting to note that Smirke had been on the Building Committee of the Athenaeum Club since 1824, which may account to some extent for the similarities of the interior of Roberts' Hall to that of Decimus Burton's Club.[8] The two main façades of the Fishmongers' Hall were not entirely free from the influence of Smirke. The Giant Ionic Order was a particular favourite of Smirke, while the attic storey on the east front recalls Smirke at his most inventive, especially in the use of large blocked masses to fuse with a Greek Revival style. The east front of the Hall was not unlike the main façade of the old Town Hall in Manchester, designed by Francis Goodwin, and erected between 1822 and 1825. Furthermore, it is very likely that Smirke, wearing his hat as consultant overseer to the Bridge approaches, had his views on Roberts' designs sought after the premium was awarded on 6 February. In any event, several disgruntled competitors assumed that it was Smirke who had got his former young assistant the first prize, and that there were wheels within wheels.[9] There were also dark mutterings about a Tory plot, since Smirke's practice was largely concerned with the Tories, but this was clearly nonsense as the Fishmongers' Company was predominantly Whig and Radical, and very much concerned with reform.

After he was awarded the premium, Roberts wrote to the Company to hope that it would not 'deviate from the customary course on such occasions, but confide to him the superintendence of the Building, convinced that no other Architect could enter so fully into the spirit of the design; and that no remuneration could compensate for the mortification of seeing another reap the benefit of the study and labor [sic] bestowed in forming it; whilst the adoption of a contrary course might, unintentionally, inflict a serious injury on the professional character of an individual'. He need not have worried. On 1 March he was interviewed, and by 12 March he was sitting with the Building Committee, taking instructions. Doubtless he had remembered Fowler's experiences over the London Bridge Competition, and this may have prompted him to write.

Thus, during 1831-2, at a time when there was political unrest over the Great Reform Bill, and Queen Adelaide was convinced she would become the English Marie Antoinette; when the first cholera epidemics struck terror throughout the land, and the first cemeteries had to be laid out in London;[10] and when Britain began an era of unprecedented development and population growth, the Fishmongers' Company and several other old-established institutions determined to express their wealth and their continuity by the erection of splendid new buildings. Indeed, as one member of the Company put it, it was hoped the new Hall would 'last for Centuries . . .' and that the public would appreciate the new building since it was to stand in 'so conspicuous a Situation'.[11]

Roberts was now firmly in the saddle as architect at a crucial time in England's history. Yet the structure of society seemed anything but secure. Quite apart from cholera, riots, and the possibility of revolution, there was a major economic depression. The manufacture of bricks was at a low ebb in 1832.[12] Many contractors had been bankrupted following the collapse of the stock market in 1825 and the crisis in banking that had ruined so many. The new Fishmongers' Hall was commenced on the proceeds of compensation following the construction of London Bridge, augmented by capital, but it was completed largely by borrowing money.

Three basic contracts were organised. The first was signed in April 1832, and concerned the concrete raft. The contract for the shell of the Hall was let in August 1832, and this also involved the finishing of the warehouse in the podium since it was essential to let these as soon as possible in order to recoup some of the finances. The last contract was let in February 1834, and involved the finishing of the interiors of the Hall itself. During 1834-5 Roberts organised the supply of all fixtures, furnishings, and fittings, by dealing directly with specialists, tradesmen, and suppliers.

The concrete raft is about eleven feet below wharf-level, an immense amount of material.[13] The contract was let to Samuel Grimsdell of Bell Lane, Spitalfields, for £1,590, the work to be completed in two months. Excavations began in April, and by June old rubble was still being removed. The depth of the excavations alarmed Sir John Rennie, who feared for the safety of his new Bridge, and who warned the

Company that filling should begin as soon as possible. Roberts immediately ordered Grimsdell to begin concreting, and to provide drains that had not been allowed for. By July, a number of accidents had occurred, which is not surprising, since 'concreting' involved mixing the gravel with lime and water, then throwing the mixture from a height of not less than six feet. While the concrete was being 'thrown', men were treading down and puddling the mass to consolidate it. The work went on section by section, each layer never more than one foot in depth. The whole of the area was covered and set before the next layer was 'thrown'. Speed and nimble feet were obviously essential, and it is amazing there were not more fatal or serious accidents. The site was very wet and unstable, so Roberts was clearly not gambling with his foundations. In fact, the concrete was poured on to a bed of 'muddy peat, in which there were a great number of old piles', presumably dating from Tudor times.[14] Matters were more complicated under the terrace foundations that had been constructed by Jolliffe & Banks in 1828. Suter wrote to the Building Committee on 5 July to point out that these foundations should not be used for a future terrace wall, and recommended that no part of any new structure should be built on the Jolliffe & Banks works. What had happened was that the coffer-dam built as an embankment had left a number of old fir piles behind. These had dried out, and decayed, and Roberts confirmed that the terrace foundation was defective. The old brickwork and timber had to be removed, and Grimsdell was instructed to extend the concrete rate.

These various problems and extras meant that the original period of two months contracted for extended to double that time. Roberts had taken on a new assistant in May, the young George Gilbert Scott, who was later to describe the foundations in a paper at the Institute of British Architects. Scott was only eight years younger than Roberts, and spent two years with him, later claiming to have made 'all the working drawings' for the Hall.[15] In fact, most of the interior drawings are dated 31st January 1834, and these are probably drawn by Scott. Roberts and his assistant moved to new premises at 18, Adam Street, Adelphi, in the autumn of 1832.

Meanwhile, a clerk of the works, one Elisha Bonner, had been appointed in April at a salary of two and a half guineas per week. A well was sunk on the site by Isaac Facer, who specialised in finding springs of 'soft water' but he had to go down two hundred and thirty feet to find water.

In July, fourteen contractors were invited to tender for the Hall buildings, and on 24 August 1832 William and Lewis Cubitt signed the contract to build for £27,750.[16] Quantities to be contracted for were to be drawn up by two quantity surveyors, a novel move at the time. One was to be nominated by the contractor, the other by the architect on behalf of the Company. The fees for both were to be paid by the contractor. An arbitration clause was added to the contract, nominating Smirke, Wilkins, and Hardwick, but none was asked to intervene since no disputes arose. Payment for work was in five parts: the first after a quarter of the work was completed in January 1833; the second up to first-floor level; the third at roof level; the fourth on the completion of the shell; and the last when the warehouses were fitted out in April 1834. Portland stone was provided at a prime cost of £11,000.

The footings were constructed of four courses of Roman cement under six courses of bricks laid in cement, and these were laid directly on the raft. The timber chain-plates through the footings were 'Kyanised' by John Howard Kyan, who had patented a new method of preserving timber by immersion in 'corrosive sublimates'. Smirke was a keen user of Kyan's process, and presumably it was he who introduced Roberts to the method.

The shell of the Hall consisted of brickwork with a stone skin. The floor of the Hall itself, between it and the warehouse-podium, was constructed of brick arches bedded in concrete, springing from cast-iron bearers that were spaced with tie-rods. Walls were of best London stocks, and the podium was clad in Devon granite. It is interesting to note that Roberts used hollow bricks for the internal brickwork. These resembled garden-pots, closed at both ends, and had been used at the General Post Office by Smirke, and at the Bank of England vaults by Soane. Nash had used hollow bricks or pot-tiles at Buckingham Palace, while William Wilkins had also built with them at the National Gallery. Hollow pots had been used for fireproof construction in some of the early mills of Shropshire, but it will also be recalled that the Romans used *amphoræ* or hollow pots for certain concrete vaults, notably at *San Vitale* in Ravenna. The main purpose was to lighten the structures, but additional acoustical advantages were found in Ravenna and also in the vaults of certain mediaeval churches. The pot-tiles in the vaults of the Banqueting Hall of the Fishmongers' Company help to create an especially felicitous acoustic for music.[17]

Roberts also used much iron, both cast and wrought, at the Hall. Two girders, each forty feet long, support the west wall of the Banqueting Hall, and these are carried on two pairs of columns at the foot of the stairs. It is interesting to note that these columns were originally to be of cast iron, clad with scagliola, but Roberts later substituted solid granite, on grounds of honesty and to give an appearance of structural strength. In addition, scagliola, in a position where it would be exposed to damage, would not be the ideal material, so red Aberdeen granite was chosen instead. The working of this very hard material had only just been perfected, and it is perhaps not insignificant that Smirke had specified red granite from the Stirling Hill quarry at Peterhead for the King's Library at the British Museum. It was this quarry that also provided the stone for the columns inside the Fishmongers' Hall.[18] Four unfluted Doric columns and four unfluted pilasters were shaped and fixed for £432. These handsome granite columns and pilasters are perhaps slightly over-slender for Greek Doric, but this appears to have been due to the need to economise, for Roberts had originally obtained prices for £516 for fluted shafts, and it seems that in the general desire for economy, proportions and detail suffered slightly.

Most of the roofs of the new Hall were clad in slate, although there was a lead flat over the roof of the staircase, and copper on 'Borrowdale's Patent Felt' over the Banqueting Hall itself.

As the carcass of the building neared completion, specifications for the interior were produced. Cubitts refused to enter into any competitive tendering, and so on 31 January 1834 Cubitts' tender for finishing the Hall, including plastering, was accepted at a figure of £17,500. In 1834, the newly perfected plate glass was used to glaze the south and east fronts.

Surprisingly old-fashioned opinions prevailed regarding the heating of the Hall. The Fishmongers' Company determined to stick to the well-tried method of heating by fireplaces, despite Roberts' pleas to introduce a system of heating via radiators. A register stove was placed in the entrance hall, made of polished steel, cast iron, and bronze.

Progress was good, and bell-hangings were carried out by John Barrow. Yellow scagliola was used for columns and pilasters, all provided by Joseph Browne's Scagliola Works. Stained glass was by Hancock and Rixon, all to designs by Roberts. All carpentry, joinery, marblework and stonework were carried out by Cubitts. Timber was oak or 'best dry Memel wood'. At the time there was great resistance to the use of American or Canadian wood, which was unseasoned, and more liable to decay than good wood imported from Danzig and Memel.

Roberts produced individual designs of all the chimney-pieces, and no less than twenty-seven of his designs survive. Black, white, and red Mona marbles were used. These designs also proved to be the basis of chimney-pieces by Roberts at Peamore House, Devon; Escot House, Devon; Toft Hall, Cheshire; and Exton Hall, Rutland. All rooms were illuminated by gas-light, provided by James DeVille of 367, Strand, who was also a brass-founder. Gas-light was provided in the entrance-hall, corridor, back-stair, basement passage, kitchen, scullery, and basement entrance. Limited gas-light was to be provided in the Great Hall and grand stair-case. Elsewhere, candles and oil-lamps provided illumination that was enhanced by an extensive use of mirrors.

Roberts' grasp of decoration was thoroughly professional. Marble, gilt, and rose-wood were his main materials, while mirrors, green silk, and damask were used in profusion. He produced exceptionally refined interiors, very typical of the décor of the Greek Revival style, and a tribute to his reticent good taste.

Unfortunately the Fishmongers' Hall was completed just when there was the beginning of a major revolt against Smirke, Soane, and all they stood for. The Greek Revival was already under attack for its flatness, and heavier shadows, greater cornices, and huge porticos were demanded by the *avant-garde*. Yet, despite the critics, one of the most perceptive anti-Greeks, W. H. Leeds, saw a great deal to praise in the new Hall.[19] Leeds saw the subtleties, and praised much of the décor. Roberts used a version of the elegant Corinthian Order of the Monument of Lysicrates in his formal spaces where decorative emphasis was desired.[20]

The final cost of the Hall was £51,533, which compared favourably with Roberts' estimate of £58,500. This was Roberts' first as well as his last major commission, for, despite his designs for a new terminus at London Bridge and much work in philanthropic housing, he never again built a major public or institutional building, either from choice or from lack of it.

In April 1840, final painting and gilding of the Hall began under Roberts' direction. The prevailing hues were cream, white, gold, bronze, black, and steel. The delicate 'chryselephantine' tones were to be obliterated by Owen Jones in his redecorations of 1865. In any case, Roberts had no further association with the Hall after 1840. His work there was done. He had completed his masterpiece.

The new Fishmongers' Hall was, in a sense, an amalgam of all the best aspects of the Greek Revival school of Smirke. It had a great deal in common with the British Museum and with other buildings by the great Sir Robert. The refined details and the splendid interiors demonstrate how much Roberts had learned from his masters. Fresh from his Continental tour, Roberts produced an assured and noble building. *The Architectural Magazine* of April 1834, however, was not excessively enthusiastic. The Hall was regarded as 'a piece of building' of which the critic could 'not at all approve, from the use which has been made of three-quarter columns in two of the elevations'. In 'other respects' the journal continued, the building was 'good'. The elliptical coffered ceiling of the Banqueting Hall caused much favourable comment and the ceilings were much admired. The entrance hall and main staircase were also appreciated. The richness of the fireplaces and mantles, doors, and especially the exquisite door-furniture can still be admired today.

Although Roberts was later to achieve fame as the architect of working-class housing, his design for the Hall can be regarded as one of the most elegant of the Greek Revival. He exhibited a drawing of the 'Banquetting Room, Fishmongers' Hall', at the Royal Academy in 1838, numbered 1118 in the *Catalogue*. It has been said (by Sir John Summerson) that after the Fishmongers' Hall, Henry Roberts' works were never so grand, while those of Scott were never so pure. There may be a great deal of truth in this, for Roberts was never again to design a building of such splendour.

Chapter Three

THE EVANGELICAL CONSCIENCE AND THE FOUNDING OF THE SOCIETY FOR IMPROVING THE CONDITION OF THE LABOURING CLASSES

To contribute to the welfare of our fellow-creatures, with a view to the glory of God, carries with it that durable happiness which the pursuit of wealth, of fame, or of fleeting pleasure, cannot afford.

Henry Roberts, in his *The Dwellings of the Labouring Classes*, London, 1867, p.28.

BEFORE GOING ON to describe the work of the Society for Improving the Condition of the Labouring Classes (with which Henry Roberts was so intimately involved), it will be necessary to set the scene by attempting to picture the extraordinary birth of the Evangelical Conscience of Victorian England.

Francis Sheppard[1] has described how the appointment of John Venn as Rector of Clapham in 1792 had far-reaching effects. Venn owed his appointment to the trustees of John Thornton who had owned the patronage of the living. All three sons of Thornton were Members of Parliament, and two were directors of the Bank of England. Henry Thornton, the youngest of John Thornton's sons, had purchased the manor house at Battersea Rise, and had invited his friend William Wilberforce to live with him there. Old Thornton had been a devoted Evangelical, and had used much of his wealth in his lifetime to purchase advowsons to ensure the furtherance of his principles. Wilberforce and the Thorntons became the centre of the circle of Evangelicals and reformers, including Charles Grant (the promoter of missionary work in the East), Edward Eliot (the brother-in-law of William Pitt), James Stephen (a convinced Abolitionist of slavery), Zachary Macaulay (also an Abolitionist), and Lord Teignmouth (later the first president of the British and Foreign Bible Society). The latter was also known to Roberts and was a Vice-President of the S.I.C.L.C.

The Clapham Sect was bound by faith, by philanthropic zeal, and by the central figure of Wilberforce. Venn went out into his parish and worked tirelessly for his calling. He inveighed against drunkenness and vice, and struggled heroically against sloth, apathy, and immorality. Venn became the model for the revival of Christian life in thousands of parishes, and was able to claim at the end of his life that every child in his parish could read and write, and that every family could be supplied with a Bible and could find a seat in church.

Venn sought to educate the poor, and, through education, he hoped that Christianity would flourish. Like other Evangelicals, he thought that attentivity, docility, submissiveness, and reasonableness were virtues that ought to be drummed into the poor. In 1799 Venn founded the Society for Bettering the Condition of the Poor at Clapham, one of the first of the London philanthropic societies, and a committee was formed which met monthly. Visitors were empowered to give financial assistance to the needy, but before further relief was given, 'information should be particularly sought concerning the moral character of the applicant, particularly if he is accustomed to attend public worship, whether he sends his children to school, and trains them in the habit of industry'.[2] The poor were thus divided into two categories: the deserving and the undeserving. Bettering meant more than the relief of immediate want: it meant extricating the poor from all future want; the instilling of good principles; the elevation of minds to a state of independence; and the raising of the poor to higher tones of character.

Clapham was the first home of the Evangelical Conscience, although there were other early centres, such as Cambridge. It was because so many members of the Clapham Sect were wealthy and prominent people that they were able to exert an influence far beyond anything their numbers might have indicated. The members of the Sect achieved much, notably the abolition of the Slave Trade in 1807, the reform of the penal code, the emancipation of Roman Catholics, the abolition of press gangs, and the prohibition of the employment of child chimney-sweeps. The Sect was also the foundation of the Church Missionary Society (1799) and of the British and Foreign Bible Society (1804). In 1802 the Sect established *The Christian Observer* as a vehicle for Evangelical Christian ideas, including opposition to duelling, to bear-baiting, and to state lotteries. The London Anti-Slavery Society was founded by members of the Clapham Sect in 1823, and in 1833 the Act of Parliament abolishing slavery in the West Indies was passed.

There is no doubt that the Evangelical Christians, of whom the Clapham Sect had been the original leaders, were in the vanguard of the formative influences in the creation of the conscience of Victorian England. As Sheppard says, never 'in the whole history of the Church of England has any group of Anglicans exerted so profound an effect on the life of the whole nation as they. The intensity of their religious faith and of their zeal for good works provided the foundation for Victorian morality'.[3] It also was the basis for the whole philanthropic movement in which Henry Roberts was so actively involved.

This brings us to a fundamental aspect of Roberts' character that it is essential to understand. Roberts was a devout and zealous Evangelical Christian, who was a personal friend of one of the most celebrated Evangelical preachers of his day, the Rev. Baptist Noel. Many people who were involved in the Society for Improving the Condition of the Labouring Classes were also members of the Clapham Sect, or had been greatly influenced by the philosophies and aims of the Sect. The members strove with immense energy to put their ideas into practice. Clapham became the model for the revival of Christian life throughout the country. In the previous chapter the fact that several members of the Clapham Sect were members of Baptist Noel's congregation at St John's Chapel, Bedford Row, has been noted.

The problem of housing in the nineteenth century was essentially in urban centres, although there were appalling conditions in the housing of the rural poor. An unprecedented growth of proletarian population in the towns caused difficulties that the free market system and *laissez-faire* could not begin to solve. The drift to the towns was becoming something that could no longer be ignored, for public amenities such as the supply of water, the removal of rubbish, drainage, and the burial of the dead[4] were no longer capable of serving the needs of the growing population. Not until the first cholera epidemic occurred in 1832 did it dawn on politicians that an enormous problem existed, for choked burial-grounds, evil-smelling streams, and foul cess-pits were thought to exude a 'miasma' that was the cause of cholera. There had been some recognition of a rising social problem following the 'Peterloo' affair of 1819, and Chartism was eyed with some anguish as a possible source of revolution. Parliament recognised the changed structure of the nation in 1832 when the Great Reform Bill became law, and franchise was greatly extended. The first joint-stock cemetery companies were promoted in the 1830s, and the *Municipal Corporations Act* was passed in 1835, giving votes to all ratepayers. In 1834 a new *Poor Law Act* was passed, initiating a workhouse test and abolishing outdoor relief, while providing a workable structure for a national network of Poor Law Boards of Guardians with their own medical officers.

Housing and public health were concerns of the Victorian age. Overcrowding, ill-health, disease, and mortality were themes returned to again and again, while water supplies and drainage were seen to be essential, although it took several cholera epidemics and much propaganda to convince the public that something was not right. one of the great figures in the sanitary reform movement was Edwin Chadwick, the first Secretary of the Poor Law Commissioners, and one of the three great members of the General Board of Health, established under the *Public Health Act* of 1848.

The local Boards of Guardians from 1836 were required to register births, marriages, and deaths, and Chadwick, by analysing these registers, was able for the first time to give a factual statement regarding the health of the country. The Commissioners were able to report to the Home Secretary figures of mortality, and the Poor Law Board was required to prepare a full report. In 1840 the Government appointed a Select Committee to inquired 'into the circumstances of large towns, with a view to improved sanitary arrangements for their benefits'. The Committee also recommended a new General Building Act and a Sewage Act.

Chadwick is probably most celebrated for his *Report on the Sanitary Condition of the Labouring Population and on the Means of its Improvement* of 9 July 1842, signed by the Poor Law Commissioners. The result was a Royal Commission on the Health of Towns which provided a report on 3 February 1845 based on the techniques Chadwick had used in the earlier *Report* of 1842. These reports contained various suggestions for improvements, including J. C. Loudon's high-rise blocks.[5]

The revelations about how the urban poor lived awakened the consciences of many sections of the public. A Health of Towns Association was formed, backed by several peers and by the young Disraeli. Not until the fearsome cholera visitation of 1848 was the *Public Health Act* passed, but in the meantime the first stirrings of action by philanthropists had begun.

The Evangelical Conscience, as aroused by the Clapham Sect, was one of the most significant strands in the pattern of social responsibility that concerns the story of Henry Roberts. Epidemics did not confine themselves to the working classes, and many people believed that it was essential to cleanse the minds and bodies, as well as the habitations, of the labouring classes before contagion more deadly than cholera destroyed the fabric of Christian society. Riot and revolution were known in Europe in 1830 and in 1848, and fears of Jacobinism were as real as the fears of disease. The vast problem of poor and overcrowded housing made it clear that legislative powers had to be sought relating to both sanitary and structural conditions of buildings. Those who had a social conscience wondered how the working classes were to be adequately housed and by whom. Workers had to live near their place of work, as wages were low and rents took a sizeable amount of the weekly wage. Pressure for accommodation was great, and most accommodation was found in single rooms in houses that had once been occupied as family dwellings by the middle classes. Over-occupation of such houses meant lack of ventilation, lack of drainage, over-taxation of water supply, and gross deprivation of privacy, decency, and basic cleanliness. Housing reformers recognised the need for standards that would give dignity back to the dwellings of the labouring classes. One of the greatest problems, however, was that of acquiring land, for housing was required near centres where the price of ground was very high. It was necessary to wean the drunkards off the bottle by example, just as Christian piety could only be achieved by example: therefore, the reformers argued, standards of good housing could only be achieved by example.

The contribution of those with an Evangelical Conscience was very great. The housing reform movement began as a result of action by groups of people imbued with a sense of duty, and with no hope of financial gain. The recognised key figure in the early philanthropic movement was Anthony Ashley Cooper, later the seventh Earl of Shaftesbury (1801–85). He became a Tory M.P. in 1826, and held junior ministerial rank under Wellington and Peel, but before succeeding to the title in 1851 had taken up a fairly independent political stance. Housing and the social condition of the poor occupied him longer than any of the causes he later championed, although his name is usually associated with the reform of the laws relating to lunacy, to factories, to the employment of women and children in mines; with the ragged school movement; with the reformatory movement; with the protection of animals; and with Evangelical and missionary zeal. One of his last involvements was to give evidence to the Royal Commission on the Housing of the Working Classes in 1884. As Lord Ashley (his courtesy title), he combined his Toryism with an active Evangelical Conscience in the field of working-class philanthropic housing. He knew many figures of the Clapham Sect.

That peculiarly Victorian phenomenon, the provision of housing by philanthropists, grew from an organisation founded (under the name of The Labourers' Friend Society in 1830) by a group that included the Bishop of Bath and Wells. The founder of The Labourers' Friend Society was Benjamin Wills. The first Annual General Meeting was held on 18 February 1832 and reported that the Society derived its origin and establishment 'principally from the zeal and humanity of an individual who for many years has dedicated his time and talents to the great object of improving the condition of the poor. From his correspondence with eminent and philanthropic men . . . and to his unremitting efforts and those of a few friends . . . the Society owes both its existence and its preservation'. The Labourers' Friend Society grew from an earlier society called the Society for Improving the Condition of the Labouring Classes, founded by Wills and his associates in 1825, but after the publication in 1825 of a book of cottage and farm designs and the erection, in 1827, of twelve model cottages at Shooters' Hill, the Society foundered through lack of support. The resurrected and renamed Society of 1830 aimed to provide small allotments of land for labourers (at moderate rents) for cultivation during leisure house, a system that the Bishop of Bath and Wells had operated on his own estates. The idea was to assist labourers to free themselves from dependence on charitable assistance and the Poor Rate.

Membership of the Society stood at about five hundred in the first year of its existence. Bishop Law and Lord Kenyon were the first Vice-Presidents. Agents were employed to interview landowners, members of the public, clergymen, and persons of influence; to arrange public meetings and publicity; and to form auxiliary associations in the provinces. During the first five years the Society recorded the grant of allotments to some seventy thousand families, a colossal number indeed. Many branch societies were formed and the plans of the Society were adopted by landowners throughout the Kingdom. Circulation of the Society's Journal, *The Labourers' Friend*, reached about one thousand four hundred copies monthly. The success of the Society encouraged its committee to promote Benefit Societies, Clothing Clubs, Loan Funds, Schools, and Dispensaries, based on the experiences of the London Companies in their Model Towns in Ulster. At meetings held throughout the country, agents argued for an improvement in the construction and design of labourers' cottages to benefit both the health and the morals of the inhabitants. The policy of disseminating information continued, but in 1844 a number of eminent people changed the direction of the Society. The Society appears to have been given a new lease of life by Sir Thomas Bernard in 1834, when the magazine *The Labourers' Friend* first appeared. The original Society's cottages for agricultural workers at Shooters' Hill were illustrated by the indefatigable John Claudius Loudon in his *Encyclopaedia of Cottage, Farm, and Villa Architecture* in 1833. When a number of influential people, including Lord Ashley, became interested in the Society, they expressed the opinion that the Society should be enlarged and its funds augmented to allow it to undertake some of the improvements it advocated. It appears that Ashley and his colleagues realised that an existing society with an established journal would be an ideal starting point for their ambitious ideas to create models, or examples, for other reformers to follow.

The Labourers' Friend reported that there had been an important change in the Society in 1844, for a 'body of gentlemen not hitherto connected with the Society' had been 'recently aroused to a sense of the necessity of making more efforts to ameliorate the condition of the labouring classes'.[6] On Saturday 11 May 1844 a meeting was held in Willis's Rooms, St James's, called by a group that included Ashley and Dr. Southwood Smith, the sanitarian who had worked with Chadwick, and who prepared Jeremy Bentham's body for permanent display at University College, London. Ashley was in the Chair, and announced that the purpose of the meeting was to form a society to be called the Society for the Improvement of the Condition of the Poor. The objects of the Society included the improvement of the dwellings of the poor, the extension of the cottage allotment system, and the introduction of Friendly Loan Societies. Henry Roberts was at this inaugural meeting, and was elected to the Committee. He donated one guinea to the Society.[7] A more powerful and influential Society capable of demonstrating (both in town and country) the benefits that would be secured for the poorer classes, and for the nation, by a better standard of housing; by the extension of the land allotment idea; and by the formation of Friendly Loan Societies, was the aim of the invigorated body. The Society recognised it would have to cope with a 'social evil of greater magnitude than any ever yet undertaken by a voluntary society'..

The idea of introducing allotments into the environs of London was floated, so that workers would grow their own vegetables 'to such an extent as materially to reduce, if not entirely eradicate, the pauperism heretofore existing in the place'.[8] It was also proposed to build a 'planned dwelling, or cottages' that would combine 'comfort with economy'.

From the Minutes of the Society for Improving the Condition of the Labouring Classes, now held by the Peabody Trust, it appears that no time was lost in setting up Executive Committees. A Secretary was appointed at a salary of two hundred pounds per annum, and a Clerk and Agent were also appointed at salaries of forty pounds and one hundreds pounds each per annum. The offices of the Society were the same as those formerly occupied by the Labourers' Friend Society at 20, Exeter Hall, the rent for which was forty pounds per annum. Roberts first attended a committee meeting on 30 May 1844. By 6 June 1844 the Queen and the Queen Dowager had transferred their patronage from the Labourers' Friend Society, and the Prince Consort had been approached regarding the Presidency. Roberts was appointed to the Dwellings Committee.

The Society for Improving the Condition of the Labouring Classes (as it became known) gained fame as a first-rate philanthropic housing society, and the allotment and loan ideas soon became secondary considerations. With the enlargement of the Society, however, the land allotment movement initially gained strength. Several suitable sites were secured, and the Society popularised the system until 1858, when the Committee was able to report that the movement had taken root throughout the country. So successful had it become that the 'work of the Society . . . was satisfactorily concluded'. Steps were taken to liquidate the land holdings by transferring the leases to other associations or to benevolent individuals. From its beginnings, the S.I.C.L.C. was eminently respectable. Queen Victoria had been patron of The Labourers' Friend Society, and as stated already, her patronage was transferred to the reformed organisation (which Roberts sometimes referred to by its old name). The Prince Consort became the President, and the Vice-Presidents included the Archbishop of Canterbury, the Duke of Manchester, Lord John Russell, Lord Ashley, Sir John Dean Paul, Bart., J. H. H. Foley, W. A. Mackinnon, M.P., and Samuel Gurney. The Committee was chaired by Lord Ashley, and included Henry Roberts, J. Dean Paul (Sir John's son), F. L. Wollaston, and Joseph Toynbee.[9] These names are significant. Sir John Dean Paul was the Chairman of the General Cemetery Company[10] and had played an important part in setting up joint-stock cemetery companies to relieve the dreadful overcrowding in churchyards. As stated in Chapter One, he owned a bank in The Strand which crashed in 1855. He was Augustus J. C. Hare's maternal grandfather, and was related by marriage to the Leycesters of Toft and to the Strathmores of Glamis. W. A. Mackinnon was an M.P. and was most active in the agitation to reform towns. He was responsible for much parliamentary work relating to the banning of intramural interment, and was a leading figure in the promotion of health in towns.

Roberts was to carry out work at Kimbolton for the Duke of Manchester, while Lord Calthorpe, Vice-Patron of the Society, a friend of Wilberforce, Evangelist and member of the Clapham Sect, was to employ Roberts as his architect at Elvetham, and owned the land on which the first model houses were built by the Society to Roberts' designs. One of the most interesting names on the list, however, is that of F. L. Wollaston, a merchant-banker engaged in trade with Genoa, and who probably introduced Roberts to Genoese society in the following decade. The Wollastons lived in Clapham, and were prominent in the Evangelical movement.

The Society was basically an exemplary organisation, and was determined to keep dividends low. In fact dividends were limited by the Charter of 1850 to a maximum of four per cent per annum, a restraint that was to have an adverse effect on finances since more attractive returns on investments could be found elsewhere (St James's Cemetery in Liverpool was paying eight per cent in 1831). Chadwick argued that the low rates of interest were commercially unwise as well as savouring of charity, two factors which must in the long run damage the philanthropic societies, both from the financial point of view and from that of the tenants. As John Nelson Tarn, in his *Five Per Cent Philanthropy*, has noted, Chadwick was firmly committed to the placing of philanthrophic housing societies on sound commercial footings in order to benefit 'the working classes'.[11] The petition for the charter of 1850 stated that 'the individual members of the Society have never sought or derived any personal profit whatever from the rents received in respect of the property purchased or taken by the Society'.[12]

Roberts attended Committee meetings with regularity. He himself was to describe the early work of the Society in his classic *The Dwellings of the Labouring Classes, Their Arrangement and Construction; illustrated by a reference to the Model Houses of the Society for Improving the Condition of the Labouring Classes, and other buildings recently erected: being an Essay, read January 21, 1850, at the Royal Institute of British Architects.*[13] The S.I.C.L.C. 'to which the Labourers' Friend Society is United' sought to execute plans as 'Models, for the Improvement of the Dwellings of the Poor, both in the Metropolis and in the Manufacturing and Agricultural Districts'. It also sought to establish the 'Field-Garden and Cottage-Allotment System, and also Friendly or Benefit and Loan Societies, upon sound principles'. The results would be reported 'with a view to rendering' the data 'available as Models for more extended adoption'. The Society also sought to form 'County, Parochial, and District Associations, Acting upon uniform plans and rules'. A further object was to correspond with 'Clergymen, Magistrates, Landed Proprietors, and others disposed to render assistance in their respective localities either individually, or as Members of Local Associations'.

The Society gradually produced a model set of rules. It found itself unable to make an effectual contribution to the formation of Friendly Societies, and concentrated on three aims:

> Firstly, to build model dwellings to demonstrate that commodious and healthy dwellings could be provided at moderate yet remunerative rents;
>
> Secondly, to issue plans calculated to promote the construction of improved dwellings for the working classes;
>
> Thirdly, to correspond with landed gentry, clergymen, and others, in order to assist in the erection of dwellings and the establishment of branch societies.

Roberts noted that few architects had given much attention to the problem of providing housing for the labouring classes as it offered 'little scope for scientific skill, and but few attractive points to an artist's eye'. He stated that he had once felt the same, but the profession should be as involved as the 'philanthropist and political economist'. The 'highest achievements of architecture are accomplished through the . . . working classes, whose skill and persevering industry conduce as much to the fame of the Architect as the steady valour of the soldier does to weave a crown of victory around the brow of his triumphant General'.[14]

To Roberts, it was clear that 'the merest fraction' of the working classes could help itself. Improvements of the condition of the labouring classes were a moral and hygienic necessity. He dwelt on the house-to-house inspection of houses in St George's parish, Hanover Square, in 1842. There, the inspection had shown that 1,465 families lived in 2,174 rooms, and slept on 2,510 beds. 929 families lived in single rooms, and 623 families had only one bed each. Poor ventilation, drainage, and water supply, together with overcrowding that 'would not be tolerated in farmyards, stables, or dogkennels', were usual. Roberts wrote that in 1846 he visited a house in St Giles's in one room of which (22 feet x 16 feet, with a low ceiling) there was no ventilation except through 'some broken squares of glass', yet forty to sixty people were living in it, with dogs and cats.

He was greatly concerned to actively operate 'Christian principles' to effect improvements in dwellings in the same way as Howard had improved prisons. Roberts contrasted the 'domiciliary comforts' enjoyed by 'those who have forfeited their free-dom as the penalty of crime' with the 'wretched homes from which at present too many of our labouring population are tempted to escape to the gin-palace or the beer-shop — those very portals of domestic misery and moral ruin'. Here was the Evangelical Conscience in full spate.

There was clearly an urgent necessity to make even 'humble abodes' dry and well-ventilated. The height of the rooms should not be less than seven feet six inches. Family dwellings should have at least three bedrooms, each with distinct and separate access. A fireplace was essential in the main bedroom. Vents for 'vitiated air' should be placed near ceilings, and chimney valves were useful for air-changes if they were properly constructed, as the heat drew the air up, and thus ensured adequate changes, although it was essential to provide a ventilated lobby or porch to avoid unnecessary draughts. Casements should open outwards, and Roberts felt zinc was useful in their construction, for if the 'quarries are well-proportioned, the effect is not so different to that of lead'.

The Society presented successive models for improved dwellings, and published them, but it was decided that no amount of description or reasoning would suffice. An actual experiment was essential. In July 1844 *The Labourers' Friend* stated that three sub-committees had been set up to deal with cottage allotments, dwellings, and loans.[15] The Society was looking for a site, and in due course one was found at Bagnigge Wells, Lower Road, Pentonville, at the top of Gray's Inn Road. The land was owned by Lord Calthorpe, and on 19 July 1844 the rent for the site was agreed at fifty pounds per annum. Twenty pounds were paid for completing a retaining wall, and Roberts' plans were approved. A lease of ninety-nine years was agreed, and Lord

Calthorpe magnanimously agreed to sell the land to the Society for that term clear of rent for the sum of one thousand pounds. On 10 October 1844 John Thompson of Camberwell (where Roberts had family connections) contracted to build ten houses 'in the rear of Pakenham Street' at a cost of £1,670. Donations had to be requested to complete the work, and many contributed, including Sir John Kennaway, Bart. (Roberts' client in Devon). Lord Calthorpe himself was serving on committees of the Society in 1845, and in July of that year potential tenants were interviewed.[16]

It was not a very promising site, for it was made-up ground (which limited the height and caused foundation problems), and was very long and narrow. There was great resistance to the securing of the land owing to opposition from the owners of surrounding property. However, the Model Dwellings consisted of a 'double row of two-storey houses, facing each other, and on three distinct plans, to accommodate in the whole twenty-three families, and thirty single females. In their arrangement, the main object has been to combine every point essential to the health, comfort, and moral habits of the industrious classes and their families, particular attention being paid to *ventilation, drainage, and an ample supply of water*'.[17] Nos. 1, 2, 4, 5, 10, and 11 were the residences of twelve families, each occupying a floor with two rooms, the larger room being 13 feet by 10 feet, and the smaller being 10 feet 6 inches by 7 feet 6 inches. 'All requisite conveniences' were provided separately for each family, 'with distinct access to the upper floor'. The eight houses, Nos. 6, 7, 8, 9, 12, 13, 14, and 15 were the residences of eight families, each having on the ground floor a living room, 13 feet 6 inches by 12 feet 6 inches, with a lobby, enclosed recess for beds, closets, and a scullery under the stairs, with a small courtyard. The upper floor of each house was divided into two small bedrooms, the larger being 12 feet 6 inches by 10 feet 6 inches, and the smaller being 13 feet by 7 feet 6 inches. The house, No. 3, was intended as the residence of the thirty females. Each woman had a room, 12 feet 6 inches by 8 feet 6 inches, approached by a corridor, and lighted and ventilated in the centre and at both ends. A sunken wash-house for the use of the inmates was provided at the back of No. 4, while another wash-house adjoining was provided for the use of the other tenants. A further three houses were built on the east side of the ground. Rents were two shillings for single rooms and six shillings per week for two-bedroomed houses.

On the basis of this exercise, Roberts estimated that the cost of the buildings was £5,325, and he allowed for £1,045 as the cost of the land. Rents were £391 per annum. Taxes and expenses, exclusive of repairs, came to £83. The return was therefore 4.33 per cent of the cost of the buildings, and 4 per cent on the cost of the land. He stated that the use of hollow bricks or tile arches in the construction of the floors would add greatly to the comfort of families lodged one above the other. If the streets could be wider, then the blocks could be taller, and access to the upper floors could be gained via galleries, or, perhaps, one stair might give access to a number of tenement apartments on each floor. Internal stairs were undesirable if they were common to several families, as the problems of cleanliness would be great.

The Bagnigge Wells scheme was the first in London to provide the working class with a new kind of housing, specially designed for the purpose, and it was the first time in London that an architect had turned his hand to such work, with anything approaching conviction (*see* Figures 3–4). The first working-class tenements in England were probably those built by the Birkenhead Dock Company in 1845 (*see* Figure 11), and there were other developments in Glasgow and Edinburgh. Thus Roberts' design was a landmark in housing history of the urban fabric. Roberts was thereafter responsible for most of the work of the S.I.C.L.C. and so he was a great pathfinder in the realms of housing design, and must be regarded as the father of the whole working-class housing movement. The Bagnigge Wells scheme was not a true innovation, however, for it resembled speculative terraces of the period, although it was soundly built and paid proper attention to hygiene and to ventilation. As a whole, however, the site was overdeveloped, accommodation was minimal, and the planning was uninteresting. Contemporary critics, including Roberts' acquaintance George Godwin (1815–88), the Editor of *The Builder*, disliked the somewhat drab rows, and particularly denounced the miserably small yards at the rear.[18] 'Anxious to examine the Society's first work', Godwin 'hastened to the site of the new houses' and regretted to say that his 'worst anticipations' were confirmed. 'The arrangement is a disgrace to the Society, and cannot surely have been seen by Lord Ashley, the Chairman of the Committee . . . These houses, model houses remember . . . are actually arranged to form a court open at one end only, and less than 23 feet in width at the widest part! The plot of ground, on which the fifteen buildings are crammed is so small, that, notwithstanding this proximity, the yard attached to each house, is literally what its name imparts in fact, or very little more. We call most urgently on the committee and the shareholders to prevent the consummation of this most dangerous mistake, or they will rear a hot-bed for infection, and throw a great impediment in the way of that improvement which they profess to seek'.[19] The estate was completed in 1846, and was open for viewing from 23 to 28 March. There were three types of accommodation: two-storey houses divided into two-room flats; houses, each with a living-room (with bed-recess), scullery, two bedrooms, and a walled yard; and a lodging house for widows, each of whom would have a separate room. Despite Godwin's severe criticisms, however, this first set of buildings won some approval, and, more important, 'liberal contributions' for the Society.[20]

The Royal Commission on the Health of Towns reported in 1844 and 1845, and the Health Act was in gestation in the late 1840s. Another important housing society, the Metropolitan Association for Improving the Dwellings of the Industrious Classes (founded in 1841) was starting to build, having spent several years getting capital in order to build on a commercial basis. Two ambitious projects were started in 1848 and 1849: the family dwellings in Old St Pancras Road, designed by W. B. Moffat; and the Mile End New Town scheme by William Beck. Roberts was interested in these developments, because the internal stair at Old St Pancras Road (Figure 14) had involved a heavy window-tax of £152 16s. 0d. per annum, although Roberts could quite see the logic of the planning. The Lodging-House by Beck at Mile End New Town incorporated a coffee-room, a lecture room, and a reading room. The two Societies became the centre of housing experiment, and the S.I.C.L.C. began to evolve schemes for lodging-houses. The next step was to exhibit a Model of an Improved Lodging-House for Working Men. Most lodging-houses of the time were a 'reproach to the Christianity of England', in the words of Roberts. The Society bought three existing lodging-houses in 'one of the worst neighbourhoods of London', Charles Street, Drury Lane, in January 1847.

They were renovated and fitted up with conveniences for eighty-two men, who were charged four pence per night, the same as less wholesome places (*see* Figure 5). The experiment was a success, and proved it was financially viable, although Roberts conceded that 'however valuable as an experiment, and calculated as a stimulant to produce highly beneficial results, the houses in Charles Street cannot be considered as the model of what a lodging-house ought to be'.[20] At one stage the Committee of the London City Mission agreed to transfer its Newton Street lodging-house for Females to the Society (this was presumably originally mooted through Roberts' friendship with Noel and other Evangelicals), but the conditions laid down by the S.I.C.L.C. were regarded as too stringent.

The S.I.C.L.C. determined to acquire freehold land in George Street, Bloomsbury, for one hundred and four men and boys. 'It is on behalf of this large, much neglected and deserving class, and with a view of showing how they may be rescued from the discomfort and contamination to which they are at present (through no fault of their own) so injuriously subjected, that the Committee propose erecting a Model Lodging-House in St Giles's'.[21] The site was acquired for £1,200 from the Committee of Woods and Forests, and Prince Albert gave £100 towards the cost of building. Subscriptions were invited and £2,657 10s. 0d. had been donated by September 1846. Tenders were obtained, that of Robert Hicks being the lowest at £3,930, and his was accepted.

This House was built to designs by Roberts (*see* Figures 6–7), who was first referred to as the 'Honorary Architect' in the Minutes of November 1847, although it appears from Roberts' own writings that he held this title from 1844. The house was five storeys high, with a basement containing kitchens and laundries. The main entrance and stair were placed in the centre of the block, and the common room and superintendent's flat were disposed on either side of the stair on the ground floor. The floors above were dormitories, privacy being assured by the erection of partition walls. There was a communal wash-room on each floor with six wash-hand basins and plentiful supplies of hot and cold water, but there was only one water-closet for every twenty-five people. The pantry had ventilated safes for the food of each inmate. There was a small library. The building was very tightly arranged, and, as a result, one half of the inmates were without direct natural light or air, although Roberts did his best to alleviate matters.[22] White tiles were used for the floor, laid on brick arches. The main stair was of stone. Ventilation to the cubicles was by shafts, the draught being assisted by gas, which also illuminated the apartments. There was also a ventilation shaft on the stair to supply fresh air to the dormitories, and there was provision for warming the air in cold weather. The washing closets were fitted up with slate shelves, with japanned iron basins. Despite the alarming lack of water-closets (the queues in the mornings must have caused great problems) the hundred and four inmates escaped the cholera of 1849, even thought the disease was particularly ferocious in the area. The cost of the land was £1,200, and that of the building was £4,289. The outlay on furnishings was £936. Receipts from lodgers came to £614 per annum. Taxes and expenses, exclusive of repairs, came to £308 per annum. The return on the buildings and furnishings was five per cent, with four per cent for the land. The rent was 2s. 4d. per week compared with William Beck's Lodging-House at Mile End New Town at 3s. 8d. per week. At that price Roberts was of the opinion that Beck's scheme was too

PLAN OF TWO OF THE TENEMENTS IN THE FAMILY HOUSES FOR
WORKMEN, ST. PANCRAS.

BUILT BY THE METROPOLITAN ASSOCIATION.

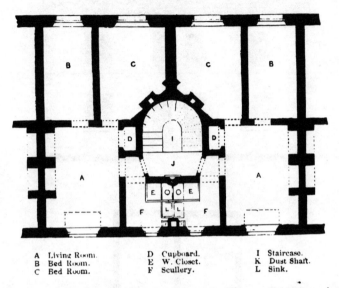

A   Living Room.   D   Cupboard.   I   Staircase.
B   Bed Room.   E   W. Closet.   K   Dust Shaft.
C   Bed Room.   F   Scullery.   L   Sink.

Fig. 14.   Two typical plans of flats built by the Metropolitan Association.
Roberts was critical of the internal stair.

PLAN OF TWO OF THE TENEMENTS IN THE FAMILY HOUSES FOR
WORKMEN, SPICER-STREET.

BUILT BY THE METROPOLITAN ASSOCIATION.

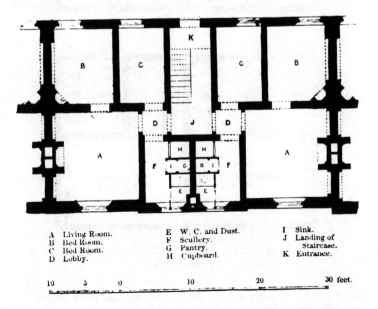

A   Living Room.   E   W. C. and Dust.   I   Sink.
B   Bed Room.   F   Scullery.   J   Landing of
C   Bed Room.   G   Pantry.   Staircase.
D   Lobby.   H   Cupboard.   K   Entrance.

10   5   0   10   20   30 feet.

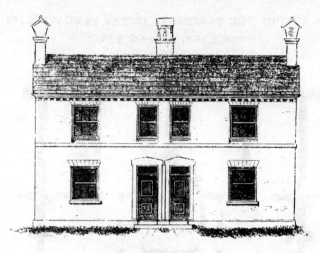

ELEVATION.

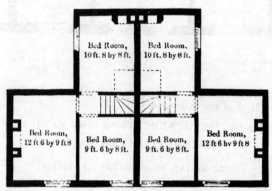

PLAN OF UPPER FLOOR.

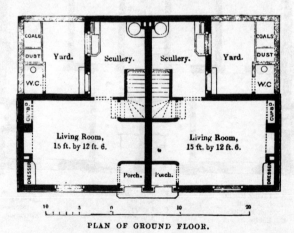

PLAN OF GROUND FLOOR.

Fig. 15.   Roberts' designs for 'Double Houses for Families
Adapted to Towns, with Three Bed Rooms each'.

expensive because of the 'luxuries'. In the event, Roberts was right, because the Metropolitan Association had to convert the Lodging-House into family flats to make it pay. However, Beck's building was adjacent to a spacious range of dwellings built by the M.A.I.D.I.C. so the facilities could be used at certain hours by families 'thus turning into good account what might otherwise be surplus accommodation'.

The third Annual General Meeting of the Society for Improving the Condition of the Labouring Classes was held at the Model Lodging House, George Street, on 18 June 1847. It is clear from the Minutes that there was a very close relationship between the Society and the London City Mission, for clergymen were sent to the Lodging-Houses owned by the Society in order to attend to the moral welfare of the lodgers. Although he never chaired a General Meeting, Roberts often chaired committee meetings from 1847 onwards.

It was obvious that the Society was moving ahead quickly with its plans. At the fourth Annual General Meeting of 18 May 1848 Prince Albert announced in the Freemasons' Hall his interest in the improvement of dwellings and his desire to arrive at the most successful model that would be an example to all. By that date Roberts had given up his Suffolk Street address and used 10, Connaught Square as his only address.

Roberts' old friend, Professor Cockerell, had projected the establishment of the Provident and Friendly Society for Building and Engineering Workmen. This was to be formed by the united efforts of architects, engineers, and builders. During this period, Roberts was to note with concern the demolition of numerous dwellings for modern improvements. This had exacerbated overcrowding, and even the 'important provisions of the *Health of Towns'* Bill would make matters worse. In 1851 Ashley was to get two Acts of Parliament, known as the Shaftesbury Acts, through both Houses. The first of these was the *Common Lodging Houses Act*[23] which affected some 80,000 transient workers, by insisting that all lodging-houses were subject to compulsory registration and inspection by the police. The second *Act* was the *Labouring Classes Lodging Houses Act* that permitted the vestries to purchase land and to build dwellings.[24]

Of course, Roberts had had early experience in the design of lodging-houses. The Sailors' Home in Well Street (now Ensign Street), Whitechapel, was the prototype of the Improved Lodging-Houses, and this building was known to Roberts. The Destitute Sailors' Asylum in the same street was designed by Henry Roberts in 1835 (*see* Figure 1) and was for a 'class below that of ordinary labourers', and therefore not within the scope of the S.I.C.L.C.

The Society proceeded to acquire further premises for conversion to lodging houses. No. 76, Hatton Gardens was purchased in 1849 on a twenty-one year lease at £56 per annum and converted for use as a lodging-house for fifty-seven women (*see* Figure 7). Hicks was again the contractor, his tender being for £637. It was closed the next year, as demand was slight in that area, and was reopened in 1855 as a lodging-house for men.

Thus ended the first phase of the work of the Society for Improving the Condition of the Labouring Classes. The success of the ambitious and commercially orientated Metropolitan Association for Improving the Dwellings of the Industrious Classes had created a spirit of rivalry and of competition. The S.I.C.L.C. had to produce an innovation, a spectacular success in order to gain support. The success of the Society's Model Lodging-House, despite the rigid rules which often drove inmates back to the less reputable private lodging-houses,[25] did actually help to improve conditions throughout London, and, ultimately, throughout the country. Nevertheless, the Society's record up to 1849 could hardly set the world afire. It was Roberts' next scheme that was to prove the most important break-through in the development of philanthropic housing.

Chapter Four

THE DESIGNS FOR MODEL HOUSES FOR FAMILIES
BY HENRY ROBERTS AFTER 1849

The question of lodging a large number of families in one lofty pile of building has been the subject of much discussion, and in reference to it the most contradictory opinions were stated before the Health-of-Towns' Commission . . . It must be obvious that in the many localities where labourers' dwellings are indispensible, it is impossible to provide them with isolated and altogether independent tenements; and therefore, though modified by local and other circumstances, it will be found the general practice in Great Britain, as well as in the large towns on the Continent, for several families of the working class to reside in one house.

Henry Roberts, *The Dwellings of the Labouring Classes*, London, 1867, p.10.

THE SOCIETY for Improving the Condition of the Labouring Classes developed its ideas to build a new tenement to house families, possibly stimulated by work that the Metropolitan Association for Improving the Dwellings of the Industrious Classes was completing at Mile End New Town.[1] The Model Houses for Families, Streatham Street, Bloomsbury, were completed in 1850, and built on a site leased to the Society for Improving the Condition of the Labouring Classes by the Duke of Bedford for fifty pounds per annum (Plates 62–63, and *see* Figures 8–11). This scheme was to prove the Society's most important contribution to the design of tenements. Early in 1848 appeals were launched for funds, but by June the Annual General Meeting learned that the money had not been raised, probably because of the disastrous famine in Ireland that had captured most of the charitable donations. In 1849 enough money had been collected, and it was not until the Annual General Meeting of that year that the Society learned that work had commenced on site.[2]

Roberts described the building at some length in his *The Dwellings of the Labouring Classes*. To him, it appeared that domestic privacy and independence for each family were essential. Like many of his Evangelical contemporaries, Roberts was shocked by 'drunkenness, domestic feuds, and vice in its most appalling forms'. He drew attention to the frequent investigations in Police Courts relating to charges of incest, rape, and murder, all of which were partially caused by intolerable overcrowding. The returns of the Registrar-General of Scotland revealed a great increase in illegitimate births in certain areas, so much so that *The Times* was able to say that such reports spoke 'trumpet-tongued' of the 'necessity for improved cottages'. The Model Houses for Families at Streatham Street, Bloomsbury, achieved these aims. One common stair led to galleries open on one side of a spacious quadrangle, and on the other side access to the entrance-lobbies of each flat was provided.

'The question of lodging a large number of families in one lofty pile of building has been
the subject of much discussion, and in reference to it the most contradictory opinions
were stated before the Health-of-Towns' Commission. Some thought it the best adapted
and most economical plan to provide in one house, with a common staircase and internal
passages, sufficient rooms for lodging a considerable number of families, giving them the
use of a kitchen, wash-house and other necessary conveniences, in common; others
objected that such an arrangement would lead to endless contentions; and be attended
with much evil in cases of contagious disease.

'It must be obvious that in many localities where labourers' dwellings are indispensible,
it is impossible to provide them with isolated and altogether independent tenements;
and therefore, though modified by local and other circumstances, it will be found the
general practice in Great Britain, as well as in the large towns on the Continent, for
several families of the working class to reside in one house.

'The important point, then, for consideration, is, in what manner can the advantages
of this economical arrangement be retained without the serious practical evils which have
been referred to?

'In providing for the accommodation of a large number of families in one pile of building, a leading feature of the plan should be the preservation of the domestic privacy and
independence of each distinct family, and the disconnection of their apartments, so as
effectually to prevent the communication of contagious disease. This is accomplished in
the model houses for families in Streatham Street, Bloomsbury, by dispensing altogether
with separate staircases, and other internal communications between the different
storeys, and by adopting one common open staircase leading into galleries or corridors,
open on one side to a spacious quadrangle, and on the other side having the outer doors
of the several tenements, the rooms of which are protected from draught by a small
entrance lobby.'[3]

The galleries were supported by a series of arcades with segmental heads, each opening
embracing two storeys. The floors of the intermediate galleries were of slate, carried
on iron beams, with iron enclosure railings. Roberts' design was influenced by the
necessity to avoid window-tax, so he argued that each gallery was an elevated street,
so that each flat, with its independent access from this elevated 'street', was a separate
dwelling-house. Unfortunately the authorities did not agree with Roberts, and the
Model Houses were at first assessed for window-tax, but the Society successfully
appealed, and Roberts' interpretation was accepted. Some £80 per annum were saved
by the Society as a result. Window-tax was repealed by the time Roberts produced
his new edition of *The Dwellings of the Labouring Classes* in 1853, and the repeal
of the tax was partly due to pressure brought to bear by the influential members of the
S.I.C.L.C. as a result of Roberts' forceful denunciations of the tax. Roberts himself
said that the abolition of the tax was probably the most important concession made
to the public call for sanitary amelioration. The outlay on the buildings was £8,860,
although the original tender by Winsland and Holland that had been accepted was
for £7,370. John Newson was one of the unsuccessful tenderers. There was a separate
contract for the hollow roof- and floor-tiles that was awarded to W. Cubitt & Co. The
Star Life Insurance Company advanced £3,500 towards the costs of erecting the
Streatham Street buildings. Rents, since the addition of six extra flats to the forty-
eight originally planned came to £745 per annum. During 1850 the Society benefited
greatly from the repeal of the duty on bricks, which had come to £300 for Streatham
Street alone.

The deep foundations of the Model Houses necessitated excavations, so the basement was formed to incorporate workshops, wash-houses, and bathing-houses for communal use. Storage space for coal and potatoes was provided in the basement. Fireproofing was provided by arches of wedge-shaped tiles or hollow bricks. These bricks, in section something like a garden-pot, were used, derived, Roberts said, from proto-types invented in France. Roberts had used them in his Fishmongers' Hall of 1833–5, and Rawlinson had specified hollow bricks for the ceilings of St George's Hall, Liverpool, after the death of Elmes. These hollow bricks were set in Portland cement in a one-to-two mix. Floors and roofs had a continuous series of abutments, except at the ends, where they were tied with $7/_8$ inch iron rods secured to cast-iron or stone springers. The roof was levelled with concrete and asphalted. Floors of bedrooms were boarded on two-inch square joists. All other floors were of Portland cement, except the basement, which was of metallic 'Lavar'. To test his system, Roberts constructed an experimental arch 3 feet 2 inches wide, spanning 9 feet 6 inches between the points of support, and rising 7 inches. Deflection was only $1/_8$ inch for three tons. The tiles did not fracture until a load of ten tons was applied, so, calculating the greatest total weight of thirty-two hundredweight, if the floor were covered with people at one hundred and twenty pounds per square foot, it would carry four times that number safely. The building was fireproof, and sound and water were prevented from 'percolating' by means of the tile or hollow-brick arches.

These Model Houses in Streatham Street were important for many reasons, not least of which were the changes in the law they heralded. The standards of construction and of accommodation were greatly in advance of their day, and perhaps because of these factors, the building was not very profitable to the Society. Rents varied from four to seven shillings each week, and these were not low compared with the usual rents in a tenement. However, the scale of charges limited the class of tenant to that of the better types of artisan. The low financial return discouraged investment, and this was the main reason why the principles of the S.I.C.L.C did not encourage philanthropic developments of such a high quality. The hopes of the Society that investors would encourage the building of tenements were dashed, and sudden rises in prices (perhaps encouraged by the repeal of brick- and window-taxes, and by the recovery after the disasters of the 1840s) made the erection of good-quality tenements impossible, except on a non-profit-making basis, or even on the principle of financial loss. As a result, the more commercially based societies and companies quickly took the initiative from the philanthropists, and Ashley's ideas that improvements of the dwellings could bring about elevation of the individual suffered an eclipse.

Before designing the Model Houses at Streatham Street, Roberts had studied other pro-totypes. Among the first blocks erected were the dwellings at Birkenhead for 324 families. These were constructed by the Birkenhead Dock Company, and were four storeys high (Figure 11). Roberts criticised these and said that the spaces between the blocks should never be less than the height of the blocks. The minimum width between blocks should be thirty-six feet, for example, if the site were really pinched, for forty-feet-high blocks. Many of the Birkenhead rooms were too small, and the internal arrange-ments precluded the segregation of the sexes. With reference to dust-shafts, Roberts stressed the importance of sealing them off to prevent gases from decomposing matter to ascend from the dust-cellar. He also emphasised that good ventilation was essential where gaslight was provided. Roberts visited the Birkenhead tenements in 1849 during the great slump in Liverpool, and found them excessively gloomy, owing to the narrow spaces between the blocks. Yet he found the nearby Morpeth Buildings, erected on the same general plan, four storeys high with a central stair to two flats per landing, much more successful, because they had access to unobstructed light and air. As a result, these flats were popular, and were tenanted at two shillings and six pence per week plus three pence per week for the supply of gas.

The Model Houses at Streatham Street survive, though the internal arrangements were altered in 1956 to designs by Frederick Gibberd and Partners in order to upgrade the accommodation. This work was carried out with the support of the old Holborn Borough Council under the *Housing Act* of 1949. In the Model Houses, Roberts established an excellent precedent. The plan was ingenious, for the access galleries all faced the generous internal court. The street elevations were simple and refined, with the lowest two storeys emphasised by banded brickwork in piers, resting on a massive plinth. The buildings avoided any hint of institutional grimness, and the internal planning was much more professional than in the Bagnigge Wells experiment.

The Streatham Street block was opened to view on 20 May 1850. It was described as a 'plain, but handsome and massive, building of very considerable size . . . suited for the accommodation of large numbers of the families of the artizan and journeyman class, with all requisite conveniences for household life complete in each dwelling with a perfect system of ventilation and drainage — managed on the newest and most approved principles — the building arrangements being wonderfully compact, and the rents at which wholesome, airy, and convenient premises can thus be let, lower than the average sums paid for the airless, lightless, and fetid rooms in which are lodged so great a proportion of the operative classes of London and of England.'[4]

The previous year had seen a particularly unpleasant outbreak of cholera that had been exacerbated in its effects by the enthusiasm of Chadwick and his fellow miasmatists for flushing out drains, thus spreading the cholera sources into the drinking water. At the Annual General Meeting of the Society on 12 July 1840 in Willis' Rooms, Southwood Smith (who was to die on 10 December 1861 and who was to be buried in the same cemetery as was Roberts in Florence) seconded a motion deploring the condition of the dwellings of the labouring classes. At that meeting was a representative of the Stradbroke family who had connections with Yoxford (where Roberts had carried out works some twelve years earlier). A National Day of Thanksgiving for deliverance was declared, and the Bishop of London (a Vice-Patron of the Society), recommended that all collections in his diocese taken on that day should be given to the S.I.C.L.C. to further the work of the Society. A sum of over five thousand pounds was raised, and a site was purchased at Portpool Lane, Gray's Inn Road. Roberts designed the new block, appropriately called the Thanksgiving Model Buildings, for twenty families and one hundred and twenty-eight single women. There was a great need for accommodation for poor, single needlewomen, who earned very low wages. An old building on the site was converted into a public wash-house. The cost of the land was £1,700 and the cost of the buildings, initially estimated as £6,865 finally came to £9,500.[5] The contractor was Samuel Grimsdell, who had built the concrete

ELEVATION.

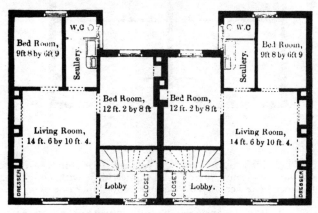

PLAN OF UPPER FLOOR.

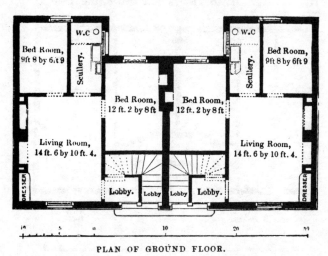

PLAN OF GROUND FLOOR.

Fig. 16. Roberts' designs for 'Double Houses Adapted to Towns, with Four Distinct Tenements on Two Floors, each having Two Bed Rooms'.

PLANS OF A DOUBLE HOUSE FOR ONE FAMILY IN EACH.

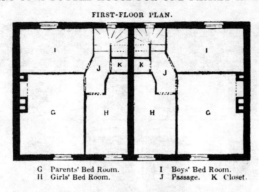

FIRST-FLOOR PLAN.

G   Parents' Bed Room.   I   Boys' Bed Room.
H   Girls' Bed Room.   J   Passage.   K   Closet.

GROUND FLOOR PLAN.

A   Living Room.   D   Fuel Store.
B   Scullery.   E   Staircase.
C   Pantry.   F   Porch.

Fig. 17.   Plans by Roberts for: (*above*) A Double House for one family in each; (*below*) A Double House with Four Distinct Tenements on Two Floors, the Upper one being approached by an Open Staircase.

Both these designs could be built in pairs or in terraces. The plan at the bottom is basically that of the Great Exhibition Houses.

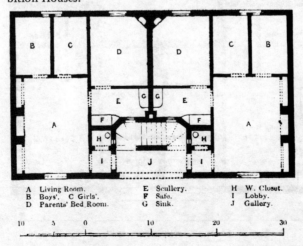

A   Living Room.   E   Scullery.   H   W. Closet.
B   Boys'.   C   Girls'.   F   Safe.   I   Lobby.
D   Parents' Bed Room.   G   Sink.   J   Gallery.

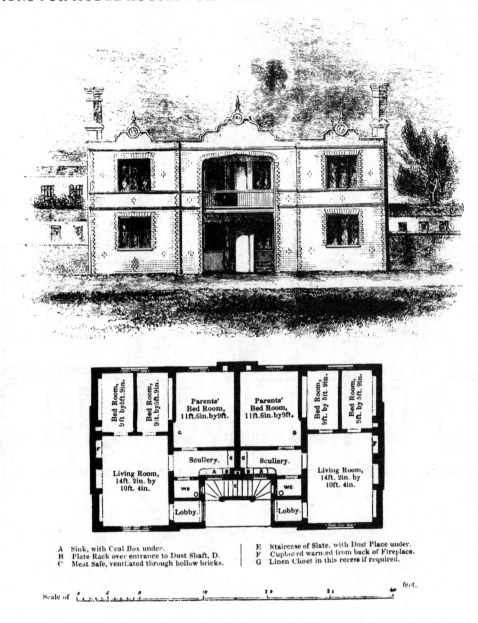

A Sink, with Coal Box under.
B Plate Rack over entrance to Dust Shaft, D.
C Meat Safe, ventilated through hollow bricks.

E Staircase of Slate, with Dust Place under.
F Cupboard warmed from back of Fireplace.
G Linen Closet in this recess if required.

Fig. 18. 'Model Houses for Four Families, Erected by Command of his Royal Highness Prince Albert, K.G., at the Exposition of the Works of Industry of All Nations, 1851, and subsequently rebuilt in Kennington New Park, Surrey'.

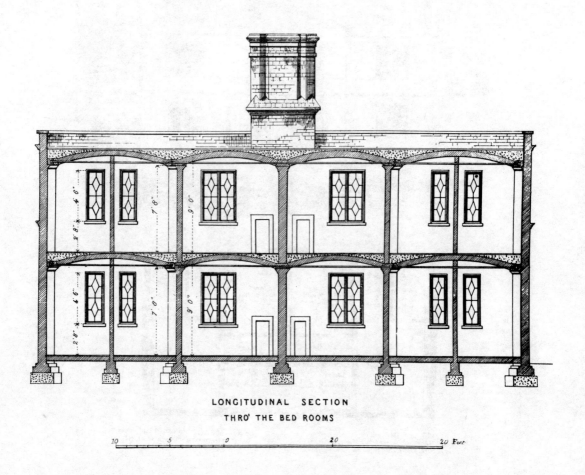

LONGITUDINAL   SECTION
THRO' THE BED ROOMS

Fig. 19a. 'Longitudinal Section Thro' the Bed Rooms' of the original Exhibition Model Dwellings.

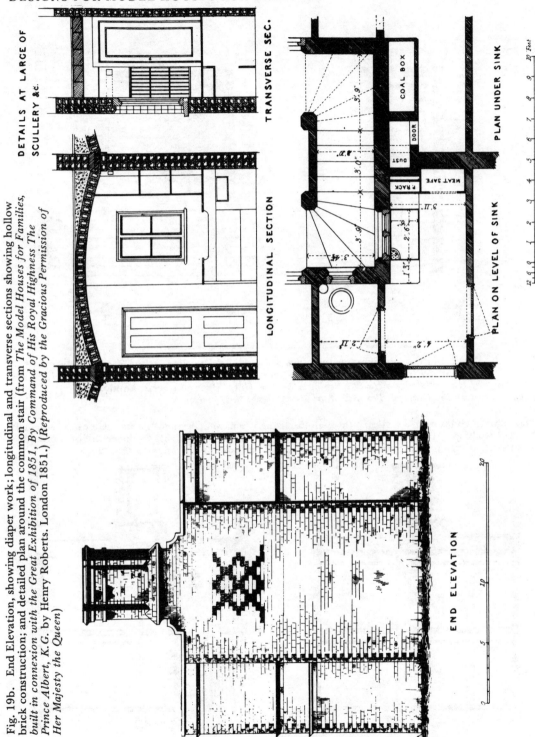

Fig. 19b. End Elevation, showing diaper work; longitudinal and transverse sections showing hollow brick construction; and detailed plan around the common stair (from *The Model Houses for Families*, built in connexion with the Great Exhibition of 1851, By Command of His Royal Highness The Prince Albert, K.G. by Henry Roberts. London 1851.) (Reproduced by the Gracious Permission of Her Majesty the Queen)

DETAILS AT LARGE OF SCULLERY &c.

TRANSVERSE SEC.

LONGITUDINAL SECTION

COAL BOX

DOOR

DUST

RACK

MEAT SAFE

PLAN UNDER SINK

PLAN ON LEVEL OF SINK

END ELEVATION

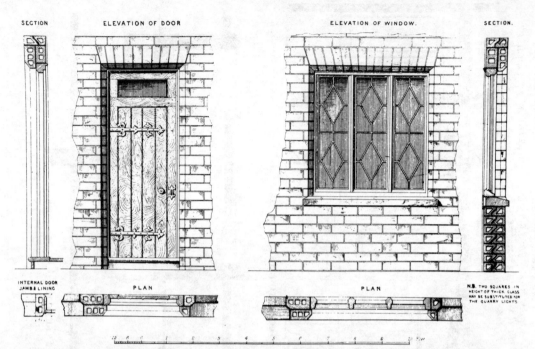

Fig. 20a.   Details of door- and window-openings of the Model Dwellings at the Great Exhibition of 1851 (from *The Model Houses for Families, built in connexion with the Great Exhibition of 1851, By Command of His Royal Highness The Prince Albert, K.G.* by Henry Roberts. London, 1851). (*Reproduced by the Gracious Permission of Her Majesty the Queen*)

Fig. 20b.   Two transverse sections, through the living rooms and through the staircase of the original Model Dwellings at the Great Exhibition of 1851. Note the ceiling heights to the centre of the vaults and to the springing. (*Reproduced by the Gracious Permission of Her Majesty the Queen*)

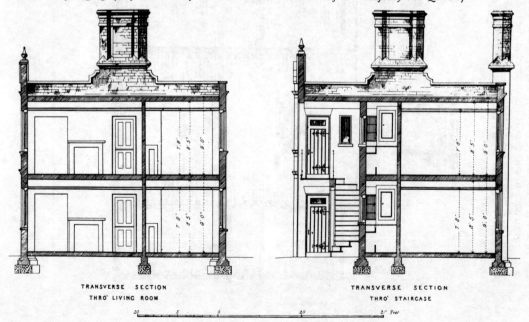

raft of the Fishmongers' Hall. The family flats were self-contained, and were approached from common stairs. Sixty-four rooms were provided for the poor women. The laundry was visited annually by about 20,000 people (Figures 12 and 13).

The most important scheme of the S.I.C.L.C. was, of course, the most celebrated of all its models (Figures 18–20 and Plate 66). This was Roberts' design for the 'Model Houses for Families erected by H.R.H. Prince Albert' at the Great Exhibition of 1851. These dwellings earned the Society the highest award of the Exhibition: the Council Medal. The original idea of erecting these Model Houses derived from a desire to bring the work of the Society to as wide a public as possible. Drawings were all very well, but a complete building could demonstrate the latest concepts of advanced housing for the working classes much more effectively. By December 1844 Roberts' plan and description of a double cottage for an agricultural district was agreed for publication, and his drawings and specification for the pair of cottages were lithographed for sale at one guinea per set. His book on the subject of the design of dwellings was then prepared for publication at the request of Lord Ashley. Roberts' ideas in *The Dwellings of the Labouring Classes* were developed further in his designs for the Great Exhibition exemplars, for his plans were infinitely adaptable. Each floor could be repeated to four or five storeys, while the pairs could become long streets of tenements. The open stair was both decorative and hygienic, and was a happy invention, since it avoided the evil-smelling enclosed access stairs of blocks erected by other Societies, as well as the necessity of long external galleries as at the Streatham Street block. This basic plan was the essence of thousands of working-class flats that followed, notably those built by the Improved Industrial Dwellings Company, of which many examples exist in Bethnal Green.

The designs for the Great Exhibition Model Dwellings derive from several years' experimentation by Roberts, with the mature planning of Streatham Street well to the fore. The Exhibition houses represent Roberts' designs at their most ingenious and compact.

As stated in Chapter One, the S.I.C.L.C. was anxious to advertise its activities by erecting an exemplar at the Great Exhibition. This was to be the first major attempt to show what could be done to house the poor at any international exhibition. It has not been possible to ascertain who was responsible for initiating the proposal, but it is clear that Prince Albert himself was very actively involved (letters survive in the papers of the Royal Commission for the Exhibition of 1851). Roberts and Shaftesbury were keen to pursue the idea, and it seems fair to give credit to the Prince as a powerful advocate (as well as financier), to Roberts as designer, and to Shaftesbury for also working hard to ensure that the exemplars were built.

The Committee of the S.I.C.L.C. first approached the Commissioners for the Exhibition to ask for a suitable site, but was rebuffed. The Prince then wrote to the Duke of Wellington stating that he wished to have a Model House erected as part of the Exhibition, but that it was impossible within the space allotted in Hyde Park. He suggested that a vacant site belonging to the Cavalry Barracks, just across the road from the Crystal Palace, would be ideal. In the letter, the Prince informed the Duke that he would have the 'house' erected at his own expense.[6] The Duke replied on 27 January 1851.[7] The old warrior was convinced that the idea was dangerous, as the soldiers would compare their quarters most unfavourably with the modern standards of construction, hygiene, and space provided in the proposed dwellings. Although the Duke was finally persuaded to relent, events proved him right, because most barracks in the country had to be modernised within the next decade.[8]

It is interesting to note that Roberts himself anticipated some of the objections. When Ashley (as he then was) wrote to the Prince on 22 January 1851 about 'Mr. Roberts' improved plans', Roberts wrote to Ashley to suggest that the Model Dwellings had to be in a prominent position to be successful as an exhibit. He suggested that the buildings could be adapted for use by married soldiers after the Exhibition closed.[9]

The 'Model Houses for Four Families' were 'Erected by Command of His Royal Highness Prince Albert, K.G., At the Exposition of the Works of Industry of All Nations, 1851'. There is a fine lithograph of the finished building by Day & Son, showing the dwellings in relation to the Crystal Palace (Plate 66).

The Model Lodge consisted of four flats for the families of the 'classes of manufacturing operatives who reside in towns' or in their 'immediate vicinity'. Each flat had a living-room, three bedrooms (each with separate access), and a scullery fitted with a sink, a plate-rack, a coal-bin, a dust-shaft, and a meat-safe. There was also a water-closet inside each flat, and the soil-pipe also doubled as a rainwater pipe to drain the flat roof. The living-room had a cupboard heated by warm air from the fireplace.[10] The most important feature of the design was the covered staircase at the front that gave access to the two upper floors. The construction included the use of hollow bricks (of which Roberts was a keen partisan) in order to secure 'dryness, warmth, durability, security from fire, and deadening of sound' as well as 'economy of construction to the extent, as compared with the cost of common brickwork, of at least 25 per cent'.[11] Roberts had patented his designs for hollow bricks, as problems of waterproofing and insulation were notorious in Victorian times. The cavities were also used for bell wires and for other services, such as water-pipes. Hollow bricks were used for the floors and for the roof, in the segmental arched form carried on iron springers held and spaced by means of tie-rods which were visible inside the rooms. No timber was used in the first floor or in the roof, and concrete was used to level off the arches. The total height of each arch was about 9 inches, measured from the point of the springing. The internal face of the walls was very smooth, and plastering was unnecessary.[12] The total cost of the four dwellings was £458 14s. 7d. which Prince Albert provided from his own pocket (Figures 18–21).

Roberts wrote to Colonel Grey,[13] Prince Albert's Private Secretary, on 17 June 1851[14] about admissions to the Model Dwellings. Roberts had arranged for a more extensive admission of the working classes, and had been in communication with the Superintendent of Police to that effect. He mentioned that several visitors to the houses had expressed their intention of carrying out the plan on their own property, and some on an extensive scale. By October 1851 Roberts reported to Colonel Grey that 250,000 visitors had seen the houses, including 7,400 on one day alone, and that these numbers themselves were a severe test of the qualities of materials and of construction. Already plans were afoot for an eight-family block at Ramsgate (Plate 70) and a thirty-six-family block at Shadwell (Plate 67), but neither of these was being built of hollow bricks. Roberts was reminded of the engagement to take down the

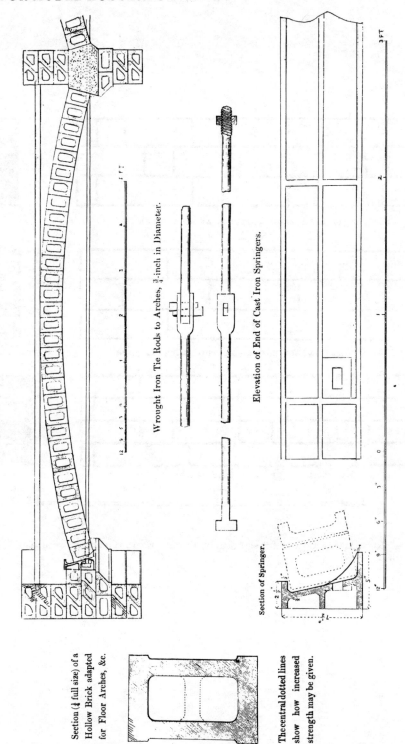

SECTION, SHOWING THE FLOOR AND ROOF ARCHES TO H.R.H. PRINCE ALBERT'S EXHIBITION MODEL HOUSES, AND THOSE TO THE MODEL HOUSES IN STREATHAM STREET AND PORTPOOL LANE.

Section (¼ full size) of a Hollow Brick adapted for Floor Arches, &c.

The central dotted lines show how increased strength may be given.

Wrought Iron Tie Rods to Arches, ¾-inch in Diameter.

Elevation of End of Cast Iron Springers.

Section of Springer.

Fig. 21. Roberts' designs for fireproof floors, used at the Exhibition Model Houses at Windsor, and at the Model Houses in Streatham Street and Portpool Lane. Note the hollow bricks (patented by Roberts) and the springers.

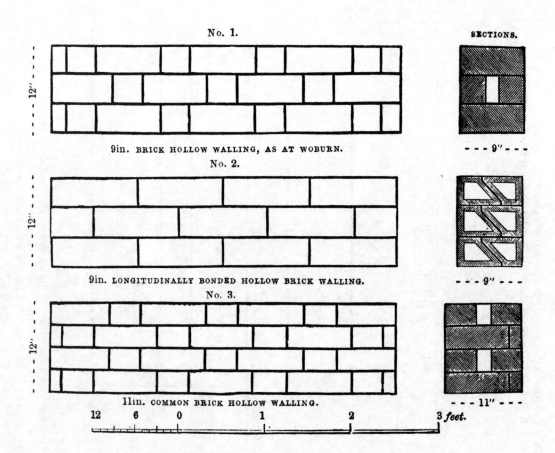

Fig. 22. Roberts' suggestions for semi-cavity brickwork. In the centre is his patent hollow brickwork.

buildings in November 1851, and he wrote to the Prince to enquire if he had any commands or reference to the houses. Roberts presented descriptions of the Model Lodges and a copy of his *The Dwellings of the Labouring Classes* to the Prince at this time. The latter work is beautifully bound in red leather, and is emblazoned with the Prince's Arms.[15]

In the Royal Archives, Windsor Castle, there is some material concerning Henry Roberts. In Queen Victoria's Journal, Her Majesty mentioned her visit to the Model Dwellings on 12 July 1851, and noted that they were 'admirably constructed by Mr. Roberts', who had 'built a great many of the new lodging houses in London'. The Queen was 'graciously pleased with what she saw', according to Roberts, who, with Lord Shaftesbury, was in attendance. On 23 October Roberts wrote a descriptive account of the houses, gave great detail of how many visitors had seen them, and reported that buildings of other houses based on his plans were under construction at Ramsgate and Shadwell.[16]

On 24 October 1851[17] Prince Albert wrote to Lord Shaftesbury about the disposal of the houses. The Prince received an application to have them re-erected at Ipswich, but he first asked if the Society for Improving the Condition of the Labouring Classes would take them over and re-erect them. Shaftesbury replied on 25 October.[18] Prince Albert was most anxious that the re-erected houses should be in the best interests of the working classes, and expressed this view in his letter to Lord Shaftesbury in 1851.[19] This letter, and correspondence from the Duke of Wellington, from Lord Shaftesbury, and from Henry Roberts, survive in the Royal Archives at Windsor Castle.

These Model Houses were popular among visitors to the Exhibition, as the numbers who saw them testify. When the Exhibition closed, the future of the cottages was debated. The design was subsequently used in a number of places, notably in Cowley Gardens, Stepney; in Fenelon Place, Kensington; in Hertford; and near Abbot's Langley in Hertfordshire. One suggestion from Lord Seymour of 23 February 1852 was that the Exhibition houses should be re-erected on Primrose Hill 'as a gate-lodge'.

These exemplars crystallised standards of accommodation that the Society sought to make the ideal. The three bedrooms separated boys from girls, and children from parents. Each flat had its own kitchen, water-closet, water-supply, fireplace, and dust-shaft, and there were built-in cupboards. Fireproof construction ensured safety. Materials were of excellent quality, and ventilation was good. Each room had a window, so that in practically all details these flats were of a very advanced standard for their time.

Roberts wrote up a description of the Model Houses in his publications, and he was quoted verbatim in *The Builder*:[20]

H.R.H. PRINCE ALBERT'S EXHIBITION MODEL HOUSES

'Amongst the vast collection of objects presented in the Great Exhibition of 1851, the visitor who estimated their real value and importance, not by the cost or labour of production, not by the artistic merit or gorgeous effect, but by their adaptation to advance the physical, the social, and the moral condition of the great masses of the people — of those who form the basis of the social edifice, would justly and gratefully appreciate the unpretending contribution made by His Royal Highness the PRINCE ALBERT, of *Model Houses for Families*, of the class of manufacturing and mechanical operatives.

'HIS ROYAL HIGHNESS had this building raised on his own account, with a desire of conveying practical information calculated to promote the much needed improvement of the dwellings of the Working Classes, and also of stimulating Visitors to the Exhibition, whose position and circumstances enable them to carry out similar undertakings, and thus without pecuniary sacrifice, permanently to benefit those who are greatly dependent on others for their home and family comforts.

'In its *general arrangement*, the building is adapted for the occupation of four families of the class of manufacturing and mechanical operatives, who usually reside in towns, or in their immediate vicinity; and as the value of land, which leads to the economizing of space, by the placing of more than one family under the same roof, in some cases, renders the addition of a third storey desirable, the plan has been suited to such an arrangement, without any other alteration than the requisite increase in the strength of the walls.

'The most prominent peculiarity of the design is that of the receding and protected central open staircase, with the connecting gallery on the first floor, formed of slate, and sheltered from the weather by the continuation of the main roof, which also screens the entrances to the dwellings.

'The four tenements are arranged on precisely the same plan, two on each floor. The entrance is through a small lobby, lighted from the upper part of the door.

'The *living-room* has a superficial area of about 150 feet, with a closet on one side of the fire-place, to which warm air may be introduced from the back of the range: over the fire-place is an iron rod for hanging pictures; and on the opposite side of the room a shelf is carried above the doors, with a rail fixed between them.

'The scullery is fitted up with a sink, beneath which is a coal-bin of slate; a plate-rack at one end, drained by a slate slab into the sink, covers the entrance to the dust-shaft, which is enclosed by a balanced self-acting iron door. The dust-shaft leads in to a closed depository under the stairs, and has a ventilating flue, carried up above the roof. The meat safe is ventilated through the hollow brickwork, and shelves are fixed over the doors. A dresser-flap may be fixed against the partition.

'The *sleeping apartments*, being three in number, provide for that separation which, with a family, is so essential to morality and decency. Each has its distinct access, and a window into the open air; two have fire-places.

'The children's bed-rooms contain 50 feet superficial each, and, opening out of the living-room, an opportunity is afforded for the exercise of parental watchfulness, without the unwholesome crowding of the living-room, by its use as a sleeping apartment.

'The parents' bedroom, with a superficial area of about 100 feet, is entered through the scullery — an arrangement in many respects preferable to a direct approach from the living-room, particularly in case of sickness. The recess in this room provides a closet for linen. In each of the bedrooms a shelf is carried over the door, with a rail fixed beneath it.

'The water-closet is fitted up with a Staffordshire glazed basin, which is complete without any wood fittings, and supplied with water from a slate cistern in common of 160 gallons, placed on the roof over the party and staircase walls. The same pipes which carry away the rain water from the roof serve for the use of the closets.

'*Constructive Arrangement*. — The peculiarities of the building in this respect are, the exclusive use of hollow bricks for the walls and partitions (excepting the foundations, which are of ordinary brickwork,), and the entire absence of timber in the floors and roof, which are formed with flat arches of hollow brickwork, rising from 8 to 9 inches, set in cement, and tied in by wrought-iron rods connected with cast-iron springers, which rest on the external walls, and bind the whole structure together; the building is thus rendered fire-proof, and much less liable to decay than those of ordinary construction. The roof arching, which is levelled with concrete, and covered with patent metallic lava, secures the upper rooms from the liability to changes of temperature to which apartments next the roof are generally subject, and the transmission of sound, as well as the percolation of moisture, so common through ordinary floors, is effectually impeded by the hollow-brick arched floors. The external and main internal walls are of patent bonded brickwork.

'The advantages afforded by the use of hollow bricks in securing an effective system of insensible *ventilation*, deserves particular notice. Fresh air is admitted from a suitable point of the exterior of the building to a chamber at the back of the living-room fireplace, where, being warmed, it may be conducted to any convenient place of exit above the level at which the fresh air is admitted. Vitiated air may be conveyed either into the chimney flue or to any other suitable place of exit through the upper wall courses.

'The glazed surface of the bricks used in the two upper-floor living-rooms, and at the foot of the staircase, shows a very superior mode of superseding all plastering and colouring.

'The fire-proof construction, and the general arrangement of the fittings, are such as have been used in the Model Houses built by the Society for Improving the Condition of the Labouring Classes under the direction of the Author, who also acted as honorary architect to this building.'

The Builder[21] also gave a very full description of the Model Houses in terms of their construction, with particular reference to hollow brickwork. The magazine illustrated the buildings and gave a full description of the brick construction:

'To make our illustration of the model houses erected in Hyde Park complete, we now give an external view of them, and to elucidate the hollow brick construction, as patented by Mr. Roberts, we add a sectional view of one compartment of the model structure placed by the "Society for Improving the Condition of the Labouring Classes", in the Exhibition of the Works of Industry of all Nations.

'The structure will be found by those who would seek it, on the north side of the building, towards the west end, in class 27. The bricks used in it, we may say, are from the following places, the straw-coloured from Aylesford, near Maidstone; the red from the Buxley Works, near Esher; and the glazed, of a grey tint, in the central compartment, were made by Mr Seagar, Vauxhall, of a clay from the North of Devon; the light-coloured glazed at the Staffordshire Potteries.

'The section is also illustrative of the construction adopted in Prince Albert's Model Houses — the span of the arches being there increased over the living rooms to 10 feet 4 inches, with a proportionate addition to their rise. The external springers are of cast iron, with brick cores, connected by wrought iron tie rods.

'The advantages derivable from the use of hollow bricks are dryness and warmth, as well as economy of construction — considerations which recommend them as a preventive of the evils that result from the absorption of moisture by common bricks and other porous materials.

'For agricultural buildings, and for inclosure, park, or fence walls, they are particularly adapted, as well as for the ordinary dwellings of the labouring classes, for schools, and for houses generally of moderate height, and with the usual weight of roofs and floors, rendering the internal battening unnecessary. Their strength may be adapted to circumstances, and where necessary be rendered equal to that of solid bricks.

'When used for partitions, or for roof and floor arches, they are fire-proof, deaden sound more effectually, and are considerably lighter than solid brickwork. As a lining to stone or flint walls, they supersede the necessity for battening, and the consequent risk of fire and dry rot is avoided. For cottage floors they are also well adapted.

'By the form adopted in the patent hollow brickwork, a perfect bond, running longitudinally through the centre of the wall, is secured; all headers and vertical joints, passing through it are avoided; internal as well as external strength is obtained; and every facility given for the fixing of floor-plates, and other timbers; whilst, by the parallel longitudinal cavities, ample security for dryness is afforded, and great facility presented for ventilation, as well as for the conveyance of artificial heat, and for the transmission of bell-wires, and pipes.

'When passing through the machine, or in the process of drying, any number may be readily splayed at the ends for gables, or marked for closures, and broken off as required . . .'

Clearly the material was adaptable, for the angles could be taken off with a trowel as readily as those of any common brick.

'The bricks for the quoins and jambs may be made either solid or perforated; and with perpendicular holes, either circular, square, or octagonal, those in the quoins may be so arranged as to serve for ventilating shafts. Stone will be found equally applicable for the quoins and jambs, and the appearance of the work be thereby improved. Hollow bricks may be made, with any good tile machine, in the same manner as ordinary draining pipes, and at about the same cost in proportion to the quantity of clay contained in them. They are more compressed, require less drying, and with much less fuel are better burned than ordinary bricks, even when waste heat, or that in the upper part of the kiln, only is used.

'The saving in brickwork effected by the use of the patent bricks, when made at a fair price, is said to be from 25 to 30 per cent on their cost, with a reduction of 25 per cent on the quantity of mortar, and a similar saving on the labour, when done by accustomed workmen. The process of drying is much more rapid than in common brickwork, and the smoothness of the internal surface of walls built with the patent bonded bricks renders plastering, in many instances, quite unnecessary, whereby a further saving is effected not only in the first cost, but also in the subsequent maintenance. If glazed on the outer face, as may be done with many clays, a superior finished surface is obtainable without plaster.'

The Model Houses were built in the winter, and there were difficulties in obtaining supplies of hollow bricks. As *The Builder* put it:[22]

'disappointments were experienced in reference to a considerable number, on which account the structure should be regarded rather as the pledge of future excellence in hollow brick construction than as its full accomplishment.

'The glazed surface of the bricks used in the two upper floor living rooms, and at the foot of the staircase, may, however, be referred to as a specimen of what can be accomplished by the skilful adaptation of fitting materials, and as highly creditable to their maker, Mr. Ridgeway, of the Staffordshire Potteries. Specimens of glazed bricks of clay from the north of Devon are also exhibited.

'Internally French plaster has been used, as drying quicker, and having a harder surface than ordinary plaster, The floors, where not of Portland cement, are laid with Staffordshire tiles, excepting to the right-hand room, first-floor, which is of lava, by Orsi and Armani. The coping is in Portland cement. The external string courses and internal cornices are the patent bonded bricks set in Portland cement, with the splayed side outwards.'

The list of materials and fittings used in the construction of the Model Houses is interesting, for names and addresses are given:

'The unglazed hollow bricks have been chiefly made by Clayton's patent brick and tile machines, to which the prize of the Royal Agricultural Society of England was awarded in 1850. The process of manufacture may be seen at the Atlas Works, Upper Park-place, Dorset-square, where detailed particulars may be obtained.

'The patent bonded facing bricks generally, and those used in the floors and roof, were made at Aylesford, near Maidstone; the red patent bonded internal bricks, at the

1a. Josiah Roberts, Henry Roberts'
father. A pencil-and-wash drawing by
Daniel Maclise, dated 1828. (*Collection of Mrs. J. C. Cuningham*)

1b. Mrs. Josiah Roberts, Henry Roberts'
mother. A pencil-and-wash drawing by
Daniel Maclise, dated 1828. (*Collection
of Mrs. J. C. Cuningham*)

2. Henry Roberts. A Silhouette of about 1812.
(*Collection of Mrs. J. C. Cuningham*)

3. Charles Roberts, brother of Henry.
A pencil-and-wash drawing by Daniel
Maclise, dated 1828. (*Collection of
Mrs. J. C. Cuningham*)

4. The sisters of Henry Roberts. Pencil-and-wash drawings by Daniel Maclise, dated 1828. (*Collection of Mrs. J. C. Cuningham*)

5. The south or river frontage of the Fishmongers' Hall, London, in 1979.

6. Henry Roberts' competition drawing for the 'Floor of Domestic Offices' of the Fishmongers' Hall, London. (*Guildhall Library, City of London*)

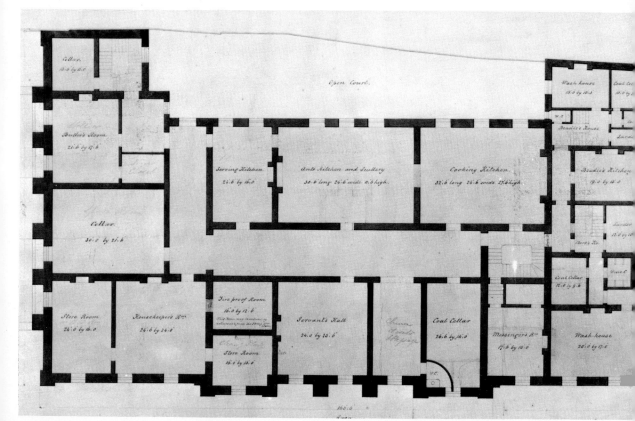

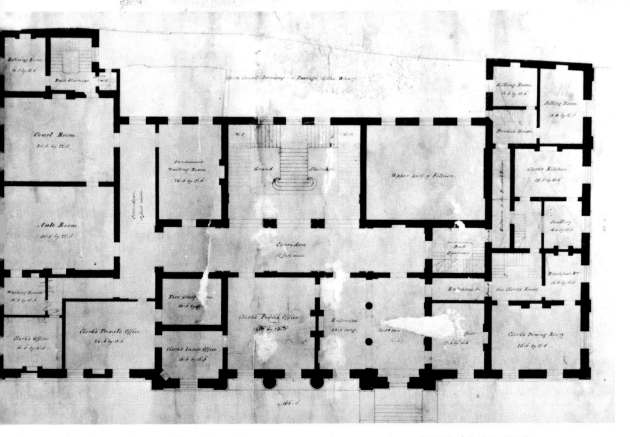

Henry Roberts' competition drawing for the ground floor of the Fishmongers' Hall, London. (*Guildhall library, City of London*)

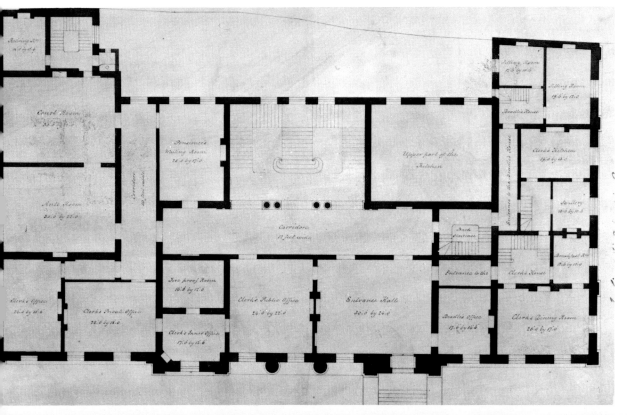

Henry Roberts' revised ground-floor plan of the Fishmongers' Hall, London, of 1832. (*Guildhall Library, City of London*)

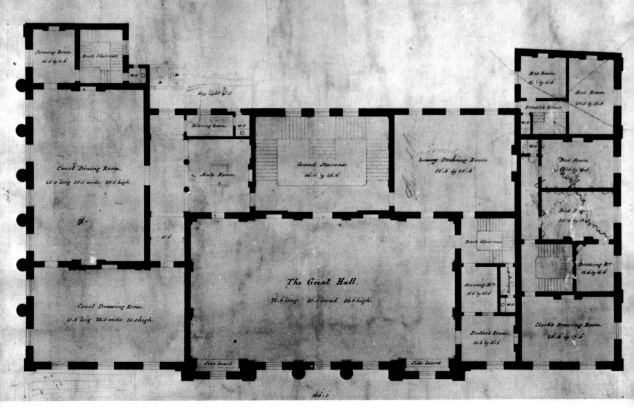

9. Henry Roberts' competition drawing for the first-floor plan of the Fishmongers' Hall, London. (*Guildhall Library, City of London*)

10. Henry Roberts' competition drawing for the east or entrance front of the Fishmongers' Hall, London. (*Guildhall Library, City of London*)

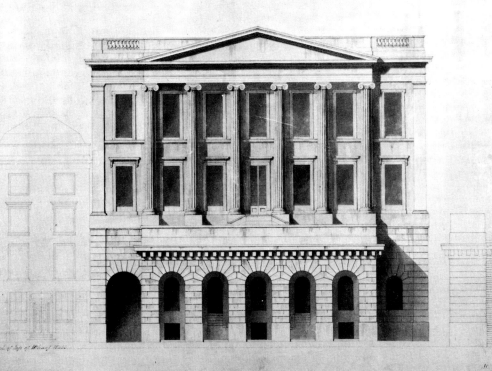

11. Henry Roberts' competition drawing for the south or river front of the Fishmongers' Hall, London. (*Guildhall Library, City of London*)

12. Henry Roberts' competition drawing for the north or Thames Street front of the Fishmongers' Hall, London. (*Guildhall Library, City of London*)

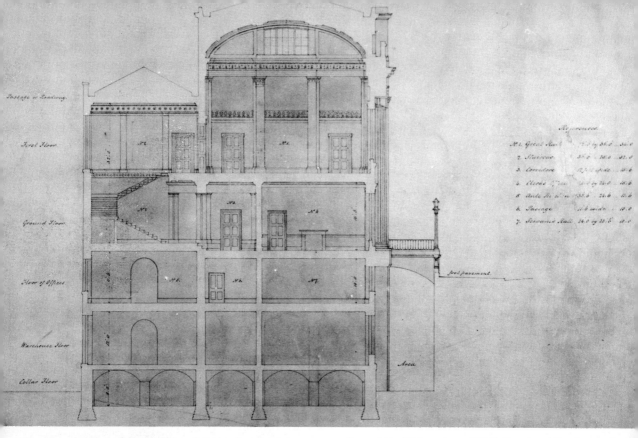

13. Henry Roberts' competition drawing for the transverse section of the Fishmongers' Hall, London. The 'ground-floor' level is halfway up on the building, with access from the approach to London Bridge. (*Guildhall Library, City of London*)

14. Henry Roberts' competition drawing for the 'Longitudinal Section' of the Fishmongers' Hall, London. (*Guildhall Library, City of London*)

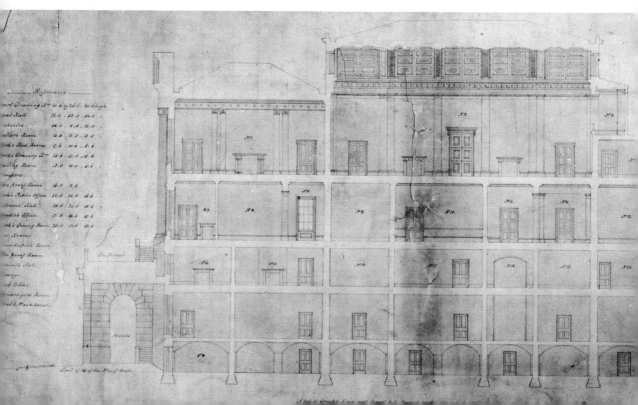

A lithograph by Day and L. Haghe of the new Fishmongers' Hall, London, from the south-east. Henry Roberts, architect. (*Guildhall Library, City of London*)

16. The Camberwell Collegiate School. A lithograph by F. Mackenzie. (*Guildhall Library, City of London*)

17. The Asylum for Destitute Sailors, London, in 1978.

18a. The basement plan of the Glebe House, Southborough, Kent, by Henry Roberts. An original contract drawing. (*R.I.B.A. British Architectural Library Drawings Collection*)

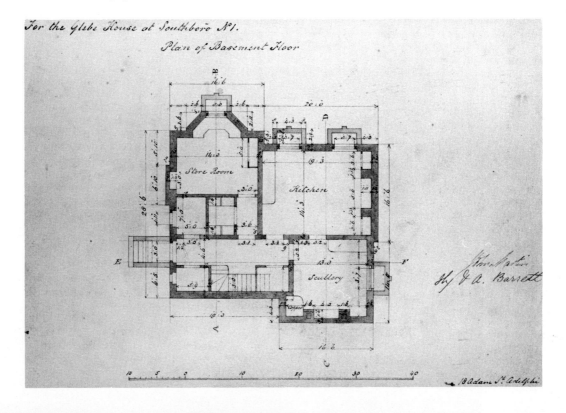

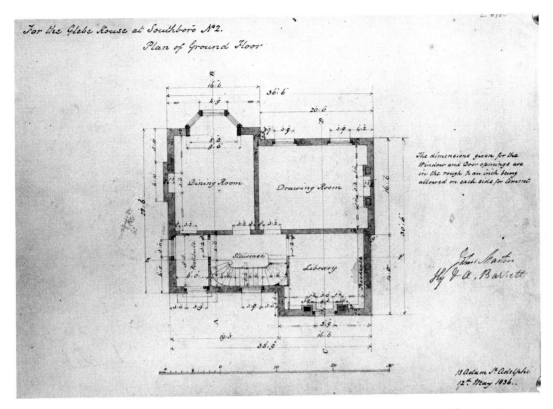

18b. The ground-floor plan of the Glebe House. An original contract drawing. (*R.I.B.A. British Architectural Library Drawings Collection*)

19a. The first-floor plan of the Glebe House. An original contract drawing. (*R.I.B.A. British Architectural Library Drawings Collection*)

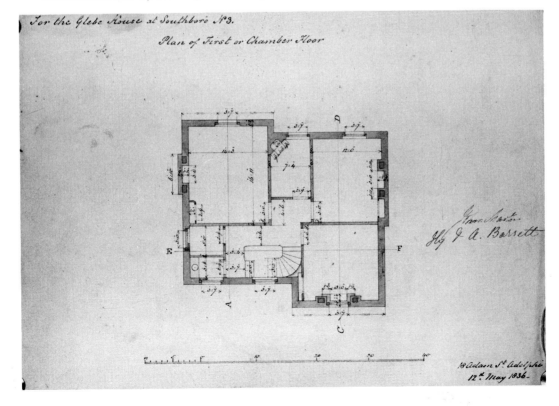

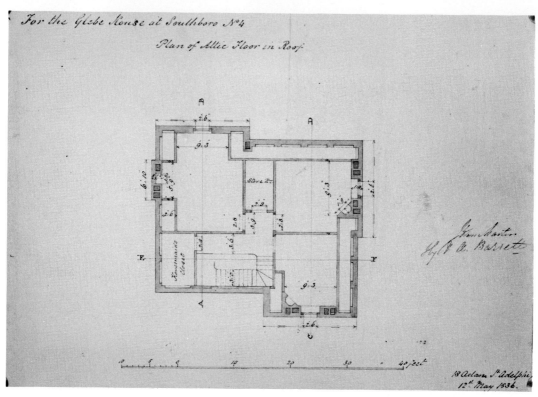

19b.   The attic-floor plan of the Glebe House. An original contract drawing. (*R.I.B.A.*
British Architectural Library Drawings Collection)

20a. The main entrance elevation of the Glebe House. An original contract drawing. (*R.I.B.A.*
British Architectural Library Drawings Collection)

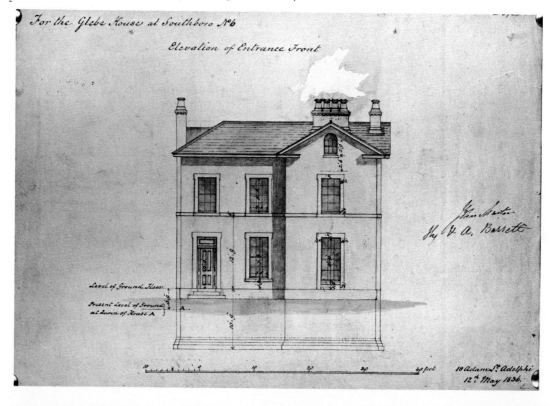

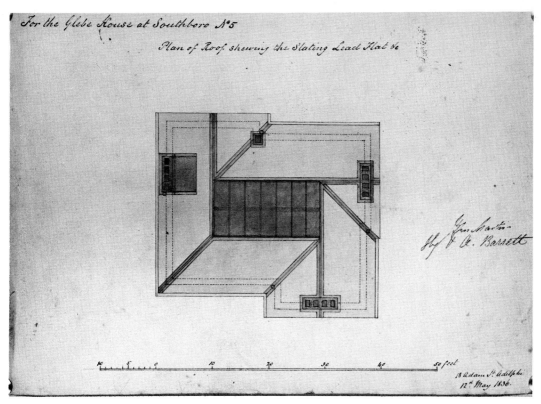

For the Glebe House at Southboro N°5

Plan of Roof shewing the Slating Lead Flat &c

Jno Martin

Hy & A. Barrett

18 Adam St. Adelphi.
12th May 1836.

20b. The roof-plan of the Glebe House. (*R.I.B.A. British Architectural Library Drawings Collection*)

21a. The garden elevation of the Glebe House. An original contract drawing. (*R.I.B.A. British Architectural Library Drawings Collection*)

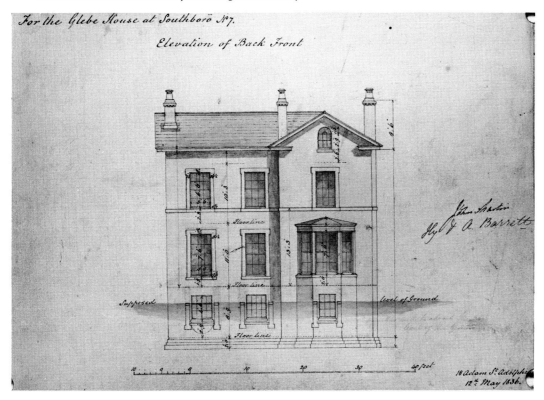

For the Glebe House at Southboro N°7.

Elevation of Back Front

John Martin

Hy & A. Barrett

18 Adam St. Adelphi
12th May 1836.

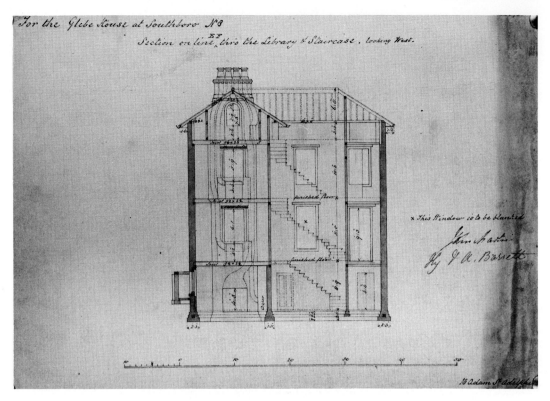

21b. Section E-F through the library and staircase of the Glebe House. An original contract drawing. (*R.I.B.A. British Architectural Library Drawings Collection*)

22a. Section C-D through the drawing room and library of the Glebe House. (*R.I.B.A. British Architectural Library Drawings Collection*)

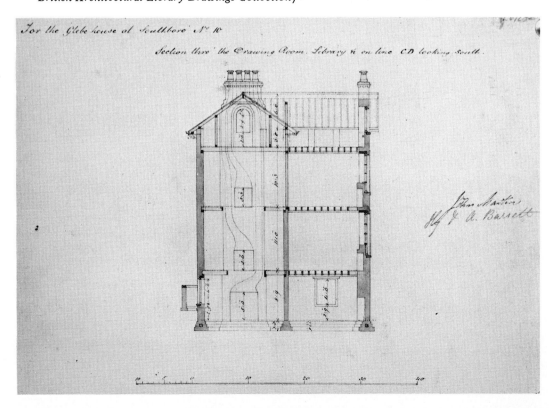

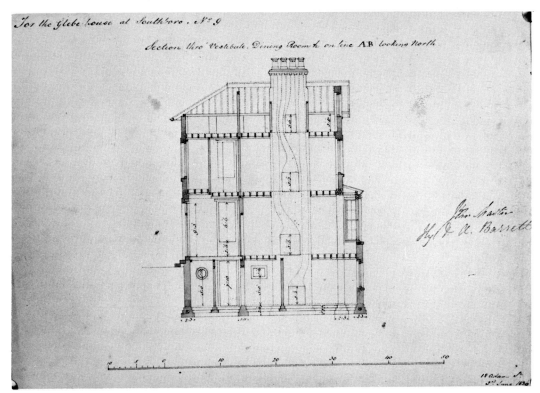

For the Glebe house at South'oro. No 9.

Section thro' Vestibule, Dining Room &c on line A.B looking North

22b. Section A-B through the vestibule and dining room of the Glebe House. (*R.I.B.A. British Architectural Library Drawings Collection*)

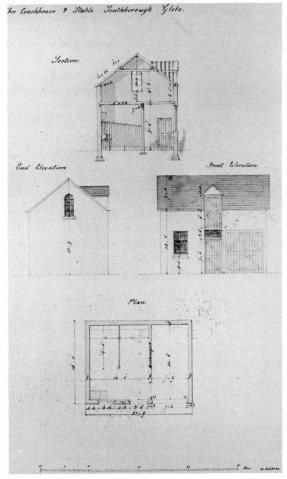

for Coachhouse & Stable Southberough Glebe.

Section

End Elevation

Front Elevation

Plan

23. The coach-house and stable of the Glebe House. An original contract drawing. (*R.I.B.A. British Architectural Library Drawings Collection*)

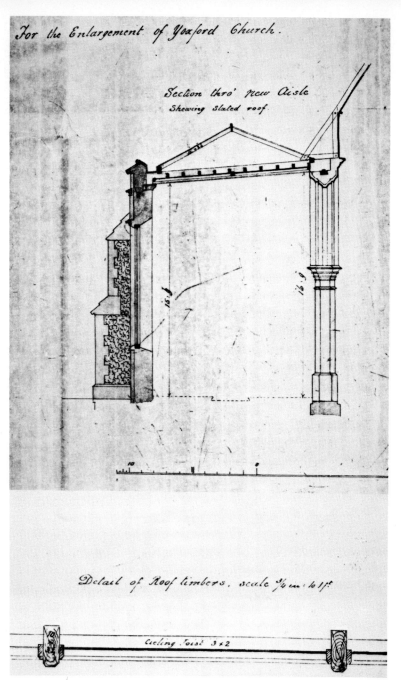

For the Enlargement of Yoxford Church.

Section thro' new Aisle
Shewing slated roof

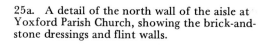

Detail of Roof timbers. scale ¾ in. to 1ft.

Ceiling Joist 3 × 2

24a. (*above left*) Roberts' drawing of the section through the new aisle for Yoxford Parish Church in Suffolk, dated 1837.

24b. (*below left*) A detail of the roof timbers of Yoxford Parish Church new north aisle (*Lambeth Palace Library*)

25a. A detail of the north wall of the aisle at Yoxford Parish Church, showing the brick-and-stone dressings and flint walls.

5b. The north aisle of Yoxford Parish Church
1 1979, showing Roberts' nave arcade.

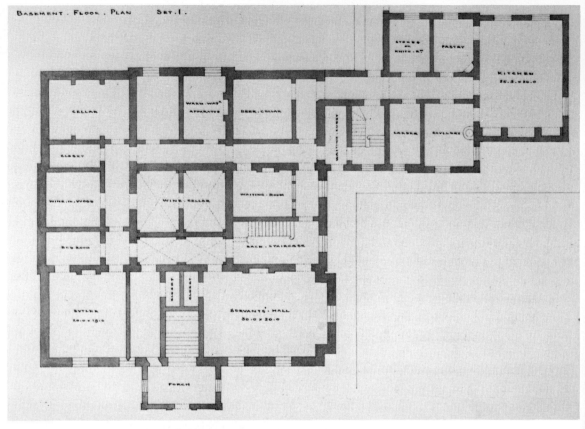

26. The basement (*above*) and first-floor (*below*) plans of Escot House in approximately its final state. (*Devon Record Office 961 M/add. 1/E29*)

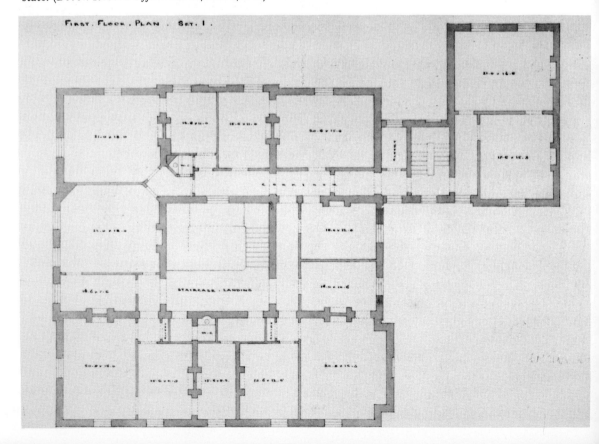

27. Henry Roberts' study of the south front of Escot House showing the attic storey and the treatment of the fenestration (*Devon Record Office 961 M/add. 1/E29*)

28a. A chimney-piece for the drawing-room at Escot House. (*Devon Record Office 961 M/add. 1/E29*)

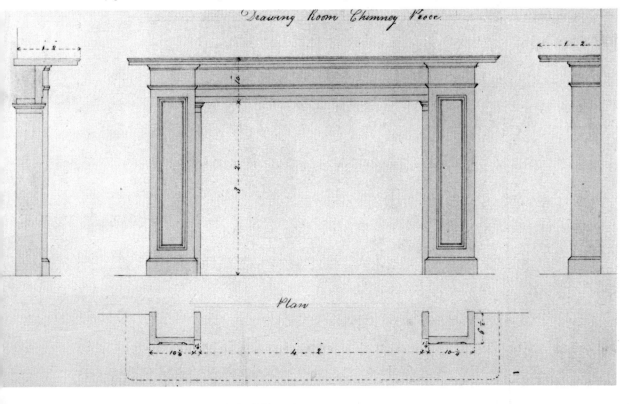

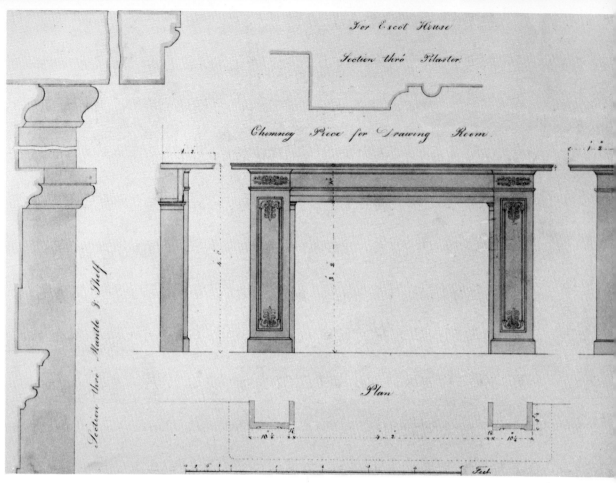

For Escot House

Section thro' Pilaster

Chimney Piece for Drawing Room

Section thro' Mantle & Shelf

Plan

28b. A more elaborate chimney-piece for the drawing-room at Escot, typical of Roberts' classical designs. There is an identical design at Toft Hall in Cheshire, as shown on Plate 53. (*Devon Record Office 961 M/add. 1/E29*)

29. Escot House in 1979 showing the terrace.

30. The front (*above*) and terrace garden (*below*) at Escot House in 1979.

1. Escot Church exterior (*below*) and interior view of the Chancel (*right*) in 1979.

32. Elvetham Church,
Hartley Wintney, Hampshire,
of 1840-41, in 1979.

33. 'The London Terminus
of the Brighton and Dover
Railroads'. Roberts' design of
1841-44 drawn by Marchant
and engraved by Adlard.
(*Guildhall Library, City of
London*)

34a. (*left*) The entrance-porch of Norton Manor, Norton Fitzwarren, Somerset, in 1979.

34b. (*above*) The entrance-front of Norton Manor, Norton Fitzwarren, Somerset, in 1979.

35a. The garden-front of Norton Manor, Norton Fitzwarren, Somerset, in 1979.

35b. The terrace at Norton Manor in 1979.

37a. The garden-front of Peamore House, near Exeter, Devon, in 1979.

36. The interior of the drawing-room of Norton Manor, Norton Fitzwarren, Somerset, in 1979

37b.   A prospect of Peamore House, Alphington, near Exeter, Devon, in 1979.

8a. Henry Roberts' designs of 1846 for the school at Sidmouth, Devon.   (*Devon Record Office 961 M/E40*)

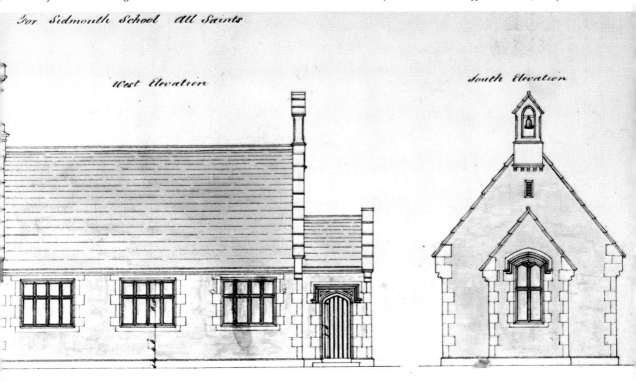

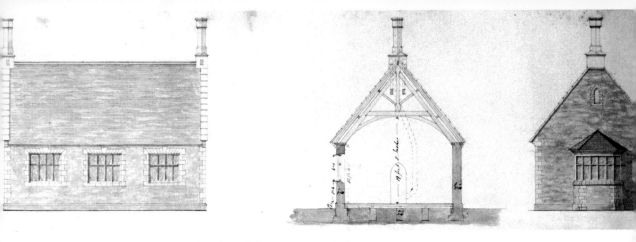

38b.   The design redrawn by the builder, W. Lee, two months later.

39a.   The school at Sidmouth, Devon, in 1979.

39b.   All Saints' Church and Schools, Sidmouth, Devon, c.1850. (*In the possession of All Saints' Church*)

40b. St. Paul's Church, Dock Street, London, from the north, in 1978.

41a. Interior of St. Paul's Church, Dock Street, London, looking west, in 1979. (*Photo: Alan Turner*)

. St. Paul's Church, Dock Street, ndon, from the south, in 1979.

41b. Interior of St. Paul's Church, Dock Street, London, looking east, in 1979. (*Alan Turner*)

42. 'His Royal Highness Prince Albert Laying the Foundation Stone of the Seamen's Church on Monday last'. An engraving from *The Illustrated London News* of 16 May 1846 (p. 321). At this ceremony Roberts read that: 'This Foundation-Stone of the Church for Seamen of the port of London was laid on Monday 11th day of May, 1846, in the eighth year of the reign of her Majesty Queen Victoria, by his Royal Highness Prince Albert, K.G., her Majesty's Consort; the Right Hon. and Right Rev. Charles James Bishop of London; John Labouchere, Esq., Treasurer; Henry Roberts, F.S.A., Architect; William Cubitt & Co., Builders'. The figure on the right is the Marquis of Abercorn. Roberts is the tall slender man immediately to the left of the Prince. (*Tower Hamlets Public Library*)

43. The Vicarage of St. Paul, Dock Street, London, c.1847, in 1978.

44a. The entrance front of the Norbiton Parsonage, Surrey, 1846. (*Surrey Record Office Acc. 1056/441*)

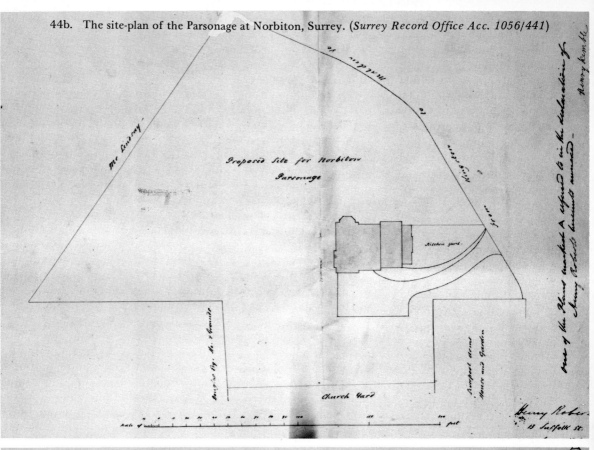

44b. The site-plan of the Parsonage at Norbiton, Surrey. (*Surrey Record Office Acc. 1056/441*)

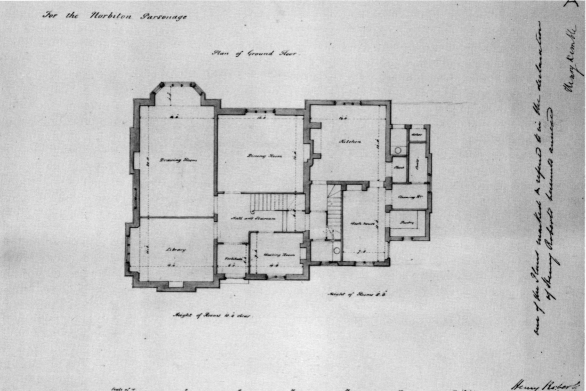

45a. The ground-floor plan of the Norbiton Parsonage, Surrey, 1846. (*Surrey Record Office Acc. 1056/441*)

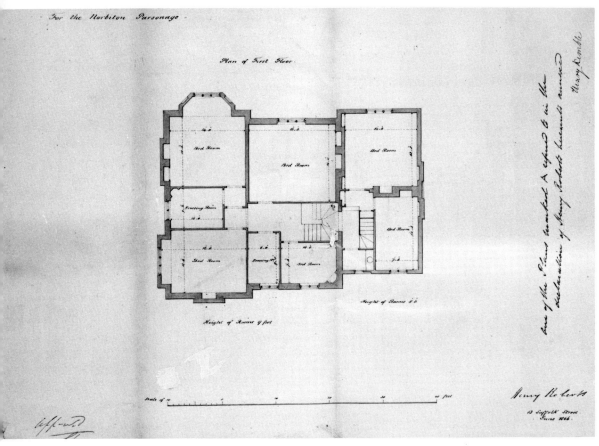

Plan of First Floor.

Height of Rooms 9 feet

Height of Rooms 8.6

Henry Roberts
13 Suffolk Street
June 1846.

45b. The first-floor plan of the Norbiton Parsonage, Surrey, 1846. (*Surrey Record Office Acc. 1056/441*)

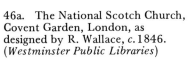

46a. The National Scotch Church, Covent Garden, London, as designed by R. Wallace, *c.*1846. (*Westminster Public Libraries*)

46b. (*left*) The National Scotch Church, Covent Garden, with adjoining schools, as enlarged by Henry Roberts in 1848. (*Westminster Public Libraries*)

47a. (*above*) The principal front of the Norbiton Schools, Surrey, of 1851. (*Surrey Record Office 264/51/1-5*)

47b. (*below*) The site-plan of the Norbiton Schools and Mistress' House, Surrey. (*Surrey Record Office 264/51/1-5*)

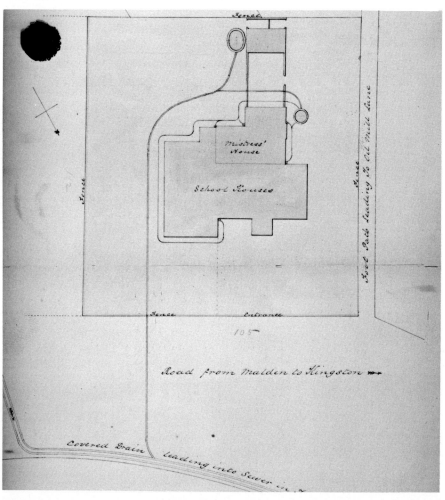

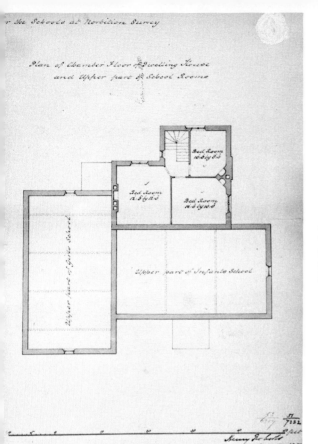

48a. Plan of the first floor of the Teachers' House at Norbiton, Surrey, with the upper part of the Schools. (*Surrey Record Office 264/51/1-5*)

48b. Plan of the ground floor of the Norbiton Schools, Surrey. (*Surrey Record Office 264/51/1-5*)

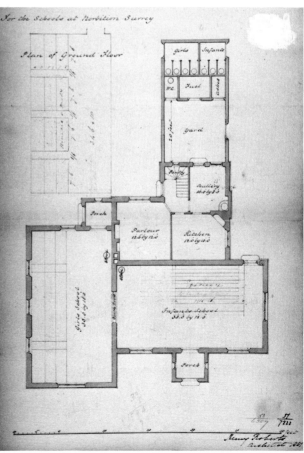

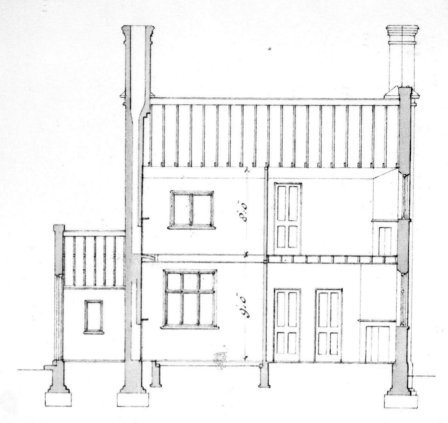

Section thro Dwelling House

50a. (*above*) The Norbiton Schools, Surrey, in 1979, showing the alterations.

49a. (*opposite above*) Section through the dwelling-house at Norbiton Schools, Surrey.

49b. (*opposite below*) Section through the school-room and the dwelling-house at Norbiton Schools, Surrey. (*Surrey Record Office 264/51/1-5*)

50b. (*below*) The rear of the Norbiton Schools, Surrey, in 1979.

51a.   Exton Hall, Rutland, in 1979. The garden in front with the chapel. The centre portion is by Roberts. Note the resemblance of the part adjacent to the chapel to the Great Exhibition houses.

51b.   Exton Hall, Rutland, in 1979. The entrance front. The part by Roberts is on the right.

52a.   Henry Roberts' extension to Toft Hall, Cheshire, in 1979.

52b. Toft Hall Cheshire.
On the right is Henry
Roberts' extension.

53. The interior of Henry
Roberts' extension at Toft
Hall, Cheshire. The fire-
place is identical to his
designs at Escot House.
Compare with Plate 28.
The design is also similar
to those for the Fish-
mongers' Hall in London.

54a. 'Proposed Church for Saint Matthews District, Nottingham'. Lithograph by Hullmandel and Walton.

54b. St. Matthew's Church Nottingham, c.1900. (*Local Studies Library, Nottinghamshire County Library*)

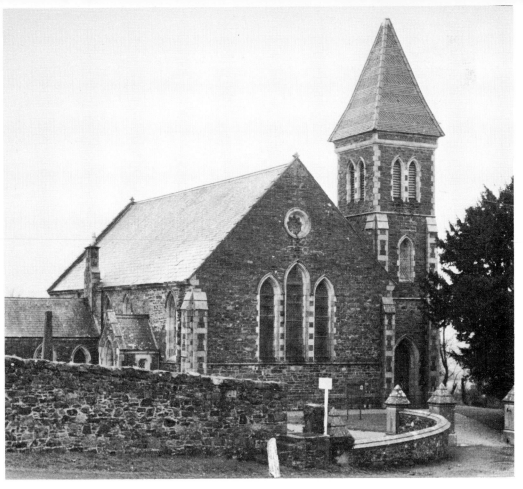

55. Wigtown Church,
Scotland, in 1979.

56. St. George's Buildings
(1852-3), London, built by
John Newson to designs by
Henry Roberts. (*Greater
London Council Department
of Architecture and Civic
Design No. 77/2828*)

57.   Gate-lodges built by the Duke of Manchester in 1853 at Kimbolton, Huntingdonshire, photographed in 1979. These are very similar to those designs shown in Figure 2.

58.   (*opposite*) An original drawing by Henry Roberts, dated 10 July 1848, showing a design for a model Lodging-House for Labourers. This design was produced for Lady O. B. Sparrow's estates in Huntingdonshire. These estates were closely connected with those of the Duke of Manchester. (*The Manchester Papers, Huntingdon County Record Office*)

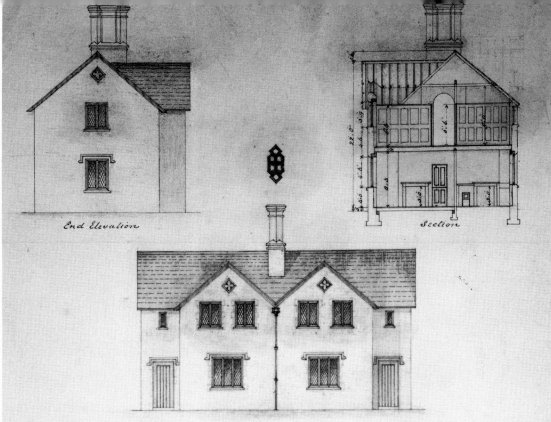

End Elevation

Section

Elevation of the Front

Plan of Dormitory Floor

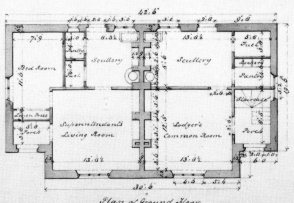

Plan of Ground Floor

59. A sketch by Henry Roberts of a house for the Manchester Estates in Huntingdonshire. (*The Manchester Papers, Huntingdon County Record Office*)

60. The *Villa Romana*, San Gaggio, Florence, where Henry Roberts died. Photographed in 1979. The proportions a not unlike those of Escot House.

51.   Graves Nos. B.VII 68-71 in the *Cimitero Evangelico degli Allori* in Florence. On the left in B.VII 68 is the grave of Henry Roberts (16 April 1803 to 9 March 1876). Next, in B.VII 69 is the grave of Lydia A.D. de Schéhavtzoff, née Roberts (19 June 1851 to 10 February 1877). Also in this grave is buried Véra de Schéhavtzoff (21 March 1876 to 20 May 1877), whose father was Pietro de Schéhavtzoff. Third from the left, in B.VII 70 is the grave of Catherine Roberts, née de Svétchine (2 March 1820 to 20 November 1905). Lastly, on the right, in B.VII 71, is the grave of Theodora Amélie Roberts (8 June 1856 to 19 March 1916). Photograph of 1979.

52.   (*left*) 'View looking from George Street' and (*right*) 'View of the Internal Quadrangle' of the Model Houses for 48 Families, Streatham Street, Bloomsbury. Two framed architectural perspectives, rendered with water-colour, from the office of Henry Roberts, and probably by him. (*The Peabody Trust*)

63a. The internal court of the Model Dwellings at Streatham Street in 1979.

64a. A detail of the open gallery at Kennington Park

63b. The exterior of the Model Dwellings at Streatham Street in 1979.

64b. The re-erected Prince Consort's Model Houses in Kennington Park in 1979.

65a. 'Elevation of Two Pair of Three Story Houses on the Plan of the Prince's Model Houses Accommodating together Twelve Families. The Roof of Ordinary Construction'. Two-storey versions of these were built as the central block of the development at Windsor designed by Henry Roberts for the Windsor Royal Society. (*Reproduced by the Gracious Permission of Her Majesty the Queen*)

65b. 'Elevation of Two Pair of Three Story Houses on the Plan of the Prince's Model Houses Accommodating together Twelve Families. The Roof of Fire Proof Construction'. A three-storey version of the original Model Dwellings at the Great Exhibition of 1851. (From The Model Houses for Families, built in connexion with the Great Exhibition of 1851, By Command of His Royal Highness The Prince Albert, K.G. by Henry Roberts. London, 1851. *Reproduced by the Gracious Permission of Her Majesty the Queen*)

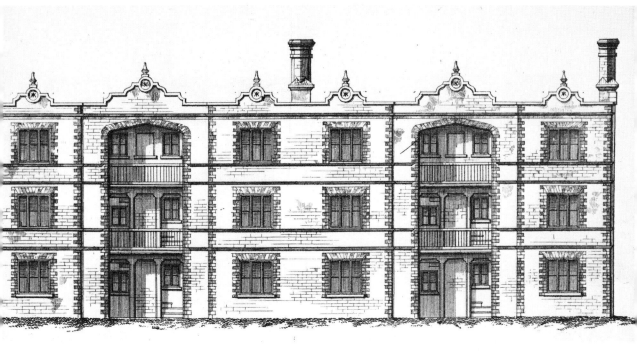

VIEW OF THE MODEL HOUSES FOR FAMILIES, ERECTED IN HYDE PARK, AT THE EXHIBITION OF 1851.
BY COMMAND OF
His Royal Highness The Prince Albert, K.G.

Henry Roberts Esq F.S.A.

66.   'View of the Model Houses for Families, Erected in Hyde Park, at the Exhibition of 1851 By Command of His Highness The Prince Albert, K.G. Henry Roberts, Esq. F.S.A. Hony. Arch.' A lithograph by Day & Son. (*Reproduced by the Gracious Permission of Her Majesty the Queen*)

67.   The Prince Consort's Model Houses adapted as a continuous run at Cowley Gardens, Shadwell. (*Kindly lent by Professor John Nelson Tarn*)

68a. The front of the Hertford Model Houses in 1978.

b. The rear of the Hertford Model Houses in 1978.

69a. The Prince Consort's Model Houses at Hertford in 1969.

70. (*below*) The pair of Model Dwellings at Nos. 1-8, Erdley Square, Ramsgate in 1957. These were based up the Great Exhibition Model Dwellings. Note the flint construction with brick dressings. Most of the hood-moulds have been destroyed, and the access to the cent stairs has been altered. Note that the Tudor arch in the centre of each block was once the entrance to the stairs and that very considerable alterations have taken place. These buildings were demolished under the Borough of Ramsgate (Erdley Square) Clearance Order No. 2 in 195 The photograph shows the front elevation looking south (*Photograph by Sunbeam Photo Ltd., Margate, kindly lent by Mr. C. E. Busson, Librarian of Ramsgate Public Library*)

69b. (*above*) The version of the same design (much mutilated) at Abbot's Langley, Hertfordshire, in 1969. (*Hertfordshire County Council*)

71a. (*above*) A view from Alexandra Road in 1979 of the 'Prince Consort Cottages' built for the Windsor Royal Society to designs by Henry Roberts.

71b. (*right*) On the left is the block modelled on the Great Exhibition Model Dwellings. The Windsor Royal Society development in 1979.

a. (*above*) The centre building for eight families at Windsor in 1979, based on the Great Exhibition Model Dwellings.

2b. (*right*) The open gallery of the centre building for eight families Windsor in 1979.

3a. (*above*) The Windsor Royal Society's scheme by Henry Roberts 1979. To the right is the centre building for eight families; left of this building is a pair of cottages with dormers based on one of the designs by Roberts for the S.I.C.L.C.; and to the far left are the cottages for four families.

3b. (*right*) The cottages for four families at Windsor in 1979. See also Plate 78.

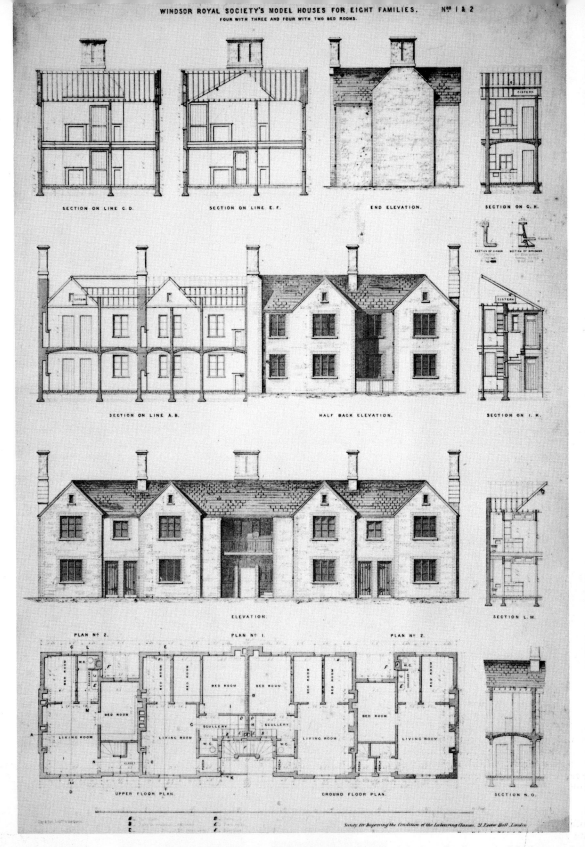

74a. 'The Windsor Royal Society's Model Houses for Eight Families'. Roberts' designs for houses with three and two bedrooms. Note the flatted arrrangement, and the fireproof construction between floors. (*The Bodleian Library*)

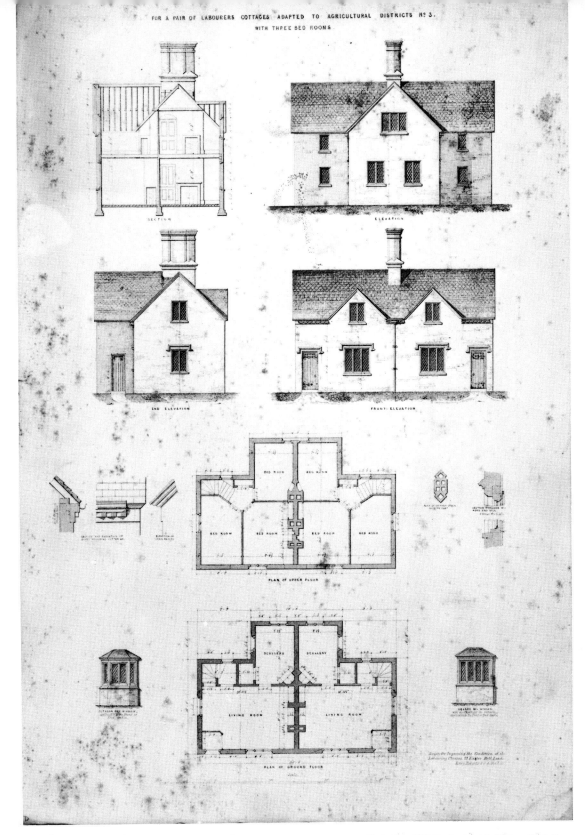

74b. Roberts' designs for a pair of 'Labourers' cottages adapted for Agricultural Districts with Three Bed Rooms'. These sheets were published by the Society for Improving the Condition of the Labouring Classes, and were sold to enable landowners to build such cottages. (*The Bodleian Library*)

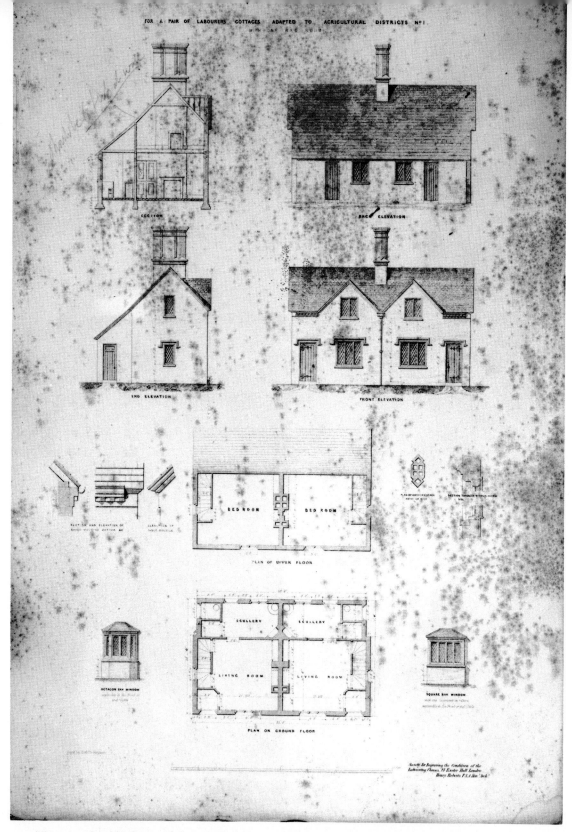

75a. A pair of 'Labourers' Cottages, with one Bed Room, adapted to Agricultural Districts'. (*The Bodleian Library*)

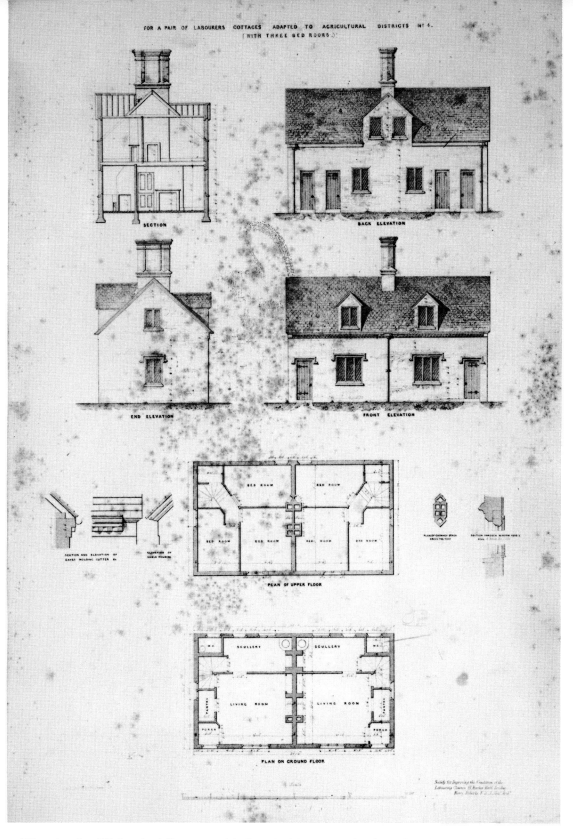

75b. A pair of 'Labourers' Cottages, with three Bed Rooms each, adapted to Agricultural Districts'. These were typical of the design sheets published by the Society for Improving the Condition of the Labouring Classes, and sold to persons anxious to build. All the designs were by Roberts. (*The Bodleian Library*)

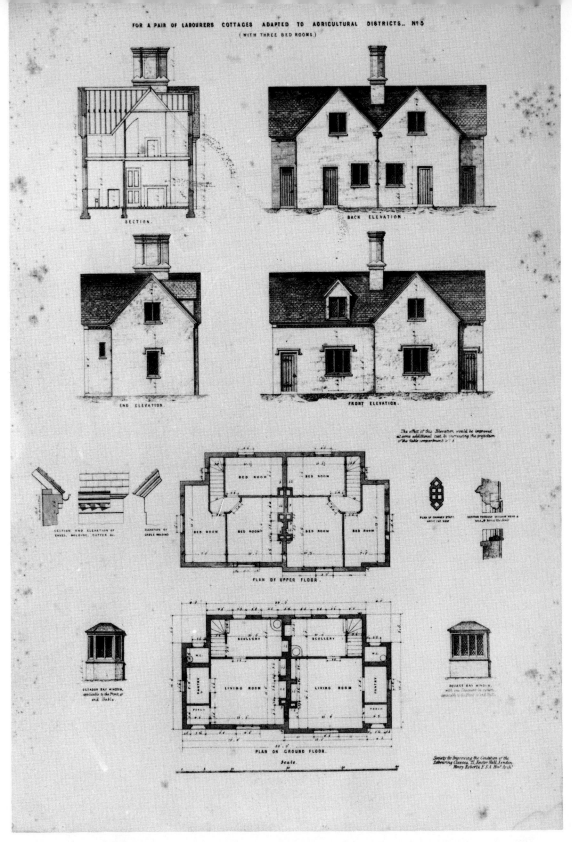

76a. A pair of 'Labourers' Cottages with Three Bed Rooms each, Adapted to Agricultural Districts'. (*The Bodleian Library*)

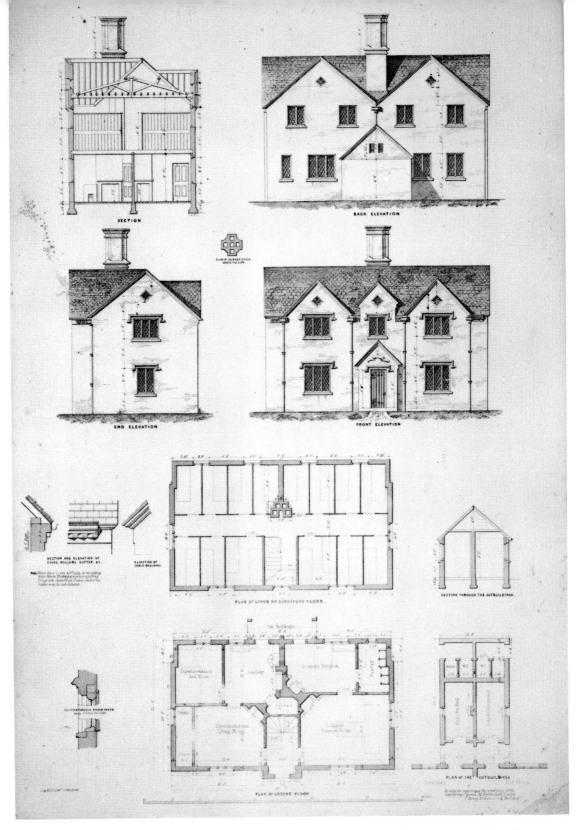

76b. A 'Lodging House for Unmarried Workmen or Labourers'. Two design sheets published by the Society for Improving the Condition of the Labouring Classes. (*The Bodleian Library*)

77a.   A pair of 'Labourers' Cottages, with Two Bed Rooms each, Adapted to Agricultural Districts'.
(*The Bodleian Library*)

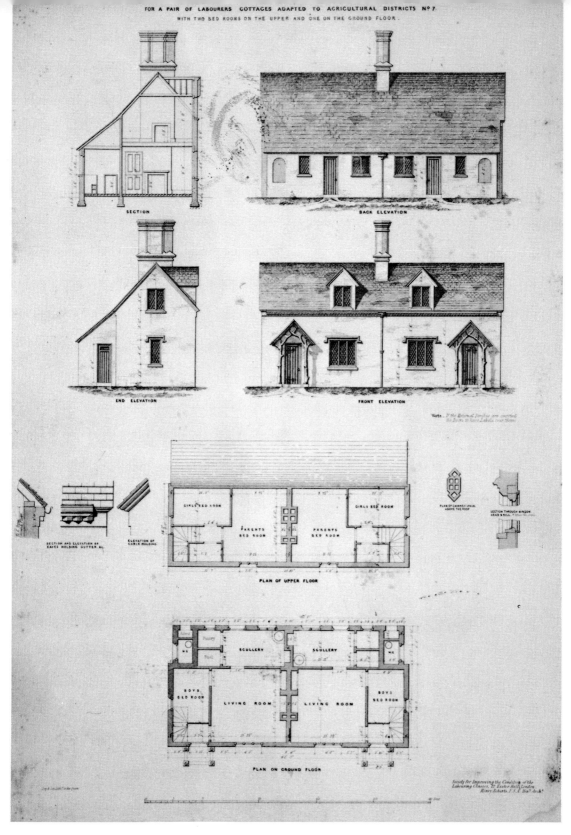

77b. A pair of 'Labourers' Cottages, with Three Bed Rooms each, Adapted to Agricultural Districts'. Design sheets published by the Society for Improving the Condition of the Labouring Classes. (*The Bodleian Library*)

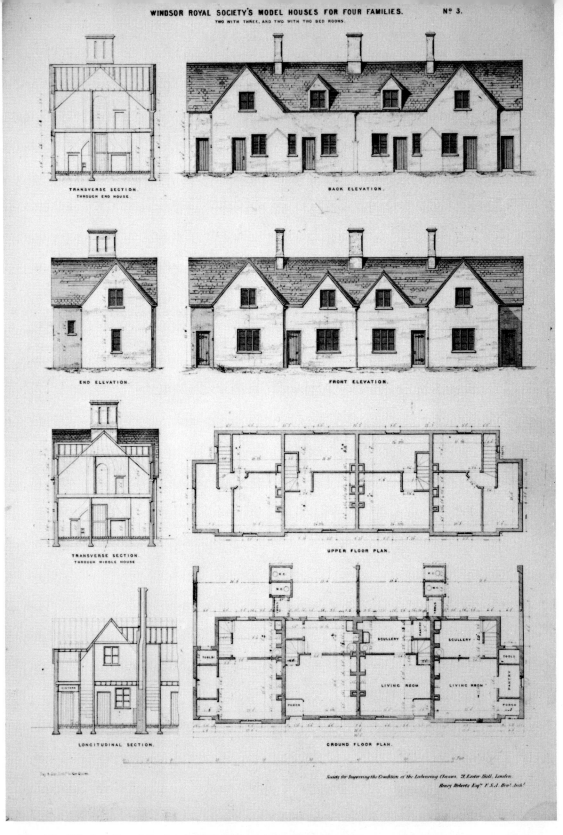

78. The Windsor Royal Society's Model Houses 'for Four Families, two with three and two with two Bed Rooms'. A design sheet published by the Society for Improvings the Condition of the Labouring Classes. See Plate 73. (*The Bodleian Library*)

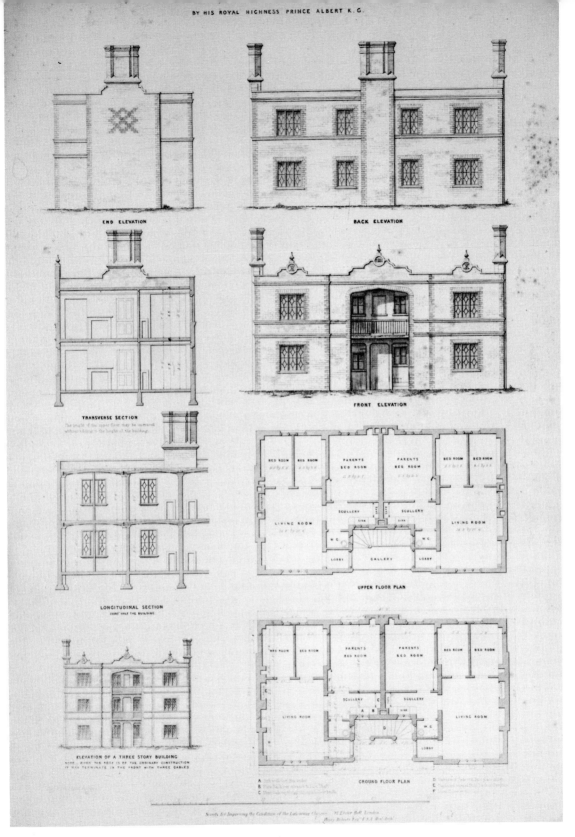

79a. A detailed and refined plan of the 'Model House for Four Families Erected in Hyde Park at the Industrial Exhibition of 1851 by His Royal Highness Prince Albert, K.G.' Note the three-storey variant. (*The Bodleian Library*)

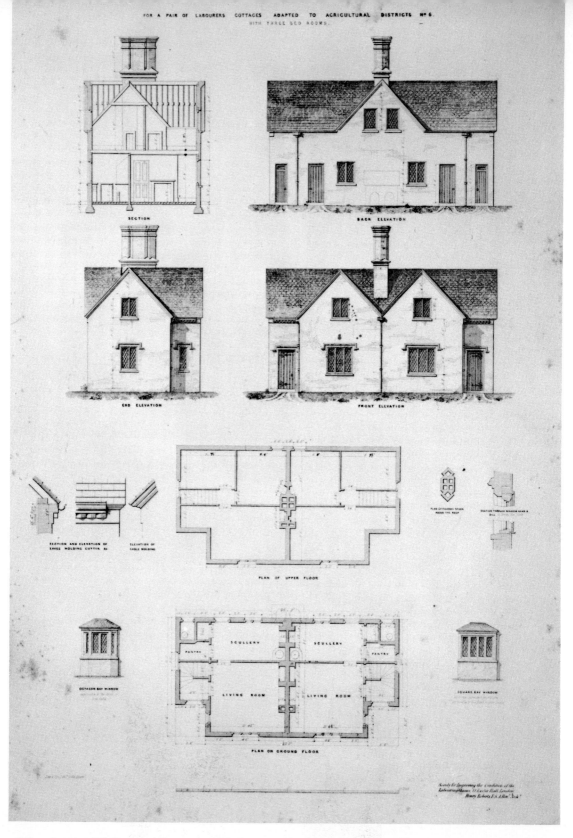

79b. A pair of 'Labourers' Cottages, with three Bed Rooms each, Adapted to Agricultural Districts'. Two design sheets published by the Society for Improving the Condition of the Labouring Classes. (*The Bodleian Library*)

80a.   The south side of Newcomen Road, Tunbridge Wells, in 1980, showing Nos. 2 (right) to 28, Newcomen Road, all designed by Henry Roberts.

)b.   Nos. 14 (*right*) to 16, Newcomen Road, ınbridge Wells, in 1980, with No. 18 in the ıckground.

81a.   The south side of Newcomen Road, Tunbridge Wells, in 1980, showing Nos. 6-8 in the foreground (No. 6 is nearest the camera). This pair is of patent hollow bricks.

b.   Nos. 18-20 Newcomen Road, ınbridge Wells, in 1980. Nos. 22-24 ɛ in the background.

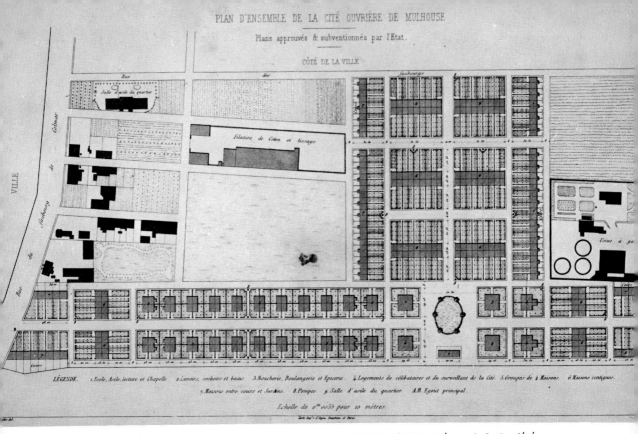

LÉGENDE. *1. École, Asile, lecture et Chapelle   2. Lavoirs, séchoirs et bains   3. Boucherie, Boulangerie et Épicerie   4. Logements de célibataires et du surveillant de la cité.   5. Groupes de 4 Maisons.   6. Maisons contiguës.*
7. Maisons entre cours et Jardins.   8. Pompes   9. Salle d'asile du quartier.   A. B. Égout principal.

Échelle de 0ᵐ.0055 pour 10 mètres.

82.   A plan of the *Cité Ouvrière* at Mulhouse, designed by Emile Muller. (*Bibliothèque de la Société Industrielle de Mulhouse*)

83.   (*opposite*) Designs by Henry Roberts for the Society for Improving the Condition of the Labouring Classes. These are based on the sheets of designs sold by the Society, while the design on the left can be positively identified at Kimbolton (Plate 57 and Figure 2), and that on the right at several places in England.

(*lower*) Cottages for the Metropolitan Association for Improving the Dwellings of the Industrious Classes at Mile End New Town (Victoria and Albert Cottages), and Alexandra Cottages at Penge, in Surrey, all based on plans by Henry Roberts. This engraving was designed by Emile Muller and printed by Thieffry and Co. of Paris. *Bibliothèque de la Société Industrielle de Mulhouse*)

84a.   (*left*) The Metropolitan Association's Lodging House known as Howard Buildings, Deal Street, Mile End New Town, in 1976. The Architect was William Beck, and the contractor was Samuel Grimsdell. The cost was £9,565, and the block was completed in 1849. Beyond are Victoria Cottages.

84b.   (*right*) Cottages completed in 1858 on the estate of the Metropolitan Association for Improving the Dwellings of the Industrious Classes at Mile End New Town, known as Albert Cottages. These were based on designs by Henry Roberts (see Plate 83). Photograph of 1976.

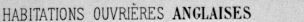

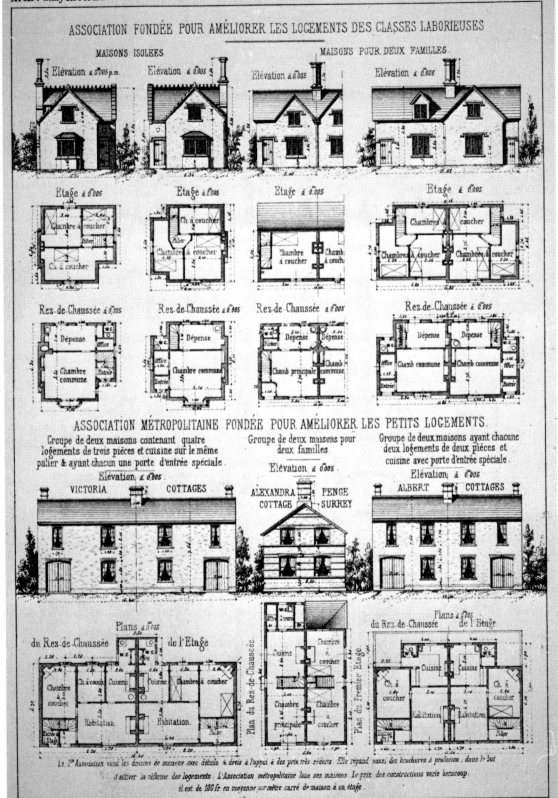

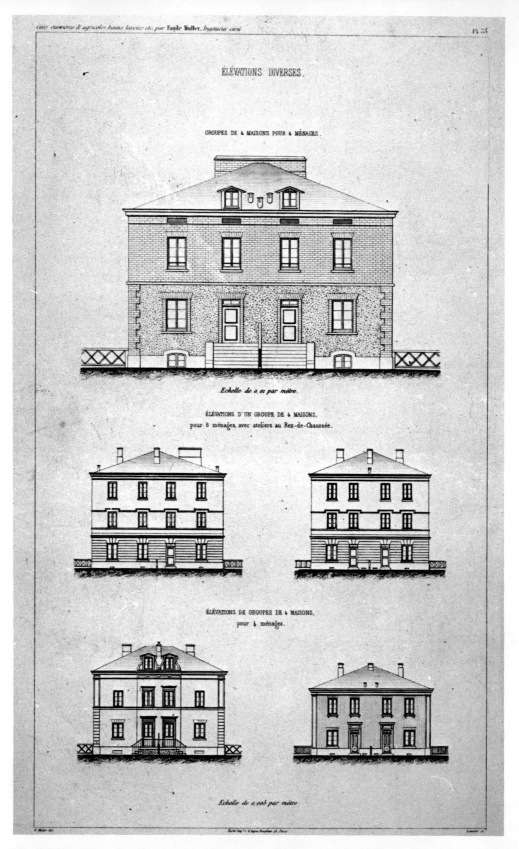

GROUPES DE 4 MAISONS POUR 4 MÉNAGES.

Echelle de 0.01 par mètre.

ÉLÉVATIONS D'UN GROUPE DE 4 MAISONS,
pour 8 ménages, avec ateliers au Rez-de-Chaussée.

ÉLÉVATIONS DE GROUPES DE 4 MAISONS,
pour 4 ménages.

Echelle de 0,005 par mètre.

85.   Different elevations for groups of four houses for four families by Emile Muller. The central design owes not a little to Roberts' work at Streatham Street. (*Bibliothèque de la Société Industrielle de Mulhouse*)

Buxley works, near Esher, Surrey; and some of the partition bricks, at Mr. Cubitt's works, Pimlico.

'The glazed bricks were made by the Ainslie Machine, at Mr. Ridgeway's, the Potteries, Staffordshire. These being the first specimens, the actual cost at which they are likely to be hereafter supplied has not yet been ascertained.

'The brick-work was executed by Mr. S. Grimsdell, Sun-street, Bishopsgate-street.

'The metallic lava covering the roof, the floor lava, and the gravel lava to the front, were laid by Messrs. Orsi and Armani, Guildhall-chambers, Basinghall-street.

'The French plaster and the Portland cement floors have been executed by Messrs. J. B. White and Sons, Millbank-street, Westminster.

'The tile floors in the left-hand ground floor rooms are from Mr. Peak, Tunstall, Staffordshire, or Macclesfield-street South, City-road Basin. Those in the right-hand rooms are from Messrs. H. & R. Haywood, Burslem, Staffordshire, and South Wharf, Paddington.

'The staining fluid used for the wood work is from Ibbotson's Varnish and Colour Works, Hammersmith.

'All the traps used in the building are those of Lowe & Co., Salford; agents, Messrs. Kennard & Co., Upper Thames-street.

'The stoves in the left-hand ground-floor rooms are from Mr. Leslie, Conduit-street; in the right-hand room is the "Cottager's Stove", manufactured by D. and E. Bailey, High Holborn. The stoves in the left-hand rooms, first floor, are from Pierce, of Jermyn-street; to the right-hand, the Prize Cottage Range, by Nicholson, of Newark, is fitted in the living-room, and suitable stoves in the bed-rooms, with fire-brick back and cast-iron chimney-piece complete, by the same maker.

'The earthenware sinks are from Mr. Ridgeway, the Potteries, Staffordshire, who has also supplied specimens of earthenware pipes, wash-hand basins, and the water-closet plans; two of the sinks are of slate.'

Letters of appreciation poured in from all over the world. The papers of the Royal Commission for the Exhibition of 1851 contain many favourable comments from royal personages in Prussia, Portugal, and other countries, addressed personally to the Prince. His Royal Highness wrote to Shaftesbury offering the Model Houses to the S.I.C.L.C. when they were removed from Hyde Park.[23] He also wrote to Roberts to convey, 'his best thanks for his exertions connected with the design of the houses', and to express his 'regret' that the Council Medal was 'merged in the one given' to the Prince 'for the Exhibition generally'. This prevented the Prince from giving Roberts the Medal, 'as it was his intention to do, had it been given exclusively for the Cottages, and the whole merit of which' he considered to be Roberts' due. In any case, the Establishment appears to have been very niggardly with honours in connection with the Exhibition, and the papers of the Royal Commission contain much acrimonious correspondence from persons who felt slighted. If Roberts complained, no record appears to have survived.

Roberts was also connected with the Great Exhibition in another capacity. He acted as designer for the exhibits of the British and Foreign Bible Society. He was responsible for a bookcase to house the Society's publications, and there appears to have been some trouble about the placing of this bookcase, for there are references to 'Mr. Roberts having been clearly informed' of the positioning of the stand and case.[24]

Owing to the Society's policy of publishing its plans, the Model Lodge was copied in many places throughout the country. One block was erected on land owned by a member of the S.I.C.L.C. Committee (Robert Dimsdale, M.P.), and a pitched roof replaced the flat. It is also worth noting that, in addition to Dimsdale, a member of another influential Hertfordshire family, Abel Smith, M.P., sat on the Committee.

Two units were built at Ramsgate in 1851-2 to house eight families. These stood at Nos. 1-8, Erdley Square (off King Street), Ramsgate, in Kent, and their appearance differed considerably from the original dwellings at Hyde Park (Plate 70). They were constructed of flint, with brick dressings, and had pitched slate-covered roofs. They were demolished under Clearance Order No. 2 in 1957. There were other model cottages based on Roberts' standard S.I.C.L.C. designs in Ramsgate at Nos. 49-51, Albert Street, but these have also been pulled down. An entire street of Model Lodges based on the 1851 Great Exhibition exemplars was erected in Cowley Gardens in the East End of London from 1851 to 1854 (Plate 67). These were built largely through the enthusiasm of Rev. W. Quekett, vicar of Hawksmoor's great Church of St George-in-the-East, and through the good offices of W. E. Hilliard, a member of the S.I.C.L.C. Hilliard was the main entrepreneur, and no less than eighty-four model dwellings were built, based on the Roberts plan for the Great Exhibition houses. When Quekett became Rector of Warrington, he carried his belief in the Model Lodge with him, and his wife laid the foundation-stone of the Church Street, Cottages, Warrington, in 1856. The cost of the four houses was £370, the money being raised in shares of one pound each. It was hoped to provide good accommodation at a moderate rent. These houses were described in *The Warrington Guardian* of 14 April 1951. Regrettably, they were demolished in 1960 by the County Borough of Warrington on the grounds that they 'were unfit for human habitation and not capable of being made so fit at reasonable expense and service of notices under the Housing Act 1957'.[25] The building was not included in the List of the Ministry of Town and Country Planning List of Buildings of Special Architectural or Historic Interest, nor was it even included in the Supplementary List. The Warrington houses had a steeply pitched roof, and bays were added. The *History* of the Society for Improving the Condition of the Labouring Classes (1854-1904) mentions the building of model houses in Den Haag in the Netherlands, and other model houses were apparently erected in St Petersburg, but these dwellings owed nothing to the external appearance of the Model Lodge. Only vestigial traces of plans by Roberts may be found, even where records of the Society tell us that Model Houses were erected in Den Haag, St Petersburg, Brussels, and in other places. Even the Warrington houses had departed considerably from Roberts' plan.

After the Great Exhibition closed, the Lodge was re-erected in 1852 by William Higgs on the present site in Kennington Park for £557 (Plate 64). The projecting porch at the rear, which was not part of the original design, was probably added at this time. The houses were to be used as homes for two attendants and as 'a Museum for Articles relating to Cottage economy to which the public may be admitted'.[26] When the outside staircase was enclosed in 1898, part of the ground-floor set of rooms was used as store-rooms and for offices, and the remainder, together with the upper rooms, was inhabited by the Superintendent of the Park.[27]

The choice of Kennington Park as a site for the Model Dwellings may not be quite guiltless of political overtones. The open lands around Bedlam, St George's Fields, and Kennington had known violence. The Gordon Riots had occurred there, and there

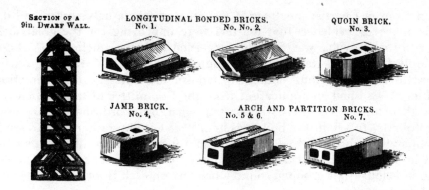

SECTION OF A
9in. DWARF WALL.

LONGITUDINAL BONDED BRICKS.
No. 1.   No. No. 2.

QUOIN BRICK.
No. 3.

JAMB BRICK.
No. 4,

ARCH AND PARTITION BRICKS.
No. 5 & 6.   No. 7.

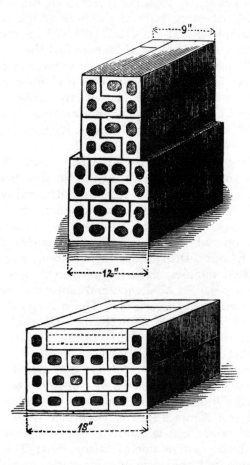

Fig. 23.   Hollow brickwork, as patented by Henry Roberts.

had been monster Chartist meetings at Kennington where ugly scenes had developed. A visible piece of evidence that matters were improving for the great mass of the people, and that Royalty was directly concerned with the amelioration of conditions, could hardly have been sited in a more appropriate place than Kennington. There had been overtures from various bodies to acquire the cottages for re-erection. Prince Albert himself had had an application from the Committee of the Ipswich Arboretum to allow them to re-erect the cottages at Ipswich, but Lord Shaftesbury was anxious (as was Roberts) to retain the buildings in or near London rather than to send them to the 'comparative obscurity' of a provincial town. Variants of the plan were constructed in several places all over the country, notably in tenements. The method of access to individual flats grouped round a balcony on each floor became a usual feature of tenement planning.

The publicity value of the Model Houses was enormous. The Society was inundated with requests for advice and for copies of Roberts' plans from all over the world.[28] Yet in many ways this design by Roberts represented the pinnacle of the Society's achievements, for models of every type of dwelling of the working classes had now been provided. The example of the S.I.C.L.C. did not encourage investment to any great extent, and soon the Annual General Meetings of the Society became noted for inertia and inactivity.[29] Instead of being the pace-setter, the Society reported on the work of other companies and societies, although it claimed that all these works had been inspired by the Society. This inertia is partly explained by the departure of Henry Roberts for the Continent. All the innovations, designs, and ideas of any originality had stemmed from the mind of Roberts. Without him, the Society was only a hollow shell.

The decline of building activity had been partially caused by rising costs, and new buildings were unlikely to be constructed by the Society from the mid-1850s. The next work was, in fact, a conversion of an existing court, and was revolutionary in that it tried to cleanse and purify a singularly unsavoury area. In 1854, with funds anonymously placed at the disposal of Lord Shaftesbury, the Society undertook to cleanse, renovate, and improve one of the most filthy and lawless courts in the parish of St Giles. This was Wild Court, Drury Lane, where about one thousand people, comprising some two hundred families, lived in fourteen houses. On 8 November Lord Shaftesbury had taken a party of noblemen and reporters over the court so that the true state of the place could be appreciated.[30] The visit was also reported in *Houshold Words* under the title of 'Conversion of a Heathen Court'.[31] Dickens later reported on progress in 'Wild Court Tamed' in the issue of 25 August 1855. Following the success two further conversions were planned at Clark's Buildings, St Giles', and at Tyndall's Buildings, Gray's Inn Lane. The converted properties were occupied by more respectable tenants. These last two schemes were completed by 1858.

The S.I.C.L.C. formed a branch at Tunbridge Wells in 1847, and a group of cottages was built (Plates 80–81 and Figure 42). The Tunbridge Wells group also ran a lodging-house. This little model estate was laid out on the south side of Newcomen Road, Tunbridge Wells, and at the eastern side of Currie Road. The lodging-house stood in Currie Road, and terminated the vista looking east down Newcomen Road. The lodging-house has been demolished, but the rest of the estate still survived in 1980.

It consisted of no less than seven semi-detached pairs of model dwellings, all designed by Henry Roberts for the Society. These houses are numbered 2–28 Newcomen Road. Nos. 2–4 form an asymmetrial pair with a large gable on No. 2, and a dormer on No. 4. The pair is constructed of Roberts' patent hollow bricks. The verges and eaves are also of patent brickwork. Nos. 6–8 are a mirror-image of Nos. 2–4, but are less altered. Nos. 10–12 form a symmetrical pair with Tudor hood-moulds, dormers, and a central chimney. This pair is constructed of ordinary red bricks, with vitrified headers. The end gables have bargeboards. Nos. 14–16 are similar to Nos. 10–12. Nos. 18–20 form a symmetrical pair with twin bargeboarded gables, and are constructed of red brick with vitrified headers. Nos. 22–24 form an asymmetrical pair, constructed of patent hollow bricks, with brick verges and eaves. This pair is similar to the pair Nos. 6–8, but is more drastically altered. Nos. 26–28 is a pair (much altered), constructed of red brick with vitrified headers, and stone hood-moulds. The gables have bargeboards. This pair was similar to Nos. 18–20, but has been considerably altered.

These seven pairs of houses have front and rear gardens, and have elaborate chimney-stacks. The estate backed on to a development of salubrious villas, and there appears to have been some local controversy about the desirability of building model dwellings on the site in question. The southern elevations have a minimum number of openings to avoid overlooking the adjoining properties. This little development, and the Windsor Royal Society's houses, are Henry Roberts' largest surviving designs for two-storey working-class housing estates. Although the Newcomen Road houses have suffered from some unsympathetic alterations over the years, the character of Roberts' design can still be appreciated. The development at Windsor is the best-preserved estate of individual dwellings by Roberts.

The last major scheme by the S.I.C.L.C. in Victorian times was a large group of model dwellings grouped around a courtyard erected at Hull in 1862, to designs by Henry M. Eyton.[32] Separate tenement flats were provided for thirty-two families. Eyton also remodelled some property in Seven Dials for the Society in 1872, but there were few further schemes produced by the Society. Nevertheless, the Society was important in the history of philanthropic housing for the work carried out under its aegis in the first decade of its existence. Practical research and publicity were the Society's greatest contributions.

Gradually, the improvement in the moral and physical condition of the occupants of the model dwellings made its impact. Tenants did not suffer from many of the diseases of the time, and they escaped the cholera epidemics of 1849 and 1854. Roberts' attention to ventilation, sound construction, and sanitation provided a practical demonstration of the advantages to the inhabitants. The Society was deluged with requests for plans and for advice. Supporters of the parent society and of its many auxiliary bodies began to erect improved dwellings throughout the country, and similar societies were formed in Europe and in the United States of America. Roberts' plans were widely disseminated and were adapted in several countries.

Before the end of the century, with the advent of public housing by local government, better houses were being constructed throughout the country, and the *rôle* of the Society became less important. Membership declined and subscriptions dwindled. The Royal Charter of 1850 had planned for such a contingency, however, and the

Society concentrated on managing its properties, repaying outstanding loans, and ploughing back any surplus that might be created. At intervals, modest schemes were undertaken, financed by raising loans, and by the sale of old buildings.

In 1900, for example, twelve flats were added to the Hull Model Dwellings, and in 1925 twenty-five flats and a clinic were erected in Holborn, called St Giles' Buildings. In 1936 a further thirty-six flats were built at Wandle House, Wandsworth, and two other buildings, Kent House at Camberwell, and York House, at Lambeth, of sixty and forty-five flats respectively, were erected. These last three blocks were built by agreement with the London County Council, and grants were given to the Society under the Housing Acts. In 1958 the Society acquired Darwin Buildings, in Southwark, and modernised the block. On acquiring this block, the Committee decided to change the Charter, and it was agreed that the name was no longer appropriate. On 13 October 1959 the S.I.C.L.C. became The 1830 Housing Society, with the aims of providing accommodation for the poorer members of the community. In the 1960s the Society merged with the Peabody Trust.[33]

Henry Roberts always emphasised the necessity for 'rigid economy' in his buildings in order to keep the rents down. He turned his attention to the urgency of housing the rural poor while respecting the landscape. He evolved designs for country cottages that were picturesque, and leaned heavily on the vernacular traditions. It is this aspect of Roberts' work that will be discussed in the following chapter.

Chapter Five

PHILANTHROPIC BUILDINGS AND DESIGNS BY HENRY ROBERTS NOT DIRECTLY CONNECTED WITH THE SOCIETY FOR IMPROVING THE CONDITION OF THE LABOURING CLASSES

> Among the various departments of Social Science, which have to late much occupied public attention, next in importance to that of popular education, may be ranked the Improvement of the Dwellings of the Labouring Classes.
>
> Henry Roberts: *The Improvement of the Dwellings of the Labouring Classes, through the Operation of Government Measures, by those of Public Bodies and Benevelont Associations, as well as Individual Efforts*, London, 1859, p.3.

ROBERTS, LIKE MANY of his contemporaries, was greatly concerned with the misery caused by the demolition of houses to make way for street-improvements, docks, or railways. Until 1853 there was little or no provision for the building of suitable dwellings for the working classes to replace houses demolished under powers granted by Parliament. 'The want of any such provision has led to incalculable misery and evil in our own metropolis; and, at the present time, similar results arise out of the gigantic and unprecedented destruction of low-class dwellings in Paris, where, however, it is now beyond doubt a part of the Government policy to disperse and to eject, at least from the heart of the metropolis, a considerable portion of the working classes. It remains to be seen whether colonies, formed in the environs without any adequate and suitable provision being previously made, do not increase the centres of discontent and political agitation, besides producing similar evils to those which resulted from our own destructions in Regent-street, New Oxford-street, and the Borough improvements, the consequences of which, in certain localities around London, were well known to the police and to medical men, in a combination of physical and moral evil as yet by no means rooted out'.[1]

Following the success of the Great Exhibition, and the powerful impact of the Model Dwellings on the public in general, many barracks were modernised. Similarly, rebuilding and modernisation programmes were begun for many groups within society. By 1859 provision had been made for lodging 3,500 ummarried policemen, and Roberts advocated the construction of dwellings for the remainder of the force, numbering some 2,500, with the families. Roberts proposed an amendment of the laws relating to the transfer of land, and quoted the benefits whereby the poor could acquire their own property by a slight increase in rent, as at Berlin, Munich, and Mulhouse. In those places, tenants could either rent their dwellings to yield a net return of four to five per cent on the outlay, with a small sinking fund, or, by paying a higher rent, for a fixed period, purchase the property.[2] Roberts very much regretted the loss of an opportunity for trying a similar experiment in London, and thought his model dwellings at Bagnigge Wells might have been ideal subjects, had they not been sold during his absence from England.[3]

Roberts advocated a discontinuance of the evils resulting from the system of demolishing cottages so that labourers would be thrown upon the mercies of neighbouring parishes. Peel himself had calculated the loss of valuable time and strength caused by a system that forced evicted labourers to walk several miles to work. Roberts suggested that government advances at low rates of interest to establish philanthropic societies might solve a number of problems. The London City Missionary Society, with which Roberts had intimate connections, advocated urgent attention should be given to the lodging-houses of London. The Royal Agricultural Society published in 1849 a letter from the Duke of Bedford that argued for improved cottage buildings, and the *Journal* of the R.A.S. consistently urged that object on the attention of landed proprietors generally. The Statistical Society of London, as early as 1842, instituted a house-to-house survey of the Parish of St George, Hanover Square, and in 1847–8, Church Lane, St Giles', was examined in detail by Colonel Sykes and Dr. Guy. The Society of Arts (again an institution with which Roberts was connected) repeatedly afforded facilities for studies of poor areas of the metropolis and invited architects to submit model plans for labourers' cottages. The R.S.A. and the R.I.B.A. (as they became) encouraged lectures on accommodation for the poor.

There was undoubtedly a movement towards the improvement of the dwellings of the labouring classes by public bodies and benevolent associations as well as by individual effort. 'Although many of the railway companies, and some other commercial bodies have, in places where dwellings for those in their employ would not have been otherwise obtainable, built them extensively, yet, as far as my own information goes, this has generally be done solely for their own convenience, and but rarely in recognition of the principle that those who have working people in their regular and exclusive employ are bound in duty to care for their domiciliary condition'.[4] Many manufacturers, as well as owners of mines and quarries, besides a considerable number of landed proprietors, however, manifested the conviction that no measures adopted for the physical and social benefit of their work-people and labourers could be complete if the state of their dwellings were to be neglected. Many employers learned that money thus invested yielded from indirect results an interest that was not to be measured by the calculation of percentage on capital.

A much wider field than that of metropolitan improvement was in fact embraced by the S.I.C.L.C., which was also called The Labourers' Friend Society. With the establishment of the field-garden, and the cottage allotment system, the main practical branch of the Society's operations was to promote the improvement of labourers. dwellings 'both in the metropolis and in manufacturing and agricultural districts',[5] by the time-honoured method of 'arranging and executing plans as models'. Needless to say, Roberts was the genius behind such plans and models. Numerous auxiliary societies were founded throughout the Kingdom and abroad. Certainly the improved health of the inhabitants of model dwellings was statistically proved, while epidemics of typhus and cholera left the fortunate tenants alone.

Roberts was greatly concerned with the financial problems of the philanthropic societies. He observed that it was necessary to site dwellings as near places of employment as possible, to save the tenants the expense of travelling. However, sites in central areas were expensive, and this taxed the ingenuity of the architect, as well as necessitating a high-density form of development. Dwellings for families were always a better investment than lodging-houses. The Thanksgiving Model Buildings in Portpool Lane, the fourth of the S.I.C.L.C.'s new range of buildings, had a public bath- and wash-house, which, 'though proving of great value to the neighbourhood', barely paid for the expenditure on them, and did not yield an adequate return.[6]

Repairs comprised a question of great importance in deciding between the profits derivable from investments in new and old buildings. The average repairs on the properties of the S.I.C.L.C. between 1850 and 1853 was ¾ per cent on the total outlay. The percentage increased in 1857, and the various philanthropic societies had to exercise a 'watchful care over the numerous small amounts forming the items of current expenditures on such establishments'.[7] The net returns also suffered from increased Income Tax. While abroad, between 1854 and 1857, Roberts urged very careful systems of detailed entries of expenses. In common with the railways and most other investments of capital in commercial undertakings, the amount of return was so greatly dependent on the management that every item of expenditure had to be accounted for. On balance, Roberts favoured 'well-constructed and conveniently arranged new buildings' rather than renovations, as the repairs would be less. The S.I.C.L.C. expended £6,700 between 1854 and 1857 in putting the old houses forming three courts into good sanitary repair. The net return, without deduction of repairs, was, on £3,303 for Wild Court, Drury Lane, some £260, or 7⅞ per cent: on £1,159 9s. 0d. expended at Clark's Buildings, Bloomsbury, it was some £46, or 4 per cent. On £2,227 10s. 7d. expended on Tyndall's Buildings, Gray's Inn Lane, it was confidently expected that a clear return of 5 per cent would be available after every deduction. Some ten years before, £1,298 14s. 2d. had been expended on putting two mens' lodging-houses into good sanitary condition in Charles Street and King Street. The average net return, exclusive of repairs, for the two houses for three years before 1853, was £227, or 17½ per cent on the outlay. Tyndall's Buildings was one of Roberts' most spectacular conversions. Before work started, Roberts surveyed the buildings, which were covered with 'indescribable filth'. As a result, he was 'as sick as a dog' on returning home. Indeed, the 'very intelligent superintendent of works, Mr. Baxindall', 'in the discharge of the disgusting duties which devolved on him, became in consequence seriously ill'.[8] The financial results, 'drawn from the experience of a professedly model society', were extremely important. 'The financial question' was significant, 'for unless the numerous societies' formed under 'the impulse of benevolent feeling' could obtain sufficiently satisfactory results to encourage further investments, then 'the direct sphere of their operations' would be 'very limited, and altogether inadequate to the necessities of the case'.[9]

In 1850, Thomas Cubitt, 'the eminent builder', had opined that 'the work undertaking is exceedingly complicated, and one which could hardly be done well, and so as to make a profit as an investment'. This opinion, understanding that 'Profit' meant something beyond a moderate rate of interest, was something Roberts agreed with.

Out of £200,000 expended on the improvement of the dwellings of the labouring classes in London, the average return, exclusive of overheads, was equal to the average borne by the aggregate of traffic receipts following a capital expenditure of £112,000,000 expended on the nine great railways diverging from the metropolis, and estimated in *The Times* as 4 per cent. However, the average profits to the original shareholders of the railways was only £1 12s. 6d. per cent.

In one respect, at least, the efforts of the Society for Improving the Condition of the Labouring Classes were fruitful to a degree. The publications of the Society were not limited to Great Britain, but were distributed all over the world in English and in translation. Many of Roberts' writings were reprinted in the United States, and a Workmens' Home for blacks was erected to accommodate eighty-seven families on the general plan of Streatham Street Model Dwellings. Another building was erected in New York to supersede a 'den of iniquity called the Old Brewery' that rivalled London's St Giles's in squalor. An association for building model lodging-houses was formed in Boston in 1851, apparently stimulated by the Rev. Abbott Lawrence, who introduced a complete set of Roberts' works to the United States. Lawrence left $50,000 for the building of model homes in Boston, and Roberts was visited by a friend of Lawrence in 1853. Published plans by Roberts reached Australia and India, where works were projected on an extensive scale.

Despite the international renown that Roberts was now enjoying, or perhaps even partly because of that fame, Roberts' relations with the Society for Improving the Condition of the Labouring Classes began to deteriorate. When Roberts was about to leave England in 1853 he was presented with a gift of plate from a group of individuals associated with philanthropic work rather than by the Society itself. Nevertheless, Roberts continued to be responsible for most of the publications and plans produced by the Society after he went abroad, and was constantly revising the plans and adding new ones to the Society's published works until he suffered the final indignity at the end of 1856. This treatment of Roberts by the Society was shabby, but, as Roberts' views became more radical, he was clearly leaving the conservative and somewhat pusillanimous lay committee of the Society behind in thinking. He became more and more convinced that the approach of the Metropolitan Association for Improving the Dwellings of the Industrious Classes was on sounder lines than the S.I.C.L.C., and said so. His differences of opinion, his new radicalism, and his personal life, as well as his growing international reputation doubtless aroused animosities with the members of the S.I.C.L.C. At the end of 1856 his appointment as Honorary Architect was terminated by the committee of the S.I.C.L.C.[10], as has already been described.

However, Roberts did not vanish from the field of working-class housing, either as an originator of ideas, as a designer of exemplars, as a powerful international influence, or as the architect of buildings. Quite apart from the fact that houses continued to be built all over the country to designs by Roberts published by the S.I.C.L.C., there is evidence that Roberts did produce some new designs for real schemes.

In 1850, the Metropolitan Association for Improving the Dwellings of the Industrious Classes purchased a strip of land at Mile End from the Trustees of the will of Sir George Osborn.[11] This site included two terraces of houses, which were let by the Association. By 1857 the dwellings in what was then Pelham Street were demolished and replaced by two parallel terraces of cottages and some shops. These new houses, only two storeys high, were called Albert Cottages, and in 1864 they were duplicated by Victoria Cottages on the rest of the site at Pleasant Row.[12] According to the *Survey of London*[13] the architect is not known. The *Survey* continued:

> 'Each flat consists of a living-room, bed-room, scullery, and sanitary facilities, and each has a separate entrance paired with that to the adjoining flat. Two terraces are built in "white" brick and two in stock brick, with red brick dressings and slated roofs. One terrace in either group faces on to a foot-way with a small front garden to each cottage'.[14]

The Albert and Victoria Cottages were intended for those who could not afford the higher rents of the family dwellings, and the immediate models were Roberts' schemes at Bagnigge Wells and for the Great Exhibition.[15] Roberts himself criticised the Association for providing housing of such low density on the site.[16]

Despite this, it does appear that the architect of the designs for the cottages was none other than Roberts himself (*see* Plates 83-84). In the 1867 edition of *The Dwellings of the Labouring Classes*, etc., 'Albert Cottages, Albert Street, Spitalfields' (actually Mile End New Town),[17] was shown, with Alexandra Cottages, Penge, Surrey. Other Penge cottages 'Built by the Metropolitan Association', were actually erected by C. H. Bracebridge, and described by him in a paper read to the National Association for the Promotion of Social Science at Birmingham in 1857.[18] Throughout his publications Roberts is meticulously careful to credit designs to their authors. In the 1867 edition of his *The Dwellings of the Labouring Classes*, etc., the Penge cottages are credited to Bracebridge, but Albert Cottages at Mile End New Town, and Alexandra Cottages at Penge are not credited to anyone, and are treated no differently to Roberts' own designs in the book. The *Bibliothèque de la Société Industrielle de Mulhouse* has a number of engraved plans by Thieffry & Cie of Paris that form a collected work by Emile Muller, the architect and friend of Henry Roberts.[19] One sheet shows designs for cottages that we know are definitely by Roberts, that were published by the S.I.C.L.C., and that were built by the Duke of Manchester on his estates at Kimbolton, Huntingdonshire (*see* Figure 2). The same sheet (Plate 83) in Muller's great work also shows the Cottages at Mile End New Town, and the Alexandra Cottages at Penge, and Henry Roberts is credited in heavy type at the top of the whole sheet as architect of everything on it. As Roberts was in England in 1858, he could easily have been architect, and even if the drawings date from 1857, he could have furnished these from Italy. They are pleasant designs, and have definite Robertsian touches. Confirmation of their authorship seems clear from the archive material at the *Société Industrielle de Mulhouse*. The widespread belief that Roberts never designed any more buildings after 1835 would seem to be no longer tenable.

This view can be countered by asking why Roberts failed to acknowledge authorship of Albert Cottages. The explanation is quite simple. Clearly he disapproved of the siting of the cottages, so he may have designed them in Italy without realising the nature of the site. As former Honorary Architect of the S.I.C.L.C. (a position from which he resigned by request of the Society in 1857), and as a close associate of that body, he may have been somewhat coy about revealing a connection with the Metropolitan Association. Perhaps, having been treated so shabbily by the S.I.C.L.C., he was tempted to move his allegiance to the rival body, but found that the personalities there were not to his taste either. In any case, as a Vice-President of the S.I.C.L.C. he would have been ill-advised to advertise any close association with another philanthropic housing body.

In his *The Improvements of the Dwellings of the Labouring Classes through the Operation of Government Measures, by those of Public Bodies and Benevolent Associations, as well as Individual Efforts* in 1859, Roberts took the opportunity to give a 'personal explanation' of his removal from the position of Honorary Architect to the S.I.C.L.C., a post he had held from the year of the establishment of the Society in 1844, on the first occasion presented since his return to England. He wrote that 'the honour of being placed among the vice-presidents of the Labourer's Friend Society was declined three months after' his resignation, 'mainly to avoid a continued appearance of responsibility without active participation in the management'. Roberts was also at pains to point out that his 'relationship to the Society' had therefore 'for a considerable time been only that of an ordinary life member'.[20] Roberts subsequently relented, and became a Vice-President, doubtless through the intervention of Lord Shaftesbury, who must have met the architect again on his return to England. Roberts' presence in England is explained by the fact that conditions in Italy were not good for foreigners during the unification campaigns.

Roberts mentioned the financial slump caused by the Crimean War that had greatly curtailed the activities of philanthropic societies. However, many societies did flourish in the provinces, notably the Association for Promoting Improvement in the Dwellings and Domestic Condition of Agricultural Labourers in Scotland, which published plans on the lines of the S.I.C.L.C. in London.

The Windsor Royal Society, formed under the patronage of Queen Victoria and of the Prince Consort, was formed in 1852, and was registered under the limited liability clause of the *Labourers' Dwellings Act* of 1855. On an investment of £6,607 12s. 2d. in new model cottages, the net return in 1858 was 5½ per cent. Roberts was able to 'look back with pleasure' to having given the plans for the first and principal range of cottages, which provided for twenty families, in tenements of various sizes. These plans were lithographed by The Labourers' Friend Society. The Windsor Royal Society, formed to promote and carry out the improvement of the dwellings of the working classes in Windsor, was constituted on the principle of a joint stock company, with a capital of £6,000, raised in £10 shares. Dividends were limited to 5 per cent, leaving any surplus available for the extension of the Society's operations. Freehold ground, between the Long Walk and the Cavalry Barracks, adjacent to what is now known as Alexandra Road, Windsor, amounting to about one acre and a half, was purchased for £288 and laid out for the erection of two rows of houses opposite each other, together accommodating about forty families. Each house had a small garden. The contract for building half these houses came to £2,240. The houses were arranged in five blocks. The centre and two corner blocks each combined two plans, while the remaining blocks were identical in plan. Four tenements were built on each of these five plans, twelve with three, and eight with two bedrooms. The centre block contained eight tenements: four on the ground floor and four above. The middle compartment was on the lines of the 1851 Model Dwellings, somewhat increased in scale, and consisted of four tenements, each flat having three bedrooms. On either side was a house arranged for two families, one above the other, with distinct entrances, and with two bedrooms to each flat. The floor between the storeys was of fireproof hollow brickwork. The next buildings, on either side, were pairs of double cottages, with living room, scullery, pantry, and three bedrooms each. Each of the end buildings comprised four cottages, each with living room, scullery and pantry, and two or three bedrooms, on the first floor. The centre building on the opposite side, which cost abour £300, combined a superintendent's residence, a bake-house, a wash-house, a bath, a fuel store, and a 3,000 gallon cistern of slate for the supply of water to all the houses. All these buildings were constructed of hollow bricks similar to those used in the Great Exhibition Model Houses. The tie-rods at first-floor level are still visible today inside the ground-floor rooms in the tenement block.

The Society for Improving the Condition of the Labouring Classes had Roberts' plans for the Windsor Royal Society lithographed 'to facilitate the adoption, in other places, of the plans of these buildings'.[21] Once more, Roberts had acted as Honorary Architect. Two years after its completion, this little estate was extended to designs by S. S. Teulon, as Roberts had gone abroad. The lodging-house was unsuccessful and was closed in 1855, but the rest of the houses remained in the hands of the Society until 1872 when they were sold to Richardson Gardner. Today, they are known as 'Prince Consort Cottages, Alexandra Road', and the estate is in remarkably good condition. Although some of the houses are now individually owned (something of which Roberts would have approved), covenants ensure that painting of windows, doors, and other exposed wood or iron is uniform. Indeed, the total amount of surfaces requiring regular painting is absolutely minimal, and an indictment of many local-authority and private-enterprise schemes of the post-war era that require costly maintenance of large areas of timber. The whole Roberts scheme at Windsor is delightful environmentally, aesthetically, practically, and architecturally. It combines his ingenious plan of the Great Exhibition Model Dwellings with plans for cottages designed for rural areas and made available by the S.I.C.L.C. (Plates 71–74 and Figures 21, 24–29).

Roberts took a great interest in the design of model dwellings for the country, as well as for the towns. John Howard's improvements at Cardington in Bedfordshire, where cottages on the estate had been rebuilt from 1756, were among the most influential of eighteenth-century model schemes. Howard required 'industry, temperance, and observance of the Sabbath' from his tenants, but left 'doctrinal opinions' to individuals. Roberts recognised that rural cottages were a 'bad investment' financially, but that was not the point. The Duke of Bedford had pointed out that landlords should improve cottages in the interests of health, education, and moral habits. Woburn was extensively rebuilt to provide model dwellings for the tenants of the Duke. Indeed, the Duke of Bedford had expended some seventy thousand pounds on improving his estate houses between 1849 and 1859, while the Duke of Northumberland laid out some hundred thousand pounds on model cottages for his lands in the same period. The Rev. C. H. Hartshorne wrote a pamphlet entitled *The System of Building Labourers' Cottages pursued on the estate of his Grace the Duke of Bedford* which was instrumental in publicising rural improvements.

Fig. 24.   The Windsor Royal Society's Cottages for the Working Classes, by Henry Roberts. The central block is based on the Great Exhibition Dwellings.

WINDSOR ROYAL SOCIETY'S COTTAGES.

ELEVATION OF THE CENTRE BUILDING.

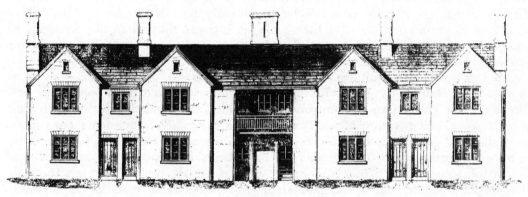

PLAN OF THE CENTRE BUILDING FOR EIGHT FAMILIES.

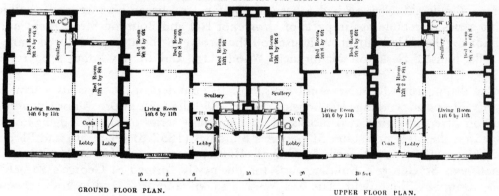

GROUND FLOOR PLAN.   UPPER FLOOR PLAN.

Fig. 25. The Windsor Royal Society's Cottages. The centre building is an adaptation of the Prince Consort's Model Houses for the Great Exhibition.

Many great manufacturers also embraced the model housing movement in order
to improve the health of their workpeople. Akroyd built new dwellings for a thousand
of his workers at Copley Mill 'intended to be model cottages, fitted up with every
convenience required in such habitations, each having its own garden plot', and the
whole well supplied with water. Roberts also referred to experiments like that at
Saltaire.

The Evangelical Conscience spread its influence abroad. Roberts mentions an
account, in French and Italian Protestant Almanacs, of a number of labourers' cottages
at Mowcop in Staffordshire, on the borders with Cheshire. These were built 'out of the
savings of money which would otherwise have been spent on the beer-shop' mainly
through Building Societies, which Roberts evidently regarded as hardly 'benevolent
institutions' on account of the high rates of interest they charged. However, he
grudgingly admitted that 'they doubtless facilitate greatly the acquisition of house-
property by the working classes'.[22]

Other schemes for building workmen's dwellings on an extensive scale were
promoted at Halifax by J. D. Taylor, and some seventy cottages were built near
Birkenhead by Price's Candle Company. Roberts himself provided plans for the builder
John Newson, of Grosvenor Mews, Berkeley Square. Newson built a tenement with an
open stair and galleries at Bourdon Street, and subsequently built three further blocks
in his own parish, and two in the city, all to Roberts' basic plans.[23] John Newson of
Grosvenor Mews, came from Woodbridge in Suffolk. He took a contract for road-
sweeping in Berkeley Square, and graduated, so to speak, via the manufacture of trunks
for itinerant maidservants, to the building industry. By 1835 Newson built Bloomfield
Terrace, Pimlico.[24] Newson had a base in Mayfair, and began his career as a builder
with a series of rebuildings in parts of Grosvenor Hill and Bourdon Street that Cubitt
had not touched. He built many houses on the Grosvenor Estate, and did well enough
to build himself Hasketon Manor near Woodbridge and to buy other property in
Suffolk.

What distinguishes John Newson from speculative builders of the previous generation
was his interest in working-class housing. In the 1850s he built in Grosvenor Hill and in
Bourdon Street the first two blocks of an important series of model lodging-houses
erected on the Mayfair Estate: St George's Buildings (1852-3) (Plate 56) and Bloomfield Flats (1854-6) as well as Oxford House, Grosvenor Market (1860), now
demolished. St George's Buildings was for the newly formed St George's Parochial
Association, but Bloomfield Flats was Newson's own enterprise, and in both schemes
the initiative appears to have been his, according to Henry Roberts, who reported
similar ventures by Newson elsewhere in London.[25] It was Roberts who provided plans
for St George's Buildings, an austere, galleried block. The Grosvenor Estate encouraged
further experiments in the field of working-class housing, not uninfluenced by Roberts
and by the exemplars of his model blocks.[26] Roberts identifies Newson's buildings as
'Grosvenor Mews: Bull Head Court, King Street, Snow Hill; Holborn Hill; and
Grosvenor Market. All resembled the dwellings in Streatham Street in their general
layout. It is not insignificant that on 6 June 1850 the Minutes of the Annual General
Meeting of the Society for Improving the Condition of the Labouring Classes reveal
that Lord Robert Grosvenor was present.

Roberts was indefatigable in his travels, and tireless in his collection of information. He studied the possibilities of building model cottages outside urban centres, thus avoiding the high prices of land in the centres, and conveying the occupants to and fro by cheap rail fares. He mentioned his visit to Paris in 1858 when he inspected a model village near the *Place du Trône* that had been built by a tailor for his work-force. The 'village' comprised seventy-six chalets, twenty-eight of which were for single people, and forty-eight for groups of families. Work shops were also provided, and an air of 'neatness and order' gave the whole 'a very pleasing effect'. In this village, the work, which was sold in the heart of the city, was carried out by workmen residing with their families. Before the construction of the model dwellings, the workers lived in 'miserable, unhealthy, and . . . high-rented dwellings'. Roberts advocated that the idea should be adopted by employers on a national scale, and said that the 'daily journey of a foreman' between the place of work and the sale 'would surely be more economical as to time and railway fare, as well as answer in every other respect the purpose of the whole body of workpeople coming to the place of the sale and returning daily'.

Roberts was gratified to note that many great proprietors of land were undertaking good works in providing model dwellings. Although these did not return a full percentage on the outlay, the efforts could not 'fail to be *repaid* by those feelings of increased contentment and goodwill which are the best bonds between a landowner and the peasantry on his estate'.

During the 1840s and 1850s the design of improved dwellings for agricultural labourers, arranged on the most economical plan, with proper regard to the health and comfort of its occupants, was repeatedly made a subject for architectural competition. In most instances, Roberts felt that the results would have been unsatisfactory but for the communications elicited from landed proprietors whose attention had been practically directed to the subject. The Marquis of Breadalbane's cottages, for example, published in the volumes of 1843 to 1845 of the *Transactions* of the Highland and Agricultural Society of Scotland, and the plans for the Duke of Bedford's cottages, published in the July 1849 number of the *Journal* of the Royal Agricultural Society, were influential and were copied by many landed gentry.

In order to clarify an adoption of plans 'which combined in their arrangement every point essential to the health, comfort and moral habits of the labourer and his family, with that due regard to stability and economy of construction, which is essential to their general usefulness, the Society for Improving the Condition of the Labouring Classes published, and have circulated extensively, a series of designs for Cottages, prepared with these special objects in view'. Terms and agreements for letting such cottages were given in the Society's publications, all drawn up by Roberts. The first plans by Roberts for a pair of cottages had been published by the S.I.C.L.C. in 1844, and by 1847 the Minutes of the Society record that many model cottages were being erected throughout the country to plans by 'Mr Roberts' (Figures 30–41).

As Honorary Architect to the Society, Roberts revised the plans and republished them in 1850, with variations in the arrangement of the 'apartments', and of the elevations, in order to achieve a 'considerable variety' by a 'judicious selection and grouping'.

Different materials were specified for different parts of the country, and Roberts stressed that it was essential to use local materials to respect the character of the areas in which it was intended to build agricultural cottages. 'No set of designs', he wrote, 'could be arranged so as to be suitable for all circumstances'. The designs could be built, however, in stone, in brick, or in flint with quoins and dressings of brick or stone. Economics suggested pairs of cottages, with chimney-stacks in the middle to ensure the greatest possible warmth. Sculleries contained brick ovens and a copper, to avoid the necessity for a fire in the living-rooms during the summer months. Sleeping apartments, usually three in number, were designed to separate the sexes, 'so essential to morality and decency'. Roberts allowed one hundred square feet for the parents' bedroom, and seventy square feet for the smallest bedroom. Living rooms had floor-to-ceiling heights of eight feet, while those for bedrooms were seven feet nine inches. Often, it was necessary to provide for the accommodation of a lodger in the cottages, in which case it was essential to give him a separate sleeping-place away from the family, usually an alcove in the living-room.

Roberts' designs for rural cottages were printed (Figures 30–41), and working drawings, with specifications and bills of quantities, were published by the Society. Rural hostels were also necessary, and Roberts produced designs for those. These 'houses for unmarried labourers' contained a library, a superintendent's apartment, and had allotments attached. Rent was two shillings per week.

It was recommended that the fronts of cottages should face south. Roberts was insistent on a good damp-proof course, and that there should be adequate drainage and water supplies. A gravelly soil was preferable to clay. Every cottage should have its own garden of one-eighth of an acre, and should have its own entrance. One well should be sunk for two or more cottages, sited to ensure that it would not be contaminated by cesspools, by liquid manure, or by drains.

The outside walls of cottages were generally in nine-inch brickwork but Roberts strongly recommended the use of his patent bonded hollow bricks to improve dryness and insulation. Sometimes he advocated the use of shortened snapped headers, leaving a cavity between. Roberts also suggested that eleven-inch cavity walls should be adopted, with two-inch closers. Unfortunately, the bonding of the two skins by bricks lessened the effectiveness of both the damp-proofing and the insulation. In flint work, it was necessary to line the inside of the walls with tiles or patent hollow bricks to ensure dryness.

Roberts also suggested that houses could be constructed of concrete, using gravel, lime, and sand, poured *in situ*. An alternative mixture was that of gravel, sand, and a tenth portion of Portland cement. Partitions were best constructed of brick or of tile rather than of wood. Hollow brick partitions had great advantages in that they improved the sound-proofing qualities of the building. Stairs were also better constructed of fireclay brick. Where hollow brick was used for the walls, the ground floors always remained warm and dry. Roberts advocated using materials that were readily available: for example, ashes of lime, smith's ashes, or pounded coke for the floors. Tiles were better for roofing than slates, being cooler in summer and warmer in winter.

Air flues for ventilation, nine inches by four and a half inches, were carried up in the jambs of the ground-floor chimney, beginning under the floor, and passing into the flue from the bedroom chimney, an opening being formed under the ceiling of the living room, fitted with plates of zinc. The bedrooms were warmed by a 2½-inch diameter pipe passing through the flue from the side of the fireplace on the ground floor, and opening into the bedroom above. Bedrooms without fireplaces had vents over the doors, or air-pipes.

Roberts advocated zinc quarry casements for windows, set in wooden frames, with oak sills set on moulded brick projecting sills. Internally, the cottages had cement dados, with chair rails, and a plaster finish above, but only in the living-room. In the other rooms, the walls were of brick, whitewashed. Rainwater was collected in tanks. Water-closets had cisterns above, to which water was conveyed by a hand-pump in the scullery.

The Minutes of the S.I.C.L.C. in 1848 record that Roberts, Seeley, and the Secretary went to Tunbridge Wells to meet the Committee of the local Association, and saw three pairs of cottages (presumably Nos. 10–20, Newcomen Road) erected to Roberts' designs (Figure 42). Oswald Mosley completed cottages to Roberts' plans on his estates in the Midlands. More houses were built in Tunbridge Wells (presumably Nos. 2–8 and Nos. 22–24, Newcomen Road) in 1850–2, and Roberts' patent hollow bricks were used in their construction. In 1850 Roberts visited Ramsgate to help to establish a local Society for Improving the Dwellings of the Labouring Classes, and it was also in 1850 that the Duke of Manchester, Roberts' client at Kimbolton, became a Vice-Patron of the Society.

The scale of influence of Roberts' designs for cottages can be appreciated even today. There are thousands of buildings recognisably based on his plans all over England, and sometimes entire estates are built of houses derived from the original published plans of Henry Roberts. Here was pattern-book architecture on the grand scale, and it is no exaggeration to say that Roberts changed the face of the countryside of Victorian England. In fact, his impact in rural areas was greater than that in the towns, although there are areas in Bethnal Green and Whitechapel that have many tenements that are based on variants of Roberts' designs.

Space does not permit the listing of all the areas where designs by Roberts based on the printed plans issued by the S.I.C.L.C. exist. Many thousands of cottages were built throughout England that owed much to Roberts' plans, even if the elevations were altered. Naseby has several paired houses that are derived from *plans* by Roberts, but in many instances designs by him were built exactly as drawn, and without modification. It would be tedious and indeed impossible to attempt a gazetteer of all such designs. However, there are numerous estate villages throughout England, notably in Lincolnshire, that were constructed by philanthropic organisations or by private individuals, based on designs by Roberts. William Burn, a friend of Roberts, built villages at South Stoke and at Revesby, and Roberts himself designed Gothic cottages at Great Gonerby in 1848 in Green Street and at Elms Farm, all in Lincolnshire. The Roberts designs were published by the S.I.C.L.C. Many other designs by Roberts were built on the Manchester estates in Huntingdonshire and on the lands of philanthropically minded persons elsewhere, including Cottesmore in Rutland, where Lord Gainsborough built a pair of cottages to Roberts' designs. The Great Gonerby houses were built by Lord Brownlow, who was later to serve on the Royal Commission for

PLANS OF THE COTTAGES FOR FOUR FAMILIES.

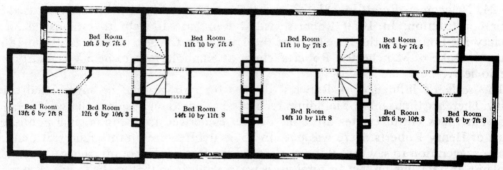

BED-ROOM FLOOR PLAN.

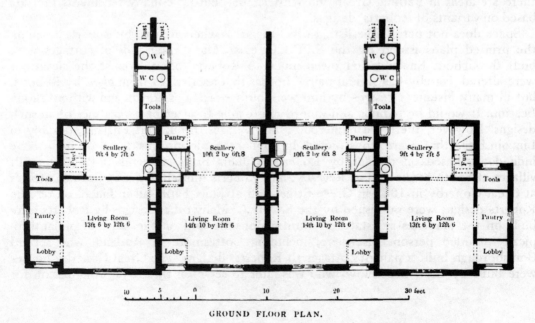

GROUND FLOOR PLAN.

Fig. 26.   Cottages designed by Roberts for the Windsor Royal Society.

WINDSOR ROYAL SOCIETY'S COTTAGES.

BUILDING WITH SUPERINTENDENT'S RESIDENCE, BAKEHOUSE, WASHHOUSE, BATH, FUEL STORE, AND TANK.

NOTE.—The Elevation of these Cottages resembles that given for the Cottages, No. 4.

PLANS OF THE DOUBLE COTTAGES.

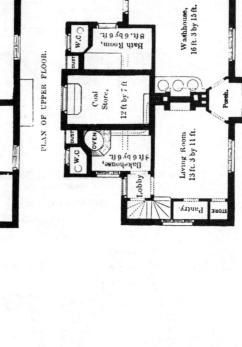

PLAN OF UPPER FLOOR.

Upper part of Washhouse.

Tank for Bath.

Lumber Loft, Water Tank over.

Bed Room, 11 ft. by 9 ft. 6.

Closet

Bed Room, 11 ft by 7 ft

PLAN OF GROUND FLOOR.

Washhouse, 16 ft. 3 by 15 ft.

W.C.

Bath Room, 8 ft. 6 by 6 ft.

DUST

Coal Store, 12 ft by 7 ft

W.C

DUST

OVEN

Bakehouse, 3 ft 6 by 6 ft.

Living Room 13 ft. 3 by 11 ft.

Porch.

Lobby

Lobby

Pantry

STORE

20

15

10

5

0

5

10

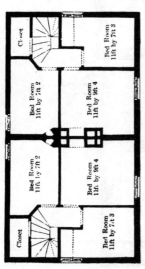

FIRST FLOOR.

Closet

Bed Room 11 ft by 7 ft 2

Bed Room 9 ft 4

Bed Room 11 ft by 7 ft 3

Bed Room 11 ft by 7 ft 2

Bed Room 9 ft 4

Closet

Bed Room 11 ft by 7 ft 3

GROUND FLOOR.

Tools or W C

Fuel

Scullery 11 ft 3 by 6ft

Living Room 12 ft 6 by 12 ft 2

3 ft 6 by 9 ft

Lobby

Scullery 11 ft 3 by 6ft

Living Room 12 ft 6 by 12 ft 2

Tools or W C

FUEL

Pantry

Lobby

10

5

0

5

10

15

20 feet

Fig. 27. Roberts' plans for the semi-detached cottages and for the Superintendent's house, the bakehouse, wash-house, baths, fuel store, and tank, all for the Windsor Royal Society.

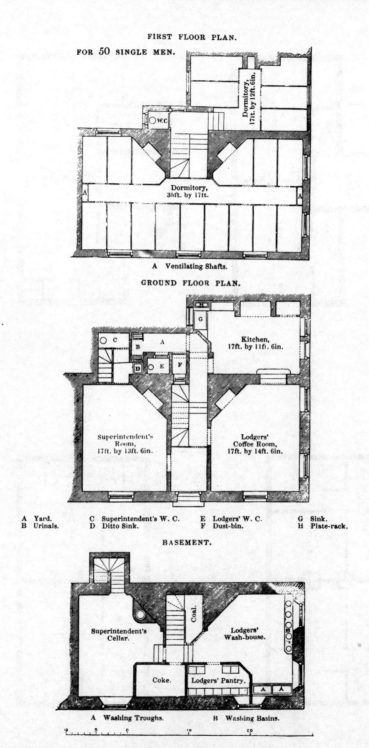

FIRST FLOOR PLAN.

FOR 50 SINGLE MEN.

Dormitory,
17ft. by 12ft. 6in.

W.C

Dormitory,
35ft. by 17ft.

A Ventilating Shafts.

GROUND FLOOR PLAN.

Kitchen,
17ft. by 11ft. 6in.

Superintendent's
Room,
17ft. by 13ft. 6in.

Lodgers'
Coffee Room,
17ft. by 14ft. 6in.

A Yard.   C Superintendent's W. C.   E Lodgers' W. C.   G Sink.
B Urinals.   D Ditto Sink.   F Dust-bin.   H Plate-rack.

BASEMENT.

Superintendent's
Cellar.

Coal.

Lodgers'
Wash-house.

Coke.   Lodgers' Pantry.

A Washing Troughs.   B Washing Basins.

Fig. 28.   Roberts' plans for the model lodging-house for the
Windsor Royal Society. Note the washing arrangements, the
coffee-room, and the dormitory.

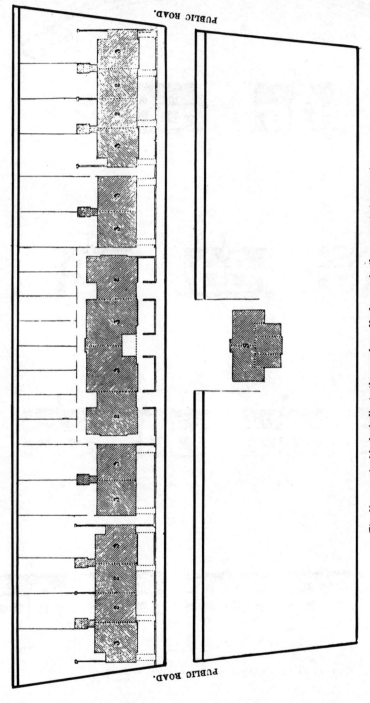

PLAN, SHOWING THE COTTAGES FOR TWENTY FAMILIES, BUILT BY THE WINDSOR ROYAL SOCIETY

UNDER THE AUTHOR'S DIRECTIONS AS HONORARY ARCHITECT, 1852-3.

The Nos. on the blocks indicate the number of bedrooms in the separate tenements.

The building S contains a residence for Superintendent, with a bakehouse, washhouse, bath, fuel store, and tank, for the general supply of the houses.

On the unoccupied space at each side of the building S, it has been proposed to erect either two blocks of houses for eight families, similar to the centre building, with a block of double cottages at the extremities; or to form a hollow square round the building S, with four blocks of five cottages, two of them facing the public roads, and the others facing the existing buildings. In either case twenty additional families would be provided for, making forty tenements in the whole.

Fig. 29.   The plan by Roberts showing the cottages built by the Windsor Royal Society in 1852-3.

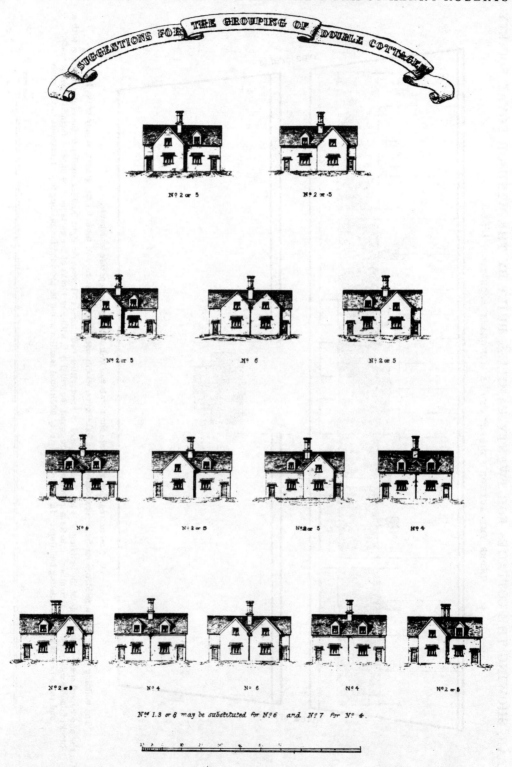

Fig. 30. Suggestions for the groupings of double cottages. These should be compared with
Plates 80-81.

FRONT ELEVATION

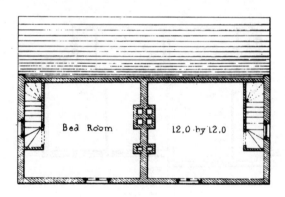

Bed Room   12.0 by 12.0

UPPER FLOOR PLAN

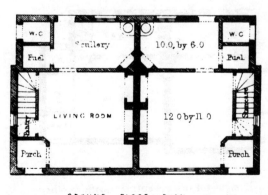

W.C   Scullery   10.0 by 6.0   W.C

Fuel   Fuel

LIVING ROOM   12.0 by 11.0

Porch   Porch

GROUND FLOOR PLAN

Fig. 31. Designs for double cottages with one bed-
room each.

FRONT ELEVATION

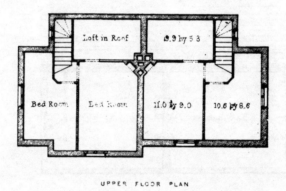

UPPER FLOOR PLAN

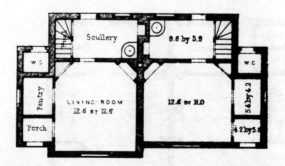

Fig. 32. Designs for double cottages with two bedrooms each. Note how Roberts used an asymmetrical composition and Tudor details.

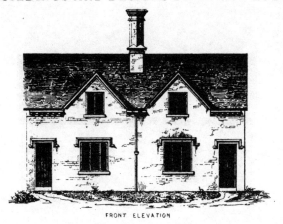

FRONT ELEVATION

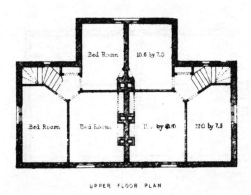

UPPER FLOOR PLAN

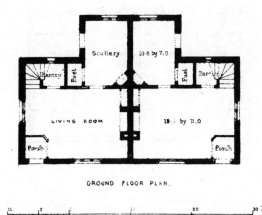

GROUND FLOOR PLAN.

Fig. 33. Roberts' designs for a symmetrical pair of
cottages with three bedrooms each.

FRONT ELEVATION

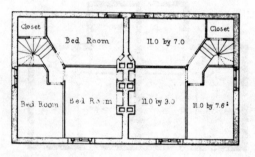

UPPER FLOOR PLAN

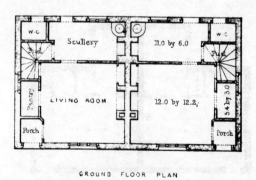

GROUND FLOOR PLAN

Fig. 34.   A variant of the symmetrical pair of
cottages, with dormer, and three bedrooms per
cottage.

FRONT ELEVATION

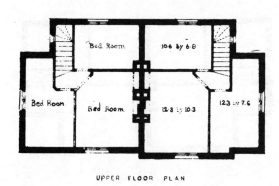

UPPER FLOOR PLAN

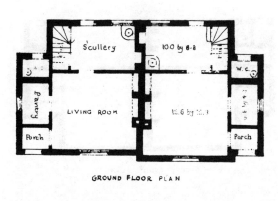

GROUND FLOOR PLAN

Fig. 35. Roberts' scheme for an asymmetrical pair
of cottages, with three bedrooms each.

FRONT ELEVATION

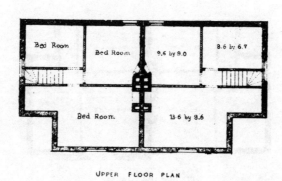

UPPER FLOOR PLAN

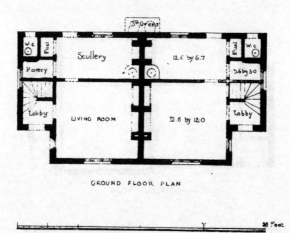

GROUND FLOOR PLAN

Fig. 36.   A symmetrical pair of cottages with three
bedrooms each.

FRONT ELEVATION

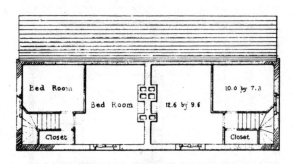

UPPER FLOOR PLAN

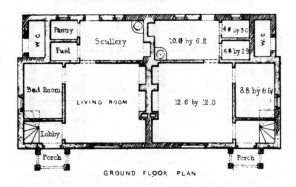

GROUND FLOOR PLAN

Fig. 37. A symmetrical pair of cottages with a
lean-to roof at the rear, and rustic porches.

FRONT ELEVATION

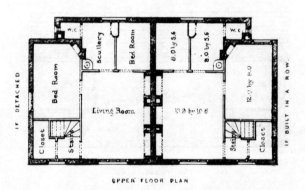

UPPER FLOOR PLAN

GROUND FLOOR PLAN

Note.. If one or two Feet be added to the depth of these Houses, another
Bed Closet 5 feet wide may be taken from the large Bed Room.

Fig. 38. A symmetrical arrangement of four flats,
each with three bedrooms, showing how Roberts
gave a domestic scale to flats.

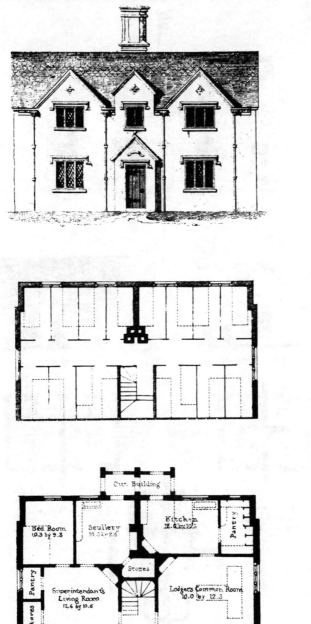

Fig. 39. Roberts' design for a lodging-house for
unmarried labourers.

THE CHARACTER OF THIS ELEVATION IS APPLICABLE TO
MOST OF THE PRECEDING DESIGNS.

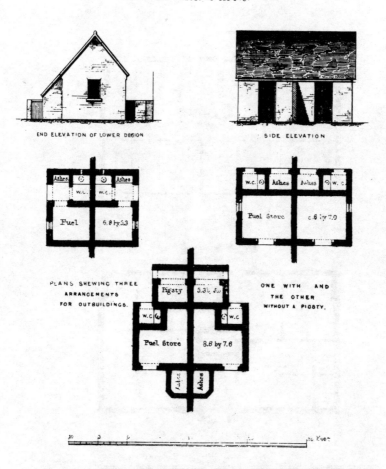

END ELEVATION OF LOWER DESIGN

SIDE ELEVATION

Ashes | Ashes
W.C. | W.C.
Fuel   6.9 by 5.3

W.C. | Ashes | Ashes | W.C.
Fuel Stove   c.6 by 7.0

PLANS SHEWING THREE
ARRANGEMENTS
FOR OUTBUILDINGS.

ONE WITH AND
THE OTHER
WITHOUT A PIGSTY.

Pigsty | 5.3½ by 5.0
W.C. | W.C.
Fuel Store   8.6 by 7.6
Ashes | Ashes

Fig. 40. Roberts' design for a pair of cottages, on an
asymmetrical plan, constructed of flint with brick quoins
and copings. The designs of the outbuildings are unusually
detailed.

ELEVATION WHICH ADMITS OF MORE ORNAMENTAL DETAILS.

ELEVATION OF THE LEAST EXPENSIVE CHARACTER

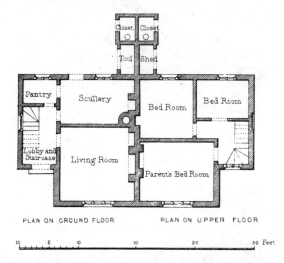

PLAN ON GROUND FLOOR   PLAN ON UPPER FLOOR

Fig. 41.   A three-bedroom pair of 'Labourers'
Cottages' with alternative elevations.

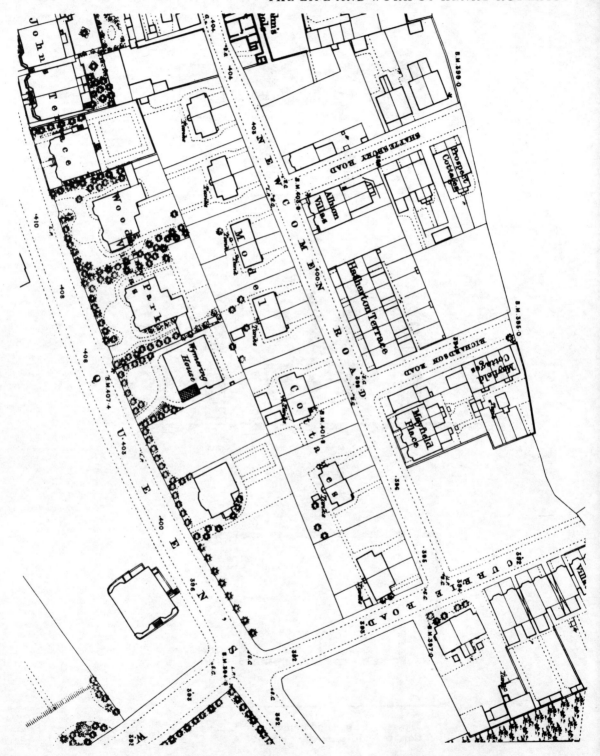

Fig. 42.   A plan of the S.I.C.L.C. Tunbridge Wells estate at Newcomen Road, Tunbridge Wells, from the 1866 Ordnance Survey, Zincographed in 1879. (*The Tunbridge Wells Reference Library, Kent County Library*)

inquiring into working-class housing. He also built an entire model village at Belton in Lincolnshire in the Tudor and Jacobean style. The houses have the basic Roberts' plans and recall his Jacobean work at Exton and elsewhere.

Apart from individual designs printed in loose-leaf form, many plans (Figures 15–21, 24–41) by Roberts were published in his *The Dwellings of the Labouring Classes, Their Arrangement and Construction: Illustrated by a Reference to the Model Houses of the Society for Improving the Condition of the Labouring Classes, with other buildings recently erected: and An Appendix, containing H.R.H. Prince Albert's Exhibition Model Houses, Hyde Park, 1851; The Model Cottages, &c. Built by the Windsor Royal Society; With Plans and Elevations of Dwellings Adapted to Towns, as well as to Agricultural and Manufacturing Districts (London, 1853).* As late as 1870, variants on Roberts' designs for paired cottages, with Tudor chimneys and a central Tudor arch reminiscent of the Great Exhibition Model Dwellings, were built on lands owned by the Duke of Marlborough at Woodstock and elsewhere. Many other estates continued to build workers' cottages that are recognisably based on the published designs by Henry Roberts. It is therefore clear that architects, builders, estate managers, and local philanthropic societies continued either to use Roberts' plans or to adapt them long after Roberts had left England. His influence remained, and it is no exaggeration to claim that his work can be seen as the basis for many thousands of nineteenth-century dwellings in every county in England.

Chapter Six

THE CAMPAIGN TO EXTEND THE BENEFITS OF A HEALTHY DWELLING TO THE LABOURING POPULATION

When recommending sanitary ameliorations to influential persons on the Continent, the misery and degradation in which vast masses of our fellow subjects are sunk, owing, in a great measure, to their domiciliary state, has been so often pointed out as a reproach to England, that the words 'Physician, heal thyself' have frequently occurred to my mind, as a call to renewed exertion for this object.

Henry Roberts: *The Essentials of a Healthy Dwelling, etc.,* London, 1862, p.42

HENRY ROBERTS sat writing a preface in the Athenaeum Club, Pall Mall, in April 1862. This was to introduce his latest publication *The Essentials of a Healthy Dwelling, and the Extension of its Benefits to the Labouring Population, with a Special Reference to the Promotion of that Object by H.R.H. the Late Prince Consort.*[1] Roberts noted in the preface that an announcement had just been made in the press of 'An unprecedented act of munificence on the part of an American merchant resident in London. In order "to ameliorate the condition and augment the comfort of the poor, who form a recognised portion of its population", George Peabody, Esq.,' had placed £150,000 in the hands of trustees who were 'to apply the fund, or a portion of it, in the construction of such improved dwellings for the poor as may combine, in the utmost possible degree, the essentials of healthfulness, comfort, social enjoyment, and economy.'

Other philanthropists had been greatly influenced by the writings of Roberts, notably Abbott Lawrence, who had left $50,000 for the erection of model dwellings in Boston, Massachusetts, U.S.A. Both the Peabody and Lawrence funds were administered to avoid any hint of charity or of alms. This was an important factor, for Roberts recognised that the receiving of charity or of alms implied a social stigma.

Prompted by the enormous success and influence of his designs for the Great Exhibition of 1851, Roberts was anxious to follow these up by means of lobbying the many people who were due to arrive in London for the Exhibition of 1862. This international exposition at Brompton was to attempt to consolidate all that had been gained from 1851, and the Prince Consort was the driving force. Originally intended for 1861, the whole matter had to be postponed for a year owing to the Prince's untimely death from typhoid in 1861. Roberts was a devotee of the National Association for the Advancement of Social Science, and of the Congrès International de Bienfaisance. Conferences of both groups were held in London to coincide with the Exhibition, and Roberts presented an important paper that became *The Essentials of a Healthy Dwelling, etc.* and was published in time for the delegates and 'fellow-labourers in the field of social improvement' to take copies home with them.

Roberts read his paper on 20 January 1862 at the I.B.A. He must have remembered giving his paper on *The Dwellings of the Labouring Classes* before the same body on 21 January 1850, for that paper was later published by the S.I.C.L.C., was subsequently translated into French, and was published in Germany and in the 'States of North America'. So, after an interval of twelve years, Roberts again gave the Institute the benefit of some of the experience gained in his 'gratuitous efforts to promote the healthfulness of our dwellings, and more especially those of the labouring population'. Roberts admitted that his subject was 'unattractive' from the 'artistic point of view', but that the Institute should give its attention to the problems of working-class housing.

He paid tribute to the work of the late Prince Consort, whose death had been a severe blow to enlightened forces in the country. Prince Albert had a reflective and highly cultivated mind, capable of appreciating minute detail as well as the grand design. Roberts had often heard the Prince speak, and referred to his attending meetings at Aberdeen of the British Association and of the International Statistical Congress in London at which the Prince Consort had delivered addresses.

Roberts set out to define what were the true essentials of a healthy dwelling. He recognised that certain aspects, though termed 'essential', could be compensated for. Where a site was not elevated, for example, it might be perfectly satisfactory if it had good soil and was well drained. The condition of health, in regard to dwellings, was achieved by a combination of factors, which Roberts tabulated:

1. The site must have access to pure air.
2. The soil must be suitable.
3. The area must be capable of efficient drainage.
4. There must be a plentiful supply of pure water.
5. The site must have a 'genial aspect'.
6. The building itself must be well designed and soundly constructed.
7. The inhabitants must be taught 'external and internal cleanliness'.

High and dry situations, having access to the free circulation of unpolluted air, whether occupied by groups of buildings, or by isolated dwellings, were regarded as ideal, while 'low and damp' situations 'surrounded by confined air' were quite unsuitable. Roberts pointed out that the military encampments of troops in the Empire offered conclusive evidence. The mortality among troops in the West Indies dropped from 120 to 20 per thousand when the camps were resited in the hills, for 'it is well ascertained that ague, dysentery, and fever prevail in localities where the surface of the ground is naturally wet and insufficiently drained, or where there exists an accumulation of decaying matter, of which one sure indication is the presence of an abundance of flies'.[2] Roberts also regarded a damp site as 'productive of mental depression and bodily feebleness, which excite a craving for intoxicating drink'. Clearly, the Evangelical Conscience was still strong. In addition, the 'embosoming in trees, or any other obstruction to a free circulation of air immediately round a dwelling' could be 'prejudicial to health, and should, therefore, be avoided'.[3] A gravelly soil was undoubtedly the most healthy, although a sandy base would be acceptable. Chalky ground had the disadvantage of porosity, so shafts had to be sunk to a considerable depth for water supplies. Tanks or reservoirs were often necessary for the storage of rainwater. Clay subsoils retained water, and were 'a frequent cause of the dampness so prevalent in the lower stories of houses in many localities — an evil felt as much in some which are elevated as those at a lower level, and a fruitful source of sickness among servants, as well as the occupants of small houses, whether in towns or in the country'. Loose soil close to a house was a 'frequent cause of damp' which might be remedied by stone flags or by asphalte. Roberts also suggested that a dry drain or an area might be formed around buildings with beneficial results. Where buildings were erected on naturally wet ground, ample drainage was essential, not only to dry the soil, but to carry off surplus water from the houses themselves. During the cholera epidemics of 1848 and 1854 in London, the percentage of mortality was higher among those living at low elevations relative to the river.

The provision of efficient drainage for dwellings as well as for the surfaces of roads and of ground was a necessity. Bad drains in the town of Windsor had caused a prevalence of 'fevers and choleraic complaints', and Roberts emphasised the necessity of ventilating sewerage systems. House drainage ought to be 'kept without the building, although the valuable modern improvement of glazed earthenware tubes with perfect sockets' had greatly reduced the risk of leakage from defective drains. Roberts was a keen advocate of traps in all pipes that discharged into the drains so that foul air could not escape into dwellings.

Cesspools under basement floors, so common before the dreadful visitations of cholera, had been the causes of sickness and death on a large scale. Roberts knew of several cases of cholera in 1849 that had been 'wholly traceable to this cause'. When 'these latent sources of mischief' were discovered, Roberts advised their immediate elimination. Even in houses of the 'first magnitude' not of recent construction, Roberts recognised that cesspools existed, causing the ground under the houses to become 'sodden with foetid matter'. The gases that became diffused throughout dwellings constituted 'one of those conditions of local impurity' and were favourable to outbreaks of cholera, fever, or other complaints. 'The abolition of cesspools within all dwellings, is therefore a sanitary measure of the first importance', Roberts declared.[4]

Roberts was a courageous advocate of the responsibility of local authorities to ensure ample supplies of pure water to towns. He denounced the contamination of rivers by 'their being unscrupulously, and at the same time most wastefully, made the receptacles of sewage'. In fact, Roberts recognised that pollution in his day had generally made rivers incapable of supplying towns with pure water. Despite improvements in London in the 1850s, the water supply of London remained 'far behind' that of the 'metropolis of the Roman Empire, and even' of many of its provincial cities. Roberts' great love for Italy comes over when he described how those who have 'traversed the Campagna di Roma can never forget the gigantic aqueducts whose ruins proclaim how abundantly and at what cost Rome was supplied with water'. Recent improvements in the supply of fresh water to Glasgow met with Roberts' approval, for Glasgow had recently been supplied with fresh water from Loch Katrine at a cost of £1,500,000. This water contained only 2.35 grains of impurity per gallon, while the water supplied to London by six companies varied from 17.72 to 21.76 grains of impurity per gallon.

Historically, wells had often been in the centres of settlements, and many had been of chalybeate or medicinal types, often associated with holy springs.[5] Unfortunately, by Roberts' day, this meant that many old wells in urban areas were situated in or adjacent to churchyards[6] so that they were 'very prejudicial to health', though the 'sparkling appearance and freshness to the taste' of the waters 'might lead to the contrary supposition'. Impurities in wells were generally caused by the infiltration from some neighbouring drain, cesspool, or other deposit of putrefying matter, such as a churchyard.

A useful medium of filtration used in drains, catacombs, and other instances in the mid-nineteenth century, was wood-charcoal, sometimes defined as the 'patent carbon filter'. The use of this filter cured many of the employees of the General Post Office of 'much internal derangement' caused by bad drains. Even in the 1860s a well at Sandgate was reported to contain 40.96 grains of impurity per gallon, while another well at Hampstead was polluted to the extent of 53.60 grains per gallon.

Roberts recognised that in the countryside, while the density of population was not as great as that in the towns, good drainage and pure water were 'no less essential', so they ought to be made the subject of 'deliberate investigation before the locality of a dwelling' was decided upon. A decent well and reasonable dryness were still 'essentials' of the healthy dwelling.

As far as the aspect of a dwelling was concerned, Roberts observed that it was often overlooked. Preferably a southern aspect should be chosen, or, if that were impossible, an outlook inclining to the east or the west would be agreeable, so that the 'rays of the sun may enter at some part of the day'. Rooms occupied at the height of the summer should have an eastern or a north-eastern aspect. In towns the difficulty of obtaining a sunny frontage was often very great, but Roberts insisted that 'the importance of having the sun's rays within the dwelling for some portion of the day, especially in rooms occupied by children or by invalids, should never be forgotten'.[7] He mentioned a 'large convalescent asylum' so arranged as to exclude the sunlight from the gallery used by the patients for exercise, and felt that the planning was 'a discredit to all concerned in its building'.

A healthy dwelling must be dry, be warm, and contain rooms in proportion to the number of occupants. The house must be well lighted and ventilated, and be free from 'noxious vapours' of any kind. In order to be dry, the house should stand on a dry foundation, and if this were not possible, Roberts suggested that artificial means be adopted, either by forming a 'stratum of concrete', varying in depth according to circumstances, but 'never less than 12 inches', or by bedding the foundations in slate or in cement, or by laying a damp-proof membrane of asphalte through the whole thickness of the wall under the floor level. Basement floors should be raised not less than about eight inches above the external surface, and if wooden floors were specified, the ground beneath them should be excavated to give a clear depth of not less than twelve inches, which should be ventilated by air-bricks built into the external walls.

Roberts recommended that floors of stone or of slate should either be hollow, resting on brick courses, or be laid on a dry bed prepared for the purposes, which would also be the case where brick or tile floors were specified. Lime and sand floors were usual in cottages, but Roberts often specified Portland cement for the floors of living-rooms in fireproof dwellings, but where much wear was expected, he preferred stone flags. Bedrooms, where not 'matted or carpeted' should have boarded floors.

External walls had two primary functions: to be weatherproof and of sufficient thickness to secure dryness and warmth; and to keep the roof up. The choice of mortar was all-important, whether brick, stone, or flint was the main material. In some instances, concrete, pisé, or cob, with a rendering of plaster or roughcast, could be used, provided foundations were dry and sound, and the tops of the walls were well protected by overhanging eaves. Roberts recommended that hollow walls were conducive to dryness and to warmth, and they could be constructed of brick, or cased with one of the materials previously mentioned, lined with brick or tile, with a hollow space between the two leaves. Naturally, hollow bricks were also recommended, and they were regarded as ideal for the lining of walls, so that the dampness would be kept to the outside. Glazing on the external faces of bricks was regarded as an effective barrier to dampness, and Roberts recorded his regrets that 'suitably glazed bricks' were not obtainable 'at a moderate price'. The smooth surfaces of glazed bricks were often ideal for internal work, on account of their cleanliness and non-absorbent properties. Colouring or whitewash was regarded as better than paper in 'common apartments', although it had to be frequently renewed.

For roofs, Roberts recommended the 'general adoption' of slate, but, because of that material's poor properties of insulation, slates should be laid on sarking or felt, or be protected by double plastering on the underside. Tiles, being warmer in the winter and cooler in summer than slate, and requiring less lead, were more economical in Roberts' day. Projecting eaves should have gutters to prevent the drip that was so often the cause of damp in the walls and foundations, and maintenance of gutters was essential to prevent the heads of rain-water pipes being blocked.

Roberts suggested fire-proof construction for roofs in town buildings. He had adopted hollow-brick fire-proof construction for the roofs and floors of the Model Dwellings at Streatham Street and Portpool Lane, as well as for the 'lamented Prince Consort's model houses at the Exhibition of 1851'. A fire at Streatham Street had proved the efficacy of Roberts' modes of construction, for no serious damage had been caused. Hollow bricks, with iron girders, were in extensive use by 1862 in Paris, based on Roberts' structural principles. Roberts acknowledged his debt to Roman constructional methods in the development of his technique.[8]

Custom had its disadvantages. Roberts pointed out that the practice of forming rooms in the roofs of buildings could cause problems, as servants (who were usually quartered in attics) tended to carelessness, and fires could result.

Referring to fire-proof construction, Roberts recalled a paper given by Sidney Smirke in 1860 'On the Use of Coke'. This material, from its lightness, was eminently suitable for vaulting, as the use of pumice or volcanic scoria had proved in ancient times.

The serious fires of the Victorian age led Roberts to consider various systems of fire-proof construction, and he urged the Institute of British Architects to give the matter 'serious consideration'. He also had strong views on materials. Wood of an inferior quality, or unseasoned, was a 'false economy', while the 'cracks and shrinkages' caused draughts that were often 'prejudicial to health'. Lead should not be used for cisterns, nor should it be used to 'convey drinking water' on account of the 'injurious effects produced by the chemical action which frequently takes place' when the water is soft. Roberts advocated varnished or enamelled iron for pipes and cisterns, and considered that slate cisterns had much to recommend them, for they kept water cool. Glazed stoneware sinks or sinks of enamelled iron got over the problem of 'offensive and unwholesome' smells that often emerged from iron or stone basins. Pipes and cisterns of paper, hardened and sealed, were also said to be satisfactory, but clearly such experiments, new in Roberts' day, did not bring long-term benefits.

Roberts was particularly concerned to provide warm dwellings that had good aspects, that were dry, that were constructed of hard and durable materials, and were planned and designed to avoid excessive draughts. He found it surprising that the effects of the British climate were not mitigated by double sashes, or casements, as was common on the Continent. This would also be a means of retaining more warmth 'from our wastefully constructed open fireplaces'.[9] He also insisted that the number and dimensions of rooms essential to health must be proportionate to the number of occupants, for 'suitable provision must be made for all that appertains to a well ordered domiciliary life, not only that of the master and mistress as well as of the children, but also that of the servants, whose health and morals it is the duty of their employers to care for'.[10]

A labourer's dwelling in the country should, according to Roberts, have an entrance lobby, a living-room, not less than 150 square feet in area, in which there should be a stove or fireplace as well as a copper and sink; and a small pantry. Above should be a parents' bedroom of not less than 100 square feet in area, and two bedrooms for children, each with a distinct and separate access. Fireplaces should be provided in at least two of the bedrooms. The 'closet' should be 'properly lighted, ventilated and drained' and there should be suitable 'enclosed receptacles for fuel and dust'. Heights of rooms should not be less than eight feet, and windows should reach 'nearly to the ceiling', and the 'top be invariably made to open'. All water-closets should have 'direct external ventilation'.

Smoking chimneys were a constant problem, and were often caused by the proximity of more lofty buildings, by trees, or by a defect in construction. Damp flues were often a cause of smoking. A narrowing of the throat of the chimney was often sufficient to ensure an upward draught.

A dark house can not only be 'gloomy and dispiriting', but is nearly always unhealthy. Light 'well diffused over all parts of a dwelling' was regarded as essential to health.[11] The abolition of window-tax and of a tax on glass had helped the reformers, but Roberts acknowledged that much time would pass before 'the evils resulting from a vicious legislation' would be swept away.

Ventilation and artificial warming were other aspects with which Roberts was intimately concerned. He drew on his experience in poor-house dormitories, in prisons, and in lodging-houses, and quoted a figure of 535 cubic feet of air per man, to be changed each hour, as 'abundantly sufficient' for health.

The continual renewal of vitiated air was a great problem for Victorian designers. Roberts stated that dwellings should be constructed so that they would, in all their parts, be accessible to pure air, and free from stagnation of any kind. Considered practically, the main question with regard to ventilation was how the vitiated air could be renewed with a supply of fresh air without the creation of draughts. 'To do this', Roberts noted, 'the air must enter copiously, and almost imperceptibly, and when used', or vitiated, 'its exit should be both continuous and complete'. Windows should be properly constructed, made to open at the top as well as at the bottom, and should be suitably placed. Chimneys act as ventilators whenever a fire is lighted in a room, for the lowest stratum of air is set in motion, and a current of air is established from crevices and doors and windows, or from any other openings, whereby much of the vitiated air is carried off. An independent supply of fresh air can be introduced into most rooms that have a fireplace by conveying it through a pipe formed under the floor, or in the wall, to an air-chamber constructed at the back of, or at the sides of the stove, in order that it may be warmed before entering the room. A separate pipe can also feed the fire with air, so that draughts are avoided.

Chimney ventilating valves were rendered more certain in action by such an independent supply of air. An independent flue was carried up in close contact with a smoke flue that was constantly in use, such as a kitchen fire. A vacuum was thus created in the independent flue, and vitiated air was drawn in. Tubular flues of pottery were ideal for this purpose. In cases where chimney valves were fixed in the flue itself, causing an ingress of smoke, the best remedy was to regulate the draught by a contraction of the vacant space over the fire.

Roberts was well ahead of his time in noting that ordinary grates are wasteful of both heat and fuel, both of which would be saved by the substitution of a stove that projected slightly into the room. Roberts had seen 'such stoves in use on the Continent', and noted that the only valid reason against their adoption in England (apart from an innate conservatism) was the difficulty of applying them to fireplaces with ornamental chimney-pieces. The intimate connection between warming and ventilation necessitates the placing of the openings for the escape of vitiated air either in the ceiling or near it. Fresh air could be admitted near the floor, or by means of a hopper, fanlight, or ventilator over a door. Roberts also used gaslight as a means of creating currents to remove vitiated air. Any form of heat was sufficient to set up convection currents which might be controlled.

Artificial ventilation by valves, fans, pumps, screws, furnaces, stoves, or other sources of heat, and a variety of contrivances by which air can be drawn out of, or forced into an apartment, interested Roberts. In one case, the space occupied by the withdrawn vitiated air is replaced by pure fresh air, while in the other case, the pure air forced into the apartment forces out the vitiated air, for the escape of which provision must be made. In both cases, a reasonable proportion between the volume of air that ought to enter, and that which should be expelled, is necessary. In order that the fresh air may be adapted for use at all seasons of the year, means must be provided (Roberts said) for warming it prior to its distribution in the apartment. Roberts advised that the best means of achieving this was by bringing the air into contact with heated fire-bricks. Roberts favoured propulsion rather than suction, because the air becomes more diffused than it does when its entrance is dependent on the withdrawal of the vitiated air by means of suction. Where German hot-air stoves or hot-water radiators were used, Roberts insisted that they should be treated as auxiliaries to open fires, because of the necessity of removing vitiated air.

Roberts clearly demonstrated his advanced views in considering heating and ventilating systems. He regretted that the science of ventilation was still in its infancy, and that 'its practical application' was not 'more employed than it would seem to be from the Report of the Government Commissioners on Warming and Ventilation'. Roberts regarded this report as having failed in placing the subject in a clear light.

He inveighed against the neglect of sanitary laws and principles. Good drainage, fresh air, and cleanliness were essential. Internal cleanliness invited proper attention to all sinks and traps, as well as to ventilation. Roberts welcomed the publication of Florence Nightingale's *Notes on Nursing*, which afforded him the means of conveying some valuable lessons on the sanitary education of servants in his *Home Reform: or, What the Working Classes may do to improve their own Dwellings*. He was clearly in the educational van, and a tireless propounder of knowledge to alleviate the results of ignorance. He noted that the middle class might contribute, less grudgingly than they frequently did, towards the cost of public sanitary improvements, and would even urge their extension, 'if they were better acquainted with the laws of health and the heavy expenses which their infringement often involves on the community, as well as on individuals'. A practical knowledge of indoor conditions might lead people to appreciate the advantages of cleanliness and good ventilation 'and to see that their benefits were extended more generally to those hives of human industry where numbers of working people congregate for many successive hours, and those partly under the deleterious influence of gas light'. Roberts noted that if, from a want of knowledge and imagination, many in the upper and middle walks of life were debarred from the full enjoyment of a healthy dwelling, the working classes were even worse off, and had no choice in the matter. Foul conditions bred intemperance, which exacerbated the problem.[12]

Unfortunately, the great publicity which philanthropic housing had been given, and the endless discussions in Parliament, bored the public at last, so that the evils of bad housing were often ignored. Roberts, in 1862, noted that the original movement of 1844 was being seriously retarded.[13] Roberts believed that if philanthropic housing had been managed to yield four per cent after the payment of all expenses and the provision of a sinking fund for the repayment of the money laid out, there would have been no difficulty in obtaining capital to build 'a very large number of improved dwellings in the metropolis' as well as in the provincial towns. Roberts believed that houses for families yielded a better return than lodging-houses, and his veiled criticism is clearly directed at the S.I.C.L.C., who were generally failing to build model houses for families after the earliest experiments with which Roberts had been concerned.

Speculative builders, or those seeking a good investment, would not consider four per cent a sufficiently remunerative return, yet Roberts was outraged that, among the many who had 'accumulated large fortunes in connection with the building trade in the metropolis', he knew of only one firm, that of Messrs. Newson & Son, who had invested part of the gains derived, in a large measure, from the labour of the working classes'. Newson built blocks to designs by Roberts, and there were other instances where individuals had built model dwellings in Edinburgh. Roberts also noted with pleasure a report in the *British Workman* concerning a village near Lowestoft, rebuilt by Sir Morton Peto. Such investment, or lack of it, however, was not surprising, for the building trade was a risky one, even in Victorian times, and the history of the development of the Ladbroke Estate, for example, is littered with bankruptcies.[14]

Henry Roberts was critical of members of his own profession who exercised 'so little influence in regard to the improvement of the dwellings of the labouring classes'. He exempted his friends Sydney Smirke, George Gilbert Scott, and George Godwin from his censures, however, for Smirke had published his *Suggestions for the Improvement of the Western Part of the Metropolis* in 1834; Scott had expatiated on the importance of practical measures in his *Remarks on Secular and Domestic Architecture*; and Godwin, as Editor of *The Builder*, had campaigned for philanthropic housing for years.

Roberts was able to assemble his arguments for housing reform under three headings:

1. Those of a legislative character, and those for which the Government was responsible.
2. Those adopted by landowners and employers generally for the benefit of their dependents, as tenants or as employees.
3. Those originating from benevolent philanthropic motives.

With regard to reforms of a legislative character, Roberts surprises by his sharpness. He contrasted the 'jealous respect for the rights of persons and property' with the 'public improvements' under 'arbitrary rule' that had been 'effected with unprecedented rapidity, on so gigantic a scale, in the metropolis of a neighbouring country' (clearly referring to Baron Haussmann's work in Paris). He thought the citizens of London had a right to complain of, 'and ought to feel ashamed of', the 'bungling and pettifogging manner' in which many of the new streets had been formed. Opportunities for obtaining 'magnificent effects' had been 'irrevocably lost'.[15] Particularly, Roberts complained of 'that great financial failure, Victoria Street', where several fruitless attempts had been made to obtain back land as sites for the dwellings of displaced persons who 'were huddled together in a frightful degree', as a result of the new streets being driven through on a compulsory basis. Indeed, Roberts was highly critical of 'the want of a compulsory provision for the displaced poor'.[16] who had been turned out by the thousand owing to railway and road construction in Victorian times. Again, he was far ahead of his time.

The same neglect on the part of the government was the cause of 'an incalculable amount of suffering in Paris, when the people who tenanted its narrow and winding streets were forcibly ejected, and often their few articles of furniture placed on the *pavé*, they themselves not knowing where to seek shelter'. Exorbitant rents were charged for temporary hovels, which the police insisted would be pulled down after three months. The morally outraged Roberts, encouraged by the fact that his work was known in France, sent a memorial to the Emperor Napoleon III which was 'graciously received'. Some amelioration of the lot of the displaced Parisians was achieved as a result.

In Britain, legislative measures to give the labouring population the benefits of a healthy dwelling had only comprised the passing of the *Public Health Act* and the *Nuisance Removal and Diseases Prevention Acts* when Roberts had first given his seminal paper in 1850. His efforts and recommendations achieved the removal of taxes on windows and on bricks under the administration of Lord John Russell; the Act for the regulation of common lodging-houses was passed largely through the offices of Roberts and of the Earl of Shaftesbury; the *Labourers' Dwelling Act*, which allowed the formation and management of independent Local Associations as joint-stock companies, with limited liability, was passed for the provision of improved dwellings; and other Bills to facilitate the construction of labourers' dwellings in Ireland and in Scotland were made law.

Roberts was enraged by the blocking of a bill in the Lords to enable landowners to raise money for building cottages on their estates. The debate showed 'how much less real interest' was shown on the whole question. Yet Parliament insisted on the insertion of clauses in some of the railway Bills that obliged the companies to provide cheap trains at hours suitable for the conveyance of working people to and from their residences out of town. A standing order, intended to apply to cases in which application was made for power to demolish houses in the paths of railways, was passed in the Lords in 1853 at the instigation of Lord Shaftesbury, but it became, in practical terms, unworkable, such was the vested interest involved.

Roberts was an advocate of 'legislative interference' as 'indispensable to the remedying' of existing evils. No adequate powers existed in his day to check the evils of overcrowding, except in common lodging-houses that were controlled by law, and except within the City of London, which was in the forefront of sanitary reform and enlightened government. Similar overcrowding was common in rural cottages. The Secretary of State for the Home Department had been urged by the Council of the National Association for the Promotion of Social Science, of which Roberts was an active member, to take advantage of the Census to obtain statistical returns on overcrowding, as had been done in Ireland, but once more vested interest blocked the appeal. Despite all the attempts by many landed proprietors, inspired by Roberts, to improve properties on their estates, many landowners were apparently quite unaware of the problem, and resented any suggestion that they should play a part in reform. Attitudes were ingrained. In some parishes, cottages were pulled down in order to relieve those responsible for improvements, so the unfortunate displaced persons were thrown on the mercy of neighbouring parishes. Roberts saw clearly that only when the working classes became owners of their own dwellings would there be any 'stimulant to forethought and general good conduct'.[17]

There was a great need to prevent building on undrained land, just as the proper sanitary arrangements were necessary. The necessity of protecting life from the influence of 'poisonous dwellings' had not been 'practically acknowledged', although the principle was already on the statute books. Roberts was pleased to note, however, that his own labours had borne fruit in some cases, both at home and abroad, mainly through his personal connections with great landowners, and through the circulation of his papers.

Turning now to measures that ought, in the opinion of Roberts, to be adopted by landowners and employers for the benefit of tenants or workpeople, the example of the Duke of Bedford was cited by the architect. His Grace had built and improved cottages on his estates in several counties, and over ten years had expended some £70,000 on such works. The Duke of Northumberland had laid out about £100,000 on improvements to dwellings on *his* estates, at an average cost of about £120 per house.

Roberts' attitude to social questions is revealing in the following passages:

'The question of a *remunerative return* on the outlay in building cottages in agricultural districts, is one which impinges so closely on that of the rate of wages, that I shall not venture on its discussion. It would be hopeless to argue this point with those who think that wages of 8s. to 9s. per week can properly maintain a working man and his family, as well as pay the rent of a healthy dwelling. With the greatly increased prosperity of agriculture, such a rate of wages appears to me unaccountable, and altogether at variance with equity and sound policy.

'The efforts made by some of our great manufacturers for the benefit of their workpeople have been in proportion to those just noticed, particularly those in Yorkshire, by Mr. Titus Salt,[18] Mr. Akroyd, and Messrs. Crossley. Many owners of mines, quarries, and works of various kinds, can bear testimony to the great benefits resulting from their expenditure in providing proper dwellings for the people in their employ.

'The same has been the case with reference to the cottages built in considerable numbers by several of the leading railway companies. The secretaries of some of them, in speaking on the subject, referred particularly to the great advantage of the men being ready at hand, in case of need, and removed from the temptation presented by public-houses. Government has acted on the same principle in regard to the Police force, and, taking the idea originally from the model lodging-houses, barracks have been built generally for those of them who are unmarried — a good precedent, which might doubtless be adopted in many other instances with much advantage to both employers and employed. In such cases a sufficiently remunerative rent can usually be charged, and its payment be guaranteed from the wages.

'A lodging-house, established at Camden-town, by Messrs. Pickford and Co., the well-known carriers, for the unmarried men in their employ, has now 60 inmates: the payment of 2s. 6d. per week by the men, and 1s. 6d. by small boys, covers all expenses, and the interest on the outlay, whilst there is "a great improvement in the men as regards orderly conduct, cleanliness, &c." When visiting this house I noticed a common carter copying a piece of music'.[19]

The third category of measures noted by Roberts was that in which reforms had been undertaken by associations or by individuals in order to aid those in need of help in housing.

The first association to begin the practical work of building model dwellings was, of course, the Society for Improving the Condition of the Labouring Classes. With an outlay of about £36,000 the Society established between 1844 and 1851 six different examples of dwellings, four of new, and two of old, with ancillary accommodation. Subsequently, in different localities, three entire courts, called Clark's Buildings, Tyndal's Buildings, and Wild Court, were taken, and the conditions of the houses (which, in two of them, were 'indescribably filthy') were completely changed. Roberts recollected the state of these houses (and the sickening effects of his minute survey of the properties) most vividly after 'the lapse of many years'.[20] These courts were fitted up as separate tenements for families, and comprised 275 rooms plus a single-men's lodging-house, with forty beds.

By 1860, the Metropolitan Association for Improving the Dwellings of the Industrious Classes had expended nearly £90,000 on ten distinct ranges of dwellings, giving a return of nearly four per cent on the outlay. On two lodging-houses for single men, there was a considerable loss, which suggested that the buildings were unsuitable for the demand.

Roberts visited a lodging-house at Marseilles which also ran at a loss as it was built too far from the centre of the town, and was too large. Smaller houses, for 50–100 men, sited near the centre, were financially viable, and Roberts quoted examples in Leeds and Liverpool. Two adjoining lodging-houses on the *Boulevard des Batignolles*, in Paris, which Roberts knew, accommodated 203 men, and had a restaurant and café on the ground floor. Yet one house failed, and had to close, which Roberts attributed to 'defective management'.

Yet there were aspects of the work carried out by the S.I.C.L.C. and other bodies that troubled Roberts. The ejection of many of the former inhabitants of the 'filthy courts' referred to above itself caused problems. While Roberts conceded that a lower density of occupancy was desirable, and in some cases 'a more eligible set of tenants' might be necessary, the ejected persons had to be housed somehow. His own conviction, surprisingly, was that the owners of unsavoury property should be compelled by law either to put it in a healthy condition, to close it, or to sell it, at a fairly estimated rate, to persons willing to undertake the necessary outlay. Roberts saw that the fact that poor property was investigated by 'philanthropic persons' was enough to give it a 'fictitious value', so that in numerous instances the object was defeated. Roberts believed that the principle involved in the prohibition of the sale of unwholesome food should apply equally to dwellings, and that legal enforcement was the only way of 'remedying the evil'.[21] These unconventional ideas had been urged by Roberts in Italy, where in Florence his representations to the Grand Duke of Tuscany had led to the issuing of a decree that empowered all municipal magistrates within the Grand Duchy to form a committee for the provision of means to cleanse dwellings that were let, and which were dangerous to the health and life of society.[22]

In some cases, individual efforts succeeded in improving old buildings so that they yielded a suitable return on the outlay. In Chelsea, the Rev. Charles Burgess and some associates established two renovated houses for families in 1851 to provide an example for others disposed to promote similar experiments. In many cases, the middle-men were the problem. Roberts quoted a report by Nugent Robinson on the Dwellings of the Poor in Dublin, in which the wretchedness of many houses was said to be mainly due to 'house jobbers' who bought up dilapidated houses, and re-let them, usually by the room. Often, the 'jobber' stayed well out of sight, but the collection of rents was left to some 'low, brutish agent, employed on commission to collect the rents by hook or by crook'. The 'jobbers' were averse to ameliorating the condition of the tenants, especially where expense was involved. Similar evils existed in English cities.

Roberts had examined a property in central London in 1861, part of which comprised dwellings for 86 families, and another part of three courts. The owner was a 'private gentleman', who derived 'his chief income from house property'. On coming into possession he desired to improve the property 'for the occupation of well-conducted tenants'. Improvements were carried out 'without pecuniary loss', and under-letting was prohibited, though occasionally a lodger was allowed.[23]

By 1862 the philanthropic housing society at Hastings had a paid-up capital of £16,000, of which £14,000 had been expended in purchasing the freehold and putting into good condition some 130 old cottages and two lodging-houses. A dividend of six per cent was paid to subscribers, while one per cent per annum was paid into a reserve fund.

Yet it was not all a case of renovation of older property, for many Societies were responsible for the erection of new buildings. In Eagle Court, the Strand Building Company erected houses for twenty-five families, and paid a dividend of 4½ per cent. The Windsor Royal Society, with Major-General F. H. Seymour as President, had £9,000 invested in new cottages (of which twenty were designed by Roberts), and in two new lodging-houses. The net return was about 4½ per cent. In addition to this Society, The Windsor Royal Association, established in 1850, promoted habits of neatness and order in dwellings, and a system of annual rewards was set up.

The Redhill and Reigate Cottage Improvement Society commenced operations by building 19 cottages, to which another 20 were added by 1862. Costs were around £120 per cottage, and a dividend of 5 per cent, reflected in cheaper ground-prices, was paid to shareholders. These cottages were near the railway station, and were very similar to the houses Roberts had designed for the Windsor Royal Society. Clearly, they had been erected from the published plans of the buildings at Windsor, which themselves were based on the 1851 Great Exhibition Model Dwellings.

Several model lodging-houses were built by the Huddersfield Improvement Commissioners under Acts of Parliament, the only instance in Britain by 1862 where municipal authorities had erected such buildings out of improvement rates at public cost. Provision was for 221 men, for 34 single females, and for 12 married couples. The Corporation of London built a large block of dwellings in the upper part of Farringdon Street, Clerkenwell, that were referred to by Roberts as being among the most important 'piles of dwellings recently built', with those erected by 'Alderman Waterlow's Industrial Dwelling Company', and the Gatliff Buildings, belonging to the Marquis of Westminster, of 1867.

Roberts' visits to Scotland led him to the conclusion that 'exertion' was 'quite as much needed' as it was in the south. The overcrowding of the poor, who were 'huddled together in gigantic buildings of seven and eight stories, divided into dwellings of one and two rooms each', in Edinburgh, shocked him. He was also appalled by the 'painful scenes' that obviously arose 'in great measure from drunken habits'.

In Roberts' paper given at the Glasgow meeting of the National Association for the Promotion of Social Science, published in the *Transactions* of 1860, there is a detailed account of numerous blocks of improved or model dwellings that had been constructed in Edinburgh during the previous decade. In many of these, cantilevered external galleries and open stairs (as advocated by Roberts) had been adopted, and in other instances where there were only two storeys, the apartments were approached on two sides, as at Pilrig Model Buildings, Leith Walk, which paid a dividend of five per cent. An Association was formed in Glasgow to cut a new street through one of the most wretched of closes, and £15,000 had been raised. Similar efforts were reported in the *Transactions* of the National Association for Social Science in Dublin in 1861.

All in all, Roberts is revealed as an advocate of measures far in advance of his time. Some of his proposals, such as those for double windows, insulated roofs, adequate air-changes, and solid-fuel stoves have not even been adopted today. His concern for suitable aspects, good insulation, and sound construction demonstrates that he was intelligently forward-looking to an extent for which he has received little credit. Had Roberts' proposals become part of housing policy in the United Kingdom, it is likely that such problems as high energy consumption and gross waste through poor insulation would not have been as great as they are in the last quarter of the twentieth century.

Chapter Seven

EFFORTS ON THE CONTINENT TO IMPROVE
THE CONDITION OF THE LABOURING CLASSES

Des, à present, tout, cela est practicable; il faut donc le pratiquer. Quand notre population si bienveillante et si ingénieuse voudra sa consacrer à de telles œuvres, elles en
comprendra bientôt l'importance extrême, et leur bienfait se répandra avec rapidité dans
tout le pays, pour le plus grand bonheur des classes laborieuses.

Henry Roberts: The Introduction to the French Edition of *Des habitations des classes
ouvrières*. Quoted in *The Dwellings of the Labouring Classes*, London, 1867.

IN 1858 HENRY ROBERTS had spent five years on the Continent 'for the recovery
of health'.[1] He was able to look back and present a fairly coherent record of progress
in the housing reform movement. Roberts' influence had already been felt in Italy.
The municipality of Genoa had been put to the expense of considerable sums to relieve
the population in narrow streets and insanitary dwellings during the cholera epidemic
of 1856. The chief magistrate of Genoa had read Roberts' works and studied the plans
for model dwellings, and a society for building improved dwellings was formed in
Genoa. The King was a shareholder, and another project in Turin also received the
backing of the House of Savoy.

The royal patronage of Queen Victoria and of the Prince Consort, and the success
of the Exhibition of 1851, drew international attention to the work of the Society
for Improving the Condition of the Labouring Classes, and to the designs of Henry
Roberts in particular. The Society had published plans and elevations of the model
dwellings, and these became widely known throughout the civilised world. Louis
Napoleon had ordered a French edition of Roberts' seminal work, *The Dwellings of
the Labouring Classes*, to be published, and, as Emperor of the French, he had encouraged urban improvement and housing experiment. Despite the criticisms of the
splendid urban layouts of Baron Georges-Eugène Haussmann, and the cramped apartments that lay behind much of the façade of boulevard or of avenue, Napoleon III was
genuinely interested in the philanthropic movement. Roberts often referred to the translation of his *The Dwellings of the Labouring Classes, their arrangement and construction*
into French in 1850 as a result of an order by Napoleon III, when President of the
Republic. He regretted that his practical suggestions had not yet been implemented.

Roberts' Model Houses at the Great Exhibition of 1851 attracted much international attention, and published plans were available at a moderate charge to those who
visited the houses. The examples of the S.I.C.L.C. and of Henry Roberts were
followed in other countries by philanthropic societies, individuals, and architects.
An immense amount of published material relating to housing for the poorer classes

began to appear from the 1850s. Extracts from these publications were later shown to Roberts by people who took a pleasure in acknowledging the influence his work was having abroad.

All the Continental movements for improving the dwellings of the labouring classes, as well as those in what Roberts called 'the North American States', were offshoots of early experiments in Britain, and were considerably influenced by the writings and designs of Henry Roberts. These movements were usually started by Evangelicals, or by those who were not associated with Roman Catholic orthodoxy. It Italy, reformers were either allies of the House of Savoy (no friends of the Papacy or of the Church), were Protestants, or were anti-clerical radicals with an admiration for the democratic institutions of Great Britain.

At the Paris Exhibition of 1855 were several examples of workmen's dwellings erected by employers. Roberts noted[2] that, in two of these, the resemblance to the Prince Consort's Exhibition Model Houses was 'strongly marked'. One set of dwellings constructed at Bourges in 1853 provided accommodation for four families on the ground floor, and for twenty single men on the upper floor, an improbable combination, one imagines. There was a major development at the *Cité Ouvrière des Verriers* at Escautpont, near Valenciennes. This comprised, in a central building, schools and other apartments used in common, with some dwelling houses, but the living accommodation was chiefly contained in two detached blocks that formed the sides of a square. Roberts approved of the repetitive recessed entrances, with galleries to the upper floor, for their 'novel' effect. Many of these experimental blocks survive today, although they have been much altered.

The indefatigable Roberts travelled widely to inspect as many philanthropic dwellings as he could. He mentioned dwellings for work-people built by the employers in Brussels (where the designs were based on Roberts' final Exhibition plan), in Lille, and at Mulhouse. In the latter town, Dr. Pinôt, Professor of Applied Sciences,[3] informed Roberts that the idea of constructing a *Cité Ouvrière* owed its origins to Roberts' seminal work, *The Dwellings of the Labouring Classes*, in its French translation. This *Cité Ouvrière* was begun in 1853 by an association of manufacturers, that developed from the *Société Industrielle de Mulhouse*, headed by M. Jean Dollfus, and it was constructed on an ambitious scale. It is particularly interesting that Eugène Véron, in his *Les Institutions Ouvrières de Mulhouse et des Environs*, published in Paris in 1866, specifically mentioned the Evangelical origins of the *Cité Ouvrière* and the Protestant Evangelical connections with England. In fact, both Guise and Mulhouse had strongly Protestant leanings, and it is not surprising that where there were already wealthy industrialists of the Protestant faith, the Evangelical Conscience would spur philanthropists to emulate the reformist movements in England. Mulhouse itself is a strongly Protestant city, and English Evangelical publications found their way their quickly. The *Société Industrielle* in Mulhouse even today has strongly Evangelical connections.

M. Emile Muller, the architect of the *Cité Ouvrière* in Mulhouse (Plate 82), the most extensive and successful model development in France, paid tribute to the publications of the S.I.C.L.C., and especially to Roberts' influential work, *The Dwellings of the Working Classes*, in influencing both the principles and the details of the *Cité*. Muller wrote or Roberts' book that 'cette œuvre, ce résumé didactique, est devenu en France, et chez toutes les nations representées ici, le point de départ, le guide sûr, le *vade-mecum* de ceux qui ont eu à se préoccuper de l'amélioration des classes laborieuses'.[4] Muller, who met Roberts at the *Congrès International de Bienfaisance* in 1856, was greatly influenced by the ideas of his English colleague, initially through Roberts' published writings and designs, and subsequently by the exchange of ideas at a personal level (Plates 83–85).

The *Société Mulhousienne des Cités Ouvrières* was founded by private enterprise and by the state, which also paid for the relevant roads and open spaces. There was a large road, planted on either side, running between the main groups of cottages, while parallel roads ran behind those cottages (Plate 82). The dwellings were arranged in detached blocks of four dwellings each, placed in the centres of square plots of open land that were divided equally between tenants. Two of these groups of dwellings fronted on the main boulevard, and two fronted on the minor or back road, an arrangement that Roberts thought was economical in terms of cost of construction, and one that allowed good internal ventilation. On balance, however, Roberts favoured houses built in pairs. The dwellings at Mulhouse were not identical, but they mostly had wide entrances equipped with stoves and sinks; staircases beyond; and three bedrooms and a closet. The ground-floor accommodation contained the living-room (with a large recess under the stairs that was big enough to contain a bed and that was illuminated by a side window). There were several rows of double houses, built back to back, each house having a narrow strip of garden. Roberts felt that the 'general appearance of the tenants indicated a decidedly inferior class' of occupants.[5] There were also communal baths, a wash-house, a bakery, and a public kitchen and restaurant (conducted by the *Société Alimentaire*). Roberts visited Mulhouse in 1856, after which date a reading-room, a school, a lodging-house, and a 'spike' for tramps were also provided. By the summer of 1860 there were 480 houses, two-thirds of which had been sold to the occupants, and 90 more were in the course of construction. The initial purchase of land allowed for the erection of 800 houses. The outlay on roads, fencing, and planting was defrayed by the French Government out of a total of ten million francs that had been appropriated to such purposes by the Emperor. Tenants had the option of purchasing the houses by gradual payments of the cost price, which compared with that of similar dwellings in England, and ranged from about £72 to £120 each. This method ensured that the capital was replaced, and no further funds had to be raised. Roberts paid tribute to the architect, Emile Muller, of Paris.

When Mulhouse became Mülhausen after 1871, the *Cité Ouvrière* became the *Arbeiterstadt*, or artisans' colony. Baedeker noted that it had been founded in 1853 by the *Société des Cités Ouvrières*, 'a society established by mayor Dollfus to improve the condition of the working classes'. It was developed to the north-west of the old town, and by 1900 consisted of about 1,000 houses of one or two storeys, each accommodating one or two families, and provided with a small garden. Even by 1900, however, the *Arbeiterstadt* was largely occupied 'by small shopkeepers and the like', as the workers moved out to the remoter suburbs.[6]

Today, the *Cité Ouvrière* is still very much recognisable, although there have been inevitable alterations to the fabric in the way of extensions, new doors and windows, and the addition of garages and outhouses. However, the pedestrian ways between the gardens, and the paired houses and terraces are of a much higher standard than the usual tenements built at the time.

Roberts also visited the *Familistère*, or Workmen's Home, at Guise, not far from St Quentin.[7] This differed from the *Cité Ouvrière* at Mulhouse, and was built by J.-B.-A. Godin-Lemaire (1817–89), 'the proprietor of extensive Iron Works, for his workpeople, about 800 in number'.[8] This *Familistère* resembled Roberts' designs for the Model Houses in Streatham Street, with its open galleries and courts, and indeed the direct ancestors of the *Familistère* were Streatham Street and Fourier's *Phalanstère*. The completed scheme consisted of three quadrangular piles of dwellings 'of imposing exterior, each having an internal court, covered with a glazed roof, and the whole forming a hollow square'.[9] There were stores for supplying the tenants with food, clothing, and fuel, and schools were also provided. The idea derived from Robert Owen's experiments and from other French Utopian visions.[10] Indeed, François-Marie-Charles Fourier (1772–1837) was influenced by, and perhaps jealous of, Robert Owen. Fourier argued for a specific Utopia in which a harmony between the interests of rich and poor, based on association, would be reached after seven historic periods had been gone through. Physically, Fourier expressed his ideas in plans for a *Phalanstère* published in *Le Nouveau Monde*.[11] This had a highly organised formal plan, with strong axes reminiscent of Baroque planning, and, within the *Phalanstère* workshops, dining-halls, finance-halls, libraries, study-rooms, residential quarters, and community-halls were to be provided. Essentially, it was a town without open streets, enclosed, heated, and ventilated, the noisier parts being connected with the centre, or *cité*, by means of covered arcades. The denizens of the *Phalanstère* were to be members with accommodation and shares, and forced equality was to be avoided since variety would be aimed at by the different qualities of the people, their occupations, and abilities. Godin-Lemaire and others attempted to put the ideas of Fourier into practice, and the *Familistère* of 1859–77 was an expression of Fourier-type ideas published in *Solutions Sociales* in 1870. Godin developed the industrial basis of his economy, abandoning communal ideas except for the use of open land. The *Familistère* was built as a unit in which the buildings were not scattered, but embraced many functions including educational facilities, so that the rest of the land would be used as an open park. Godin also adopted the covered-street idea of Fourier in the great covered courtyards of the residential blocks. In 1880 the whole complex was handed over to a workers' co-operative as a self-sufficient going concern.[12] This co-operative was still active in 1939, and the original factory had increased in size. Today, the factory flourishes, and the *Familistère* is in very good repair.

Roberts' admiration for certain developments by the people Karl Marx referred to as 'Utopian Socialists' might indicate to orthodox Marxists that his attitude was unscientific and Utopian according to the dialectic method, because Roberts based his hopes on the amelioration of the conditions of the working classes through individual benevolence and enterprise.[13] Yet Roberts' recognition of the necessity for legislation and compulsion, and even of State interference, and his uncharacteristic bellicosity on such matters[14] puts him firmly in the radical camp. Perhaps his frustrations with benevolent philanthropy, and his Continental experiences, pushed him towards

Socialism. As with many other Evangelical Christians of the period, Roberts appears to have moved steadily to the left politically, so that by the late 1860s he was advocating compulsory purchase, state interference, and other measures to alleviate housing conditions.

Roberts also noted that an entire village of wooden chalets had been constructed outside Paris by a clothing manufacturer. There were also two spacious workshops, and access to central Paris was by train. However, although Napoleon III had set aside ten million francs for the encouragement of philanthropic housing, Roberts was displeased to note that only in very few instances had the options been taken up. The Emperor's fund was intended to provide one-third of the outlay, the rest to be raised by private enterprise or by municipalities. Roberts was disgusted to find that most persons 'engaged in the enterprise to any extent appear to have done so exclusively as a commercial speculation, expecting to derive a considerable pecuniary profit, and uninfluenced by benevolent motives'.[15] Furthermore, it seems that the leading French philanthropic society suffered greatly through the 'misconduct' of its secretary, 'a similar misfortune to that which befell one of the earliest established Societies of London', causing a 'very serious discouragement to the work'.[16] Much information was disseminated in France at the time. Two reports were produced by Le Vicomte A. de Melun and Le Baron H. de Triquete, and were presented to the *Congrès International de Bienfaisance* that was held in London in 1862.[17]

Roberts was in Paris again in the autumn of 1866, and noted 'with pleasure' that private enterprise was responsible for a number of 'suitably arranged dwellings' giving a return of eight per cent. Roberts did not fail to notice that private enterprise was more successful financially than the Societies. Roberts particularly mentioned the building of workmen's dwellings in Russia, and he referred to projected buildings for St Petersburg. In Berlin, the Hohenzollerns patronised a philanthropic housing society that was the first in Europe to be modelled on the English example, according to Dr. Huber, the secretary. Indeed, Roberts himself had noted the close interest that the Prussian princes took in the work of the S.I.C.L.C. when they visited England. Copies of several letters from the Prussian princes to the Prince Consort concerning the Great Exhibition and the Model Houses survive among the papers of the Royal Commission for the Exhibition of 1851.

Indeed, it appears that the Berlin philanthropic housing society followed the example of the Society for Improving the Condition of the Labouring Classes, and was under the personal patronage of the King of Prussia. Roberts met King William on two occasions, and 'Had the honour of conversing with his Majesty' ('whose enlightened and personal interest' in philanthropic housing was well known) on the subject dear to his heart. The Prussian Royal House was stoutly Evangelical in outlook. During the 1860s several meetings of the Berlin society were presided over by H.R.H. Prince Frederick William (whose wife was the Princess Royal, daughter of Prince Albert and Queen Victoria), and capital of £34,655 was raised. Dwellings for 218 families were built, and 31 workshops were constructed. Dividends were around four per cent. Annual additions to the reserve fund came to just over £3,000, of which one half was repaid to the tenants.[18] It is perhaps worth noting that the Prussian connection was further strengthened through the friendship of the Prussian diplomat, the Chevalier de Bunsen, with Lord Ashley, which began on 15 January 1834, according to Hodder. Bunsen remained a close friend of Shaftesbury all his life, and was also a friend of Augustus J. C. Hare and his family.

Another society, the *Alexandra Stiftung* was founded by order of Tsar Nicholas of Russia in 1852. The Tsar gave 1,000 ducats to the funds, which stood at £21,388 in 1858, partly through donations and partly through loans at four per cent. With the intention of constructing suitable dwellings in St Petersburg for the working classes of that city, an architect was sent to London during the 1860s to study philanthropic housing. In due course several houses were built by private enterprise.

In Frankfurt-am-Main, another society, founded 'on a strictly commercial principle', began a successful operation under the 'guidance of its energetic and philanthropic promoter, Dr. Varrentrapp, who also visited England to see buildings designed by Roberts and others.[19] Roberts was personally approached by 'a gentleman from Bremen' who wanted advice on 'the carrying out of an extensive undertaking' which involved the erection of workmen's houses on land belonging to the Church, and situated outside the city. In this case, the Church authorities offered the ground at 'remarkably favourable terms', while the 'projectors' only sought very low rates of interest. To Roberts, these facts proved 'the earnestness of all engaged in this good cause, and how really anxious they are to meet the necessities of a case . . . most intimately connected with the well-being of the masses of the population'.[20]

As in Britain, the rate of interest sought in philanthropic housing ventures was usually four per cent, with a small sinking fund for paying off the capital. In some cases the dividends were five per cent, but on the Continent the tenants were afforded the opportunity of becoming the owners of their own dwellings by a small payment in addition to the rent. Dwellings were thus regarded almost as savings banks, and the scheme was 'found greatly to stimulate habits of forethought and sobriety'.[21]

The ideas of philanthropic housing, and the designs of Roberts, were disseminated throughout Norway, Denmark, Sweden, the Netherlands, and Belgium. Following the *Congrès Général d'Hygiène* in Brussels in 1852, the Belgian Government published an instructive series of resolutions on the construction of dwellings. Enlightened views on philanthropic housing were advocated by two international congresses held under the patronage of the King and the Royal Princes of the Belgians. Similarly, in Bavaria, in several smaller German states, and in Switzerland and in Italy, many model houses were built as a result of the writings and published plans of Roberts.

In Sweden, thirteen model blocks were built in Stockholm, and capital was raised for building a *Cité Ouvrière* at Gothenburg. In Amsterdam, no less than three housing societies were established, paying dividends of four per cent. In three of the industrial valleys of the Jura, as well as in Geneva, Basel, and other cities in Switzerland, model dwellings were built that owed much to Roberts' prototypes. In France, the Government's ten-million franc fund that was available for one-third of the outlay on the model dwellings was responded to rather slowly by the public.

Roberts' ideas fell on fertile ground in Italy, where he resided after he left England. Both the Grand Duke of Tuscany and Cardinal Antonelli personally expressed to Roberts their interest in promoting the cause of sanitary dwellings for the poor in the Italian states over which they had influence. In 1854, the Grand Duke issued a decree for enforcing the cleansing and 'rendering wholesome' of dwelling houses occupied by persons other than the owner. Roberts was less successful in promoting his ideas in Naples, where 'the shadow of foreign intervention and propagandism proved a barrier' to all his efforts.[22] Roberts was enthusiastic about the model dwellings erected for one hundred families in Florence. A lecture was delivered in that city by the Marchese Carlo Torrigiani, who, in his *Della Abitazioni del Povero*, acknowledged Roberts and England as the sources for his ideas.

Roberts' great love for Italy is proved by his long residence in that country, and by the affectionate way in which he writes of it. Sanitary improvements had long been needed in Italy, a fact Roberts had noted from his visits to Rome and Naples in 1828-9. One of the earliest and best examples of philanthropic housing was in Florence, the city in which Roberts was to make his home, and in which he was to die in 1876. This block housed 100 families, and another range like it was built in 1867. In the same year, Roberts was able to rejoice that Naples was 'greatly benefiting by its emancipation from a rule so jealous of the semblance of foreign interference', and recalled that in 1855 the British Ambassador had cautioned him against any 'attempt to diffuse any of that light which even Cardinal Antonelli had spoken of as being especially needed in Naples'.[23]

Roberts' first paper, read before the Institute of British Architects, together with printed plans of the Streatham Street dwellings, was widely distributed in the United States of America. Partly through the offices of Abbott Lawrence, American Minister in London during the Great Exhibition of 1851, several model dwellings for families, five storeys high, were constructed in New York and in Boston. In New York the return on capital was four per cent, and in Boston it was six per cent, although the buildings in Boston owed their existence to the legacy of $50,000 bequeathed by Abbott Lawrence. Colonel Lawrence, Abbott Lawrence's son, told Roberts that the experiment had been a great success, and yielded a good return, so that money was available for the construction of additional dwellings.

In 1867 Roberts could look with some satisfaction at the results of his labours. It is not given to many men to see the children of their imaginations go forth and multiply throughout the world. The ideas of Roberts were readily accepted by enlightened persons throughout Europe and America. He was known to many sovereigns and princes, while his acquaintance with the great of many lands was enormous.

The British example was a potent one. Many measures had been adopted by individuals to encourage the working classes to help themselves. Queen Victoria gave respectability to two philanthropic societies by honouring them with royal patronage, and the labourers' dwellings actually owned by the Queen set an example which many landowners and philanthropists sought to emulate.

While Roberts noted that much had been done to fulfil a desire to place a Bible in the dwellings of all the Queen's subjects, he felt that the 'actual state of vast numbers' of the dwellings themselves might present obstacles 'to the profitable reading of that book'. Roberts felt that a weighty responsibility, that rested 'much more extensively on the upper and middle classes . . . than is generally admitted', needed to be pressed home and actively pursued. The example of the late Prince Consort was quoted. Roberts declared that his 'loss must be long and deeply felt in every branch of effort connected with the objects of social science'.[24] The Model Houses for the 1851 Exhibition have already been described. A year after the Exhibition, a lodging-house for married soldiers was built near Vauxhall Bridge Road by an association of officers of the Battalion of Guards which was later bought by the Government. The Minister of War later instigated the building of separate dwellings for the married non-commissioned officers and men at the Chatham Garrison, and a grant of £30,000 was made by Parliament for achieving the same objects elsewhere, at the 'instigation of that great friend of the soldier ... and of the labourer ... Lord Herbert'. His Lordship was also involved in improving the dwellings of the rural population.

Scarcely any of the illustrious Europeans who visited the Great Exhibition failed to examine the Prince Consort's Model Dwellings, and few returned to their own countries without some of the publications written by Roberts. According to Roberts, his designs for the Exhibition houses gave the philanthropic housing movement an impulse greater than that it received from any other single effort. His descriptive accounts of the building were translated into German and French, and a German edition was published in Berlin. These Model Dwellings were the basis for many designs all over the Continent and in America, but Roberts pointed out that the example in London that bore the closest resemblance to the original structure was at Cowley Street, Shadwell, where W. E. Hilliard caused houses for 112 families to be built on the general plan of the Prince Consort's Exhibition Model Houses. The erection of these cottages (which gave a return of seven per cent) produced excellent results in the neighbourhood. Tenants became 'sensible of the discomforts and evils of their unwholesome dwellings', and so other landlords found it necessary to improve their old houses. In Lambeth, on the property of the Prince of Wales as Duke of Lancaster, a considerable range of model dwellings, with shops on the ground floor, was built at a cost of £16,000. Lord Kinnaird, a Vice-Patron of the S.I.C.L.C., built some renovated model lodging-houses in Peter Street, Westminster, and promoted similar schemes on his property in Dundee. Roberts felt that every town ought to have such model lodging-houses, with advertisements placed at all the railway stations to advertise their existence. Roberts also noted the work of 'Miss Burdett Coutts' at Bethnal Green, and the buildings designed by H. A. Darbishire.

The growth of Benefit Building Societies[25] caused Southwood Smith, Roberts, and other reformers, some worries as they feared many of the houses built in connection with these societies would be 'inconsistent with a healthy and convenient dwelling'.[26] Roberts felt that poor standards of design would be remedied by 'the circulation of sound views on the subject through the medium of Mechanics' Institutions and kindred associations'. He advocated the exhibition of suitable plans for the dwellings of working people, as well as of 'collections of domiciliary appliances conducive to health and comfort'. Indeed, a collection of sanitary and other appliances adapted to the circumstances of the working classes had been formed under the direction of Henry Roberts at the offices of the Society for Improving the Condition of the Labouring Classes in 1850, and this led to the exhibition of a stand of model appliances at the Crystal Palace in 1851. Roberts hoped to see this collection continued and increased when, at the close of the Exhibition, the houses were removed to Kennington Park, and a proposal to that effect was made by Roberts to the Chief

Commissioner, Lord Seymour. The practical value of such a collection was recognised at the *Congrès Général d'Hygiène* in Brussels in 1852, when Roberts proposed that the utility of establishing in each country, and in principal centres of population, a kind of museum where models, plans, and specimens of materials relating to hygienic amelioration and progress should be recognised by all. Roberts' friend, Twining, had established an Economical Museum at Twickenham, near the railway station, which expanded on Roberts' own collections at the offices of the S.I.C.L.C.

Roberts' recognition of the necessity to diffuse knowledge on sanitary matters led him to follow up his declarative resolution regarding the establishment of illustrative Museums by proposing a new resolution at the *Congrès International de Bienfaisance* at Brussels in 1856. The resolution declared that 'it is of public utility that the working classes be enlightened by all possible means in regard to the improvement and keeping of their houses in good order. It declares that the instruction of the young in the labouring classes ought to comprise all which relates to the benefits resulting from good ventilation, and the evils resulting from humidity. Lastly, it thinks that the study of the science of preserving health is one which ought to be rendered accessible to all'.[27] The unanimous adoption of this resolution by the representatives of upwards of twenty different countries recognised the widespread extent of the ignorance prevailing as well as the serious nature of the problem.

The *Transactions* of the National Association for the Promotion of Social Science contain many contributions by Roberts. The *Transactions* of 1858 contain reports of the *Congrès International de Bienfaisance*.[28] The second Congress was held in Frankfurt in 1857, and members included Bethmann-Hollweg, Rogier, Ducpétiaux, Varrentrapp, and Schlemmer. The industrialist Akroyd gave a paper. The *Transactions* of 1860[29] reveal that Roberts was in Glasgow that year giving a paper, and that he gave another paper in Liverpool in 1858 to the National Association. Again, Roberts' aristocratic connections must have drawn him to the Association, for the Hon. Arthur Kinnaird and Sir John Kennaway, Bart., were on the Committee of the Association.

In these illuminating *Transactions* Roberts states unequivocally that the great project at Mulhouse was started after the appearance of the French translation of his *Dwellings of the Labouring Classes*. When the plans of the Streatham Street dwellings were published in the *North American Review* in 1852, model dwellings were built in Boston and other places.

Roberts gave a paper on 'Measures taken by Employers for Promoting Habits of Prudence and Forethought' (that is, insurance) at Burlington House in London in 1862.[30] In 1863 Roberts heard a paper by the Provost of Leith largely dealing with the evils of cesspools.[31] Roberts was also concerned with providing the labouring classes with wholesome food,[32] and he referred to his papers at Liverpool (1858), Glasgow (1860), and London (1862). His papers included information on 'Continental Establishments for the economical Supply of the Working Population with Wholesome Dressed Food'. Soup, meat, vegetables, bread, wine, and desserts were provided on a meal-ticket system at Geneva, Grenoble, Linden (near Hanover), and Mulhouse. Very cheap but nutritious meals were provided for the working classes. In 1864 Roberts was again in London,[33] and suggested the need for education on sanitary matters. Clearly he was following the ideas of Southwood Smith (his friend and the associate of Shaftesbury and Bunsen), who had died in Florence in 1861. In 1865 Roberts contributed papers on Mulhouse and Guise,[34] and referred to a paper by George Godwin on the *Familistère* at Guise.[35]

Quite apart from the main philanthropic societies, there were others that developed, including the Ladies' Sanitary Association, the Female Domestic Mission (connected with the distribution of Bibles), and the Meetings for the Instruction of Mothers. Similar associations were formed in Europe and in America. The Evangelical Conscience went hand in hand with good plumbing and sobriety.

Roberts was able to note the beneficial results of sanitary improvements in several large British cities, but he was still outraged by the 'great number of deaths that occurred annually through ignorance of elementary hygiene' and because of a culpable neglect of powers to improve matters by the authorities. The contrast between the acceptance by the public of many annual deaths caused by disease and the charitable public reaction to the accidental death of a few miners was illogical and inexcusable to Roberts. A parallel might be drawn today between the occasional air crash, and the annual toll of deaths on the roads, or as a result of smoking or other abuses.

Roberts was aware that when recommending 'sanitary ameliorations' to influential persons on the Continent, the misery and degradation of so many Britons (that could be ascribed to their domiciliary state) were reproaches to the nation. He felt that Britain should put its own house in order before criticising Europe or America.

A great many agencies would be necessary to bring about the reforms that Roberts sought. He quoted the improvements in the prisons, which were no longer 'hotbeds of fever' in his day. Better hygiene in barracks and in hospitals had halved the mortality of the inmates, a fact reported by Gladstone when Chancellor of the Exchequer.

At the Ninth Annual General Meeting of the Congress of German Political Economists at Hamburg in August 1867, attended by 305 members, the subject was 'The Dwellings of the Poor in Large Cities'. It was recognised that it was a condition of health to have pure air and more room, and to have clean, dry dwellings. Popular treatises on Sanitary Science were in the lists of books used by the National Schools in Ireland, and lectures on sanitary science were begun in many cities in Italy, France, Prussia, and Bavaria.

On 30 November 1867 Roberts sat at his desk in his home, the *Villa Niccolini*, in the Florentine suburb of Bellosguardo, to write his *Report on the Dwellings for the Working Classes, in connection with the International Exhibition in Paris, 1867*. This was reprinted for *The Labourers' Friend*, the magazine of the Society for Improving the Condition of the Labouring Classes, in January 1868. In this *Report*, Roberts mentioned lodging-houses erected by order of Napoleon III at the Avenue Bourdonnaie in Paris. This block had an internal stair, and had no features to distinguish it from other buildings in the vicinity, so it fitted into the urban fabric which consisted of buildings that were mostly four or five storeys high. Yet Roberts was critical of the planning, for it was necessary to pass through a bedroom to get to the living-room. Newton and Shephard had built a block for 42 families in the Avenue Dumesnil, using a method of construction in mass-concrete that Roberts had advocated in 1850 However, Roberts was to reserve most of his praise for the *Société des Cités Ouvrières* at Mulhouse, which had built in fourteen years houses for 800 families, of which 700 houses had been purchased by their occupants. The work of Emile Muller and of Jean Dollfus (whose name is still celebrated in the designation of streets in Mulhouse) aroused Roberts' greatest admiration. Here was a memorial to his own efforts to improve the condition of the labouring classes.[36]

Italian versions of *Home Reform* or *Advice to the Labouring Classes* were also printed. *Consigli ai Braccianti per Migliorare le loro case* 'di Henry Roberts' was published in Rome and in Florence in 1873. The concern of Roberts for the poor of Italy was not untinged with a certain Evangelical zeal to convert the Italian Papists by Good Works and Protestant Bibles. His daughter, Theodora Amélie, was to continue the Evangelical cause long after Roberts' death. There was also a most interesting connection with Garibaldi in that Shaftesbury saw in Garibaldi an agent not only of liberal reform, but of anti-Papist forces. A similar attitude of Evangelical fervour was expressed in Shaftesbury's support of Prussian arms, with their 'Teutonic and Christian glory', against the 'stay of Anti-Christ, the power by whose bayonets the Pope reigns in Rome' during the Franco–Prussian War of 1870-1.[37]

Copies of working drawings were also purchased in quantities by French, Italian, and German philanthropic housing societies.[38] Roberts himself reported that he had received through the Prussian Consul-General two copies of German translations of descriptions of the 1851 Model Dwellings at the Great Exhibition.[39] Bunsen seems to have known Roberts well, and was certainly on intimate terms with both Shaftesbury and Augustus Hare. Bunsen was also closely involved with Shaftesbury in the establishment of the bishopric in Jerusalem, a scheme that was designed to advance the Evangelical movement, to curb France, to 'nullify the Pope and to exalt Prussia' and England.[40]

One of Roberts' last works was his little pamphlet, *Efforts on the Continent for Improving the Dwellings of the Labouring Classes. Similar in the Main to those Commenced in England by the Society for their Improvement.*[41] In this booklet, printed by the Claudian Press, Roberts stated that he had spent the 'greater part' of the twenty years since 1853 'in Italy for the benefit of health'. He mentioned the large numbers of houses for workmen erected in Belgium, and progress in Italy through his aristocratic connections. An examination of the many plans of working-class housing, published largely through the efforts of Emile Muller, is sufficient to show how much the international movement to ameliorate the conditions of the working classes owed to the pioneering work of Henry Roberts, not only in the direct derivation of plan-forms, but in the interpretation of his writings. Emile Muller himself acknowledges the importance of Roberts,[42] and the Englishman's name recurs in the literature of working-class housing on the Continent.[43]

Chapter Eight

THE INFLUENCE OF HENRY ROBERTS ON LEGISLATION CONCERNING WORKING-CLASS HOUSING IN VICTORIAN BRITAIN

> The repeal of such taxes as the duty on bricks, and on windows, which pressed heavily on the construction, whilst they impeded the healthy condition of houses, was of much importance to the dwellings of the poorer classes, and was a valuable concession made to public feeling by the administration of our noble president, Lord John Russell.
>
> Henry Roberts: *The Improvement of the Dwellings of the Labouring Classes through the Operation of Governing Measures, by those of Public Bodies and Benevolent Associations, as well as Individual Efforts*, London, 1859, p.11.

HENRY ROBERTS had a great number of books and pamphlets published in his lifetime.[1] Quite apart from these works, he had many papers published in the *Transactions* of the National Association for the Promotion of Social Science:[2] in the *Transactions* of the British Association for the Advancement of Science;[3] and in the *Proceedings* of the *Congrès International de Bienfaisance*, particularly 1862. Roberts also reviewed legislative measures, including those of 1866-7.

In this chapter an outline of legislative changes and of the aftermath of Roberts' activities will be attempted. While there had been individual philanthropic efforts to improve the dwellings of the labouring classes, concerted action only began after the ravages of the cholera epidemics of the 1830s, followed by the 1837 outbreak of typhus fever. Only after these disasters did the Government department charged with the care of the poor (the Poor Law Commissioners) institute a searching medical inquiry that revealed the appalling state of housing to a largely ignorant nation.

Early reformers, like John Howard, Dr. Chalmers, and Dr. Gilly, had been in the vanguard of the early promotions of sanitary and constructional improvements before the publication of a seminal work by Henry Roberts' friend, the architect Sydney Smirke. The *Suggestions for the Architectural Improvement of the Western Part of London* appeared in 1834, and in it Smirke had advocated the amelioration of the housing conditions of the poorer inhabitants. The poor had suffered greatly in the cholera epidemic of 1832, and in 1837 typhus had claimed thousands of victims in the East End. As a result, the Poor Law Commissioners requested Dr. Southwood Smith to enquire into the sanitary condition of the poor, while Dr. Neil Arnott and Dr. Kay (later Sir J. P. Kay Shuttleworth, Bart.) examined the states of other metropolitan districts. Dr. Southwood Smith's house-to-house survey of Bethnal Green and Whitechapel showed up an appalling state of affairs. A second report of 1839 revealed statistics of disease, of premature mortality, and of physical and moral degradation on a colossal scale. In the East End, in the year ended 25 March

167

1838, out of 77,000 persons who received parochial relief, no less than 14,000 were the victims of fever.

The effects of the reports of the Commissioners produced a very deep impression on the public and on the legislature, and a combination of distinguished statesmen and philanthropists was formed with the intention of devising remedial measures.[4] The Health of Towns Association was thus formed in 1839. A Committee of the House of Commons was set up in 1840 to pursue investigations, while the subject of improving the dwellings of the labouring classes was taken up in the House of Lords by the Bishop of London, Dr. Blomfield, the father of the eminent architect. The first legislative remedial measures were introduced and carried through the House of Lords in 1841, but, owing to the prorogation of Parliament, never reached the Commons. Continued interest in the subject led in 1842 to the publication by the Poor Law Board of the *Report* of an Inquiry into the Sanitary Condition of the Labouring Population. Lord Stanley was able to refer to this *Report* in 1857 as a 'text-book of sanitary research'.[5]

In May 1842 a Royal Commission for inquiring into the states of large towns and of populous areas was set up. Illustrious members included the Duke of Buccleuch and the Duke of Newcastle. The Commission was asked to inquire 'as to how far the condition of the poorer classes of the people, and the salubrity and safety of their dwellings, may be promoted by the amendment of the laws, regulations, and usages'. The first *Report* of the Commission came out in 1844, and the second in 1845. The evidence that the Commissioners amassed was staggering, and the sources of the epidemics that destroyed so many people were traced to the insanitary dwellings of the labouring classes.

The investigations traced to the condition of the houses of the labouring classes most of the leading causes of the excessive sickness and mortality shown by the returns of the Registrar-General. In addition, the conditions of the dwellings were so poor as to suggest to the Commission a possible source of the recurring epidemics that carried off fifty per cent of the children born while yet in childhood; destroyed the heads of families in the prime of life; and deprived the poorer members of society of about one-third of their natural term of existence.

The first results of the various unpleasant disclosures enshrined in the various *Reports* were the establishment by philanthropists of the two great societies that were to work out and exhibit practical remedies for the social evils that resulted from the state of the dwellings of the labouring classes. These two societies were, of course, the Society for Improving the Condition of the Labouring Classes and the Metropolitan Association for Improving the Dwellings of the Industrious Classes. The remedies proposed by the societies would recommend themselves 'to extensive adoption by stimulating owners of existing houses, from self-interested motives, to improve and render them healthy abodes, and at the same time afford the evidence of practical results in support of appeals to the Legislature for a somewhat unprecedented interference with private property'.[6]

Roberts declared unequivocally that the Metropolitan Association was 'based on the sound and only principle on which it can be reasonably expected that the construction of improved dwellings for the labouring population in towns can be effected on a scale at all adequate to their necessity, viz. that of an investment of capital, with the prospect that, under good management, a fair return on the outlay will be realized'.[7] The S.I.C.L.C. 'was established as a professedly model institution, under the patronage of Her Majesty the Queen; H.R.H. the late Prince Consort having been its President, and the Earl of Shaftesbury, Chairman of the Committee'.[8] This Society received 'benevolent contributions to the extent of about one half its expenditure in the construction of a series of model or improved dwellings, adapted to the various circumstances of the industrial classes, and the renovation of numerous dwellings which were previously in a wretched and altogether unhealthy condition'.[9] The S.I.C.L.C. aimed at demonstrating by experience, and that with a judicious expenditure and moderate rents a fair return might be obtained from money invested. The Society took precedence in the practical commencement of exemplars, but the Metropolitan Association did not begin to build until after its incorporation by Royal Charter in 1845.

The earliest and most important legislative results of the pioneering *Reports* were the passing of the *Public Health Act* of 1848, and of the *Nuisances Removal and Diseases Prevention Act* in 1848 and 1849, with their subsequent amendments. The *Local Government Act* of 1858 effected important changes, and provided for an extensive application of local government to the carrying out of sanitary and other improvements, without recourse to a central executive or to Parliament. By this *Act* the sanitary functions of the General Board of Health were transferred to the Privy Council, and, for the purpose of carrying them out, a medical officer was attached to that department of the Government. The *Local Government Act* was amended in 1860, and again by the provisions of the *Sanitary Act* of 1866. The *Nuisances Removal and Diseases Prevention Acts* of 1848 and 1849 were amended in 1855 and again in 1860, while the second part of the *Sanitary Act* of 1866 provided for further amendments. The Regulations under the *Sanitary Act* of 1866, issued with the sanction of the Home Secretary of State, could become oppressive, Roberts felt, 'unless very carefully considered'.[10] They could also become 'perplexing in their applications', for Roberts argued for uniformity in interpretation. The *Sanitary Act* was described in the *Report* on the sanitary condition of the City of London[11] as requiring 'a very close and constant supervision of the houses of the poor'. Letheby also regarded the Act as an 'important amendment of the *Nuisances Removal Acts* of 1855 and 1860', for it not only enlarged the definition of a nuisance, but it added considerably to the power of the local authorities dealing with nuisances.[12]

In 1851 an *Act* was passed to enable parishes or boroughs (containing not fewer than 10,000 inhabitants) either to build new houses, or to adapt old ones, with a view to the provision of better lodgings for the labouring classes. Power was also given to raise money and to defray the expenses out of the poor rates, such houses being made self-supporting as far as possible.

In the same year, at the instigation of Lord Shaftesbury, an *Act* was passed for regulating common lodging-houses, a piece of legislation described by Roberts as 'a measure second only to the Public Health Act as to its necessity and the importance of its results'. This legislation was amended in 1853, and was made compulsory in its operation in that local authorities were bound to carry it into effect. Conditions of cleanliness, proper ventilation, the avoidance of overcrowding, and the separation of the sexes were enforced, all aspects of proposed reforms that Roberts had been championing for a very considerable time. This legislation was intended to help the itinerant artisans or labourers who had not the means to procure a better home. Roberts was to note that 'the want of a power enforcing such regulations generally, in all tenements in towns let at low weekly rents to the working population, which was granted in the city of London in 1851, and there operates most beneficially, has long been felt and urged in various ways: to what extent "The Sanitary Act, 1866", will effect the much desired improvements remains to be seen'.

As a direct result of the activities of the two great pioneering societies and of the efforts of Henry Roberts, a Bill entitled The *Labourers' Dwelling Act* was passed in 1855 to promote the building of dwellings for the labouring classes and to provide for the registration of Joint Stock Companies formed for that purpose. This legislative measure greatly facilitated the formation and general management of independent local associations (conducted on the principle of Joint Stock Companies) with limited liability. Bills were also passed with the same view applicable exclusively to Scotland and Ireland to facilitate the building of cottages for labourers in 1860.

In 1866 an *Act* was passed to enable the Public Works Loan Commissioners to make advances towards the erection of dwellings for the labouring classes, whereby the carrying out of powers granted in the *Act* of 1851 was greatly facilitated. Railway, Dock, and other companies that employed large numbers, and private individuals who held land for an unexpired term of not less than fifty years, were included in the provisions of this *Act*, which was amended in 1867.

The two legislative measures adopted in England for the repeal of duties that pressed heavily on the construction or tended to impede the healthy condition of houses were directly the result of the work of Henry Roberts. These were Window Tax and a duty on bricks. At Streatham Street, Roberts regarded the gallery access to the flats as external streets, while the official view was that the building was one block. Roberts and the Society argued persuasively against the official view, and the government had to agree eventually to repealing Window Tax as a result. In due course the House of Lords adopted a Standing Order with a view to ascertaining the necessity for enforcing the building of suitable dwellings for the working classes in lieu of any that might be demolished under powers granted by Parliament for the carrying out of public improvements, or by the works of large companies.

Roberts regarded that the most necessary legislative measures to be adopted after 1867 should be those 'imperatively obliging owners of unhealthy dwellings either to put them into a good sanitary condition, to part with them to those who would do so, to close them, or to pull them down'.[13] In such cases, property 'would then cease to have the fictitious value which now generally renders it an unprofitable or an inadequately remunerative investment to those who, from benevolent motives, seek the ownership with a view to its renovation. The Bills hitherto introduced into Parliament with this view do not appear to have received that deliberate consideration which the difficulties surrounding it render necessary, in order to their being fully met'.[14] In other words, Roberts was advocating twentieth-century legislation that only recognised the site value of unfit or sub-standard dwellings.

Roberts attributed the climate in which legislative reforms had been enacted to the many people involved in ameliorating the condition of the labouring classes, including the societies and the great landowners. He also paid tribute to benevolent industrialists like Titus Salt, Akroyd, and others. He especially noted the contribution of 'the example of the late Prince Consort . . . particularly to the impulse it received on the Continent'.[15] Landlords, according to Roberts, were 'beginning to find that tenants' insisted on having good cottages, 'because good labourers are otherwise unobtainable'. Roberts himself was responsible for many designs for improved cottages, and so was an agent of real reform in both country and town. His plans were readily available in printed form not only in the British Isles, but on a world-wide basis. His influence was immense, as an examination of later plans by European architects in the archives of the *Société Industrielle de Mulhouse* makes clear.

In the towns, Roberts' 1851 Great Exhibition exemplars provided the prototypes for many later buildings. They 'had always been intended as a prototype capable of vertical and lateral expansion'.[16] Sydney Waterlow 'took the single staircase "unit" and built it up to five floors in height, the practical maximum for "walk-up" flats in the last century, and eventually he added several units, together making a terrace. The staircase was centrally placed, giving access to an open balcony on each floor, from which two tenements were reached. This much did Waterlow and Allen take from Roberts' design, but the internal planning of the dwellings they worked out for themselves, on the whole with less satisfactory results than if they had adopted Roberts' own plan in its entirety'.[17] A study of plans by philanthropic organisations, and by local authorities, and by benevolent industrialists demonstrates that the plans by Henry Roberts were not only the basis upon which most later designs were built, but that in almost every case, Roberts' plans of the 1850s were more ingenious, and certainly more self-contained than even plans of the 1890s. The London County Council Boundary Street Estate, begun in 1893 as a result of the *Housing Act* of 1890, did not have self-contained water-closets, for example, and the planning was far inferior to that of Roberts' exemplars forty years previously.

It is interesting to consider the 'remarkable flurry of legislative activity', as Professor Anthony S. Wohl puts it,[18] that occurred between 1850 and 1880. That the activities of Henry Roberts, both as a tireless lecturer and writer, and as a designer of exemplars, played no small part in this activity cannot be doubted, although many commentators have failed to recognise the fact. Some forty major *Acts* of Parliament that were concerned with public health were passed. But the Government gradually 'came to appreciate that working-class housing constituted a set of problems quite distinct from those associated with public health, and gradually housing legislation began to embrace a concept of coherent slum clearance and urban renewal'.[19] As Professor Wohl states, by 1880 'the problem of the supply of houses for the labouring classes, rather than the cleansing of already existing houses, was beginning to attract the attention of politicians'.[20]

The history of legislation from 1850 is bound up with the names of both Shaftesbury and Roberts, and gradually Shaftesbury, as the leading parliamentary voice for reform, adopted Roberts' view that specific legislation was needed to improve the conditions of the labouring classes. Indeed, Shaftesbury's desires to see better housing were expressed in terms that are Roberts' own of that date. The 1851 *Acts*, known as the Shaftesbury Acts, were the *Common Lodging Houses Act*[21] and the *Labouring Classes Lodging Houses Act*.[22] The first established the principle of registration and inspection of lodging-houses, and the second permitted the vestries to purchase land and build housing, borrowing the necessary money using the rates as security. In 1851 the *City Sewers Act*[23] extended the *Act* of 1848 in that it permitted the right of inspection of common lodging-houses to all residences, prohibited cellar-dwellings, and made the demolition of houses possible on grounds of general public health. The *Nuisances Act* of 1855 helped to establish an effective inspectorate.

In 1855 there was further legislation. The *Metropolis Local Management Act*[24] made it necessary for every vestry to appoint a medical officer of health in London, and laid the foundations for a public-health inspectorate in local government. The *Nuisances Removal Act*[25] insisted that overcrowding was a danger to public health, and was the first attempt to control overcrowding outside the lodging-houses. The *Metropolitan Building Act*[26] put the district surveyors and the operation of the *Building Acts* under the control of a new centralised authority in London: the Metropolitan Board of Works.

Roberts had carried out surveys of buildings and courts for the S.I.C.L.C. Sir John Simon, when medical officer to the Privy Council, worked towards the simplification and consolidation of sanitary reform, and employed Dr. Hunter in 1865 in a survey of overcrowding in towns. The published arguments of Roberts were of singular importance in encouraging such surveys, and from Hunter's research emerged a dreadful tale of widespread overcrowding. The *Sanitary Act* of 1866[27] was the result of the efforts of Simon and of Hunter, and, ultimately, was inspired by the sound reasoning of Henry Roberts in his various books dealing with the condition of dwellings.[28] The *Act* was 'a major landmark in the development of public health activity and central-local relations in the nineteenth century'.[29] It insisted on the joining of all houses to main sewers, and limited the uses of cellars as habitable rooms. It contained provisions to control overcrowding, using standards of air space per occupant to define overcrowding. Roberts had long argued for such standards to be set.[30] The National Association for the Promotion of Social Science, with which Roberts and his friends were so closely connected, began to agitate for further compulsion in controlling the condition of housing.

The repeal of the Window Tax in 1851, directly as a result of the work of Roberts, and the repeal of further taxes on bricks in 1850, on glass in 1860, and on timber in 1866 freed the building industry from harsh taxation, and the benefits were considerable. The climate of opinion that led to their repeal was largely the creation of Henry Roberts, whose writings and lectures constantly reiterated his opposition to such taxes. There were also changes in the laws relating to the sale and exchange of land that helped the development of artisans' dwellings. Companies wishing to acquire land had been hindered by the law of mortmain, by which corporations were prohibited from holding land without licences.[31] In addition, company law made the setting-up of model-dwelling companies risky and expensive. The *Limited Liability Acts* of 1855 and 1862, and the *Dwelling Houses for the Labouring Classes Act* of 1855[32] helped to ease the establishment of companies to build housing for the working classes. The

Labouring Classes Dwelling Houses Act of 1866[33] enabled companies, local government, private individuals, and railway and dock organisations to borrow from the Public Works Loan Commissioners at four per cent interest for up to one half of the total value of the land and buildings, repayable over forty-one years.[34] The legislation included standards of construction for dwellings, and it was stated that each tenement should have its own water-closet. Sizes of rooms were also laid down. Clearly the original inspiration for this legislation came from the published works of Henry Roberts, from his tireless advocacy of sound common sense and of businesslike principles, and from his widespread influence as a lecturer, pamphleteer, and moulder of opinion.

The costs of raising money to build housing for the working classes created great difficulties even in the halcyon days of loans at four per cent. The Society for the Encouragement of Arts, Manufacturers, and Commerce had recommended three-and-a-half per cent loans for the purpose. Shaftesbury had called for one-and-a-half or even a two per cent rate of interest, as the vast majority of workers earning less than twelve shillings a week could only afford two shillings maximum in rent. The abolition of taxes on building materials, and the provision in legislation for public loans over long periods at low rates of interest indicated that the Government began to recognise that the open market could not provide an answer to the housing problem in central areas. Effectively, Government subsidies in the form of loans below the market rate created a climate in which philanthropic societies could flourish, and by 1875 over a quarter of a million pounds had been lent.[35] Roberts himself had long argued for cheap loans to offset the costs of land in central areas, and he had been one of the first to recognise that workers on low wages could not afford high rents and so would continue to inhabit the insanitary overcrowded dwellings at rents (exorbitant though they were) they could afford.

The 1860s saw legislation passed for which Roberts had argued consistently and convincingly since the 1840s. Tax reductions or abolition of duty on building materials aided private enterprise; low-interest Government loans helped the philanthropic dwelling companies; and two *Acts* relating to overcrowding and sanitation gave local authorities powers of entry, of cleansing, and for preventing overcrowding. However, many authorities were not keen to prosecute for insanitary overcrowding because of the dangers of great numbers of evictions. As Roberts had argued, power to evict was only proper where there was an obligation to rehouse. He had been particularly critical of the behaviour of railways and docks, which had the power to evict, but which exacerbated the housing problem by not providing housing to replace that which had been destroyed.

In order to get over this problem, the M.P. Torrens introduced a Bill to set up local municipal government as a major agent of slum clearance and of urban renewal.[36] Unfortunately the Bill ran into considerable opposition from those devoted to *laissez-faire*. Roberts himself had argued strongly for new legislation throughout the 1850s and 1860s, and it is clear he was firmly convinced of the need for radical Government measures to help philanthropic societies, private individuals, and, if necessary, public interference with private interests for the common good. Roberts, like Torrens, was one of the first commentators to recognise that the terrible housing problem needed a radical approach that would run contrary to the principles of *laissez-faire*. Roberts had insisted on the need to create healthy dwellings in order to secure health, fitness, and decent behaviour among the working classes. Moral and intellectual improvement, he argued, could only be achieved if the dwellings were uncrowded, self-contained, well-ventilated, dry, and well-designed. Torrens also recognised the truth of Roberts' arguments, and Torrens' remarks concerning the health of the working classes echo those of Roberts in his many pamphlets and books, even to the extent of almost verbatim quotation.

Unfortunately Torrens' Bill was rendered virtually toothless by a Select Committee of the House of Lords, on which Shaftesbury and the Bishop of London sat. Indeed Shaftesbury's attitude towards Torrens is also reflected in the S.I.C.L.C.s treatment of Roberts in 1856, and is very likely due to Roberts' increasing insistence that *laissez-faire* in housing was not entirely the solution and would not solve the problem alone. Indeed, the success of the S.I.C.L.C. was entirely due to Roberts, and when he ceased to be involved, the Society became unimportant as an innovator, as a provider of exemplars, and as a driving force. It settled down to be a respectable, orthodox philanthropic Society, and lost its position as a leader of the movement to promote improvements. When the *Artizans' and Labourers' Dwellings Act*[37] was passed, it was shorn of all its armaments. Some vestries attempted to become active under the *Act*, but the pitfalls were great, and most local authorities ignored the *Act*. While Shaftesbury and others recognised the necessity of destroying foul dwellings, they were less willing to accept the defeat of *laissez-faire* by creating legislation that would force action to rehouse the evicted. Unquestionably, Roberts' arguments in his published works from the 1860s onwards were increasingly radical. He thus became a leader in the movement for legislative reform, and helped to create a climate in which interference with the rights of both the individual and of private property became acceptable.

Roberts' papers to the National Association for the Promotion of Social Science, and to many other bodies, were very influential. The Conservative Party was to be instrumental in helping to promote urban reform and Roberts' ideas, partly because Gladstone's Liberals were curiously uninterested in the challenge of urban problems, and partly because *laissez-faire* was essential to Gladstonian Liberalism. The *Artisans Dwellings Sites and Transfer Act*[38] was a Conservative enactment that helped the sale of land by local government to individuals and to companies willing to build artisans' dwellings.

Professor Anthony S. Wohl has admirably traced the story of gradual consolidation of legislation in his work.[39] The *Artizans' and Labourers' Dwellings Improvement Act*[40] was still fairly permissive but it contained compensation clauses and to local authorities it gave powers for rehousing. It further stimulated work by bodies like the Peabody Trust. Subsequently there were amendments which created powers whereby an owner of property that was scheduled for demolition or alteration could compel the local authority to purchase his dwelling, thus causing additional waves of caution to break among the vestries. Later *Acts*[41] lowered the rate of compensation, which was calculated on the market value minus the estimated costs of repairs or of the abatement of the nuisance. The *Artizan's Dwellings Act* of 1882[42] enabled vestries to demolish buildings which were either unhealthy or prevented other buildings from being healthy through the obstruction of light and air. At the same time it only obliged the Metropolitan Board of Works to rehouse half the number of persons evicted in any scheme.

Roberts' demands for new standards to ensure sound buildings that were safe and healthy were largely met by the *Metropolis Management and Building Amendment Act* of 1878,[43] while his arguments in favour of creating conditions where the working classes could buy their property were taken account of in the *Chambers and Offices Act* of 1881[44] and in the *Public Works Loan Act* of 1879. The culminating *Act* that resulted from the work of the Royal Sanitary Commission was, of course, the *Public Health Act* of 1875,[45] which consolidated the sanitary, abatement of nuisance, and public health enactments. It also defined overcrowding, and made it illegal even if only one family were involved.

The *Act for Consolidating and Amending the Acts relating to Public Health in England* gave existing authorities (town and borough councils, Boards of Improvement Commissioners, local Boards of Health formed under the *Public Health Act* of 1848, Local Boards formed under the *Local Government Act* of 1858, and the Boards of Guardians), powers to control conditions. The Local Government Board established standards for housing, and these standards became the base for all bye-laws relating to level, width, and construction of sewerage; to the structure of walls, foundations, roofs, and chimneys; to the space around buildings and the ventilation of buildings; to the drainage of buildings; and to their closure if unfit.

The Legislation up to 1875 laid the foundations of a national policy of slum clearance as well as a code for house-builders. New stimulus was given to the solving of the housing question, many new organisations were established, and some of the older associations were galvanised into further action. Until 1890 private enterprise was the main agency through which the working classes were housed. Professor Tarn has described the architectural and spatial solutions that occurred under the 1875 *Act.*[46] The Metropolitan Board of Works displaced great numbers of people, cleared several acres of slum property, and ensured that the housing agencies rehoused the displaced. Professor Tarn has shown that in one instance an average of 540 people per acre were housed in airless and insanitary courts. The areas cleared were developed by sixteen schemes at 660 persons per acre, but the new buildings, though barrack-like, were a great improvement in terms of construction, sanitary arrangements, and ventilation. Such densities demonstrate the problems of housing enough people on central sites to be able to attempt to make the venture an economic proposition.

In the 1880s the National Association for the Promotion of Social Science (a body with which Roberts had been actively concerned, and which had friends of Roberts, including the Hon. Arthur Kinnaird, on its Committee) pressed for further sanitary reforms, and urged that suburban areas should be brought under the control of the urban authorities. The huge losses incurred by the Metropolitan Board prevented further action in demolition and rehousing. The result was that Parliament had to set up a Select Committee which met in 1881. In 1882 it produced a *Report* that dealt with existing legislation. This *Report* pointed out that legislation from 1868–75 was based on 'the principle that the responsibility of maintaining his house in proper condition falls upon the owner, and that if he fails in his duty the law is justified in stepping in and compelling him to perform it'.[47] Existing laws assumed 'that houses unfit for human habitation ought not to be used as dwellings, but ought, in the interest of the public, to be closed and demolished, and to be subsequently rebuilt. The expropriation of the owner is thus a secondary step in the transaction, and only takes place after the failure of other means of rendering the houses habitable'.[48] Legislation from 1875 was based 'upon a different principle'. It contemplated 'dealing with whole areas', where the houses were 'so structurally defective as to be incapable of repair, and so ill placed with reference to each other as to require, to bring them up to a proper sanitary standard, nothing short of demolition and reconstruction'. Accordingly, the local authority, 'armed with compulsory powers', could at once enter as a purchaser, and on the completion of the purchase, could proceed 'forthwith to a scheme of reconstruction'.[49]

Unfortunately, high compensation, expensive procedures, and the requirement to sell the land solely for housing contributed to the considerable costs of implementing the so-called 'Cross Acts'. Evidence was given to the Select Committee that dwellings which were unfit should be valued only in terms of site value and any materials retrieved from their demolition, and this evidence was accepted. It became an important principle of subsequent housing policy, and was something for which Roberts had argued in his lectures and in his pamphlets. In 1882 the *Artizans' Dwellings Act*[50] was passed, and set out new machinery to reduce compensation and to reduce the obligation to rehouse the displaced, so freeing land for other purposes. In 1883 Parliament passed another *Act*, the *Cheap Trains Act*,[51] an enactment that Roberts had proposed years earlier. This gave the Board of Trade powers to insist that the Railway Companies should provide cheap travel on suburban lines (in return for tax relief) so that workers could move out to the new, cheaper suburbs. Of course cheap trains were to enable a new type of suburban development to evolve. Bedford Park was one of the earliest and most distinguished examples of a type of garden suburb which Roberts had seen could be possible.

Roberts had complained of 'the bungling and pettifogging manner in which many of our new streets have been formed, and fine opportunities for obtaining magnificent effects irrecoverably lost'.[52] He also complained of the 'want of a *compulsory*[53] provision for the displaced poor'.[54] Roberts had referred to 'clauses in some of the railway bills obliging the companies to provide certain cheap trains, at hours suitable for the conveyance of working people to and from the precincts of their residences out of town'.[55]

During the 1880s there was considerable literary activity which has been more than adequately covered by others.[56] In 1884 a Royal Commission was appointed to investigate the housing of the working classes that included Lords Carrington and Salisbury, the Prince of Wales, J. E. C. Bodley, Sir Charles Dilke, Cardinal Manning, Lord Brownlow, G. J. Goschen, The Bishop of Bedford, W. T. Torrens, Jesse Collings, G. Godwin, Lord Shaftesbury, Sir Richard Cross, Samuel Morley, H. Broadhurst, and the Hon. E. L. Stanley. The Commissioners heard much evidence of overcrowding that led to incest and promiscuity, something that Henry Roberts had been arguing thirty years before. The evidence that working-class housing was far too expensive, and that widespread problems existed was overwhelming. Even Lord Shaftesbury had to admit that existing legislation (that he had been instrumental in watering down on the grounds of protecting private interests) was inadequate. The work of the Commission painted a dismal picture, and indicated that philanthropic remedies were no longer capable of coping with the problem, while the vestries were not implementing existing *Acts*. The *Report* of the Commission was published in 1885, and stressed that overcrowding was a major problem, caused by high rents and by the necessity of artisans to live near their work, something Roberts had pointed out in the 1850s. Indeed, nearly all the findings of the Royal Commission simply confirmed what Roberts had been saying all along.

The *Report* began modern legislation to solve the problem of working-class housing, for it indicated clearly that the laws of supply and demand in cities had created terrible problems. It pointed out that overcrowding was caused by the relationship between wages and rents. The *Housing of the Working Classes Act*[57] was passed in 1885, and introduced the principle of state intervention in housing. It was denounced by many as a Socialist measure in that central government was accepting the idea of subsidies in the form of land and low interest for the supply of working-class accommodation. The powers of an owner to require a local authority to purchase insanitary dwellings were revoked. The first steps towards the approval of municipal Socialism for housing had been taken.

The scandal of the Jack the Ripper murders in Whitechapel in the autumn of 1888 drew national attention to the dreadful conditions in London's East End.[58] This was the last straw. So great was the publicity and so terrible were the appalling murders that public opinion swung behind more draconian reform. The result was the passing of the *Housing of the Working Classes Act* of 1890[59] which organised sanitary and housing legislation on a national basis, and at last provided the armoury for slum clearance. The Kingdom moved towards the twentieth century as a more responsible society, with stringent controls over building development, open space standards, and sanitation. In addition, state interference was accepted. The 1890 *Act* was only the beginning of a great number of later laws that were to develop as a result of the pioneering work of the Victorian reformers, notably Henry Roberts. This watershed enshrined much of what Henry Roberts had advocated in the 1850s, 60s, and 70s. Roberts was the original mind behind the reforms that became law in the last decade of Queen Victoria's reign. His was the guiding spirit that took working-class housing from insanitary hovels and created new, hygienic dwellings. The safety, the health, and the quality of life of a very great part of the population can be attributed to the efforts of Henry Roberts, the architect and thinker who influenced two generations of reformers in the field of working-class housing, as well as the law-makers themselves.

Chapter Nine

A SUMMING-UP.
THE IMPORTANCE OF ROBERTS AND AN EVALUATION
OF HIS IDEAS AND OF HIS ARCHITECTURE

To show how man can help man, notwithstanding the complicated state of civilized
society, ought to be the aim of every philanthropic person; but it is more peculiarly the
duty of those who, under the blessing of Divine Providence, enjoy station, wealth and
education . . .

Prince Albert, at the Annual General Meeting of the Society for Improving the Condition
of the Labouring Classes, 18 May 1848.

BY ANY STANDARDS, Henry Roberts had a successful career as an architect. After
the splendours of the Fishmongers' Hall (designed while he was still in his twenties) he
managed through his aristocratic and Evangelical connections to carry out a number of
important commissions for country houses, extensions, and churches throughout the
country. The Fishmongers' Hall is unquestionably his masterpiece (Plates 5-15), but
the fine terminus building at London Bridge was not undistinguished (Plate 33). The
country houses at Alphington (Plate 37), Escot (Plates 26-30), and Norton Fitzwarren
(Plates 34-36) are all solid, workmanlike, and pleasing, while the additions at Exton
(Plate 51) show a sensitivity to the existing buildings and to the site. Escot is an
unusually massive and unconventional building, with an ingenious plan. The churches
are generally undistinguished, though inoffensive, but they are all cast within an
unmistakeably Evangelical mould. Roberts handled Gothic uneasily, and his larger
churches at Nottingham and Whitechapel, though competent, are clumsily composed
(Plates 54 and 40-41). Escot church (Plate 31) is a simple nave with a chancel, and is
perhaps his most successful essay in ecclesiastical Gothic, while Hartley Wintney (Plate
32) is a solid piece of mechanical Romanesque. Wigtown is not elegant, but is in a dour
Presbyterian tradition found throughout Scotland (Plate 55). In fact the latter church
is so Scottish that it is perhaps a tribute to Roberts' skill that he was able to produce
such a convincing specimen of native lowland Scots kirk architecture. Additions to
existing buildings, such as those at Toft (Plates 52-53), or Yoxford church (Plates
24-25), are handled tactfully.

It is with his work for the improvement of housing for the working classes,
however, that Roberts becomes of international importance. The early experiment
of 1844 on Lord Calthorpe's land was not earth-shaking, but the achievements at
Streatham Street and for the Great Exhibition were. These were perhaps the most
influential exemplars of model housing ever designed, and they became world-famous.
The designs were distributed throughout the civilised world, and the plans set new

standards for hygienic and healthy dwellings. It was largely through Roberts' efforts that the iniquitous taxes on windows and on bricks and on other building materials were repealed, and Streatham Street was the test-case. Streatham Street (now Parnell House) was a masterpiece, a design of the highest distinction, and an indictment of those architects who could not accept that cheap housing was 'architecture'. The Model Dwellings for the 1851 Exhibition were not only immensely ingenious, but they were in advance of the planning of their day, and were infinitely capable of variation. The plans could be repeated upwards *and* horizontally, and they caused a sensation when they were published. Roberts' basic plan was copied throughout Europe and in America, although the external appearance of the dwellings was not usually followed. As an exhibition building Roberts' design was far more important in its impact for the mass of the people than Mies van der Rohe's Barcelona Pavilion, or any of the far more famous exhibition buildings erected in this century. The basic plan form was still in use in the twentieth century.

Roberts' designs for Lodging-Houses and Model Dwellings set new standards of accommodation for the poor. He was the man who translated desirable theory into practice. Roberts was the practical man and the theoriser of the Evangelical Conscience. The practical Christianity of the Clapham Sect was to bring about reforms of a revolutionary nature through men like Wilberforce. Evangelical zeal was to be behind the life of Lord Shaftesbury, and reforms went far beyond the erection of a few model dwellings. Roberts approached his work as a reformer from a social, moral, professional, and religious point of view.[1] Like the French designers of the *Phalanstère*, and other pioneers, Roberts was interested in communal planning, and indeed was one of the first to succeed in integrating communal uses with the residential quarters. There were communal wash-houses at his Bagnigge Wells scheme, communal areas at the George Street Model Lodging-House, and at other such schemes. At Streatham Street, however, there were communal open spaces, communal galleries, and communal workshops, as well as wash-houses. At Windsor there was also a bake-house. Roberts was particularly anxious to give a heart to his schemes by providing communal facilities, and he greatly admired the pioneering experiment at Guise, where shops, schools, and even a communal hall were provided. Roberts was one of the first visionary planners whose ideas were quickly taken up by others in many places in Britain. Later developments at Bournville, Saltaire, Port Sunlight, and other places were extensions of proposals that had initially been made by French radical thinkers, and that had been first tried in a modest way by Robert Owen in Great Britain. Jeremy Bentham, of course, had proposed a *Panopticon* and other ideas that had more of an influence on the European Continent than in Britain. Nevertheless, it is interesting that both Henry Roberts, for the S.I.C.L.C., and William Beck, for the M.A.I.D.I.C., were the first architects of modern times to plan communally for the working classes in Britain. That the ideas of providing communal facilities such as workshops and libraries in tightly planned urban blocks should have been pioneered in the 1840s in Britain is significant. Roberts was always closely in touch with radical ideas for reform in Europe, and his experiments are closely allied with the more famous experiments of Fourier, Godin, Owen, Saint-Simon, Cabét, and others. The fact of the matter is that Roberts was able to persuade a group of Evangelical Christian philanthropists to incorporate facilities that were advocated by radical Europeans, notably Frenchmen (of whom English Evangelicals were deeply suspicious), into buildings designed by him for the S.I.C.L.C. He was also able to publish radical ideas in his collected writings issued by the Society. There is no doubt that Roberts was deeply influenced by, and interested in, radical notions, no matter from whence they came. His intellectual curiosity was such that he could appreciate a good idea at once, despite its origins. Shaftesbury was so deeply prejudiced against France and all ideas that emanated from France, that he was unable to see with Roberts' clarity of vision.

Cleanliness, education, sobriety, and godliness could only be achieved if the poor had decent housing. The work of the Clapham Sect became a model for the nation to follow. Most of Roberts' rich clients had connections with the Evangelical movement, with Clapham, with Shaftesbury, or with the various philanthropic organisations. The Fishmongers' Company was connected with University College and with Benthamite notions of reform, but otherwise Roberts was mostly associated with Tory Evangelicals. The key figures in Roberts' career were the Seventh Earl of Shaftesbury, the Rev. Baptist Wriothesley Noel, and the Hon. Arthur Fitzgerald Kinnaird. Through them Roberts was introduced to the London Missions, to various Evangelical bodies, and to Associations for promoting education, social science, cleanliness, and better conditions among the poor. Noel himself had the Thorntons, Wilberforce, and Zachary Macaulay (all members of the Clapham Sect) in his congregation at Bedford Row, and he was a leading figure in the attempts to evangelise France as well as England. The Evangelical movement tended to support causes like those of Garibaldi and Mazzini, and was militant in its attempts to bring Protestantism to Roman Catholic Ireland, Italy, and France. Shaftesbury himself was vigorously anti-Papal in his activities, and sympathised with Prussia in 1870-1 on the grounds that Prussia was Evangelical while France supported the Pope. The Prussian connection went back to the appointment of Alexander as first Anglican Bishop of Jerusalem. Lord Calthorpe was a leading Evangelical, as were Sir John Kennaway, Bart., Kennaway's son, the Hon. Arthur Fitzgerald Kinnaird (later the tenth Baron), Kinnaird's wife, Sir John Dean Paul, Bart., the Earl of Galloway, and many others who knew Roberts. J. A. Giles was an Evangelical, and Roberts himself was firmly of the Evangelical persuasion. Sir Harry Verney, Bart., another client of Roberts, was at Harrow with the young Ashley-Cooper, later Earl of Shaftesbury. The Duke of Manchester was also involved in philanthropic and Evangelical activities. The Prussian Bunsen was also an Evangelical and a philanthropist, as was Southwood Smith.

Henry Roberts had a very big network of clients, all of whom were connected either by blood or by marriage, or through philanthropy or Evangelical Christianity. The friendship with the Noels survived Baptist Noel's death in 1873, for Roberts nominated his 'friend Ernest Noel Esquire of No. 6, Albermarle Street' to be a guardian of his daughter Theodora Amélie during her minority.[2] Ernest Noel was also known to Augustus J. C. Hare. The Evangelical fervour survived Henry Roberts too, for his daughter Theodora Amélie Roberts (1856-1916) was the founder and for thirty-five years Directress of the Medical Mission at Florence.[3]. When Theodora Amélie's Will was proved, probate was granted to Frederick Albert Roberts, Francis Hare Clayton (who ultimately inherited F. A. Roberts' house at Grayswood) of 10, Lancaster Place, and Thomas Boston Bruce of the Temple on 3 June 1916.[4] £3,200 in stock was left in trust for the Florence Medical Mission, and £2,500 was to be divided among five other charities. The report in *The Times*, referring to her total estate of £18,745, inaccurately refers to her brother, but an examination of the Will[5] makes it clear that the 'brother' is in fact her cousin, Frederick Albert Roberts. The Will gave Theodora Amélie's address as *27 Lungo-il-Mugnone (Viale Milton)*,[6] and the beneficiaries were her late mother's 'Secretary and Amanuensis', Elena Casella *née* Giglioni. The silver plate that Lord Shaftesbury presented to Roberts in 1853 was already in England, and was left to Frederick Albert Roberts. Other monies were left to Edith Annie Roberts, Frances Gay Roberts, and Eva Maria Roberts, daughters of her cousin Charles Gay Roberts. Most of Theodora Amélie's money was invested in the London Brighton and South Coast Railway, clearly a residue of Henry Roberts' estate, and a reminder of Henry's and Josiah's interest in railways in the 1840s. From the Will it is clear that the Schéhavtzoffs were cousins of the de Swetchines, and so Lydia A. D. Roberts married a relative. Pierre de Schéhavtzoff was still alive when Theodora Amélie made her Will, for he is referred to as her brother-in-law. Considerable sums were left to the Medical Missionary Association of 49, Highbury Park, and the bulk went to the Florence Medical Mission. There was a proviso, however, for, if on the 'advice of the *Table Vaudoise* of the Waldensian Church in Italy, the Florence Medical Mission' was not being carried forward on 'distinctly Evangelical lines' then the funds would stop. The zeal of the 1830s as shown by the Clapham Sect, by Noel, Shaftesbury, and Roberts, had not waned.[7]

Henry Roberts was not only the chief theorist and practical man in the field of working-class housing. He was aware of the need to educate the masses to eat properly, to use leisure fruitfully, and to become versed in hygiene, both personal and domestic. His pamphlets *The circulation of a pure and instructive literature, adapted to the capacities and means of the labouring population*, and *La réforme domestique, ou conseils aux personnes de la classe ouvrière pour l'amélioration et la bonne tenue de leurs demeurs*, together with his various papers given to the *Congrès International de Bienfaisance*, show him to have been intensely aware of the wider issues involved in the bettering of the condition of the labouring classes.

It becomes clear from Roberts' own writings, especially where he is concerned with a rational approach to housing, to hygiene, to adequate food, warmth, and clothing, to light, and to air, that he was moving away from the original philanthropic paternalism to something akin to Christian Socialism. His advocacy of compulsory purchase, of Government action to prevent land for building houses being excessively expensive, and of better standards heralds the ideas of later generations of social reformers.

As has already been established, Roberts was just as concerned with improving the dwellings of the labouring classes in the country as in the towns. Early inspections of conditions in the East End of London by Drs. Southwood Smith, Neil Arnott, and Kay, revealed a state of things that was profoundly shocking. Yet conditions in rural areas were not pleasant either, and commentators such as James Silk Buckingham painted an appalling picture of the sanitary state of cottages in Ireland, England, and Scotland.[8] Roberts himself drew attention[9] to the returns of the

Registrar-General for Scotland in which alarming rates of illegitimacy were reported in country districts where cottages were grossly overcrowded.

The work which Roberts carried out for the Windsor Royal Society was to bear fruit, just as his many designs for model cottages were to be copied throughout the Kingdom. The Society for Improving the Condition of the Labouring Classes published plans, working drawings, and specifications for model cottages designed by Roberts from 1844 onwards, and also published his designs for the Windsor Royal Society. The first plan and description of a 'double cottage for an agricultural district' by Roberts was agreed for publication in December of 1844[10] and each set of plans was offered for sale at a guinea a set. During the course of the next ten years Roberts produced a great number of model plans for agricultural cottages. These were greatly varied, and incorporated every possible type of material that was likely to be available locally (Figures 30–41). Roberts also encouraged the use of his own patent hollow bricks (patented in 1849) for the construction of these cottages, and always allowed a small number (about 20,000) of these bricks to be manufactured privately before he charged any royalty. The Duke of Manchester built several cottages on his Huntingdon estates using the hollow bricks which he had had made locally. These cottages are precisely in accordance with Roberts' published designs. Throughout England there are thousands of cottages built to Roberts' designs, or derived from those designs, either from the patterns sold by the S.I.C.L.C., or from one-off plans produced for landowners. The designs reproduced here identify the commonest types.

Considerable publicity was given to designs for labourers' cottages, not only in England, but in France, where an account of the village of Mowcop, Staffordshire, was published. The vehicle for publicity in Italy was 'an Italian Protestant Almanac'.[11] The Evangelical movement was again behind the housing reform movement, even in Roman Catholic Italy, where radical ideas were promoted by forces opposed to clerical authority. It is not surprising that the anti-Papist Evangelicals found fertile ground for their ideas among liberal, nationalist, and anti-clerical Italians.

Roberts argued passionately that the weighty responsibility for providing housing for the labouring classes rested on the upper and middle classes to a much greater extent than was officially admitted. Roberts argued that conditions were generally so bad that 'tens of thousands of human lives' were 'sacrificed annually in Great Britain through ignorance and the culpable neglect of means' that were within the nation's power to remedy. Yet, 'owing to the noiseless and almost imperceptible way in which such multitudes' were carried off by preventible diseases, there was no 'manifestation of the practical sympathy so justly shown by the public, when, through some lamentable accident, a score, or perhaps hundreds', were suddenly deprived of life, and their families of the means of subsistence.

After Roberts retired to Italy in 1853, the housing movement, in the words of Professor Tarn, 'had been searching for fresh inspiration, the injection of more money', and perhaps for 'the arrival of some dynamic personality willing to face the problems of rising building costs and soaring land values'.[12] Both Waterlow and Peabody brought practical help, but by 1860 the housing movement had scarcely advanced, although Roberts' ideas and even his plans were being adapted by Waterlow's Improved Industrial Dwellings Company. As Professor Tarn has noted, many 'of the men who, twenty years before had been filled with the zeal of Young England or the enthusiasm of an Evangelical Sanitary reformation, were ageing, discredited, or disillusioned. Some, it is true, had great tenacity, like Lord Shaftesbury, but many of this group were bewildered by the failure of the movement to gain momentum. One of the few who remained with interest undimmed was Henry Roberts, the original architect to the S.I.C.L.C., a sick man, forced to live most of the year in Florence, but with his beliefs in the efficacy of model housing unchanged. His rare visits to London came to be regarded with considerable interest . . . '.[13]

Professor Tarn has pointed out that Roberts was 'an exception, an architect of no small ability who, by choice, had given up a growing commercial practice, to devote his energies to housing reform. In 1862 he was probably the greatest living authority on the planning and construction of model dwellings'.[14]

During the 1860s the whole subject of housing became of fundamental concern to society as a whole, and occupied much time at meetings of learned societies.[15] The architectural profession had first debated the matter when Roberts gave his seminal paper at the Institute. In 1864 The Society of Arts organised a conference that set out the full magnitude of the problem, with its causes and effects and probable solutions.[16] Additional legislation was proposed; improvements without changing legislation were considered; and the *rôle* of the Society was debated. The conference decided that the law could be improved if housing societies could borrow money at lower rates of interest and with fewer requirements relating to security. Other recommendations were that the laws relating to conveyancing should be simplified, that control of lodging-houses should be strengthened, and that all commercial undertakers demolishing houses for other purposes should be obliged to build an equal number of houses elsewhere.

The many pamphlets produced by Godwin and others during the 1860s were either extensions of what Roberts was saying, or the words of Roberts rephrased. The agitation by the various societies, such as those of Arts and for the Promotion of Social Science, were addressed by Roberts, whose works were known throughout the reform movement. Many of the recommendations by the reformers were embodied in the *Public Health Act* of 1848 and in the *Working Classes Dwelling Houses Act* of 1866. Architects like Godwin, Darbishire, and Eyton (the architect of the S.I.C.L.C. dwellings at Hull), all gave lectures on the improvement of the dwellings of the labouring classes during the 1860s, the texts of which contained little that Roberts had not already published. In fact, all through the 1860s, it was still Roberts who led the field with ideas, facts, and thought, as his vast output of lectures, pamphlets, and books proved.

The basis of Evangelical and sanitary reform was to live on in the work of Octavia Hill, who believed that self-help was an important factor in educating the poor. She was a grand-daughter of Dr Southwood Smith, Roberts' old friend and colleague who was to be buried in the same cemetery in Florence as was Roberts.

Part of what Roberts, Octavia Hill, and others had been agitating for was to be accomplished in a Bill introduced to Parliament by William Torrens in 1866. This was designed to deal with insanitary houses where owners refused to take action themselves, and contained powers of compulsory purchase, demolition, or repair. However, when Torrens' Bill became an *Act*, in 1868,[17] it only provided for the local authority to secure improvements by repair or demolition: the parts that made provision for rebuilding were dropped. This *Act* accorded with Roberts' own notions, but as it was to be implemented by the vestries and by the district boards, the chances of efficaciousness were reduced. The principle of official interference with private property was a major change in housing policy.

During the 1860s an enormous amount of literature dealing with health and housing problems appeared. Roberts himself contributed much to the debate.[18] In due course, Gladstone appointed a Royal Commission in 1869 to investigate the sanitary administration of England and Wales. The history of the various sanitary reforms have been adequately dealt with by J. N. Tarn,[19] by Anthony S. Wohl,[20] by Francis Sheppard,[21] and by Donald J. Olsen,[22] among others. The great watershed was the *Public Health Act* of 1875[23] which gave to the town and borough councils, the Boards of Improvement Commissioners, the Local Boards of Health formed under the 1848 *Public Health Act*, the Local Boards formed under the 1858 *Local Government Act*, and the Board of Guardians, powers to control conditions in towns or districts.

During the 1870s it had become obvious to many thinkers, including Roberts, that stronger powers were necessary to provide decent housing. *The Report of the Special Dwellings Committee of the Charity Organisation Society*[24] argued for greater powers to be given to municipal authorities. In 1875, too, the *Artizans' and Labourers' Dwellings Improvement Act*[25] became law. This *Act* did raise problems. The Society for Improving the Condition of the Labouring Classes, for example, was concerned about the difficulty of housing displaced persons between demolition and rebuilding, and, with Octavia Hill, was concerned about a new tendency to think in terms of housing the poor on other than strictly commercial principles.[26]

These *Acts* began a development that was to lead inexorably to state intervention in housing. Many of their provisions enshrined the arguments of Henry Roberts, but the drift away from individual responsibility and the shouldering of the burden by the state would not have pleased him entirely. Nevertheless, the last months of his life must have been interesting for him as he saw much of his life's work to improve the dwellings of the labouring classes come to some sort of fruition in *Acts* of the British Parliament. Nevertheless, the lack of official recognition of the momentous and essential *rôle* he himself had played in arriving at such legislation must have irked him. For fourteen years after 1875 the Metropolitan Board of Works was to carry out enormous schemes, while there was, in the words of Professor Tarn,[27] 'an Indian summer of private enterprise' when the Peabody Trustees and other philanthropic societies were actively involved in considerable developments.

However, not until the 1890s were the last bastions of *laissez-faire* removed when the *London Government Act*[28] reorganised the administration of the capital. Under the 1890 *Housing Act* many high-quality schemes were brought into being, including the 1893 L.C.C. Boundary Street Estate, yet even these were not as advanced as Henry Roberts' scheme for Streatham Street that had self-contained sculleries. In fact, the more Roberts' designs for Streatham Street and for the Model Houses at the Great Exhibition are examined, the more advanced they appear, for in the latter W.C.s were included in the self-contained dwellings, something the L.C.C. was not providing forty years later.

It was not only in the fields of ingenious and economical planning, the provision of completely self-contained family units, and the development of safe, strong, light, and fireproof construction that Roberts excelled and led the way forward. He also provided experimental communal facilities, not only in the lodging-houses, but in the apartment-blocks for families. An examination of his plans also demonstrates that he provided adequate storage facilities for working-class families, something that most council houses have consistently failed to do even up to the present day. It is no exaggeration to state that Henry Roberts was not only one of the best and most advanced planners of economical housing in his own time, but that in over a century his basic ideas have not been greatly improved upon, and, in terms of construction, contemporary building failures demonstrate that his experimental forms of construction were also in general more sound. His use of concrete in foundations, in floors, and in roofs, combined with the lightness of hollow-pot floors and walls, shows that he was a major innovator, an original mind, a great improver, and an inventor of some importance. The fact that Streatham Street, the Fishmongers' Hall, and the charming dwellings at Windsor survive so well today is a testament of his soundness in the design and construction of buildings. The dwellings at Windsor are particularly notable for small areas requiring painting, something of which Roberts was always mindful.

An examination of Roberts' writings and designs for housing shows him to have been far in advance of his time. The Streatham Street buildings and Great Exhibition houses are unquestionably the finest examples of model housing of the nineteenth century. Indeed, as already stated, cheap mass-housing of the twentieth century has hardly advanced on Roberts' basic ideas. The designs of Henry Roberts were flexible, adaptable, and capable of being used in infinite variety, upwards or sideways. The Streatham Street flats have never been surpassed for their ingenuity or dignity, while the adaptability of the 1851 Model Dwellings has been echoed in countless twentieth-century schemes.

The wide publicity given to the Great Exhibition houses made the plans familiar to architects all over the world. Even De Klerk's Henrietta Ronnerplein Estate in Amsterdam, of 1922, had flats based on the Great Exhibition plans, and there are thousands of examples of late-nineteenth and twentieth-century plans for flats that are basically to Roberts' designs.

Roberts was one of the chief architects of Victorian housing reform, in every sense of the word. He was not only one of the chief theorisers, but he was also one of the most successful executive designers. His was the greatest influence during the 1850s and 1860s, and, indirectly, when his ideas became part of received opinion, he was the guiding force in the movement to house the poor adequately until well into the present century. He was the man who translated the Evangelical Conscience first into exemplars of decent dwellings, then into eloquent arguments for national reform, and finally into the beginnings of modern housing. Henry Roberts is the unsung hero of housing and of sanitary reform. It is amazing that his achievements have largely gone unnoticed by contemporary commentators.[29] To a considerable extent, Henry Roberts is the father of modern ideals of good housing. He was certainly one of the most important figures in a movement to promote hygienic dwellings in both town and country, and his concern for the poor went far beyond mere basics, but extended to culture as well.

Roberts did not turn to philanthropic housing because he was a failure, or because he had not had success as an architect in the wider world. On the contrary, he had enjoyed a very considerable success, and had had the patronage of a wide circle. His buildings were always sound, and were frequently distinguished. His greatest architectural works are undoubtedly The Fishmongers' Hall, London Bridge Station, Escot House, Exton Hall, Peamore House at Alphington, Streatham Street, and the Model Dwellings for the 1851 Exhibition. Yet his written works must not be underestimated, nor must his designs for rural dwellings that changed the face of the Victorian countryside.

Architects like Scott and Butterfield have been the subject of research because they built so much, and perhaps because their buildings were so prominent. Roberts changed the appearance of rural England, and ultimately his ideas (through the widespread copying of his published exemplars) changed urban England too. His views finally altered the whole concept of housing the labouring classes. He was a major influence on developments abroad, and was acquainted with nearly all the housing architects and philanthropists of his day. He addressed all the major conferences that dealt with the problems of ameliorating the condition of the labouring classes from the mid-nineteenth century until his death in 1876. He was in regular correspondence with most of the innovators and influential bodies in the field, and his exemplars became the models for many architects in many countries to follow. His plans for the Great Exhibition were the basis for all the successful subsequent designs for working-class flats, and are the genesis of many much-praised buildings of the twentieth century including housing in Amsterdam and elsewhere. He was the first architect to design fully self-contained flats for the labouring classes. His designs were at least seventy-five years ahead of their time, and in some respects, notably his provision of storage, his awareness of the need to provide buildings requiring a minimum of maintenance, and his attention to detail, have never been surpassed. He was one of the most humane, inventive, and original minds of the Victorian age, and his best designs for working-class housing were brilliant. His influence has been enormous, not only through his exemplars, but through his ideas, his lectures, his books, and his pamphlets. There is no doubt that Henry Roberts was the true father of civilised housing conditions for the mass of urban people. He deserves a greater recognition at the hands of historians than has been his fate hitherto.

An Evaluation of Roberts as man and Architect

The study of the Life and Works of Henry Roberts, Architect, has gone into exhaustive detail. It has described all Roberts' known works, both written and architectural, and has established the authorship of a number of buildings, such as the Sidmouth School and several railway structures, not previously attributed to him. For the first time, details of his appearance and of aspects of his personal life have emerged from the obscurity of time, largely through the discovery of surviving members of his family and their kindness in making reminiscences and documentary material freely available for study. The invaluable help of the Cuningham family is gratefully acknowledged, for without this even the physical appearance of Henry Roberts would not have been determined. The curious circumstances of the burial, exhumation, and reburial of Roberts in a different Florentine cemetery have helped to establish the precise dates of birth and death of himself and of his immediate family, as well as leading to further facts concerning the history and interests of the Roberts connections. The very full details, bibliography, and illustrative coverage in the study itself set out the facts as far as it is possible to go, but a few more words are necessary to elaborate on the small number of hypotheses and conjectures that appear in the study. In addition, this brief essay will attempt to give a personal view of Roberts as a man, as an architect, and as an influence, and will try to assess the quality of his work. The present essay is therefore a rounding-off of the original study, and a considered reflection on Roberts as he appears after a long period of closely examining the man and his achievements.

First of all, what can be made of Roberts the man? Initially, when commencing the study proper, he appeared remote, enigmatic, and oddly obscure, but gradually a picture of him emerged that is both interesting and deeply moving. The delightful drawings by Maclise, illustrated on Plates Frontispiece–4, show an attractive and handsome family of obviously prosperous background. The very choice of Maclise points to a certain social standing, while the not unfashionable address in an elegant terrace in Camberwell does not suggest any whiff of straitened circumstances. Roberts' father was a successful merchant, with business backgrounds in the United States and in London, and, from the evidence in surviving papers in the hands of the Cuningham family, was accepted by Philadelphian society in 1798. Josiah's connections in London were also considerable, for he was a South Australian Colonisation Commissioner from 1835–40, and the family retained Australian and American ties until well into the present century. Henry Roberts was a handsome, thoughtful, sensitive-looking young man (Frontispiece), and was clearly a gifted student. Scott himself noted that Roberts was 'gentlemanly, religious, precise, and quiet', and was of 'independent circumstances'. It has not been possible to establish from whom Henry Roberts derived his fortune (which was mostly tied up in the Equitable Reversionary Interest Society and in Guaranteed Railway Stock), for his father died leaving only a small sum. The architect may have been given his fortune quite early in his career by his father, or he may have been left money by his mother, who appears to have been an American. Roberts was obviously not dependent upon his architectural practice, although that was successful and mixed. Whatever the source of the capital of Henry Roberts, it was substantial, and gave him an unusual degree of freedom very early in his career.

In one sense Henry Roberts was fairly typical of a type of young, middle-class Englishman of the first half of the nineteenth century: he was deeply religious, and imbued with the Evangelical Conscience that did so much to form the powerful currents and forces of Victorian Britain. Eighteenth-century spiritual torpor had been rejected by the generations influenced by Wilberforce and by the Clapham Sect, and Roberts was not alone in his high-mindedness and devotion to the Evangelical cause. Concern for the spiritual, educational, and moral welfare of the masses was a feature of the Evangelicals, who, in the view of a number of scholars, did more to influence the tone of society than did any other single body or factor of the period. The Evangelicals were practical, sober, earnest, hard-working, and deeply committed Christians who led the way in social reform. In another sense Roberts was atypical, in that almost alone among his fellow-professionals, he concerned himself with a practical alleviation of the problems of poor housing, and became a great innovator and proselytiser, excelling in the field. There were other architects who designed working-class housing, but none in Britain became so single-minded; none produced work of such outstanding quality as Streatham Street or the 1851 Model Dwellings; and certainly none was regarded as such an expert in the subject, nationally and internationally, as was Roberts. He was in the vanguard of developments in exemplary housing, and had much to say on all aspects of working-class housing, including sound buildings, good ventilation, adequate light and air, heating, nutrition, and public health. It would be superfluous to repeat here what has been discussed fully in the study itself, but it is important to emphasise the fact that Roberts was able to understand the problems of designing very small houses, unlike most of the celebrated architects of his time.

After the 1851 Exhibition the fortunes of Roberts clearly changed. His surviving relatives are still intensely proud of his achievements, but his apparently sudden opting out needs further clarification. The family was quite open and adamant about the unfortunate liaison Roberts had with a working-class lady, and that this had a catastrophic effect on his standing with the S.I.C.L.C., as well as with the aristocratic and royal Establishment: the honours that should have been his did not materialise. This information came from a surviving relative who heard it first-hand from Roberts' nephew: this nephew (F. A. Roberts) was close to Roberts himself. This evidence must be regarded as of the utmost importance. Documentary proof in published sources, minute-books, and memoranda does not exist, but reminiscences of an intelligent and erudite octogenarian relative who knew Roberts' nephew well must be regarded as a prime source. Without the family evidence we would have no clue about the appearance of Roberts, of his parents, or of his siblings, and very little in the way of of private correspondence, American connections, or ephemera. Such evidence cannot be discounted or overlooked: to do so would be irresponsible. What is more, verbal reminiscences about Australia and America tie in with documentary evidence, so the witnesses in the family must be regarded as reliable. There are other points to be considered apart from the strict sexual morality of the Evangelical Christians of the period that was intolerant of adultery. Roberts had had a very bad press in *The Ecclesiologist*, a paper that carried considerable weight in architectural circles. Scott himself states in his *Personal and Professional Recollections* (*op. cit.* p. 203) that 'so imperious was . . . (the law of the ecclesiologists) . . . that anyone who had dared to deviate from or to build in other than the sacred "Middle Pointed" well knew that he must suffer . . . '. Scott also refers to the 'tyranny' of *The Ecclesiologist*, and makes it clear that its voice was respected and feared by members of the profession for the weight it carried. Canon Clarke confirms this view, and Eastlake, in his monumental history, shows that the Ecclesiologists carried their ideas forward with the fervour of a moral crusade. Roberts' Whitechapel and Nottingham churches came in for vitriolic abuse from *The Ecclesiologist*. Now although the magazine was originally associated with the Liturgical or High Church Movement, by the 1850s it was a powerful and influential organ of criticism that could make or break reputations: Bassett Keeling was to be mauled by *The Ecclesiologist*, and bad notices had the effect of putting committees off, such was the 'tyranny' to which Scott refers, and Keeling was firmly in the Evangelical camp. It would be a great mistake to assume that Evangelicals were not affected by *The Ecclesiologist* criticisms, as the case of Keeling makes clear. The impact of the S.I.C.L.C. housing exemplars could be severely curtailed if the Honorary Architect's designs were castigated by powerful critics. In 1851, too, Roberts ran foul of the British and Foreign Bible Society for which he had designed a stand at the Great Exhibition. The *Minutes* of the *Proceedings* of H.M. Commissioners for the Exhibition are unusually sharp when recording this point, and the Commissioners also were offended by an error of Roberts who had been 'clearly informed' of the position of the Society's stand, and had got it wrong. The subsequent retreat to Italy by Roberts in 1853, and his own published remarks about his 'protracted residence on the continent, *partly*[30] for the recovery of health', point to the possibility of some kind of breakdown, perhaps caused by the stress over his personal life, his poor notices, his quarrel with the Commissioners and the Bible Society, disappointment over the lack of official recognition in the form of an honour for his work for the S.I.C.L.C., and, probably most of all, his over-exertion in the cause of the Society. The association with the failed banker, Sir John Dean Paul, cannot have helped. The fact that Roberts was married to a Russian, and that the Crimean War broke out in 1854, lasting until 1856, would have been socially unpleasant. Subsequent shabby treatment by the S.I.C.L.C., by which the removal of Roberts from the post of Honorary Architect was assured by abolishing the post, points to a determination that cannot be explained by the inconvenience of Roberts' being in Italy. The Society quite obviously was not going to tolerate Roberts as its architect any longer, and Roberts' refusal of the title of Vice-President of the Society suggests more than an ordinary tiff, although he subsequently (1867) relented and became a Vice-President. It says a great deal for the influence, status, example, and work of Roberts that after 1853 the S.I.C.L.C. largely stagnated. The driving force had been Henry Roberts: that is clear as crystal.

Roberts emerges as the best type of early Victorian: industrious, earnest, inventive, deeply religious and humane, dedicated, and committed to improving the lot of his fellow human beings. His writings are sensible, full of facts, reliable historically, and very interesting. He was able to live a long life after his departure from England, and he did not waste those years. In fact he became better known internationally as an expert on the dwellings of the labouring classes. When he died he left substantial sums, and his daughter carried on his Evangelical convictions by directing the Florence Medical Mission until her death. As a man of some means, he was able to settle money on his wife when he married, and his own fortune at his death was, by today's standards, very considerable. He belonged to a breed perhaps best described as 'gentlemen-architects'. His connections and clients were all drawn from the upper echelons of society, with a pronounced leaning to the Evangelically inclined members of the aristocracy and landed gentry. Kinnaird, Manchester, Gainsborough, Leycester, Galloway, Kennaway, Welman, and Calthorpe were all men of wealth and substance, and all were staunch Evangelicals with an interest in philanthropy. Lords Kinnaird, Calthorpe, Gainsborough, and the Duke of Manchester were rich, even by Victorian standards, and by those of the 1980s were very rich indeed. Roberts himself had clearly enjoyed a comfortable childhood, and his addresses at Camberwell, Suffolk

Street, Adelphi, and Connaught Square, were not those of a struggling beginner with no capital behind him. Although Roberts designed the Fishmongers' Hall, several buildings including the terminus for the Brighton and Dover Railway, and two substantial houses for aristocratic clients, most of the rest of his general practice consisted of major extensions to country houses, a few churches and schools, a parsonage or two, and sundry small works. The bulk of his *œuvre*, apart from the aforementioned buildings, consists of working-class housing, most of which he appears to have designed *gratis*, in an honorary capacity. He had a modest income from the royalties on his patent hollow bricks, but otherwise he contributed most of his professional life to writing, lecturing, and exchanging information about the improvement of the condition of the poorer strata of society. Only a man free from economic burdens could have done that. His status in society was therefore substantial, and he was on almost equal terms with the aristocratic members of the S.I.C.L.C., many of whom were also his clients.

Roberts was married to a member of the Baltic Russian aristocracy, and was on friendly terms with the royal houses of Prussia and Italy, with the ruling elements in France, and with the Northern Italian aristocracy. The latter, although nominally Roman Catholic, was closely associated with reform, with anti-clericalism, with English Liberalism, with the cremation movement (itself radical and anti-clerical in Italy), and with philanthropic housing. It tended to be a feature of Evangelical activity to side with elements opposed to the authority of the Roman Catholic Church, and in his writings Roberts often associates that Church with the forces of anti-progressive reaction to the amelioration of the condition of the working classes, notably in Naples and the Sicilies. Lord Shaftesbury himself was notoriously anti-Catholic, while the vigorous Protestantism of Catherine and Theodora Roberts has already been fully chronicled in the study itself. It is clear that Roberts remained true to his Evangelical principles until his death, and that he believed it was the duty of professional and wealthy men to improve the lot of the poor, not only for physical reasons, but for educational, moral, and spiritual ones as well.

Having looked at Roberts the man, it is important to consider him as an architect, for there is no doubt that he had great gifts. He received a rigorous classical training, notably in the office of the great Sir Robert Smirke. Scott noted that Roberts had thoroughly absorbed much of the lessons of Smirke's buildings: a refined Greek Revival style, a facility for massing and for robust composition, and an attention to fine details second to none. Perhaps even more important for the future career of the young Roberts was Smirke's insistence on good foundations, sound construction, and an intelligent use of modern techniques of building. It says much for Roberts' structural expertise that when the Fishmongers' Hall was partially burned and blasted in the Blitz in September 1940 the brick-vaulted floor construction survived. The riverside range was burned from the ground up, and the roof over the main staircase was destroyed, although the stone steps and the landing on its iron cantilevers survived.

There can be no doubt about the fact that, by general consensus, the Hall of the Fishmongers' Company at London Bridge was Henry Roberts' most distinguished work of architecture in the public, civic sense. Never again, as Summerson has written, was Roberts' architecture so grand. The Hall was a suitable ornament to the North bank of the River, and provided a splendid architectural foil on the Western side of the viaduct to London Bridge. In terms of planning, massing, composition, urban design, and exquisite detail (both inside and out), the Fishmongers' Hall was a work of the highest refinement: a Greek Revival building of supreme quality with a pronounced flavour reminiscent of Smirke's best work. The Ionic Order is almost the same as that used by Smirke on the prostyle hexastyle portico of the former Royal College of Physicians building in Trafalgar Square. Not only did the Fishmongers' Hall form part of a scheme of metropolitan improvement for which Smirke was the overseer, but it possessed interiors that were among the most elegant of the whole Greek Revival. The formal and decorative Corinthian Order of the Monument of Lysicrates was used to great effect inside the Hall, and Roberts' deft handling of Greek motifs has earned his interior design at the Hall a place in Wiebenson's *Sources of Greek Revival Architecture* as an example of a distinguished work in the style. The Chryselephantine colour schemes, the discreet guilding, and the extra touches of richness in the chimney-pieces, stoves, and granite columns in the lobby all added up to an ensemble of considerable distinction, even in an age of architectural giants. The chimney-piece designs, themselves of the utmost refinement, and superb examples of Greek Revival detail, were to reappear at Toft, Peamore, and Escot. They testify to Roberts' unerring eye when it came to Grecian detailing. At Fishmongers' Hall the exquisite subtlety of the slightly battered architraves, the entirely unmechanical and authentically Greek Revival designs for everything from chimney-pieces to fenders, and from friezes to office desks and partitions, point to a thoroughly professional and dedicated classicist who was absolutely sure of his touch even to the last detail of moulding or colour. Roberts supervised the design of everything in the Hall. The wonderfully soft and delicate colour-schemes were praised by no less a critic than Leeds, and something of their original qualities may be appreciated when reading contemporary descriptions and studying the papers, drawings, and specifications at Guildhall Library. Owen Jones largely obliterated Roberts' colouring with the intense hues he favoured, although he could not destroy Roberts' admirably solid three-dimensional ornament. Subsequent redecorations by Crace and Bodley in turn changed much of Jones' work, but Goodhard-Rendel began a process of lightening the Victorian decorations more in accord with Roberts' scheme. After the War certain changes were made to the planning of the court-room, but the Banqueting Hall, staircase, and other rooms were sensitively restored, and much of Roberts' original colouring in the scagliola, chimney pieces, and ceilings, has been revived. The Fishmongers' Hall can be counted as one of the very finest of all Greek Revival buildings in Great Britain, and possesses an interior that is today perhaps the best example of the style. The recently restored staircase is particularly felicitous.

Yet by the time the Hall was completed in 1840 the Greek Revival was already out of favour, and the building consequently did not attract the acclaim it might have won had it been finished a decade earlier. Nevertheless the Hall reveals much about Roberts as a designer and as a practising architect. He was thoroughly at home with the classical style, and especially with Greek detail; he advocated only the best materials; he was especially careful with foundations and structure; he was modern and progressive regarding heating, ventilation, and construction; he was an urban designer of subtlety, exploiting different levels and a *piano nobile* idea; and he was an interior designer and detailer with an eye for colour, profile, and rich effects without vulgarity. As the drawings show, his draughtsmanship displays great sensitivity and feeling for refinement, and, as the building shows us today, the realised scheme has a rare quality and architectural integrity. As a classicist of the Greek Revival school of Smirke, Roberts could produce work of the first rank. Never again was Roberts to design a building to such a standard, and never again, except in a few interiors, was he to display his facility for Greek Revival as a style to such an extent. At Toft, Escot, and Peamore the classical Grecian civilities were still observed in Roberts' designs for chimney-pieces and interiors generally, despite the disconcerting Jacobean exteriors of both Toft and Peamore.

The ultra-refinement of the Fishmongers' Hall was succeeded by a second classical style favoured by Roberts in a few of his buildings. This was a robust and masculine Italianate manner. Two buildings in the Italianate style deserve mention; the railway terminus at London Bridge, with its tower, pedimented architraves, and toughly rusticated arches through which goods and carriages could progress; and Escot House in Devon. As the terminus, an architecturally fitting approach to a main line, no longer exists, Escot will have to serve as the chief work in Roberts' Italianate style. The classical restraint, the severe attention to relationships between solids and voids (Plates 26–30), and the hard, uncompromising detail of the exterior all derive from the training under Smirke (leavened, no doubt, by Roberts' travels in Italy), but the ingenious planning, using the *piano-nobile* idea again recalls the arrangements of levels at the Fishmongers' Hall. The entrance to Escot House is through the podium, and that of the Hall is at the *piano-nobile* level. In both cases the unusual planning and response to the difficulties of the site are most brilliantly handled, creating impressive massing of the outside, and interiors of great subtlety. The plans of both buildings can be found on Plates 6–14, and 26–28, of the study itself. Photographs of the exteriors (Plates 5, 15, 29, 30) are also included. The refinements inside Escot House owe a great deal to the Hall, and in several cases chimney-pieces are identical to those in the earlier building (Plate 28). At Escot, too, a round-arched manner on one elevation that is specifically Italianate points to a move away from the icy precision of the Greek Revival. Apart from the designs for the Glebe House at Southborough (Plates 18–23), the Asylum at Whitechapel (Plate 17 and Figure 1), and the vicarage at Whitechapel (Plate 43), Roberts' classical training was only to be apparent in his designs for Model Dwellings and in a few country-house interiors.

With the Gothic style Roberts was not at ease, and it would be difficult to quarrel with some of the criticisms of his designs for churches in *The Ecclesiologist*. At Yoxford Parish Church, however, his North aisle (Plates 24–25) is perhaps his happiest essay in Gothic, but there he was using details already established in the Southern façade of the church. Nevertheless the flintwork, dressings, tracery, and nave arcade are self effacing and authoritatively well mannered. Significantly, Yoxford is in the Perpendicular style that, of all Gothic periods, is the most regular, and therefore nearest the classical organisation with which Roberts was most at home. Escot Church is a very small and economically controlled essay in Early English, with a Decorated chancel (Plate 31), but is not of especial distinction. Furnishings are mean. The other designs for Gothic churches at Whitechapel (Plates 40–41), Nottingham (Plate 54), and Wigtown (plate 55), it must be admitted, are run-of-the-mill and indisputably dull. Elements are clumsily juxtaposed, detail is commonplace, and compositions are lumpishly inelegant. There is no hint of the assured classicist of the Fishmongers' Hall in these insipid and coarse buildings. Cheap Gothic churches were put up in numbers during the nineteenth century: some were strangely barbaric, like Bassett Keeling's weird 'acrobatic Gothic' or Chester Cheston's fantasies; some had a degree of distinction, like Pearson's designs for Freeland or Vauxhall; but, most sadly to say, were of little architectural note, and it is into this category that Roberts' designs for churches must regretfully be relegated. The Romanesque church in Hampshire (Plate 32) that Roberts designed for Lord Calthorpe is worthy but pedestrian, with an inappropriate Gothic spire, and an undistinguished interior. The Church of Scotland building at Wigtown is dour in the extreme, its only virtue being that it looks *echt*-Scots (Plate 55).

It is difficult to state definitively what Roberts would have made of the Gothic style had he considerable funds at his disposal. His former pupil Scott could be deplorably mechanical and dull, even when such funds were available, yet sometimes rose to heights of real distinction. It is probable that Roberts was too much of a classicist to be really at home with the Gothic style, and one suspects his Evangelical mould precluded a full-blooded attempt to provide the proper richness that convinced Gothic Revivalism demanded. Classicism, after all, remained a vital force in Presbyterian Scotland and Northern Ireland long after it was *passé* in England, and there can be no doubt that Evangelicals, like Presbyterians, were happier with classicism, which had no Catholic overtones. It must be remembered that the Gothic Revival style was closely associated with Pugin, Roman Catholicism, *The Ecclesiologist*, and the High Church party, all of which were viewed with suspicion, if not hostility, by Evangelicals. Gothic, in the hands of an Evangelical architect, was often rather bare and lacking in a full commitment, notably in the detail, interiors, and furnishings. Even chancels, to the Evangelicals, were suggestive of more than a whiff of Popery. By 1840, however, to build for the Established Church at all, Gothic was *de rigueur*, even if the Evangelical element was dominant, and so a host of unconvincing and mean-looking Gothic churches, designed by unconvinced architects, sprang up all over Britain.

Designs by Roberts for the Camberwell School (Plate 16), for the Norbiton Schools (Plates 47–50) and Parsonage (Plates 44–45), for the house on the Manchester Estates in Huntingdonshire (Plate 59) for the School in Sidmouth (Plates 38–39), all employ late-Gothic, Tudor, and seventeenth-century motifs culled from Jacobean sources, but none is of any real distinction. Norbiton and Camberwell Schools were especially thin and unconvincing essays in the Perpendicular style, somewhat gimcrack and mean in their appearance and detail (Plates 16, 47–50). More substantial buildings where gables, mullioned and transomed windows, Jacobean details, and late-Gothic occur in profusion, as at Norton Fitzwarren (Plates 34–36), Toft (Plates 52–53), Exton (Plate 51), and Peamore (Plate 37), are moderately successful, yet only at Norton and Exton is the period detail carried completely inside the buildings, and only at Norton is the house a new structure, erected from scratch. Even then, although the quality of the materials and workmanship is sound, the design is curiously uneasy. Rather coarse and unconvincing joinery and plasterwork do not suggest anything of the refinement of

Roberts' classical buildings. Similar detailing to that at Norton occurs at Exton, although there is a severe classical dining-room that recalls the Henry Roberts of twenty years earlier. At Peamore the interiors are classical, with Greek chimney-pieces, and the same curious anomaly occurs at Toft. Of course Roberts' work at Peamore, Toft, and Exton consists of substantial extensions to existing buildings, and use is made of Greek detailing developed for the Fishmongers' Hall (Plates 37, 51–53).

Thus in his general practice we are really left with one building of substantial excellence: a masterwork of that last phase of English Greek Revival. Apart from London Bridge Station and Escot House, most of the other buildings designed by Henry Roberts cannot be claimed as especially fine, although tactful additions, like those at Yoxford, Exton, or Toft, clearly point to an architect of sensitivity perhaps caught in an unsympathetic national fashion for un-classical architecture, and responding as best he could to a number of stylistic notions for which he had little taste or enthusiasm. The thoroughly classical training that Roberts had enjoyed, and his Evangelical roots, did not endear him to the Gothic Revival. Had the story ended there the name of Henry Roberts would only have survived in the context of the Greek Revival: it is safe to say that the other buildings of his general practice would not have earned him any niche of immortality or of especial distinction.

It is with the designs for model housing that Henry Roberts achieved international fame and a sure place in history. His pecuniary circumstances, his religious beliefs, and his inquiring mind led him to specialise, and indeed to lead the field, in the subject of ameliorating the condition of the labouring classes. No young man of conscience, bred into an Evangelical family where the ideals of the Clapham Sect burned brightly, could fail to respond to the sights and smells of abject poverty he witnessed while travelling in Italy in the 1820s; nor could he fail to see that conditions in England were anything to be proud of, at a time when Chartism and talk of revolution were in the air, and when the railways were starting to cut their ways through the urban and rural fabric. The horrors of the first cholera epidemics, economic problems, and an atmosphere where reform was about to change the power structure of Britain could not but impress an intelligent and gifted young man with a sound education and an Evangelical conscience that was clearly well developed.

The first philanthropic residential development with which Roberts was concerned as an architect was the Sailors' Asylum at Whitechapel. He then became involved with the Society for Improving the Condition of the Labouring Classes, which was revitalised and refounded in 1844, and Roberts was a member from the very beginning of the renewed organisation. He designed all the exemplary buildings for the Society, and he played an enormous part in publicising the movement as well as the exemplars themselves. His first designs for the Society to be built as a large-scale exemplar were the Bagnigge Wells model dwellings, and here the classical style, even to the extent of having vaguely Greek–Revival architraves around the ground-floor windows and doors, and including string-courses and vestigial cornices, was well to the fore (Figure 3). This was an experiment, and it attracted adverse criticism, but Roberts quickly learned from his mistakes. The George Street Model Lodging-House used typical late-Georgian sashes, and so was firmly within a classical tradition of tall town-house, warehouses, and offices (Figure 7). Portpool Lane was a robustly classical composition with a banded base, massive, almost Roman, arched elements for the staircases, hefty string-courses, and a crowning cornice of some weight (Figures 12-13). As in George Street, the windows were of the sash type, with skewbacks over. A sound classically trained architectural mind was clearly at work when these ingenious designs were conceived (Figures 1, 3, 4, 6, 7, 12, and 13).

Roberts' brilliant scheme for the Model Dwellings at Streatham Street once more displays the classical assurance that had been missing in his Gothic essays elsewhere. The simple nobility of the exterior, with its banded base, rigorously classical relationships of solids to voids, and overall proportions, was not to be improved upon in terms of architectural dignity (Plate 62). The ingenious galleries (important for reasons already discussed fully in the study proper), with the tall arcades in the courtyard, help to make the main space contained in the block architecturally interesting and humane in scale (Plate 63). The planning and legislative aspects have been thoroughly set out previously, but the architectural qualities need further emphasis. Streatham Street is not only a watershed: it was virtually a new type of building, almost perfected in this one brilliant design. The site was very restricted, and Roberts rose to the occasion with imagination and a professionalism that seem to make the design effortless and completely right, so unlike the uncomfortable massing of the Whitechapel church, for example. The classical proportions, sensible materials, and lack of frippery make Streatham Street a work of the highest distinction. The street façades of the block are variants on a type of domestic architecture in London that had been known for a century or so. Sash-windows in the simplest of openings, arranged with an eye to pleasing proportion, were elements Roberts used to considerable effect and with immense assurance (Plates 62-63).

The Model Dwellings designed for the Great Exhibition were also distinguished and ingenious, based on plans that could be extended upwards or repeated on either side (Figures 18-20). The plan was certainly the basis of much later work, notably of Waterlow's Company, and of many other organisations, and it established a precedent for minimum accommodation, self-contained, well-built, adequately ventilated, and fire-resistant. However, the overt use of an architectural language with a Tudoresque flavour is less convincing for this type of building than is the uncompromising classicism of Streatham Street. The ornaments above the staircase well and over the window-bays appear as afterthoughts, and detract from the integrity of the design as a whole. A comparison of the Exhibition designs with the adaptation of the plans at Windsor (Figure 25, Plates 71, 72) demonstrates how much more successful were the cases where Roberts eschewed ornament in working-class housing. In fact the Windsor development as a whole is an admirably homogeneous scheme, with a use of materials carefully chosen to reduce maintenance to a minimum. The Windsor scheme incorporates different designs for model dwellings that Roberts had produced for the S.I.C.L.C., but with standardised details and materials. The result demonstrates how successfully these designs harmonised with each other, not only because of the colour and texture of the materials, but because the scale and proportions of each block are closely related. The dormers and gables, serene and balanced fenestration, and carefully designed chimneys owe much to a vernacular tradition with which Roberts was clearly familiar, and thus the buildings appear uncluttered and timeless. When Roberts introduced late-Gothic hood-moulds, Dutch gables, and the like, his designs for cottages became somewhat self-conscious and certainly less successful than those at Windsor. The latter scheme is much more successful architecturally than the Tunbridge Wells estate (Plates 80–81), for example, as the Kentish development has large amounts of unnecessary and expensive Gothic detail, most of which has not worn well. The Windsor scheme (Plates 71–73) relies on good proportions, the simplest of materials, and detail that requires little or no maintenance. As a result the Windsor group still looks fresh, and has weathered well, while the Tunbridge Wells scheme is decayed and run down. Variations on Roberts' plans for cottages that he produced as standard designs for the S.I.C.L.C., and that were printed and sold freely, occur in great numbers throughout England. Although the elevations do not usually follow Roberts' designs, but were often reworked to suit local requirements by estates surveyors and architects on the spot, the plan-forms Roberts had produced for the Society were used. His contribution to the quality of rural life as well as to the appearance of working-class housing in the country was therefore not negligible. Typical pattern-book designs for rural dwellings are shown on Plates 74–77, 79, and Figures 30–41, all by Henry Roberts. These were the bases for countless cottages erected all over the country, although the external appearance varies greatly.

In the study itself the design of the Albert and Victoria Cottages at Mile End New Town is attributed to Henry Roberts on the basis of the published sheet produced by Roberts' friend Emile Muller (Plate 83). Some further explanation concerning the attribution is due. These cottages were built by the M.A.I.D.I.C. The sheet, printed by Thieffry & Cie, can be found among many other works by Emile Muller in the *Bibliothèque de la Société Industrielle de Mulhouse*, a Protestant Evangelical organisation that was completely committed to the ideals shared by Roberts. Emile Muller was a talented architect, a friend and colleague of Roberts, and was as painstaking and careful as Roberts himself. He was a stickler for accuracy, and the suggestion that he might have made a mistake in his attribution is highly unlikely. Now cottages were built at Penge by the Metropolitan Association to *plans* by Bracebridge (acknowledged by Roberts in the 1867 edition of *The Dwellings of The Labouring Classes*), and these were described by him in a paper given at Birmingham in 1857. The W.C.s were outside. Other designs at Penge called Alexandra Cottages, and attributed to Roberts on Muller's plate, have internal W.C.s, and a type of banded elevation not unlike some of Roberts' known designs. Alexandra Cottages were also built by the Metropolitan Association, as were Victoria and Albert Cottages at Mile End New Town, which also had internal W.C.s. The banding of the brickwork of these designs recalls certain features used by Roberts: even Muller followed aspects of the Streatham Street elevations in some of his designs (Plate 85).

Significantly, Roberts, like Muller, is always careful to credit designs to their authors, and states in the Preface to the 1867 edition of his great work that it was his 'invariable aim' to give credit to others and to acknowledge all sources. He castigated plagiarism in print, and clearly felt very strongly about the attribution of designs. In the same 1867 edition, Roberts credits *plans* of some cottages (not those in Muller's sheet) to Bracebridge, but Albert Cottages at Mile End New Town and Alexandra Cottages at Penge are not credited to Bracebridge and are treated no differently in the book to any other designs by Roberts himself. The planning of Victoria and Albert Cottages, and of Alexandra Cottages, with their self-contained accommodation and internal W.C.s, as well as the above facts and the *stylistic* aspects of banding, simple fenestration, and detail, point to Roberts. The definitive attribution to Roberts by the thoroughly reliable Muller, who, it must be emphasised, was in constant touch with the Englishman (who was a personal friend), does seem to suggest the reasonable proposition that Roberts was the architect. Now Roberts does not actually state that he was the designer, but nor does he say he was the architect responsible for several other published designs for model cottages that are known to be by him because they are mentioned in the Minutes of the S.I.C.L.C.; because they are credited to Roberts on some of the individual sheets sold by the S.I.C.L.C. complete with specifications; and because original drawings showing some of these designs, and signed by Roberts (Plate 58), exist among the Duke of Manchester's papers. It must be remembered that Albert Cottages were built at Mile End New Town in 1857, the very year that Roberts resigned his position as Honorary Architect to the S.I.C.L.C., although the move to unseat him was made at the end of 1856. It is likely that word of Roberts' involvement with the Metropolitan Association reached the ears of the S.I.C.L.C in 1856, and this may have precipitated matters that had been on the boil since 1852, and that were presumably exacerbated by the War of 1854–6 against the country of Roberts' wife. It must also be remembered that Roberts was inclining more to the view of the Metropolitan Association in respect of the financing of working-class housing, and after the Great Exhibition and his failure to obtain proper recognition for his labours, it is not at all unlikely that he transferred more than a theoretical allegiance to the M.A.I.D.I.C.

The Penge developments also began in 1856–7, but Victoria Cottages were not added to Mile End until 1864, three years before Roberts was prevailed upon to become a Vice-President of the S.I.C.L.C. Roberts is known to have criticised the Association for providing housing at such a low density at Mile End. The probable explanation is that at some time (perhaps 1855 or 6) Roberts provided designs for cottages, some of which were erected at Penge, and the type that could be made into terraces provided the basis for the developments at Mile End New Town, although Roberts had not intended the designs for an urban site. The ultra-simplified cottages at Mile End New Town appear to owe their existence to the mind of Roberts, both in terms of planning and architecture.

Having considered the evidence both documentary and stylistic with some care, and knowing that Muller was an obsessionally careful recorder of fact, as was Roberts, this is not an unreasonable conclusion at which to arrive. After all, Roberts had declared that the Metropolitan Association was 'based on the sound and only principle on which it can be reasonably expected that the construction of improved dwellings for the labouring population in towns can be effected on a scale at all adequate to their necessity, viz. that of the investment of capital, with the prospect that, under good management, a fair return on the outlay will be realized'.

One final stylistic point needs to be emphasised (Plates 83–84). Victoria Cottages (1864) had splayed brickwork around all openings, recalling aspects of the Windsor scheme, and, perhaps most significantly, had casement windows of a type common in France and in Central Europe, but not in London or even in England. The published designs, both in Muller's work and in Henry Roberts' 1867 edition of *The Dwellings of the Labouring Classes* (the year in which he relented and became a Vice-President of the S.I.C.L.C.), show sash windows, but Continental-type casements occur in Victoria Cottages only: Albert Cottages were built with sash windows. The design of the casements derives from Continental practice, and is similar to casements at Mulhouse, with which Roberts was very familiar. Both Victoria and Albert Cottages were in fact cottage flats, a type of building not usual in London, although it was common on the Continent. The influence of Muller is very likely, both in the design of the windows and in the arrangements of flats on the principle of dwellings in the *Cité Ouvrière* at Mulhouse. Roberts published designs for cottage flats himself (Figures 16, 38). It would appear that Roberts was reconciled to the S.I.C.L.C. around the mid-1860s, when the Society set in motion plans to publish the sixth thousand, revised, and augmented edition of *The Dwellings of the Labouring Classes*, with *The Essentials of a Healthy Dwelling*, and *The Benefits of a Healthy Dwelling*, all part of the same volume, 'with Plans and Elevations of Dwellings adapted to Towns and to Rural Districts, by Henry Roberts, F.S.A., Fellow of the Royal Institute of British Architects, Honorary Member of the Academy of Fine Arts, Florence, &c., a Vice-President and formerly Honorary Architect to the Society for Improving the Condition of the Labouring Classes', which came out as one tome in 1867. It is this large and monumental edition that includes the Albert and Victoria cottage flats, treated in no different way to other designs (the authorship of which is in no doubt) included in the book. As a new Vice-President of the S.I.C.L.C. Roberts would not have broadcast his association with the Metropolitan Association: such a course would not have appeared proper to him. He did, however, include the designs for Mile End New Town in a section of the book where *all* the other designs are known to have been by him. The only *plans* not by Roberts are a plan of two flats built by the Birkenhead Dock Company (and acknowledged as such) on the same sheet as a plan of two flats at Streatham Street; plans of two flats built by the Metropolitan Association, the authorship of which is acknowledged (as always with Roberts) in the text; and plans of cottages *built* by Bracebridge (again acknowledged) for the Metropolitan 'Society' [*sic*] at Penge.

It must be emphasised that these Bracebridge plans are *not* the same as those other Penge designs attributed by Muller to Roberts, and shown on Plate 83. Roberts would never plagiarise, and he would never publish any design or quotation without acknowledging the author. As an architect and writer he referred bitterly to 'unacknowledged use' of his own work by others, and stated categorically that he 'invariably' gave credit to architects and writers. The title-page of the book states that plans are by Roberts, and nowhere in the text or in the notes is there the slightest hint that the Mile End New Town cottage flats are by any hand other than Roberts. There the case for the authorship of these interesting and unusual (for London) buildings must rest. In the view of the present writer the work by Muller, the personal friend and colleague of Roberts, clinches the matter, for Muller, like Roberts, acted as a clearing-house for information on the housing movement, and can be relied upon, for he gives chapter and verse for all his statements, and no errors by Muller have been discovered in the course of the study (Plates 83–84).

Henry Roberts was the original mind behind the pioneering experiments in housing design, and was, in a very real sense, the father of the working-class housing movement. He and the Society were starting from scratch with the Bagnigge Wells scheme, and although that development was marked by sound construction, good sanitation and ventilation, and a certain dignified restraint in the architecture, it was not a great innovation in terms of the fabric. Its main significance was that it signalled a change in the history of housing and in the relationship between the architect and the community as a whole; that it was the first scheme in a sequence of change that led to the ending of *laissez-faire* attitudes to the problems of dealing with the poorer classes; and it was the first skilled work entirely designed as a purpose-made development suited for its use by an architect of real stature. Thereafter the works of Roberts and of the Society are marked by originality and a notable lack of repetition: every type of exemplar was tried and built; printed plans were prepared for sale; and even rehabilitation schemes were pioneered a century and a quarter before they became fashionable in architectural circles. The quality of intellect behind the design and detail of the Model House for the Great Exhibition is undeniable, and the ingenuity of the planning and construction can still impress. Architecturally the Exhibition buildings are beautifully controlled and have a strong personality making them instantly memorable. The designs were even more successful when simplified further, as at Windsor, where Roberts' entire ensemble provides a delightful and intimate environment of high quality, with agreeable spaces, and buildings that are an object-lesson in relatively maintenance-free detailing (Figures 24–29). As a designer of exemplary housing Roberts advocated the building of independent dwellings, fully self-contained, and in the planning he was mindful of the need to segregate male from female children (incest was rife in overcrowded dwellings), and to give parental privacy. Roberts brought his Christian principles into his designs, and recognised the need to give the poorer classes dignity, privacy, hygienic surroundings, and decency in their dwellings.

Turning to Roberts as an influence, only a few words are necessary here, for the study itself covers the ground. As already stated, he was the main force behind the practical exemplars of the S.I.C.L.C., and he also greatly extended the influence of that Society and of its ideas by writing descriptions of his own designs for publication, by producing a great number of plans for model dwellings that were printed and sold by the Society (and realised in various forms throughout the country), by writing and lecturing a great deal on the benefits of sound, dry, ventilated, hygienic, and well-planned buildings, and by disseminating information on the housing movement in his lectures, pamphlets and books. His reports from abroad that were published in *The Labourers' Friend* showed that he was not only thoroughly familiar with developments in the United Kingdom, but that he was up-to-date on all aspects of the amelioration of the condition of the labouring classes throughout Europe and America.

Henry Roberts unquestionably made the most important contribution of the middle decades of the nineteenth century to the whole housing movement. He became a respected expert, both nationally and internationally, and, almost alone among his profession, concerned himself with the practical problems of designing cheap and wholesome dwellings for the labouring classes, although his friend Muller held a similar position in France. Roberts' visits to France, to Germany, to Switzerland, to

International Conferences on housing, and to England, aroused considerable interest, and he gave a number of important papers that were published in one form or another. Roberts' was the first authoritative voice in the housing movement *from an architectural point of view* to be raised in favour of interference in personal liberty for the common good, and many of his proposals, even his advocacy of compulsory purchase of slum property at site-value only, eventually became enshrined in the machinery of legal powers held by the State and by local authorities. Henry Roberts was one of the first architects to argue for new social forces in the land. He was critical of his fellow professionals for not providing useful contributions to urban housing theory. As a planner, Roberts was skilful and inventive, and his three-dimensional achievements, notably at Streatham Street, at Windsor, and at the 1851 Exhibition, rose above the utilitarian to heights of real architectural quality. The solid advances pioneered by Roberts in planning and privacy, hygiene and dignity in Streatham Street alone were not to be surpassed in Britain in the nineteenth century, and only with some of the London County Council developments at the end of the century did working-class housing designs begin to reach the point where Roberts had left off.

Although Roberts left England in 1853, and ceased his career as a successful architect in the conventional sense, his significance does not end there. For the rest of his life he was a tireless traveller, commentator on the housing scene, pamphleteer, proselytiser, lecturer, consultant, and indefatigable correspondent with others in the housing movement. There can be no doubt that, by 1862, when he was in Britain on a lecture tour, he was the prime authority on the design of model dwellings. His suggestion that the space standards for which he had long fought must not be reduced, but that State intervention in housing should be accepted in order to finance the continuance of those standards was radical indeed for the period, and doubtless caused eyebrows to be raised in all sorts of quarters. While realising the financial implications of the philanthropic organisations, it is quite clear that Roberts saw that private investment was not enough to ensure wholesale improvements in housing. State intervention to help, on a massive scale, was heady stuff in the political climate of 1862. Roberts was far ahead of his time in more than one narrow architectural sense: his Evangelical Conscience led him inevitably to foresee the type of public involvement in housing that was not to materialise until almost the end of the century. As is stated in the study proper, Henry Roberts is the true father of civilised housing conditions for the mass of the people. His was arguably among the most humane, inventive, and original minds of the Victorian age, and much of his architectural work, including the Fishmongers' Hall, Streatham Street, the Exhibition Houses, and the Windsor scheme, is of undeniable quality. His enormous output in terms of publications, going into several revised editions, had repercussions throughout Europe, and his work was translated into a number of languages.

The preparation of the study of the Life and Work of Henry Roberts has occupied several years. The man who at first appeared to be a faceless enigma has emerged as an interesting personality, deeply humane, highly gifted and intelligent. An architect of real stature when working within a classical framework, Henry Roberts was not at home with Gothic, and not quite at ease with Jacobean. The great hall for the Fishmongers' Company is an outstanding design, and is one of the most distinguished buildings of the Greek Revival in the British Isles. The original and ingeniously planned schemes for working-class housing have no real precedent, and were not to be equalled, let alone surpassed, for decades. The writings are absorbing, detailed, and reliable: they are a mine of information. Having lived so close to Roberts for so long, one can only feel humbled by his immense achievements, saddened by the personal tragedies of his life, and deeply moved by his humanity and practical sense of caring. Having handled some of his personal possessions, letters, and pieces of ephemera that fortunately survive among the papers of the family, and having found his elusive grave at long last, one feels immeasurably close to the man. There is a sense of deep understanding, of knowledge of a very human story, and an appreciation of the sterling qualities of his surviving buildings. Roberts was not dull, not boring, not mediocre, and certainly not someone who can be passed over or ignored. His contribution to the Greek Revival was distinguished; his involvement in the exemplary housing movement was original, innovatory, and as distinguished; and his tireless dissemination of information provided a powerful stimulus to reformist bodies working throughout Europe and America. In the Evangelical cemetery in Florence, his grave shaded by a wall and by mature trees (Plate 61), lies a great man, perhaps one of the best of all eminent and not-so-eminent Victorians. To refer to him as a Victorian, although he was born in America in the reign of George III, is a reasonable thing to do, for his religious and humanitarian attitudes are firmly Victorian. The Fishmongers' Hall, the Camberwell School, the early railway buildings, the Asylum, the Glebe House, and Yoxford were all built in the reign of William IV. Thereafter everything Roberts produced can be attributed firmly and chronologically to the Victorian age. His was a life that embodied the chief virtues of the time: prudence in financial matters, a thorough grasp of professional expertise, immense industry, benevolence towards the less fortunate, a willingness to experiment and develop new ideas, ability to give full attention to *minutiæ* and detail, and a deeply felt humanity based on Christian virtues. To call Roberts a great man is hardly an exaggeration, although full recognition of his merits was not to be given to him in his lifetime. It is to be hoped that the present study redresses a balance that is long overdue: Roberts was a rare and extraordinarily gifted man whose position in the pantheon of Victorian architects should be better known.

REFERENCES

References for the Introduction

1. London and New York, 1973. *See* Bibliography.
2. Notably by Dyos, H. J., and Wolff, Michael (eds.). *The Victorian City. Images and Realities.* London and Boston, 1973.
3. Including Butterfield, Pearson, Shaw, 'Greek' Thomson, and many others.
4. *See* the Bibliography.
5. Although there was a pioneering paper by John Fletcher on Roberts, written for the Architectural Association in 1950, and a subsequent study by Anthony MacIntyre at the same school in 1974. *See also* Foyle, A. M. *The Builder,* 2 January 1953.
6. Curl, James Stevens. *The Victorian Celebration of Death.* Newton Abbot, 1972, p.21. *See also* the same Author's *A Celebration of Death.* London, 1980.
7. For a revolting description *see* Buckingham, James S. *National Evils and Practical Remedies, with the Plan of a Model Town.* London, 1849. *See also* Curl, James Stevens. *European Cities and Society.* London 1970, p.129.
8. Curl. *The Victorian Celebration of Death, op. cit.*
9. *Report on the Sanitary Conditions of the Labouring Population and on the Means of its Improvement.* 9 July 1842.
10. *Ibid.*, p.233.
11. Tarn, John Nelson. *Five Per Cent Philanthropy. An account of housing in urban areas between 1840 and 1914.* London and New York, 1973, p.1.
12. *See* Rosenau, Helen. *The Ideal City. Its Architectural Evolution.* London, 1974, pp.143–52. *See also* Curl, James Stevens. *European Cities and Society, op. cit.*, pp.128–48.
13. *See* Benevolo, Leonardo. *The origins of modern town planning.* London, 1967, pp.39–84. *See also* Tarn, *op. cit.*, p.3.
14. *Report on the Sanitary Conditions* etc., p.273.
15. Curl, James Stevens. 'A Chartist Estate in Hertfordshire. Heronsgate, formerly O'Connorville'. *Country Life.* 3 March 1977.
16. The source is Roberts himself. *See* Bibliography.
17. Walter Curl, or Curll, was Bishop of Winchester when the Civil War broke out.
18. Ireland has a great number of Anglican 'Cathedrals' that have had no bishops for nearly a century and a half.
19. *Dictionary of National Biography.*
20. *See* Curl, James Stevens, and Sambrook, John. 'E. Bassett Keeling, Architect, in *Architectural History. Journal* of the Society of Architectural Historians of Great Britain, vol. 16, 1973, pp.60–9.
21. For an admirable account of the period *see* Clark, Kenneth. *The Gothic Revival. An Essay in the History of Taste.* London, 1962, pp.150–74. *See also* Clarke, Basil F. L. *Church Builders of the Nineteenth Century. A Study of the Gothic Revival in England.* Newton Abbot, 1969, pp.72–106.
22. An Arminian followed the doctrine of James Arminius or Harmensen, a Dutch Protestant theologian, who opposed Calvin, especially on predestination.
23. *See* entries in *the Encyclopaedia Britannica*, in Chambers' *Encyclopaedia*, Everyman's *Encyclopaedia*, and the *Dictionary of National Biography*, to which the present writer is indebted.

24. *See* Curl, James Stevens. *A Celebration of Death*. London, 1980.

25. Tarn, *op. cit.*, p.4.

26. Details of these buildings are given later in this study.

References for Chapter 1 — *An Outline of the Career of Henry Roberts*

1. 1851 Census.

   P.R.O. H.O.107/1467/Folio 328. Kensington Parish.

   A list of persons resident at 10, Connaught Square, revealed the following information:

   (a) Henry Roberts, head, married, aged 47, architect, British subject, born Philadelpha [*sic*], U.S.

   (b) Catherine Roberts, wife, married, aged 31.
       It appears from the Census that she was the daughter of the Governor of Tula, Russia, but this is not so. 'Governor' was an inaccurate translation of *Gubernia*, a Tsarist administrative region equivalent to an English county. Catherine was therefore born in the *Gubernia* of Tula.

   (c) Olivia M. P. Roberts, daughter, unmarried, aged 2.

   (d) Elise Pfeil, visitor, unmarried, aged 33, born in Russia.

   (e) Ann Thompson, governess, unmarried, aged 27, born in Devonport, Devon.

   (f)* Joseph Poole, servant, widower, aged 48.

   (g)* Mary Ann Goddard, servant, unmarried, aged 30.

   (h)* Louisa Jones, servant, unmarried, aged 20.

   (* = places of birth not noted.)

   Incidentally, Thomas Allason, architect and surveyor of the Ladbroke Estate, aged 60, was at 7, Connaught Square in 1851. Help by Mr. John J. Sambrook with the gathering of this material is gratefully acknowledged.

2. Information from Roberts' tombstone in the *Cimitero Evangelico degli Allori* in Florence, copied by the Author in April 1979.

3. Information provided by Miss Constance-Anne Parker of the Royal Academy of Arts, and from Census of 1851 (P.R.O. H.O. 107/1467/Folio 328. Kensington Parish. All the ages and dates from these three sources tally.

4. *M.S.* note in Hitchen, W. E. *Surrey at the opening of the XXth century*, published in Brighton in 1907, and now in Haslemere Library. Reference kindly provided by Mrs. S. Joyce Soutter.

5. The Author is grateful to the Rev. and Mrs. J. C. Cuningham for hospitality and for much help.

6. Information kindly provided by Mr. Ward J. Childs, Archivist III of the Department of Records, City of Philadelphia.

7. These survive in the collection of Mrs. J. C. Cuningham.

8. These Maclise drawings also survive in the collection of Mrs. J. C. Cuningham.

9. The silhouettes of Henry and his younger brother Frederick show heads and profiles that are very alike. These silhouettes (in the collection of Mrs. J. C. Cuningham) are identified on the backs in the handwriting of Frederick Albert Roberts.

10. This portrait is in the collection of Mr. M. C. Cuningham.

11. Hodder, Edwin. *The History of South Australia*. London, 1893. Vol. I, p.38. Reference kindly provided by Mr. J. H. Love, Principal Archivist of the State Library of South Australia. *See also* the handwritten note in Hitchen. *Op. cit.* in Haslemere Library (*see* note 4).

12. Information from Mr. J. H. Love.

13. Information from Mrs. S. Joyce Soutter and from Mrs. J. C. Cuningham.

14. A copy of this Certificate is in the collection of the Author.

15. Mrs. J. C. Cuningham kindly made them available for study.

16. Mr. John J. Sambrook kindly obtained this information.

17. Information from various street- and trades-directories, and from MacIntyre, Anthony. An unpublished study for the Architectural Association in 1974.

18. Information about F. A. Roberts has been kindly provided by Mrs. S. Joyce Soutter of Chiddingfold. Further facts about Josiah and Frederick Albert Roberts are contained in a handwritten note in the copy of Hitchen, W. E. *Surrey at the opening of the XXth Century*, published in Brighton in 1907, and now in Haslemere Public Library. Mrs. J. C. Cuningham has been very informative about the family, and has made papers and other material available for study. Miss Stella Frend was instrumental in putting the Author in touch with Mrs. Cuningham.

19. Although Theodora Amélie Roberts died in Italy, she left a small estate in England.

20. Information from the handwritten note in Hitchen, *op. cit.*, and from the Will of F. A. Roberts.

21. The Wills of Henry, of Theodora Amélie, and of Frederick Albert Roberts.

22. Colvin, Howard. *A Biographical Dictionary of British Architects 1600–1840*. London, 1978, pp.320-1.

23. *The Builder*. XXV, 1867, p.761.

24. Cruden, R. P. *History of Gravesend*, London, 1843, p.490.

25. Records of the Incorporated Church Building Society in Lambeth Palace Library.

26. The bridge has a carved inscription attributing it to Fowler.

27. H. S. Goodhard-Rendel's card-index of churches in the R.I.B.A. Library. *See also* the *Transactions* of the R.I.B.A. XVIII. 1867.

28. Loudon, J, C. *Encyclopaedia of Cottage, Farm, and Villa Architecture*. London, 1846, p. 979.

29. Boase, Frederic. *Modern English Biography*. London, 1965. *See also* the *Dictionary of Architecture*. VII. London, 1887, pp.51-2.

30. For various items relating to early works by Roberts *see: The Civil Engineer*. VI. London, 1842, pp. 403-54; *The Civil Engineer*. XXIII. London, 1859, pp. 237, 325, 373; *The Illustrated London News*. IV, p. 76; and the *Transactions* of the Society (later the Royal Society) of Arts. XLII, 1824, pp. xlvi, xlvii.

31. *See* Curl, James Stevens. *A Celebration of Death*. London, 1980, for the history of Kensal Green Cemetery.

32. Brett-James, N. G. *Mill Hill School 1807-1923*. Reigate, 1925, pp.60, 65, 66, 89. *See also* Colvin, *op. cit.* For information about the Claytons, *see* Aveling, Rev. Thomas W. *Memorials of the Clayton Family*. London, 1867. *See* especially pp. 313 and 355.

33. Information from the Cuningham Family.

34. Holford, G. *An Account of the Penitentiary at Millbank*. London, 1828, pp. xxxi-xxxii. *See also The Builder*. LXIII. 1892, p. 474.

35. Crook, J. Mordaunt. 'Sir Robert Smirke: A Regency Architect in London'. The *Journal* of the London Society. March 1968.

36. Colvin, Howard. *A Biographical Dictionary of British Architects 1600-1840*. London, 1978, p.742.

37. Britton and Pugin. *Public Buildings in London*. II, 1828, pp.219-23.

38. Crook, J. Mordaunt. *The British Museum*. London, 1972.

39. Britton and Pugin, *op. cit.* edited by Leeds.

40. Crook, J. Mordaunt. 'The Custom House Scandal'. *Architectural History*. VI, 1963.

41. Colvin, *op. cit.*, p.742.

42. *Ibid.*   43. *Ibid.*

44. Crook, J. Mordaunt. 'The Building of Lincoln County Hall'. *Lincolnshire Arch. Soc. Reports* IX, 1962.

45. Papworth, Wyatt. *The Dictionary of Architecture*. 1852-92.

46. Colvin, *op. cit.* p.743.

47. The archives of the Royal Salop Infirmary.

48. Royal Academy Schools Register. Information kindly provided by Miss Constance-Anne Parker of the Royal Academy of Arts.

49. When he recorded he visited the *Albergo di Poveri* in Naples.

50. *See* Roberts, Henry. *The Dwellings of the Labouring Classes*, London, 1850.

51. Scott, Sir George Gilbert. *Personal and Professional Recollections*, London, 1879, pp. 73–5.

52. The Fishmongers' Hall.   53. Scott, *op. cit.*   54. *Ibid.*

55. *See* the *Companion to the Almanac*, 1836, pp.219–20. *See also* Blanch, W. H. *Ye Parish of Camberwell*, London, 1875, p.307.

56. Scott, *op. cit. See also The Mirror of Literature, Amusement, and Instruction*, 30 January 1836. *See also The British Almanac* of 1836.

57. Scott, *op. cit.*

58. *Ibid.*

59. Roberts' father, Josiah Roberts, lived at 10, Camberwell Terrace, from 1822 until 1847. This was Henry Roberts' address on the Royal Academy Schools Register.

60. Minute Book of the Society of Antiquaries of London. Vol. 37, 1835–39. Information kindly provided by Mr. F. H. Thompson, General Secretary of the Society.

61. MacIntyre, *op. cit.*

62. Roberts himself is the source, in a footnote in the 1867 edition of his *The Dwellings of the Labouring Classes* etc., p.15.

63. London, 1841.

64. Information about the life of Noel from the *Dictionary of National Biography*. Information about the family connections of the Noels and other families from Debrett and Burke.

65. Copy of the Marriage Certificate in the collection of the Author.

66. *D.N.B.* Other information kindly provided by the Rt. Hon. the Earl of Gainsborough.

67. According to Lord Gainsborough both names were favoured from the seventeenth century, from the time of Sir Baptist Hicks, Lord Campden (*ob.* 1629), who is buried in the mortuary chapel in the Church of St James, Chipping Campden.

68. Information kindly provided by the Divisional Reference Librarian, Tunbridge Wells, Miss J. Mauldon. Further information from Roberts' Will, and from the memorial to Gay in Bidborough Church. *See also* Skinner, F. A. *Bidborough – A Parish History*, Bidborough, n.d. I am indebted to the Rev. Skinner for hospitality and help.

69. Records of the Incorporated Church Building Society at Lambeth Palace Library. Further information kindly provided by the County Archivist, Norfolk Records Office, from the Institution Book. *See* the Wills of Henry and Frederick Albert Roberts.

70. For the Manchester information, the Author is indebted to Miss Constance-Anne Parker and to Mrs. Margaret De Motte. *See also The Builder*, 22 September 1849, p. 451.

71. 961 M/E 29. Correspondence survives in Devon Record Office.

72. *The Builder*, XXV, 1867, p.761.

73. These were exhibited at the Royal Academy in 1839.

74. Family connections from Debrett, Burke, and from Lord Kinnaird.

75. Minute Book of the Society of Antiquaries of London. The Author acknowledges help from the General Secretary and the Librarian of the Society. The Minute Book Volume is No. 37, 1835–9, *See also The Architectural Magazine*, Vol. IV, 1837, p.360.

76. Boyle's *Court Guide*. Information kindly provided by Mr. J. S. Skidmore of the Royal Society of Arts.

77. *See* Leeds, W. H. *Supplement* to Britton and Pugin's *Public Buildings in London*, London, 1838, pp. 21–32. *See also Country Life*, 19 January 1939. The fullest account of this building is found in Metcalf, Priscilla, *The Halls of the Fishmongers' Company*, London and Chichester, 1977, pp. 117–56.

78. This was demolished in 1867.

79. Weale, John. *A New Survey of London*, Vol. I. London, 1853, p.268. *See also* Roberts, *op. cit.*,

80. The drawings and the contract survive at the R.I.B.A. Drawings Collection. Mr. John Harris and his staff have been most helpful in making copies of these.

81. Records of the Incorporated Church building Society in Lambeth Palace Library.

82. Exhibited at the Royal Academy in 1838. The drawings survive in the Devon County Record Office, Ref. 961/E 29.

83. Mentioned in Roberts' obituary notice at the R.I.B.A.

84. Spreat, W. *Picturesque Sketches of the Churches of Devon*, London, 1842, No. 69.

85. The plans survived at Claydon House at least until 1978. They have been impossible to locate in 1979.

86. The bound volume of contract drawings by Teulon survived at the house in 1978.

87. Exhibited at the Royal Academy in 1842.

88. *See* Gotch, J. A. *The Growth and Work of the RIBA*, London, 1934.

89. Information provided by Mr. G. L. E. Lindow, Secretary of The Athenæum in a written reply to the Author's query.

90. Information from MacIntyre, *op. cit.*

91. MacIntyre, *op. cit.*, and the Minutes.

92. London and Croydon Railway Company Minutes, 1834–35 and 1839–40.

93. *See The Civil Engineer*, 1843, VI, pp.403, 454. *See also The Illustrated London News*, 15 February 1851.

94. 3 February 1844, pp. 75–6.

95. Colvin, Howard, *op. cit. See also* the *Companion to the Almanac*, 1843, pp. 248–9, and 1844, pp. 239–41.

96. *See* Elmes, J. *Metropolitan Improvements*, London, 1831, pp. 146–7. *See also* Metcalf, Priscilla, *op. cit.*, for an excellent summary of the climate of the day.

97. Curl, James Stevens, 'Stepney Rediscovered', *Country Life*, 4 May 1972.

98. Colvin, *op. cit.*, information from Fletcher and MacIntyre.

99. Roberts himself is the source. He repeats the history of the Society in many of his writings.

100. *See* Curl, James Stevens, 'Taking the Waters in London', *Country Life*, 2 and 9 December 1971, and 11 and 18 November 1976.

101. The Minutes of the Society for Improving the Condition of the Labouring Classes.

102. Sheppard, Francis. *London 1808–1870: The Infernal Wen*. London, 1971. *See also* Wohl, Anthony S. *The Eternal Slum. Housing and Social Policy in Victorian London*, London, 1977. Olsen, Donald J. *The Growth of Victorian London*, London, 1976 is also useful.

103. *D.N.B.*

104. *The Builder*, IV, 1846, p.241. *See also The Ecclesiologist*, VI, 1846, pp. 34–5. For Information about Elliott, *see The Sailors' Magazine* for 1836 (p. 236), and for 1846 (p. 270).

105. *The Ecclesiologist*, VI, 1846, p.34. *See also The Illustrated London News*, VIII, 1846, p.321. *See The Builder*, IV, 1846, p.241.

106. The drawings of the School survive in Devon County Record Office ref. 961 M/E 40. Information from the church records.

107. Surrey Record Office. Acc. 1056/441. *See also* Smith. A. E. *Norbiton Church, 1842–1942*, n.d.

108. Manuscript made available by Mr. C. G. Walmsley, great-grandson of T. T. Walker.

109. The *Dictionary of National Biography* is the main source of information on Cumming, and there are prolix and sycophantic memoirs of him in plenty, practically all of which are very similar. I am further indebted to the staff of the Westminster Public Libraries for help with material.

  For information on Lord Ashley and his Milleniarist tendencies, *see* Battiscombe, Georgina. *Shaftesbury. A Biography of the Seventh Earl 1801–1885*, London, 1874.

  For further attitudes of a violently anti-Roman Catholic nature, *see* Hare, Augustus, J. C. *The Story of My Life*, London, 1896.

110. Battiscombe, Georgina. *Shaftesbury. A Biography of the Seventh Earl 1801–1855*, London, 1974, pp.99–103.

111. *Ibid.*, p. 103.   112. *Ibid.*

113. Sheppard, Francis. *London 1808–1870: The Infernal Wen*, London, 1971, p.243.

114. *Ibid.*, p. 246.

115. Scott, *op. cit.*

116. *The Times*, 16 April 1847. Information also from a copy of the Marriage Certificate in the Author's possession. Help from Mr. John J. Sambrook in finding this information is gratefully acknowledged.

117. *Dictionary of National Biography.*
118. Olivia Maria Pauline Roberts. Register of Births at St Catherine's House of September 1848 (Kensington, III. p. 336) states that Olivia Maria Pauline Roberts' birth was duly registered. Miss Roberts appears to have died very young, and her death may have contributed to Roberts' illness.
119. Information from the Will of Henry Roberts, a copy of which is in the collection of the Author. Further information from the tombstones of the Roberts family in Florence.
120. This speculation is based on the fact that she is not mentioned in the Will. It has not been possible to trace her date of death, and she may have died abroad.
121. Roberts is described as a 'Bachelor' on the copy of the Marriage Certificate of 15 April 1847 in the possession of the Author.
122. *See* Foyle, A. M. Article in *The Builder* of 2 January 1953. *See also* Tarn, J. N. *Working-class Housing in 19th-century Britain.* Architectural Association Paper Number 7. London, 1971, and Tarn, John Nelson. *Five Per Cent Philanthropy. An account of housing in urban areas between 1840 and 1914.* London and New York, 1973. The Author is also indebted to Dr. Foyle for making his papers available for study.
123. *See* Chapter II.
124. The Surrey Record Office. 264/51/1–5.
125. *The Architects', Engineers' and Building Trades' Directory* of 1868, p.133.
126. *Ibid.* 127. *Ibid.*
128. *The Builder*, II, 1844, p.630; III, 1845, p.1.
129. *The Builder*, V, 1847, pp.286–7.
130. *The Builder*, VII, 1849, pp.325–6; VIII, 1850, pp. 49–50.
131. *The Builder*, VIII, 1850, p.369.
132. *The Builder*, IX, 1851, pp.311–2.
133. *The Builder*, X, 1852, pp.468–9.
134. Surrey Record Office. 264/51/1–5.
135. Scottish Record Office. H.R. 355/6/1. R.H.P. 7802–7811, Register House Plans. The main references are the minutes of the Heritors of Wigtown (H.R. 355/1, No. 32); the minutes approving the new church (H.R. 355/1, No. 36); letters from 10, Connaught Square, London, from Roberts (H.R. 355/6/1, No. 41); correspondence regarding the appointment of Haydon & Company as heating engineers (H.R. 355/6/1, Nos. 33–35); and a letter from Roberts dated 23 March 1855 (H.R. 355/6/1, No. 42).
136. Messrs. James D. Galbraith, George P. Mackenzie, and Ian Grant, all of H.M. General Register House, Scottish Record Office, Edinburgh, have given painstaking help in unravelling the affairs of Wigtown Church. Miss Anne Riches has also been most kind.
137. The Minutes of the S.I.C.L.C. kindly made available by the Peabody Trust.
138. *The Architects', Engineers', and Building Trades' Directory*, 1868, p.133.
139. *Ibid.* 140. *Ibid.*
141. Documentary evidence regarding Toft Hall is somewhat limited. Dr. W. V. Wadsworth and Mr. E. G. M. Leycester-Roxby have given invaluable help. For further notes on Toft, *see* Hare, Augustus J. C. *The Story of My Life*, London, 1896, and the same author's *Memorials of a Quiet Life*, London, 1876.
142. *The Architects', Engineers', and Building Trades' Directory*, 1868, p.133. The Duke of Manchester was married to a native of Wigtown who was known to the Galloway family. For Kimbolton Castle itself, *see* Oswald, Arthur. 'Kimbolton Castle Huntingdonshire' in *Country Life*, 5, 12, 19, and 26 December 1968.
143. Minutes of the S.I.C.L.C.
144. Records in Huntingdon County Record Office, M.B. 46, Letter Book, M.S.
145. *See* the Bibliography.
146. *See* Foyle, A. M., *op. cit. See also* Sheppard, F. H. W. (ed.). *The Survey of London*, Vol. XXVI, London, 1956, pp.34–6. Roberts himself has much to say on the subject.
147. *The Builder*, 25 February 1854, pp.98–9.

148. *The Builder*, 22 July 1854, pp.390–9. *See also* Roberts, Henry, *The Dwellings of the Labouring Classes*, p.57 *et seq.*

149. *The Ecclesiologist* of April 1854, XV, p.142. Further information kindly provided by the Lincolnshire and Nottinghamshire County Archivist. All details are from MSS in the local collections. *The Nottingham Journal* of 18 January 1856 carries a report of the consecration. *See also The Nottingham Evening Post*, 28 September 1953, and *The Guardian Journal*, 21 May 1956.

150. Curl, James Stevens and Sambrook, John. 'E. Bassett Keeling, architect'. *Architectural History*, 16, 1973, pp.60–9.

151. Minutes of the S.I.C.L.C.

152. *The Builder*, 28 May 1853, p.348.

153. Information from the Cuningham family.   154. *Ibid.*

155. Roberts, Henry, *The Improvement of the Dwellings of the Labouring Classes through the operation of government measures* etc., London, 1859, p.24.

156. Pollock, John, *Wilberforce*, London, 1977, pp.233, 234, 262, 266, 278, 280, 296, and 302.

157. Battiscombe, Georgina, *Shaftesbury. A Biography of the Seventh Earl 1801–1885*, London, 1974, p. 281.

158. Roberts, Henry, *The Benefits of a Healthy Dwelling* , etc., London, 1862, p.64. *See also* The *Transactions* of the British and Foreign Sailors' Society for 1836, p.236.

159. Curl, James Stevens, *The Victorian Celebration of Death*, Newton Abbot, 1972.

160. Minutes of the S.I.C.L.C., 21 July 1851.

161. *See* the *Transactions*, p.583. The paper was read in 1858 in St George's Hall, Liverpool. General plans for model dwellings based on Prince Albert's Model Lodge for Upper Frederick Street, Liverpool, were shown. These were designed by G. Williams, after Henry Roberts.

162. *Transactions* of N.A.P.S.S., 1860, pp.766, 775, 779.

163. *Ibid.*, 1862, pp.775, 750.

164. Referred to, most inaccurately, in various papers, as 'M. Delfons'.

165. Roberts, Henry, *Efforts on the Continent for Improving the Dwellings of the Labouring Classes*, Florence, 1874. This little pamphlet gave Roberts' addresses of the Athenæum Club, London, and the Villa Romana, Florence.

166. *The Builder*, 11 November 1876.

167. The Will of Henry Roberts, a copy of which is in the collection of the Author.
The main beneficiaries of Henry Roberts' Will were:
    1. 'Catherine Roberts née de Swetchine', who already had a Marriage Settlement. Nevertheless, Roberts directed his Executors to arrange to pay her an annual sum as well as to transfer shares in guaranteed Railway Stock and in the Equitable Reversionary Interest Society to her. Most of Roberts' houshold goods, furniture, linen, plate (except the testimonial plate), pictures, and effects went to Catherine.
    2. Lydia Anastasie Davy and Theodora Amélie Roberts were each left some money, their father's books, and the testimonial plate presented by Lord Shaftesbury in 1853.
    3. Charles Roberts of St John's Wood Park, and *his* sons, Charles Gay Roberts of Haslemere, and Frederick Albert Roberts of Stroud were also left some residual estate.
The Guardians of the daughters were Catherine Roberts, Charles Roberts, and Ernest Noel of 6, Albermarle Street, London. The Executors were Catherine, Charles, Charles Gay, and Frederick Albert Roberts. Charles Roberts died before Henry, so Francis Stephen Clayton of 10, Lancaster Place, Strand, was appointed a Trustee and Executor in his place.
It is interesting to note that Francis Hare Clayton was finally to benefit from the Will of Frederick Albert Roberts, and that the testimonial plate passed into the possession of F. A. Roberts, and ultimately to F. A. Roberts' great-niece, Mrs. J. C. Cuningham, formerly Miss Dixon.

168. The Author thanks his wife and daughter for helping him to locate the grave.

169. *Registro Alfabetico delle Persone Tumulate ne Cimitero di Pinti.*

170. The *Registro Alfabetico* in the *Cimitero degli Inglesi* was obviously incorrect, for the surname would have been Schéhavtzoff, *née* Roberts.

171. *See* the *Transactions* of the National Association for the Promotion of Social Science. Most of the family connections discussed in this chapter have been established from *D.N.B.*, from Boase, from Burke's *Peerage* and *Landed Gentry* (various editions), and from Debrett. Other information has been kindly provided by the Rt. Hon. the Earl of Gainsborough, by Mr. E. G. M. Leycester-Roxby, by Sir Ralph Verney, Bart., by the Lord Kinnaird, and by Mrs. J. C. Cuningham.

References for Chapter Two — *The Rebuilding of the Hall of the Fishmongers' Company*

The main sources are to be found in Guildhall Library, City of London. These are: the Court and Committee Minutes of 1825-7 (M.S. 5571, Vol. 13; M.S. 5573, Vol. 12); the Court and Committee Minutes of 1827-31 (M.S. 5571, Vols. 13, 14; M.S. 5573, Vols. 12-14); the Court and Committee Minutes of August 1831–March 1832 (M.S. 5571, Vol. 14; M.S. 5573, Vol. 14; M.S. 5843, Files 1, 2, 7, 8, 10, 14, 15, 17); the competition drawings in Guildhall Library; the Court Minutes of March 1832–August 1835 (M.S. 5571, Vols. 14 and 15); the Committee Minutes of March–July 1832 (M.S. 5573, Vol. 14); the Building Committee Minutes of July 1832–July 1836 (M.S. 5837, Vol. 2); papers 1832-5 (M.S. 5834, 5841, 5843, 6242, 7288); and drawings nos. 1-22, with details, sheets, etc. Many drawings from Roberts' office, many apparently by Scott, survive. For the finishes, *see* Court and Committee Minutes (M.S. 5571, 5573, 5834 and 7278). Roberts' competition entry includes sheets 3-12, consisting of three elevations, two sections, and five plans, all of which survive at Guildhall Library. Nos. 1 and 2 were very likely a perspective and a plan of the basement. The model does not appear to survive, unfortunately. The description of his entry is in M.S. 5843, files 10, 17. The identifying letter is dated 31 December 1831 in M.S. 5843, file 2. There are excellent accounts of the rebuilding of the Fishmongers' Hall in Metcalf, Priscilla: 'The Fishmongers' Hall Competition 1831' in *Guildhall Studies in London History*, 1977, and in Metcalf, Priscilla: *The Halls of the Fishmongers' Company*, London and Chichester, 1977, pp.117-56. The permission of both Dr. Metcalf and of the Fishmongers' Company to quote from this latter work is gratefully acknowledged. Dr. Metcalf's work has provided a useful framework on which this chapter is based.

1. *See* the Court and Committee Minutes 1827-31 (M.S. 5571, Vols. 13, 14; M.S. 5573, Vols. 12-14; M.S. 5837, Vol. 1).
2. *See* Boase, Frederic, *Modern English Biography*, London, 1965.
3. Colvin, Howard, *A Biographical Dictionary of British Architects 1600-1840*, London, 1978, pp.798-9. *See also* Curl, James Stevens, *The History, Architecture, and Planning of the Estates of the Fishmongers' Company in Ulster*, Belfast, 1981.
4. *See* M.S. 5846, file 1. Suter's report and drawings are in Guildhall Library.
5. *The Architectural Magazine*, Vol. II, 1835, p. 236. The Hansom-Welch correspondence ran from January to July, pp. 16, 18, 20-3, 238, 325-6.
6. *See* Exhibition catalogue.
7. *See* Crook, J. Mordaunt, 'Sir Robert Smirke: a Pioneer of Concrete Construction'. *Transactions* of the Newcomen Society, Vol. 38, 1965-6, pp.5-22. *See also* Crook, J. Mordaunt, *The British Museum*, Harmondsworth, 1972.
8. *See* Sheppard, F. H. W. (Ed.), *The Survey of London*, Vol. XXIX, London, 1960, p.387.
9. *See* M.S. 5843, file 15.
10. *See* Curl, James Stevens, *The Victorian Celebration of Death*, Newton Abbot, 1972.
11. Letter from William Smith dated 23 February 1832, M.S. 5843, file 14.
12. *See* Hobhouse, Hermione, *Thomas Cubitt*, London, 1971, p.318.
13. *See* M.S. 5843, file 14, 31 March 1832.
14. *Transactions* of the Institute of British Architects, 1857-8, p.43.
15. Scott, George Gilbert, *Personal and Professional Recollections*, London, 1879, pp.73-5.

16. M.S. 5843, files 14 and 3. *See also* Hobhouse, *op. cit.*, pp.27–9.

17. *See* Hobhouse, *op. cit.*, pp.308–9. *See also The Builder*, 17 May 1851, pp.311.2. *See also* Roberts, Henry, *The Dwellings of the Labouring Classes*, London, 1850, p.11.

18. M.S. 5843, file 11. *See also* Gwilt, J., *Encyclopaedia of Architecture*, London, 1842.

19. *See* W. H. Leeds in his edition of Britton and Pugin's *Public Buildings of London*, London, 1838, p.24.

20. *See* Wiebenson, Dora, *Sources of Greek Revival Architecture*, London, 1969, p.67, n.22. Other buildings where this Order was used were Decimus Burton's Charing Cross Hospital, William Brooks' School of Oriental Studies, London Institute, Finsbury Circus, of 1815–16, and Thomas and Lewis Cubitt's Eaton Square, of 1827. The source for the Order was, of course, Stuart, James and Revett, Nicholas, *The Antiquities of Athens*, London, 1762–1830.

References for Chapter Three – *The Evangelical Conscience and the founding of the Society for the Condition of the Labouring Classes*

1. Sheppard, Francis, *London 1808–1870: The Infernal Wen*, London, 1971, pp.202–46.

2. Hennell, Michael M., *John Venn and the Clapham Sect*, London, 1958. *See also* Wollaston, H. W. A History of the Wollaston Family. An unpublished typescript in Guildhall Library, City of London.

3. Sheppard, *op. cit.*, p.206.

4. *See* Curl, James Stevens, *The Victorian Celebration of Death*, Newton Abbot, 1972.

5. The complicated history of urban reform and hygiene is beyond the scope of this study. The best modern studies are found in Wohl, Anthony S, *The Eternal Slum. Housing and Social Policy in Victorian London*, London, 1977; in Sheppard, Francis, *op. cit.*; and in Olsen, Donald J., *The Growth of Victorian London*, London, 1976.

6. *The Labourers' Friend*, New Series, No. 1.

7. *The Labourers' Friend*, June 1844, p. 27.

8. *Ibid.*, pp.1–2.

9. The Minutes of the Society for Improving the Condition of the Labouring Classes, *passim*.

10. Curl, *op. cit.*

11. Lewis, R. A., *Edwin Chadwick and the Public Health Movement, 1832–1854*, London, 1952, p.117.

12. Quoted in Tarn, J. N., *Working-class Housing in 19th-century Britain*, London, 1971, p.5.

13. London, 1850. Revised Edition 1867. Roberts forgot that the prefix 'Royal' was not added until some sixteen years after he had given his paper.

14. Roberts, *op. cit.*, p.33.

15. *Ibid.*

16. The Minutes of the S.I.C.L.C.

17. Roberts, Henry, *The Dwellings of the Labouring Classes, etc.*, London, 1853, p.6.

18. *See The Labourers' Friend*, April 1846, p.50; May 1846, p.73. *See also The Builder*, Vol. III, 1845, p.1.

19. *The Builder, Ibid.*

20. Roberts, *op. cit.*, p. 10.

21. *The Labourers' Friend*, July 1846, p.116.

22. *See The Builder*, V, 1847, p.287. *The Quarterly Review*, CLXIII, December 1847, p.142 also carries a criticism.

23. 14 and 15 Victoria, Cap. XXVIII.

24. 14 and 15 Victoria, Cap. XXXIV.

25. *See* Appendix.

Appendix I to Chapter Three

Societies formed for similar purposes as those of the Labourers' Friend Society, named in *The Labourers' Friend*:

Aberdeen Association for the Improvement of the Dwellings of the Labouring Classes.
Alcester and District Labourers' Improvement Society.
Appledore Labourers' Friend Society.
Association for Promoting Improvement in the Dwellings of Agricultural Labourers in Scotland.
Bandon Labourers' Friend Society.
Blythling Hundred Labourers' Friend Society.
Bridgend Labourers' Friend Society.
Brighton Association for Improving the Dwellings of the Industrial Classes.
Burham Labourers' Friend Society.
Chard, Ilminster, and Crewkerne Labourers' Friend Society.
Cork Labourers' Friend Society.
Dorchester, Weymouth, and Cerne District Association for the Improvement of the Working Classes.
Dundee Model Lodging House Society.
East Peckham Labourers' Friend Society.
East Somerset Labourers' Friend Society.
Essex Labourers' Friend Society.
Exeter Labourers' Friend Society.
Edinburgh — Rosemount Association for Providing Dwelling Houses for the Working Classes.
Glasgow Association for the Establishment of Model Lodging Houses.
Hadlow Labourers' Friend Society.
Hastings Cottage Improvement Society.
Hereford Society for Improving the Dwellings of the Poor.
Herefordshire Garden and Cottage Association.
Hertford Building Company.
Hertford Labourers' Friend Society.
Kensington Association for Providing Improved Dwellings for the Labouring Classes Ltd.
Lambeth Association for Providing Improved Dwellings for the Labouring Classes.
Lambeth Operatives' House Building Society.
Leeds Artisans' Cottage Company Ltd.
Liverpool Labourers' Dwelling House Company Ltd.
London Labourers' Dwelling Society.
Maidstone Labourers' Friend Society.
Manchester and Salford Association.
Marylebone Association for Improving the Dwellings of the Industrious Classes.
Midlands Industrial Dwellings and Sanitary Association.
Mid-Somerset Labourers' Friend Society.
New York Association for Improving the Condition of the Poor.
Northampton Artisan and Labourers' Friend Society.
North Herefordshire and South Salop Agricultural Labourers' Improvement Society.
Nottingham Cottage Improvement Company.
Oakley and Drummer Labourers' Friend Society.
Ongar Labourers' Friend Society.
Paris Association for Improvement of Habitations of the Working Classes in France.
Peckham. *See* East Peckham.
Plaxtol Labourers' Friend Society.
Redhill and Reigate Cottage Improvement Society.
Roding Labourers' Friend Society.
Roothings Labourers' Friend Society.
St Albans Labourers' Friend Society.

Societies formed — *continued*

    St George's, Hanover Square Parochial Association for Improving the Dwellings of the Labouring Classes.

    St Thomas' District Labourers' Friend Society.

    Salopian Society for Improving the Condition of the Industrial Classes.

    Stewponey Association for the Improvement of the Condition of the Labouring Classes.

    Stockbridge Labourers' Friend Society.

    Strand Building Company.

    Taunton and West Somerset Labourers' Friend Society.

    Thirsk Labourers' Friend Society.

    Tonbridge Labourers' Friend Society.

    Torquay Labourers' Friend Society.

    Tunbridge Wells Association for Improving the Condition of the Labouring Classes.

    Waterford Society for Improving the Dwellings of the Labouring Classes.

    West Dorset Labourers' Friend Society.

    West Kent Labourers' Friend Society.

    West Surrey Labourers' Friend Society.

    West Suffolk Society for the Improvement of the Condition of Labourers.

    Westminster Association for Improving the Dwellings of the Working Classes.

    Wexford Labourers' Friend Society.

    Willesden Labourers' Friend Society.

    Windsor Royal Society for Improving the Condition of the Working Classes.

    Worcester Labourers' Friend Society.

    Worcester Association for Improving the Dwellings of the Labouring Classes.

    Worksop Labourers' Friend Society.

Places where other unnamed Societies are reported in *The Labourers' Friend:*

    Amsterdam, Aylesbury, Bath, Birmingham, Boston (U.S.A.), Bournemouth, Blackheath, Bradford, Brighton, Bristol, Brussels, Chorley, Cerne Abbas, Derby, Devizes, Dublin, Dudley, Frankfurt-am-Main, Genoa, Gillingham, Greenock, Halifax, Halifax (Nova Scotia), Henley-on-Thames, Hythe, Ilminster, Leeds, Macclesfield, Maidstone, Melksham, Naples, Newcastle-upon-Tyne, Newton, Norwich, Notting Hill, Oxford, Paris, Ramsgate, Reading, Ringwood, Shrewsbury, Southall, Southampton, Sunderland, Taunton, Warrington, Wellington, Weymouth, Wimbledon, Wolverhampton, Woolwich.

Appendix 2 to Chapter Three

A typical set of rules drawn up by the S.I.C.L.C. relating to the duties of the Superintendent of the Lodging-House for Unmarried Workmen and Labourers at the Society's Lodging-Houses.

'The Superintendent, together with his Wife, are expected to set an example of sobriety, decorum, and exemplary conduct, abstaining from whatever might in any degree countenance in the Lodgers an infringement of the Rules for the general regulation of the house.

'He must faithfully account for all monies received by him or his wife from the Lodgers, at such time, and in such manner, as is required by the owner of the house.

'He is to keep a book, in which, besides a regular entry of the names, period of occupancy, and payments made by each Lodger, a Record shall be kept of any particular circumstance which may occur, either of the nature of complaint or otherwise.

'The Superintendent is to occupy, free of rent, the apartments appropriated to him, and he will be allowed Fuel, Candles, Salt, Soap, and such other necessary articles as may be required for keeping the house in proper order.

'He is to be responsible for all the Beds, Bedding, Furniture, and other effects in the House, and, as far as is in his power, to preserve them as well as the building and fixtures from injury.

'He is, together with his wife, to keep the House, the Bedding, Furniture, &c., scrupulously clean, and, to the best of his ability, conduct the establishment according to the Rules laid down for his government; in addition to which, the following instructions are to be carefully observed:—

1. No Lodgers to be admitted who are filthy in their persons, or of known bad character.

2. Although it is a Rule of the House that each Lodger will pay his rent in advance, yet, as from time to time it may occur that Lodgers of whom the Superintendent has reason to form a good opinion may, from want of employment or other causes, be unable to pay, he may give credit to such for two weeks, but not longer, and this indulgence is not to be extended to more than three at any one time; in every such case the arrear may be paid gradually, but with as little delay as possible.

3. As it respects the notice required from a Lodger before he leaves the house, although the Lodgers are weekly tenants, if, under peculiar and unforeseen circumstances, a tenant is obliged to leave the house suddenly, or if he has been a tenant for three months, any money paid by him in advance may be returned to him.

4. The due observance of the Rules to which every Lodger subjects himself on his admission is to be enforced by the Superintendent: and in the discharge of this somewhat difficult part of his duty, he is expected to combine firmness with kindness, and to abstain from all needless and vexatious interference with the Lodgers.

5. In the management of the establishment, strict regard to economy must be observed, so as to prevent all waste of the articles to be provided for the Lodgers, which will comprise Fuel, Candles, Salt and Soap.

6. In reference to the Books placed under the care of the Superintendent, he is to keep a list of them, and to enter regularly the name of every Lodger to whom they are lent, and to see that they are returned in good order.'

Appendix 3 to Chapter Three

A typical set of rules drawn up by the S.I.C.L.C. relating to the Lodgers.

'Rules of the Lodging-House for Unmarried Workmen and Labourers at the Society's Lodging-Houses.

'The Lodgers are to be admitted by the week, on payment of .... per week, in advance, and are to be subject to the following Rules, which are intended for the general comfort of the inmates, and the good order of the Establishment:—

1. The House to be open from Five in the morning till Ten o'clock at night, subject to alteration according to the season of the year and to the occupations of the Lodgers.

2. The Lamp in the Bed-Room to be lighted from Nine o'clock in the evening to Half-past Ten o'clock, when it is to be extinguished.

3. As the occupancy is by the week, each Lodger must give the Superintendent at least two day's notice, before the end of the week, if it be his intention not to remain, otherwise it will be considered that his occupancy is continued.

4. Each Lodger will be provided with a box and locker, for the security of his property, the keys of which will be delivered to him on depositing the sum of One shilling, to be returned on the re-delivery of the keys. All property belonging to the Lodgers must be considered as under their own care, and at their own risk.

5. Each Lodger will be provided with a tray, two plates, a basin, a jug, a cup and saucer, or a metal cup, a knife, fork, and two spoons, which are to be under his own care, and on leaving the House, they are to be returned to the Superintendent in a sound state.

6. The property of the Establishment is to be treated with due care, and, in particular, no cutting or writing on the Tables, Forms, Chairs, or other articles, and no defacing of the Walls, will be permitted. Any damage done by a Tenant is to be made good at his expense, or any article entrusted to him for his use, which may be lost or broken, is to be reinstated at his expense.

7. No spiritous liquors to be brought into the House, or drunk there. No person to be admitted or allowed to remain in a state of intoxication. No one, excepting the Lodgers, to be admitted into the House, excepting with the permission of the Superintendent.

8. No card-playing, gambling, quarrelling, fighting, profane or abusive language, will be permitted; and it is expected that the Superintendent and his Wife will be treated with respect: their duty in promoting the comfort of the Inmates will be to see that these Rules are strictly observed.

9. Habits of Cleanliness are expected in the Lodgers, and any person guilty of filthy or dirty practices, or rendering himself offensive to the other inmates, will not be permitted to remain in the House. Smoking cannot be allowed in the Living-Room or Bed-Room, but in the Kitchen only.

10. A wilful breach of any of the above Rules will subject the party to immediate exclusion from the House; but any money paid by him in advance will be returned after deducting the rent then due, and the amount of any damage which he may have done to the property.

11. It is expected that every Lodger will so conduct himself on the Sabbath, as not to desecrate the day.

12. For the benefit of those who may wish to avail themselves of the opportunity, the *Holy Scriptures*, and other books of an interesting and instructive character, will be lent by the Superintendent, in the hope that the Lodgers in this House will be thereby induced to spend their leisure hours in a profitable manner, as intelligent and accountable beings'.

Appendix 4 to Chapter Three

Roberts' Suggestions for Terms and Agreements for Letting Cottages.

'Terms and Conditions of Letting the Cottages belonging to .... Situated in the Parish of .... and County of ....

1. The Rent to be paid punctually, as per Agreement.

2. All Rates and Taxes in respect of the House to be paid by the Landlord.

3. Either party may terminate the Tenancy at any time, by giving a week's notice for that purpose.

4. Only one Family will be permitted to reside in a Cottage, and the Tenant is not to underlet or take in a Lodger, or carry on any trade or business therein, or keep poultry or a pig, without leave first obtained in writing from the Landlord or his Agent.

5. The Windows are to be kept clean, and the Ground-Floor Chimneys are to be swept once in Six Months. No alteration — by fixing or removing shelves or other fixtures — is to be made, without permission of the Landlord or his Agent.

6. General outside repairs are to be done at the expense of the Landlord.

7. The Windows, Ovens, and Coppers, are to be kept in repair by the Landlord, and the cost of such repairs to be repaid by the Tenant; as well as the cost of white-washing once a year, with the making good of any damaged plastering.

8. The Fences to be kept in repair by the Landlord, and cost of repair to be re-paid in equal proportions, by the Tenants of the Cottages enclosed within such Fence.

9. The re-payment agreed to in the Clauses numbered 7 and 8, as above, to be made by the several tenants, within one week after payment thereof shall have been demanded by the Landlord's Agent.

10. The Tenant to clear away the ashes, and to remove all manure, &c., which may have been laid near the Cottage, every week.

11. The Gardens in front of the Cottages to be kept in good order, and the Cottages themselves in a neat and tidy state, to the satisfaction of the Landlord or his Agent.

12. Free access to be given, at all times, to the Landlord, his Agent, Servants, or Workmen'.

FORM OF AGREEMENT

.... does hereby agree with .... to take of him the Cottage .... from week to week, at the weekly rent of .... to be paid by the said .... to the said .... at the end of each week, subject to the terms and conditions above specified.

As witness their hands, this .... day of .... 185............

Witness ....
....

References for Chapter Four — *The Designs for Model Dwellings for Families by Henry Roberts after 1849.*

1. *See* Curl, James Stevens, 'An Indictment of Bad Planning. Mile End New Town', *Country Life*, 10 November 1977.
2. *The Builder*, VII, 1849, p.325; *The Labourers' Friend*, January 1848, p. 2; *Ibid.*, February 1848, p.18; *Ibid.*, June 1848, p. 81; *Ibid.*, August 1849, p.113.
3. Roberts, Henry, *The Dwellings of the Labouring Classes*, London, 1853 edition, p.10.
4. *The Labourers' Friend*, June 1850, p.83.
5. *Ibid.*, July 1850, p.97; July 1851, p.97. *See also The Builder*, Vol. VIII, 1850, p. 287.
6. The original of the letter is in the Royal Library at Windsor Castle. A copy is in the papers of the Royal Commission for the Exhibition of 1851. Mr. Anthony James very kindly made these papers available for study. RA.F.24/66.
7. His handwriting is execrable. RA.F.24/74, 75. The letter is nine sides long.
8. *See* Foyle, A. M. Article in *The Builder* of 2 January 1953. *See also* the Duke's letter of 25 May 1851.
9. Papers of the Royal Commission for the Exhibition of 1851.
10. *The Brick Builder*, 1851, pp.122-4.
11. *Official Descriptive Illustrated Catalogue of the Great Exhibition, 1851*, Vol. II, pp.774-5.
12. Foyle, A. M., *op. cit.*
13. Papers of the Royal Commission for the Exhibition of 1851. Further letters are in the Royal Archives at Windsor Castle.
14. RA.F.24/153.
15. It survives in the Royal Library at Windsor Castle.
16. RA.F.25/64.
17. RA.F.25/65.
18. RA.F.25/66.
19. Papers of the Royal Commission for the Exhibition of 1851.
20. *The Builder*, Vol. IX, 1851, pp.311-2, and 343.
21. *The Builder*, Vol. IX, 1851, pp. 343-4.
22. *The Builder*, Vol. IX, 1851, pp. 311-2.

23. Mr. Anthony James has been most helpful in showing the Author through the mass of material.

24. *Minutes of The Proceedings of Her Majesty's Commissioners for the Exhibition of 1851*, London, 1852, pp. 373-5.

25. *See The Warrington Guardian*, 14 April 1951, and correspondence relating to 107-113, Church Street, Warrington, especially papers of the Borough Engineer and Surveyor, kindly made available by Dr. A. M. Foyle. *See The Labourers' Friend*, 1851, p.90 for the houses at the Great Exhibition; *Ibid.*, 1852, p. 82 for a description of ten houses at Ramsgate on Henry Roberts' plan; *Ibid.*, 1854 for a report that in May twenty-four more houses were completed at Shadwell. This information was kindly provided by Dr. A. M. Foyle in the papers he so generously made available for study.

26. L.C.C., Kennington Park Papers (deposited by H.M. Office of Works with the Metropolitan Board of Works).

27. L.C.C. Minutes, 24 May 1898.

28. The monthly reports in *The Labourers' Friend* after 1851 emphasise this point.

29. *The Labourers' Friend*, July 1853, p.97.

30. *Ibid.*, December 1854, p. 187. *The Builder*, Vol. XII, 1854, p.589.

31. Dickens, Charles, *Household Words*, Vol. X, 16 Dec. 1854, p. 409.

32. *The Labourers' Friend*, November 1848, p. 186; *Ibid.*, July 1850, p.97. *See also The Builder*, Vol. XXI, 1862, p.890, and *The Labourers' Friend*, January 1863, p. 582.

33. Much of the information in this Chapter is derived from the Minutes of the S.I.C.L.C., now held by The Peabody Trust.

Appendix 1 to Chapter Four

   'Expenditure on, and Revenue from Model Houses.

   'The following statement of the cost of land — expense of construction — amount of rents received, and annual expenditure connected with the several buildings belonging to the Society for Improving the Condition of the Labouring Classes, will be interesting to those who contemplate similar undertakings:—

   1. Model Buildings, Bagnigge Wells, for 23 families and 30 single females, commenced in 1844. Cost of land, 1045*l.*; outlay on the buildings, 5325*l.*; average rents per annum 391*l.*; taxes and current expenses, exclusive of repairs, 83*l.*, per annum, leaving a return of about 4.33 per cent. on the cost of the buildings, and of 4 per cent. on the cost of the land.

   2. George Street Model Lodging House for 104 single men, commenced in 1846. Cost of land 1200*l*; outlay on the buildings, 4289*l.*; outlay on the furniture, 936*l.*; average receipts from the lodgers, 614*l.*; per annum. Taxes and current expenses, exclusive of repairs, are 308*l.*, per annum, leaving a return of about 5 per cent. on the cost of the building and furniture, and of 4 per cent. on the cost of the land.

   3. Streatham Street Model Houses for 54 families, commenced in 1849. The land is rented at 50*l.* per annum. The outlay on the buildings has been 8860*l.* The rents since the addition of six tenements to the forty-eight originally provided, are at the rate of 745*l.* per annum. The ground-rent, taxes, and current expenses, exclusive of repairs, are 235*l.* per annum, leaving a return of 5.75 per cent. on the amount of outlay.

   4. Thanksgiving Model Buildings, Portpool Lane, Gray's Inn Lane, for 20 families, 128 single women, and a public wash house, commenced in 1850. Cost of the land, 1700*l.*; outlay on the buildings, 9500*l.* The amount of revenue derivable from the whole cannot yet be stated, owing to the length of time required for bringing into full operation the washing establishment, for which there is reason to believe increased accommodation will be required. The house for single women has filled more slowly than the family houses, which found immediate occupants at fair remunerative rents.

5. Charles Street Lodging House, for 84 single men. Amount of outlay on repairs, adapting and furnishing, 1163*l.*, average receipts from the lodgers, 415*l.* per annum. Rent, taxes, and current expenses, exclusive of repairs, amount to 222*l.* per annum, which leaves a clear return of 17 per cent. on the amount of outlay.

6. Hatton Garden Lodging House, for 57 single women. Amount of outlay on repairs, adapting and furnishing, 1045*l.* This house has been let as a depôt for female emigrants at a fixed rent, returning 7½ per cent. on the outlay.

'The total expenditure on the six buildings above described, with the furniture of the lodging-houses, is 31,118*l.*, and on the land or site of three of the buildings is 3945*l.*; the net return, exclusive of repairs, from those fully occupied, being at the rate of about 6 per cent. on the buildings and furniture, and of 4 per cent. on the land.

'In reference to the outlay of repairs, the experience of the Society shows that, taking new and old buildings together, and including the furniture, an average expenditure of ¾ per cent. per annum is sufficient.

'It should be observed that the revenue as shown above, might be easily augmented by raising some of the rents to the full value of the property; this applies particularly to the Model Buildings, Bagnigge Wells, the cost of which it has been already noticed was increased by peculiar circumstances. Moreover, the experience gained in the arrangement and construction of these houses, as well as the removal of duties on building materials since their construction, ought to facilitate the erection of similar buildings at a diminished cost'.

Appendix 2 to Chapter Four

Roberts' arguments against the Duty on Bricks, published as an appendix to his work on *The Dwellings of the Labouring Classes*.

'THE INJURIOUS EFFECTS OF THE DUTY ON BRICKS

'When the foregoing Essay was read at the Institute of British Architects, the Author mentioned that the hollow tiles used in the construction of the roofs and floors of the Streatham Street Model Houses for Families were passed free of duty by the Supervisor, on the ground of their being roof and floor tiles, and not intended to be used in the construction of walls. A few days after this statement had been made, an officer from the Board of Excise called on him for some explanation, and he was referred to the clause in the Act 2 & 3 Vict., Cap. 24, which specially exempts roof-tiles from duty; the Board have, however, decided, not only that they are liable to duty as bricks, but that double duty shall be charged on account of the external dimensions, cubing to more than 150 inches, although the actual cubical contents of clay is less than 140 inches. Such a decision appears to be in direct opposition to the Act, which provides explicitly for ascertaining the cubical contents of bricks, where any doubt may arise to the rate of duty to which they are subject, and explicitly states that it shall be decided by pressing the clay into a mould 10 inches long, 3 inches thick, and 5 inches wide; and if the clay is not more than sufficient to full such mould, "the bricks shall be deemed and taken to be bricks not exceeding 150 cubic inches, and subject to the lower rate of duty".

'A more striking proof of the injurious effect of this impost, as well as of the present system of levying it, can scarcely be instanced. The use of a mode of construction, calculated to prove generally beneficial, as securing the important advantages of rendering roofs and floors fire-proof, sound-proof, and water-proof, with a degree of lightness otherwise unobtainable, is thus likely to be impeded, and the dwellings of the lower classes deprived of the benefit which would result from the general adoption of a system calculated to add essentially to the comfort and durability, not only of the lowest, but of the highest class of buildings.

'The duty on bricks, levied according to the letter of the Act, offers a sufficient barrier to the exercise of inventive skill — in turning to the best account a material which providence has placed so largely at the command of the architect for the benefit of his fellow-creatures; but when double imposts are levied where the law does not enact them, he cannot but sigh for the legislative adoption of free-trade principles in reference to articles of home produce and manufacture, as well as those of foreign growth and product'.

Appendix 3 to Chapter Four

Henry Roberts' Specification for the Model Dwellings erected at the Great Exhibition of 1851.

SPECIFICATION

Of Work to be done in Erecting a Block of MODEL HOUSES FOR FAMILIES, *containing Four Distinct Tenements*

THE PLANS, ELEVATIONS, AND SECTIONS FOR THE SAID BUILDING ARE TO BE STRICTLY ATTENDED TO FOR FORM, DIMENSIONS, AND ESPECIALLY FOR THE CONSTRUCTIVE DETAIL, AS WELL AS FOR ALL OTHER PARTICULARS THEREIN SET FORTH, SUBJECT ONLY TO SUCH VARIATIONS AS MAY BE RENDERED NECESSARY BY PECULIARITY OF SITUATION, OR OTHER CIRCUMSTANCES, AND WHICH SHALL BE AGREED ON AND DEFINED IN WRITING'

NOTE:—The items thus marked (*) must be agreed upon before a Contract can be made.

EXCAVATOR

Dig out the trenches of sufficient depth and width to receive the footings of foundation walls as shown on the sections; fill in and ram to the brickwork when built.

If the ground be sufficiently good and firm for the foundations, the trenches are only to be excavated to the average depth of 1 ft., perfectly level and even to receive the brick footings.

* If the ground be loose, in order to obtain a firm and even foundation, which is *indispensable*, and must be specially observed, the trenches are to be increased in depth and filled up to the footings with a stratum of concrete, not less than 1 ft. 6 in. thick, and at least 9 in. wider than the footings, formed of clean coarse gravel and grey stone lime, in the proportion of eight parts of the former to one part of the latter, well incorporated, and mixed with a due proportion of water, being thrown in from a stage at least 6 ft. high.

* Excavate for drains, cesspools, tanks, &c., as may be required by the situation.

All the superfluous earth to be levelled round the building, or removed to such part of the ground as may be directed.

All rubbish to be cleared away at the completion of the works.

BRICKLAYER

The whole of the bricks, whether hollow or solid, are to be of the best quality of their respective kinds, hard burnt, sound, and well-shaped.

The mortar to be composed of fresh stone lime and clean sharp sand, in the proportion of three parts of sand to one of lime, well mixed.

All the cement used, to be the best Roman, unless otherwise specified.

The common stock brickwork to rise four courses to a foot, and the hollow brickwork three courses to a foot precisely, unless otherwise specified.

The footings are to be two courses deep of common stocks, the first course to be 18 in. and the next 14 in. wide in mortar; the next two courses to be the fair work, also in stocks, on which must commence the hollow brickwork.

A dust bin is to be formed under the staircase with 9 in. wall of common stocks or hollow bricks, and of the dimensions shown on the plans, 5 ft. deep from the ground floor line to top of footings, at which level a solid brick flat paving must be laid and grouted with cement on a bed of concrete at least 3 in. thick.

Where there is any reason to apprehend the rising of damp, a course of strong slate well bedded in cement should be built under the first course of hollow bricks, or a coat of metallic lava, five-eighths in. thick, should be laid on.

* According to agreement, to be noted at the foot of this Specification, the walls are to be built either with the patent bonded hollow bricks or with good stock bricks.

If hollow bricks are used, the constructive details must be in strict conformity with those given in the plans, elevations, and sections. The external walls having the inclined face of bricks set outwards, and at the string courses the internal backing up to be in 6 in. partition bricks.

All the walls are to be of the height and thickness shown on the drawings, great care to be taken in carrying them up perpendicularly and horizontally.

The external and the 9 in. internal walls, with the 6 in. partitions, are to be built in mortar. The 4 in. partitions are to be set in cement with two tiers of hoop iron bond, properly connected at the angles.

All window and door arches, and the large arch over staircase recess are to be cut and set in cement, and tuck pointed; also, all external strings to be in cement.

Two courses throughout, immediately under the ground floor level – viz., the upper course of common stocks and the first course of hollow bricks, are to be set in cement with two rows of strong hoop iron bond laid in between them. Three courses all round the building, at the first floor and roof levels, commencing with the sailing course under the springings of arches, and including the 9 in. and 6 in. internal walls to be set in cement with two rows of strong hoop iron bond laid in on top of second course.

Great care must be taken to securely connect the hoop iron bond at all the angles and cross walls, and the overlaps to be turned at least 12 in long.

The smoke flues are to be carried up as shown on the drawings, 9 in. square when finished, properly pargetted and cored; or they may be circular, 10 in. diameter.

26 cast-iron bricks and 48 ventilating valves will be supplied by the proprietor, and must be allowed for and built in by the contractor in such places as shall be directed, to communicate with the smoke flues and warm air chambers behind the living-room fire-places, also with the external atmosphere, and air flues of an average length of 2 ft. to be formed through the hollow bricks to each.

Form a dust-shaft 14 in. by 9 in. in the clear, well rendered with cement, and left perfectly smooth. The Shaft to be commenced 2 ft. 8 in. below the ground-floor line in the situation shown on the drawings, and carried up at least 4 in. above the finished surface of the roof for ventilation to the dust-bin, &c.; this shaft is to serve also for the transmission of the water supply, service, and waste pipes.

Cast-iron abutment springers are to be built in the external walls, and connected with wrought iron tie rods through the building. The end tie rods are to pass through a course of the hollow bricks.

The upper floors and roofs are to be formed of hollow brick arches, turned in cement on proper centering. They are to be 6 in. deep over the living-rooms, parents' bed-rooms, and staircase, and may be 4¼ in. deep over the small bed-rooms, lobbies, and water closets. Special care must be taken to have the centering sufficiently strong and well shored up, in order to prevent the slightest settlement or deflection taking place while the arches are being turned, and the centres are not to be removed under eight or ten days after their completion.

The floor arches are to be levelled up with concrete, averaging 4 in. thick, properly prepared to receive cement or lava flooring. The roof arches are also to have a levelling of concrete, averaging 6 in. thick, laid to a fall of at least 1½ in. to 10 ft., and properly prepared for, and covered with, a coat of metallic lava, at least ¾ in. thick, with a skirting all round, averaging 5 ft. high, turned into joint of brickwork.

* If any of the floors are to be boarded, the concrete must there be omitted (for description, *see* Carpenter's Work), and if boarded on ground-floor, air-bricks must be built in for ventilation.

The chimney stacks above the roof are to be carried up to the height, &c., as shown on the drawings. The bases and caps are to be formed of splayed bricks set in cement.

The external work to be of an uniform colour, carefully selected, with neat flat drawn joints.

The walls to the whole of the interior are to be worked fair for colour or limewhite.

The soffit of the floor and roof arches are to be cleaned, and prepared for whiting.

* According to agreement, and if the nature of the soil and locality be sufficiently dry, the ground-floor may be laid with hollow bricks, dowelled at the heading joints, or the ordinary paving tiles, bedded in cement on a layer of concrete 4 in. thick. If arches are used, the skewbacks must be formed on the upper course of footings in cement.

The area to staircase to be covered with the gravel lava on a bed of concrete 6 in. thick.

All the door and window frames to be built in and pointed, with good hair mortar.

Form ornamental gables with ramps, &c., on front parapet, and similar ramps to the chimney stacks, as shown on the drawings.

Form hollow brick corbels or sailing courses 12 in. long, to receive end of steps to staircase against main wall.

The newel wall to staircase to be built according to drawings with hollow bricks in cement, and 4 in. corbel stone or brick caps to piers, and to receive lintels.

Hollow brick lintels to be formed over all internal, and the inside of external doors, also over the 4 ft. 3 in. recesses in living rooms, by passing 1¼ in. T iron bars through the hollow of bricks, and grouting the same solid with cement. Two bars are to be used in the 9 in. walls, and one in the 4 in. partition walls, each to be 12 in. longer than the respective opening. The latter of these lintels may be dispensed with if desired.

The chimney pieces in the living-rooms to be formed of hollow bricks with small chamfered angles or arrises, the jambs to be 9 in. wide and to project 4½ in. The mantel to be 4½ in. deep, and project 4½ in. set in cement. The mantel to have 1¼ in. T iron passed through hollow of bricks, and grouted solid with cement, the shelf to be of slate as described in Slater's Work.

A dust door, or valve, to be built in under the slate shelf adjoining the sink in each scullery, and a proper shoot to be formed with bricks in cement leading into the shaft, well rendered in cement and left perfectly smooth.

Set the grates in the living and bedrooms. Those in the living-rooms are to have hot-air chambers formed behind them.

* Lay in a sufficient quantity of 4 in. and 6 in. glazed drain pipes with socket joints set in cement, to convey soil and waste from water-closets and sinks to the sewer.

* If there be no sewer in the immediate vicinity, a cesspool must be formed 8 ft. deep from the overflow, and 5 ft. clear diameter in 6 in. hollow bricks on end, or in two half-brick rims, the outer one set in mortar, the inner one in cement, the bottom brick flat and two courses plain tiles set in cement. The whole to be rendered with cement and doomed over, with manhole in centre, covered with a strong stone. An overflow drain, with proper syphon trap, to be laid from the cesspool to some convenient escape.

MASON

Provide and fix in cement 4 in. tooled and splayed York templates to ends of all the cast-iron girders and springers of the sizes necessary to secure perfect bond with the patent bonded hollow bricks.

* Provide and fix to all internal walls in cement 3 in. tooled York springers 14 in. wide, chamfered both edges for floor and roof arches, unless they be of brick in cement.

Provide and fix 3 in. ditto ditto 8½ in. wide, built in over entrance doors and water-closets in walls against staircase, to receive narrow arches over lobbies and water-closets.

Provide and fix three pinnacles in Portland cement, Caen or Bath stone, moulded according to drawing, and set same in cement to ornamental gables in front.

Provide and fix to all the ground-floor windows, and those in the staircase, tooled York sills, properly sunk, weathered, and throated, 11 in. wide and 4 in. thick, with back edges fair tooled for inside, and grooved on top for metal tongue in oak sill.

* In localities where there is any difficulty in procuring stone for window-sills, &c., they may be formed of hollow jamb bricks, 10½ in. long, set in cement, to project 1½ in. with the splay upwards, and on a slight inclination to form weathering or drip for water.

Provide and fix 2½ in., tooled York back hearths to all the fireplaces; also, 2 in., rubbed York slabs to the same, 1 ft. 6 in. wide, and 1 ft. 6 in. longer than their respective openings. The latter may be dispensed with if the floors are in Portland cement.

SLATER

The staircase is to be of 1½ in. slate treads and 1 in. risers. Winders top and bottom, as shown on Drawings, with rounded nosings, and the risers grooved into treads both edges. The treads are to be set on corbels built out of the brickwork for that purpose on the wall side, and to be built 2½ in. in the newel wall. The upper winders are to be suspended with proper irons 1½ in. by 1½ in. over the window arches, the whole to be well put together with good cement, and left perfectly clean at the completion of the building.

Provide 1½ in. rubbed slate steps and risers 12 in. wide and 5 in. high, morticed for door frames, with rounded nosings, and properly bedded in cement.

Provide and fix 1½ in. rubbed slate landing in one piece, built in the walls at each end, and resting on cast-iron girder one side, and the other on the newel wall of staircase, forming a gallery of communication to the upper houses.

Provide a cistern of 1¼ in. slate, properly grooved and bolted together with oil cement in joints, to contain not less than 250 gallons, and fix the same on the roof raised on hollow brick piers 8 in. high over the ventilating shaft from dust-bin; cut all necessary holes for the Plumber for pipes.

Provide in each scullery a sink of 1 in. slate 2 ft. 4 in. by 1 ft. 4 in. inside dimensions, with tops, sides, and fronts to coal-box underneath, all the arrises to be either chamfered or rounded off, the whole to be made in strict conformity to the drawings, put together with screws and nuts and oil cement, and fixed in the most secure manner. — *Note:* These sinks can be provided ready made in slate or cast iron, including the fittings to coal-box underneath, and will only require fixing.

Provide and fix three ¾ in. rubbed slate shelves in each safe — the bottom shelf to have rounded edge. These shelves are to be kept ½ in. from the back wall for the purpose of ventilation.

Provide ½ in. rubbed slate for the centre compartment in each of the three light windows to the small bed-rooms. (For fixing, *see* Carpenter's, &c., Work).

Provide and fix 1¼ in. rubbed and rounded slate mantel-shelf over the fireplaces in each living-room 7 in. wide in the clear, and to project 3 in. at each end, the corners to be rounded. These shelves must be built in the wall at least 3½ in., and fixed as the work is carried up.

PLASTERER

Twice white or colour all the ceilings and walls throughout the building internally.

The whole of the first floor is to be laid with patent Portland cement, at least 1 in. thick, properly floated and finished with a trowelled face on a levelling-up of concrete, as described in Bricklayer's Work.

* The ground-floor is to be laid with hollow bricks bedded in cement, dowelled at heading-joints on concrete, 4 in. thick. (*See* Bricklayer's Work.†)

† In some parts of the country, lime and sand floors are very much used, and found to last, when well made, upwards of forty years. The following description of the mode of working them may be useful: A foundation or substratum should be prepared, about six inches thick, with coarse gravel or brickbats, and lime core, well beaten to a level surface; in damp situations tar may be added to this concrete, on which is to be laid the lime and ash floor, thus prepared: Take good washed sand, free from all earth and small stones, together with the ashes of lime, fresh from the kiln, in the proportions of two thirds of sand and one-third of lime-ashes. (Where obtainable, the substitution of one-third portion of smiths' ashes, or pounded coke, for one half of the sand, increases the durability

* The coping to the parapet to be in Portland cement 1½ in. wide, 3 in. thick, properly weathered and throated both edges, and cored out with two courses of plain tiles in cement, to be continued round the ramps, &c., to gables in front, and to end chimney stacks. Jamb bricks, No. 3, in cement, may be used for the coping where preferred.

Properly weather with Portland cement all external strings and sailing courses.

CARPENTER AND JOINER

All the timber and deals used are to be of good quality, free from sap, shakes, large, or dead knots.

Provide all centering for floor and roof arches, and turning pieces to apertures.

* If any of the floors are boarded on the arches, they must be of 1 in. yellow deal straight joint, well nailed to joists 2 in. by 2 in., cut out 1 in. to fit the crown or curve of arch, notched and nailed on sleepers 3 in. by 2 in. The joists not to exceed 12 in. apart.

Provide and fix proper solid, wrought, rebated, and chamfered window frames, and mullions of deal 4½ in. by 3 in. with oak sunk, weathered and throated sills, grooved on underside for metal tongue in stone sill, 1¼ in. staffbead or ¾ in. double chamfered fillet, 2¼ in wide mitred round inside to stop joint of brickwork.

† The living-room window frames in three lights are each to have a galvanized wrought-iron casement, hung in the centre compartment with hinges, turnbuckle, and proper stay-bar fastenings, the other two compartments to have T iron cross bars, properly fixed across the centre to divide each light into two squares.

The three light window frames to the small bed-rooms to have the centre compartments blanked with ½ in. rubbed slate, properly bedded and screwed therein; the other two comparments in these windows to have casements hung as those in the living-rooms.

One casement of the same description to be hung in each of the two-light window frames to the parents' bed-rooms; the other light in each window to have T iron bar fixed across the centre as before.

The sculleries are to have two-light window frames divided into two squares high, as those to living-rooms; the upper square of one compartment in each window to be provided with an iron frame or casement hinged on T iron cross bar, to open downwards with iron rack fastening complete.

The water-closets to have one-light window frames divided into two squares, the upper one being in an iron casement hung to T iron cross bar, with rack fastening as to sculleries. (For Glazing, see Glazier's Work; and for Iron Casements, &c., see Smith.)

The entrance doors to be 1½ in. square framed, filled in with ¾ in. wrought, tongued and beaded boards, with panel 8 in. deep, formed at top for glass to be stopped in with beads, hung with 3½ in. butts to solid, wrought, rebated, and chamfered frames, 4½ in. by 3 in. A ¾ in. chamfered fillet, 2¼ in. wide, to be nailed round inside of frame to stop joint of brickwork. Fix a 9 in. rim lock, one 9 in. barrel bolt, one pair of ornamental straps, and ditto escutcheon to keyhole, to each door.

The dusthole under stairs to have a 1 in. proper ledged door, hung with 3 in. butts to proper, solid, wrought, and rebated frame, 4½ in. by 3 in. dowelled into slate sill, and to have a 6 in. deadlock.

The internal doors to be 1½ in. square framed, four panels, hung with 3 in. butts to 1½ in. wrought, rebated, chamfered, and staff-beaded linings; those in the 9 in. walls to be 6½ in. wide, and those in the 4 in. partitions to be 3½ in. wide. The staffbeads to be mitred round on one side (see Drawing), and one bow latch to be fixed to each door.

---

and hardness of the floor.) Mix the sand and lime-ashes well together, and let them remain in a body for a fortnight, in order that the lime may be thoroughly slaked; then temper the mortar, and form the floor with it, three inches thick, well floated, and so worked, that it be not trodden on until it has laid for three days; it should then be well rammed for several successive days, until it becomes hard, taking care to keep the surface level; after that, use a little water and smoothe it with a trowel; keep the floor free of dirt, and when perfectly dry it may be rubbed over twice with linseed oil, which gives the appearance of stone instead of sand.

The price paid for such floors is about 6d. per yard for labour, and 8d. per yard for materials.

† If ornamental casements be adopted, they are to have zinc bars with galvanized wrought iron frames, as are shown in the elevations.

A cupboard to be formed in the 14 in. recess in each living-room, with 1½ in. deal framed fronts and square framed doors in two heights, hung with 3 in. butts, and to have lock, knobturnbuckle, &c., fixed complete, each cupboard to be provided with four 1 in. shelves, wrought and fixed on proper bearers.

A closet in each of the parents' bed-rooms to be formed as shown on the drawing, with 1½ in. framed fronts, and 1½ in. square framed 4 in. panel doors, to correspond with room doors, hung with 3 in. butts, and to have good lock, knobturnbuckle, &c., fixed complete. Provide and fix in each of these closets a ¾ in. double chamfered hook rail, 3½ in. wide, with No. 4 iron hat and cloak pins screwed thereon.

A safe is to be formed in each scullery, as shown on the drawing, with 1¼ in. framed fronts, and doors hung with 3 in. butts, and to have knobturnbuckle, &c., fixed complete. One ¾ in.deal wrought end 14 in. wide, to be provided and fixed to each, with fillets screwed on to receive ¾ in. slate shelves. A box ventilator, fitted with perforated zinc and valve, to be let in these ends. (For Shelves, *see* Slater's Work.)

A plate rack is to be provided and fixed in each scullery, over one end of the sink, 3 ft. high, 1 ft. 6 in. wide, and 8 in. deep, framed in three heights and covered with ½ in. rounded top.

A 1¼ in. deal frame clamped table top, 4 ft. 6 in. by 2 ft. 6 in. to be provided in each living-room, hung with 3½ in. butts to the window board, to fall down or turn up against the window to form shutter. Deal framed angle brackets, hung in proper frame, or to 1 in. grounds, 3 in wide, securely fixed to the wall to support the flap when used as a table. A 4 in. neck bolt to be screwed to the window mullion, to secure the flap when used as a shutter.

The following 1 in. deal wrought shelving, 9 in. wide, to be provided and fixed on ¾ in., chamfered all round, hook rail 3½ in. wide, and plain wrought iron brackets.

The scullery in each house to have 9 ft. 5 in. of shelving in two lengths, fixed on one side and end with the same length of hook rail, and one iron bracket. 5 ft. of shelving in each of the small bed-rooms over the doors, with 2 ft. 6 in. run of hook rail, and two iron hat and cloak pins screwed thereon. 9 ft. 6 in. of shelving in each of the parents' bed-rooms over the doors, with 5 ft. of hook rail, one iron bracket, and three iron hat and cloak pins screwed thereon. Two hook rails in each living room, level with the top of doors, one 3 ft. and the other 4 ft. 6 in. long.

A ¾ in. hook rail as before, 3 ft. 6 in. long, with three iron hat and cloak pins screwed on, to be fixed in each entrance lobby.

SMITH AND FOUNDER

Provide and fix a cast iron girder, 7½ in. deep, 7/8 in. thick, with bottom flanges 3 in. wide on the inside to receive slate landing, top flange to be 2 in. wide, 1½ in. deep, chamfered both upper edges, to project ½ in. full on either side, and to have 9 in. bearing on the walls at each end, properly calked and bedded on lead seating laid on stone template.

Provide and fix cast iron railing across the staircase opening, and on the cast iron girder, 3 ft. 3 in. high, as shown on the Drawings.

Provide and fix cast iron railing on staircase landing, over newel wall, with ¾ in. round bars 4 in. apart, 7/8 in. square bottom rail 3 in. up from slate, and a flat round top rail 2 in. wide, ¾ in. thick, with one cast iron plain newel capped with top rail, and securely fixed to slate landing by means of screw and nut.

Provide and fix cast iron springers in external walls to receive floor and roof arches, in two lengths, coupled and bolted together in the middle with ½ in. bolts and screws. These springers are to be cast as shown in the Drawings.

Provide and fix four ¾ in. wrought iron tie-rods to each floor and roof with heads, screws, and nuts, coupled on each main cross wall , properly let into stone springers, to tie in the roof and floor arches through the building; these rods are not to be placed more than 7 ft. 6 in. apart, excepting over the back rooms; the tie rods at ends of springers are to pass through the hollow parts of bricks in the outer walls as shown in section.

Provide three suspension irons 1½ in. by ½ in., to support three upper winders in staircase, one 19 in. long, another 12 in. long, and the other 9 in. long, turned at each end, and let into brick and under the slates. (For fixing, *see* Slater's Work.)

Provide 16 galvanized wrought iron casements, with one T iron cross bar in each, for living-room and bed-room windows, with brass butt hinges, turnbuckle, and stay-bar fastenings complete — size, 4 ft. 1¼ in. by 1 ft. 3½ in. opening in rebate to wood frame.

Provide No. 12 T iron cross-bars, with ends turned to let in and screw to wood frame, of living-room and bed-room windows 1 ft. 4 in. long.

Provide No. 3 ditto casements for scullery windows, 1 ft. 5¼ in. by 11⅛ in., hinged to T iron cross bars, prepared at each end to let in and screw to wood frame, and to have proper iron rack fastenings over centre. No. 1 ditto casement for scullery, window under the staircase, 1 ft. 3 in. by 11⅛ in., hinged as last, &c.

Provide No. 4 T iron cross-bars, prepared at ends as last, 11⅛ in. long for scullery windows in the compartments without casements.

Provide No. 4 ditto casements similar to those in the sculleries for the water-closets, 1 ft. 5¼ in. by 11⅝ in., hinged to T iron cross-bars, &c.

The whole of the iron in connection with these casements and bars to be of good quality and galvanized. (For fixing of these casements and bars, *see* the Carpenter's and Joiner's Work.)

Note: The whole of the above galvanized iron casements and T iron cross-bars, &c., can be supplied ready for fixing.

* FURNISHING IRONMONGERY

Provide No. 18, 12 in. air bricks, and No. 8, 4 in. ditto.

Provide, also, No. 16, 12 in., and 16, 7 in. wall-ventilators; 12, cornice ditto; and No. 4, box ventilators with valve for the safes in sculleries. Also, No. 4, dust doors to be fixed in the sculleries. (For the fixing, *see* Bricklayer's Work.)

Provide and fix two strong plain scrapers, let into stone blocks.

A 9 in. strong two-bolt iron rim lock is to be provided for each entrance door, with proper box staples and large iron knob handles.

One pair of ornamental straps and one keyhole escutcheon to be provided for each entrance door, and also one 9 in. strong barrel bolt.

All the internal doors are to have 4 in. bow latches, with night bolts and brass knob furniture, except the doors leading into the sculleries, which are to be without night bolts. A 6 in. dead lock to be provided for the dust-hole door under stairs.

Provide for the living-rooms four Nicholson's prize cottage ranges, and for the eight bed-rooms, stoves with fire-brick back and cast-iron fronts by the same maker, whose address is Newark-on-Trent.

Note: The fixing of the locks, bolts, latches, &c., is included in the Carpenter's and Joiner's Work.

PLUMBER

Provide 24 lbs. of 4 lb. lead for seatings to cast iron girder and springers.

The water-closets are to be fitted up with Ridgway and Co.'s earthen pans; the water is to be laid on with 1¼ in. iron gas pipe and the supply regulated by Dann's improved valve, with strong iron chain or rod, pull, and handle. These closets are to be connected with the junctions cast on the stack or soil pipes for the purpose, if necessary, with a short length of 4 in. lead socket pipe, and made good with red-lead cement. The pans must be firmly fixed to the floors by means of screws bedded head downwards in the cement floors, and the other ends to be provided with nuts to secure the pans.

The water to be laid on to the cistern with ¾ in. iron gas pipe, and Dann's improved ball valve. The cistern to be provided with a trumpet-mouthed overflow pipe, with 1 in. washer and waste.

The water to be laid on to the sinks with ¾ in. iron gas pipe, with all necessary bends and elbows, and connections, and each to be provided with a ½ in. round water-way brass cock. These pipes are to be branched from the 1¼ in. service pipes to the water-closets.

* Provide and fix to each sink one of 'Lowe's' patent brass grates and traps, with 2 in. lead waste pipe conveyed to a main pipe down one angle of the dust shaft into the drain, unless cast-iron sinks are used, and have Lowe's traps fitted to them.

Provide and fix 2 stacks of rain water and soil pipes 4 in. clear diameter, with proper junctions for water-closets and heads, &c., complete.

GLAZIER

Glaze the windows with good 21 oz. sheet glass, properly bedded with good putty in the wood frames and iron casements, except those in the staircase to the sculleries and water-closets, which are to be glazed with ¼ in. rough plate glass properly bedded, &c. All the wood and iron work to be thoroughly primed before the glass is put in. Clean and leave in perfect repair the whole of the glass at the completion of the works.

The upper panel in the entrance doors to be glazed with 3/8 in. rough plate glass, bedded and stopped in on both sides with beads.

PAINTER AND STAINER

Properly prepare and paint three times, in good oil colour, all the cast iron springers, girder, tie-rods, and railings, all piping and other iron work; the first two coats to be red lead and the other stone colour. The railings and all exposed iron work to have one extra coat of stone colour or such plain colour as may be directed.

Properly prepare, stop, and stain, in imitation of oak, and once varnish all the internal and external wood work.

The whole of the work before described or referred to, with everything necessary for completing the Model Houses, according to the full intent and meaning of the plans, although not particularly specified, must be done by the Contractor in a good and workmanlike manner. He is to find all requisite materials and implements, with scaffolding, &c., and to deliver up the building, free from all rubbish, in a complete and perfect condition, and keep it in the same at his own expense for twelve months after its completion, excepting any damage which may be done by the Tenant.

No extra works are to be charged for, but such as are agreed upon at the time, and an order in writing given to the Contractor. The value of all extra work or omissions, or any other deviation from the specification or drawings, which may be directed by an order in writing, is to be ascertained and determined by some competent architect or surveyor, selected by the Employer, and his decision thereon is to be final and conclusive.

Statement of the Number of Hollow Bricks required in Building the
Model Houses for Four Families

Note: The No. of Bricks refers to the Drawing, Page 14; and in the quantities due allowance is made for waste.

Of No. 1. — External Patent Bonded Hollow Bricks. 18,500
             Of which 859 should be cut in or marked for halves, 850 in
             three quarters and quarters; 250 to be mitred at one end for angles
             to strings, chimneys bases, and capping.

Of No. 2. — Internal Patent Bonded Hollow Bricks 4,870
             Of which 175 should be cut in, or marked for halves,
             and 150 in three quarters and quarters.

Of No. 3. — Quoin and External Jamb Bricks, 10½ inches long 2,450
             Ditto   ditto   7½ inches long 100
             Ditto   ditto   4¼ inches long 400

Of No. 4. — Internal Jamb and Angle Bricks, Square, 9 inches long 1,500
             Ditto   ditto   both angles canted   9 inches long 430
             Ditto   ditto   one angle canted   9 inches long 670
             Ditto   ditto   ditto   5¼ inches long 480

Of No. 5. — 4¼ in Partition and Arch Bricks, 11¾ inches long 3,100
             Of which 100 should be cut in or marked for halves
             and 50 in thirds.

Of No. 6. — 5¾ inch Partition and Arch Bricks, 11¾ inches long. 5,800
             Of which 200 should be cut in or marked for halves
             and 100 in thirds.

ESTIMATE

Of the several Works required to be done in Building MODEL HOUSES FOR FOUR FAMILIES, *according to the Plans and Constructive Detail of those erected by* H.H.R. PRINCE ALBERT, *in Hyde Park*

EXCAVATOR AND BRICKLAYER

Yds.	ft.	in.		at	£	s.	d.
22	0	0	Cube excavation and levelling	6d.	0	11	0
			* Cube concrete of good clean gravel and gray stone lime, well mixed together, in the proportion of 8 parts of the former to 1 of the latter, if necessary, about 35 yards				
	12	0	* Run 4 in. glazed earthen drain pipes with bends and junctions, and including digging and laying the same with socket joints, well bedded in cement (required length to be ascertained)	8d.	0	8	0
	20	0	* Run 6 in. ditto ditto ditto ditto	10d.	0	16	8
			* No. 1. Cesspool 8 ft. deep from the overflow, and 5 ft. clear diameter formed with 6 in. hollow bricks on edge or in two half brick rims, the outer one set in mortar, the inner one with the bottom of brick flat and two courses plain tiles in cement. The whole to be rendered with cement, and doomed over with manhole in centre, covered with a strong stone. A 6 in. glazed overflow drain with proper syphon trap to be formed and carried to some convenient escape (this will not be required if there be good drainage).				

Rods	ft.	in.		at	£	s.	d.
1	73	0	Superficial reduced common stock brickwork in foundations, the first or lower course to be 18 in. wide, the next or second course to be 14 in. wide, with two courses fair work on same, and including 4 feet extra depth for dust bin under stairs	£8 15s.	11	2	6

Yds.	ft.	in.		at	£	s.	d.
377	4	0	Superficial 9 in. reduced hollow brick external walling, in mortar, with neat flat drawn joint, worked fair for colour inside, and including all strings and sailing courses, as shown on the elevations and sections, which are to be set in cement	3s. 4d.	62	18	4
5	0	0	Ditto ditto set in cement	5s.	1	5	0
80	0	0	Superficial ditto ditto, internal walling, worked, fair for colour or limewhite, and including sailing courses as before	3s. 4d.	13	6	8
29	2	0	Superficial 6 in. hollow-brick partitions in mortar, worked fair for colour, sailing courses as before	2s. 6d.	3	13	1
114	4	6	Superficial 4 in. ditto ditto in cement, ditto for colour, but without sailing courses	2s.	11	9	0
140	6	0	Superficial 6 in. ditto ditto, floor and roof arches turned in Roman cement, and including centering, &c.	3s. 10d.	26	19	2

Estimate – continued

Yds.	ft.	in.		at	£	s.	d.
56	0	0	Superficial 4 in. ditto ditto, ditto, and including ditto over small bed-rooms, lobbies, and water closets	2s. 8d.	7	9	4
111	0	0	Superficial concrete, average 6 in. thick, laid to a fall and floated to receive metallic lava on roof arches	1s. 2d.	6	9	6
95	0	0	Superficial ditto ditto 4-in. thick, and properly levelled on arches to receive Portland cement, lava, or tile floors	9½d.	3	15	2
118	0	0	Superficial metallic lava laid on roof, and including skirting about 6 in. high	3s. 9d.	22	2	6
5	6	0	Superficial gravel lava and concrete 6 in. thick at foot of staircase between lobby doors	4s. 6d.	1	5	6
2	0	0	Superficial brick flat paving, grouted with cement, to dust bin, on concrete 3 inches thick	2s.	0	4	0
190	0	0	Superficial cleaning off and preparing soffit of floor and roof arches for limewhite	4d.	3	3	4
	112	4	Superficial cut and tuckpointed window and door arches, and including the large arch over staircase opening	2½d.	1	3	5
	98	0	Superficial extra only for cement (instead of mortar) to ½ brick arches over windows, doors, and archway to staircase	1¾d.	0	14	3½
	16	0	Run labour to circular cutting 9 in. wall to back of arch over stairs	3d.	0	4	0
	23	0	Run ditto ditto ditto 9 in. wall to ramps for coping	3d.	0	5	9
	429	0	Run extra only for cement and two rows hoop iron bond round building, three courses high at floor and roof levels, including cross walls	1½d.	2	13	7½
	215	0	Run ditto ditto ditto two courses high, to foundation, as specified	1d.	0	17	11
	153	0	Run 1¼ in. T iron, in No. 33 pieces, passed through hollow of bricks, and grouted solid with cement, to form lintels over internal doorways	4d.	2	11	0

	at	£	s.	d.
No. 3. Chimney shafts, each 6 ft. 8 in. high with 4 flues, containing about 67 ft. superficial of reduced (or 14 in.) work in mortar, including bases and caps, either moulded or cut, and set in cement. The whole finished with neat flat drawn joints	£4	12	0	0
No. 50. Labour cutting skewbacks and mitres to window and door arches	2d.	0	8	4

–continued on following page

Estimate − continued

	at	£	s.	d.
No. 4. Chimney pieces formed with hollow bricks, having chamfered angles, jambs 9 in. wide and 4½ in. projection; mantle, 4½ in. deep and 4½ in. projection, with 1¼ in. T iron passed through hollow of bricks, and grouted solid with cement. The shelf to be of 1¼ in. rubbed and rounded slate, 7 in. wide in the clear, with rounded corners, the whole fixed, complete, and painted	8s.	1	12	0
No. 24. Door and window frames bedded and pointed in hair mortar	1s.	1	4	0
Coring to No. 12 flues and dust-shaft provided for by measuring work solid.				
No. 26. Labour only to fixing air bricks and forming flues, average length, 2 feet	4d.	0	8	8
No. 48. Ditto ditto ditto internal ventilators	4d.	0	16	0
No. 4. Ditto ditto ditto dust-doors under sinks	1s.	0	4	0
No. 4. Ditto, and materials to do., ranges in living rooms	12s. 6d.	2	10	0
No. 8. Ditto ditto stoves to bed-rooms	5s.	2	0	0
		£206	11	9

MASON

	at	£	s.	d.
No. 2. 4 in. tooled York templates, 1 ft. 6 in., by 1 ft. 6 in., with one corner splayed off and bedded in cement for iron girder to landing of stairs	3s. 7½d.	0	7	3
No. 8. 4 in. ditto ditto 1 ft. 3 in., by 1 ft. 3 in., for cast iron springers, with splay edges, to work in with the hollow bricks, and bedded in cement	3s. 6d.	1	8	0
No. 8. 4 in. ditto ditto 1ft. 6 in. by 1 ft. 3 in., splayed and bedded in cement under ends of short cast-iron springers	4s.	1	12	0
* No. 6. 3 in tooled York springers for arches, 16 ft. long 14 in. wide, with both edges splayed, bedded in cement, properly cramped at heading joints, and No. 4 cross grooves in each, to receive tie rods	16s.	4	16	0
No. 4. 3 in. ditto ditto ditto 7 ft. 4 in. long, 8½ in. wide, for lobby water-closet floor and roof arches, and bedded in cement in wall next staircase	4s. 6d.	0	18	0
No. 4. Ditto ditto 8 ft. long, over small bed-rooms	6s.	1	4	0

− continued on following page

* Common stocks or hollow bricks, set in cement, may be used for these springers, at a cost of 6d. per foot, run - *see* Specification.

Estimate — continued

	at	£	s.	d.
No. 3. Portland cement, Caen or Bath stone moulded pinnacles, and fixing same in cement	12s. 6d.	1	17	6
† No. 4. Tooled York window sills, 11 in. by 4 in., sunk, weathered, throated, and grooved on top for lead tongue in oak sill, 5 ft. long	10s.	2	0	0
No. 2. Ditto ditto ditto 3 ft. 6 in. long	7s.	0	14	0
No. 5. Ditto ditto ditto 2 ft. 9 in. long.	5s. 6d.	1	7	6
No. 4. Ditto ditto ditto 1 ft. 9 in. long	3s. 6d.	0	14	0
No. 4. 2½ in. tooled York back hearths to living rooms, 3 ft. 2 in. by 1 ft. 2 in.	2s. 6d.	0	10	0
No. 4. 2½ in. ditto ditto for bed-rooms, 1 ft. 2 in. by 1 ft. 2 in.	11d.	0	3	8
No. 4. 2½ in. ditto ditto ditto, 9 in. by 9 in.	6d.	0	2	0
No. 4. 2 in. rubbed York slab to the living rooms, 4 ft. 8 in. by 1 ft. 6 in.	7s.	1	8	0
No. 4. Ditto ditto bed-rooms, 2 ft. 8 in. by 1 ft. 6 in.	4s.	0	16	0
No. 4. Ditto ditto ditto 1 ft. 11 in. by 1 ft. 6 in. — NOTE: These 2 in slabs may be dispensed with if Portland cement floors are used	3s.	0	12	0
No. 2. Iron scrapers and stones, letting in and running with lead, and fixing same	5s.	0	10	0
		£20	19	11

SLATER

| No. 4. 1 in. rubbed slate sinks, 2 ft. 4 in. by 1 ft. 4 in., 6 in. deep at back and 3½ in deep at front, inside dimensions, with soap shelf at one corner, Lowes' 4 in. brass grate and trap and letting in; including two ends of ¾ in. finished rubbed slate, 2 ft. 2 in. by 1 ft. 6 in.; with inch front to coal-bin underneath, about 3 ft. 7 in. long and 10 in. high, fixed at ends with screws and nutts: also two ¾ in. tops, fixed to drip into sinks, one 1 ft. 6 in. by 1 ft. 3 in., the other 1 ft. 9 in. by 1 ft. 6 in., with rounded edges and corners; a ¾ in. shelf to be fixed under the smaller top of each sink, to form a box at end next scullery door. The whole to be properly grooved and screwed together, joined with oil cement, and fixed complete | £3 | 12 | 0 | 0 |
| No. 1. Cistern of 1¼ in. slate, to contain not less than 250 gallons, with all necessary holes cut for supply, service, and waste, and fixing same on roof on hollow brick piers 8 in. high | £5 10s. | 5 | 10 | 0 |

— continued on following page

† *See* Specification respecting brick sills, the cost of which will be 6d. per foot run.

Estimate — continued

	at	£	s.	d.

No. 1. 1½ in. rubbed slate landing, 11 ft. 6 in. by 4 ft., including all sawn edges, notches, sunk channel for water, 2 in. by ½ in., bedded on walls and cast iron girder complete: and including the staircase of 1½ in. ribbed slate treads and risers, with winders top and bottom. The risers grooved into treads top and bottom, including rounded nosings, pinnings, &c. complete, 2 ft. 10 in. wide, and 22 ft. 3 in. girt down the centre.   10   0   0

No. 4. 1½ in. rubbed and rounded slate steps and risers to doorways, notched and morticed at each end for door frames, 3 ft. 4 in. long and 12 in wide, rise 4½ in wide. — NOTE: Slate shelves for safes included in carpenter's work.   5s.   1   0   0

     £28   10   0

PLASTERER

Yds.	ft.	in.		at	£	s.	d.
691½	0	0	Superficial — Twice colour or lime-white to ceilings and walls	1d.	2	17	7½
*95	0	0	Superficial Portland cement flooring, to first floor only	2s. 3d.	10	13	9
*95	0	0	Superficial hollow brick flooring to ground floor, as specified, on a bed of concrete, 4 in thick	3s. 4d.	15	16	8
*	109	9	Run Portland cement coping, weathered, throated, and including all angles, stoppings, &c., and core to ditto of two courses of plain tiles in cement, size 12½ in. wide and 3 in thick. Hollow jamb bricks, No. 3, may be used if preferred	1s. 2d.	6	8	0½
*	26	0	run ditto circular ditto ditto to ramps	2s.	2	12	0
	314	0	Run ditto, weathering to all external sailing courses and strings, 3 in wide	½d.	0	13	1

     £39   1   2

CARPENTER AND JOINER

No. 24. Turning pieces for window and door arches   9d.   0   18   0

No. 1. Centre 10 ft. 6 in. span, 13 in. soffit, for arch over staircase   0   3   8

For floor and roof arch centering, *see* Bricklayer's work

No. 1. Inch proper ledged door, hung with 3 in. butts to fir wrought and rebated frame, 4½ in. by 3 in., to dust place under stairs, 5 ft. by 2 ft. 5 in. outside of frame   15s.   0   15   0

— continued on following page

Estimate — continued

	at	£	s.	d

No. 4. 1½ in. square framed doors, 6 ft. 9 in. by 2 ft. 7½ in., filled in with ¾ in. tongued and beaded boards, with panel at top for and including ⅜ in. rough plate glass, 1 ft. 11 in. by 8 in. stopped in on both sides with beads, hung with 3½ in. butts to fir wrought, rebated, and chamfered frames 4½ in. by 3 in.; ¾ in. wrought and chamfered fillet or stop, mitred and nailed round inside, 2½ in. wide **27s.** **5 8 0**

No. 4. Ditto four panel square framed doors hung, with 3 in. butts to 1½ in. wrought, rebated, chamfered, and staff beaded linings, 3½ in. wide, staff beads to be mitred and nailed round on one side; opening of brickwork, 6 ft. 8 in. by 2 ft. 3 in. for water-closets **19s.** **3 16 0**

No. 8. Ditto four panel square framed doors, hung with 3 in. butts to 1½ in. linings as before; opening of brickwork, 6 ft. 8 in. by 2 ft. 5 in. to children's bed-rooms **20s.** **8 0 0**

No. 4. Ditto ditto ditto 6 ft. 8 in. by 2 ft. 8 in., to parents' bed-rooms **22s.** **4 8 0**

No. 8. Ditto ditto ditto hung to 1½ in. linings, as before, 6½ in. wide, ditto, 6 ft. 8 in. by 2 ft. 8 in. to living rooms **24s.** **9 12 0**

No. 4. Ditto deal cupboard fronts to living rooms, with doors hung in two heights, including 3 in. butts, locks, turnbuckles, &c. Mitred staff bead and No. 4. 1 in. wrought shelves and bearers, 6 ft. 8 in. by 3 ft. and 1 ft. 2 in. deep, fixed complete **30s.** **6 0 0**

No. 4. Ditto ditto ditto in parents' bed-room, with doors hung in one height, to correspond with room doors, including hinges, &c. &c., as before, 1¼ in. rounded top; a ¾ in. double chamfered hook-rail, with No. 4 iron hat and cloak pins fixed therein, 6 ft. 8 in. by 3 ft. 9 in. and 10 in. deep **24s.** **4 16 0**

No. 4. Three light window frames for living rooms, opening of brickwork, 4 ft. 6 in. by 4 ft. 6 in., with fir solid, rebated, and chamfered frame and mullions, with oak sunk, weathered, and throated sills, 1¼ in. window board, and 1¼ in. staff bead, mitred round inside, prepared for glazing, in frame in two heights with ¾ in. T iron cross bar in centre. The centre compartment to have a wrought iron casement, hung with hinges, and with proper strong stay bar fastenings, and including all labour, &c., in fixing same complete **26s. 8d.** **5 6 8**

No. 4. Three light ditto ditto to childrens' bed-rooms, same size, with frame, &c., as before, but the window board to be fixed in two lengths to the outer compartments, with 1¼ in. staff bead mitred round each, the centre compartment to be stopped in with ½ in. rubbed slate, bedded in putty, and screwed to frame; wrought iron casements hung to the outer compartments, with fastening, &c. **36s. 6d.** **7 6 0**

No. 4. Two light ditto ditto, opening of brickwork, 4 ft. 6 in. by 3 ft., with fir frame and T iron cross bars, as before, and with wrought iron casements, hung in one compartment with proper star bar, fastenings, &c., complete with window board, staff beads, &c. **20s.** **4 0 0**

— continued on following page

Estimate — continued

	at	£	s.	d.
No. 4. Two light window frames to sculleries, opening of brickwork, 3 ft. 2 in. by 2 ft. 3 in., with fir frame and mullions, as before, with ¾ in. T iron bar, as last. The top square on one side to have an iron casement hung to the T iron cross bar, to open downwards, with proper rack and knob fastening, complete	14s. 8d.	2	18	8
No. 4. One light ditto ditto to water-closets, opening of brickwork, 3 ft. 2 in. by 1 ft. 2 in., with fir frame, as last, and glazed, the upper square to open, as in scullery	11s. 8d.	2	6	8
No. 4. Deal plate racks, 3 ft. high, 1 ft. 6 in. wide, and 8 in. deep, framed in three heights with ½ in. top, fixed complete in sculleries	6s. 6d.	1	6	0
No. 4. Safes in sculleries, 5 ft. 3 in. high by 2 ft. 3 in. wide, formed with one ¾ in. wrought end, 14 in. wide, and 1¼ in. square framed front and doors, hung with 3 in. butts, knob, turnbuckle, &c., and No. 3. ¾ in. rubbed slate shelves (including bottom) to each, all fixed complete	18s.	3	12	0
No. 4. 1¼ in wrought and frame clamped table tops, 4 ft. 6 in. by 2 ft. 6 in. hung with 3½ in. butts to the window board (4 in. wide), including two framed angle brackets hung to proper frame or 1 in. grounds; one 4 in. brass neck bolt to each, and the corners of top rounded, all fixed complete	13s. 6d.	2	14	0
No. 4. 1 in. deal wrought shelves, 9 in. wide and 9 ft. 5 in. long, in two lengths on one side and end of sculleries, with ¾ in. chamfered hook rail, 3½ in. wide, fixed underneath, and including No. 1 wrought iron bracket to each, fixed complete	6s. 3d.	1	5	0
No. 8. 1 in. Ditto ditto ditto, 5 ft. long and 2 ft. 6 in. run, ¾ in. chamfered all round hook rail, 3½ in. wide, with 2 iron hat and cloak pins screwed on, in children's bed-rooms	2s. 3½d.	0	18	4
No. 4. 1 in. Ditto ditto ditto, 9 ft. 6 in. long and 5 ft. hook rail, as before, and No. 1 iron bracket and 3 iron hat and cloak pins to each, in parents' bed-rooms	5s. 2d.	1	0	8
No. 4. ¾ in. chamfered all round hook rails, 3½ in. wide 4 ft. 6 in. long, and No. 4 ditto ditto 3 ft. long, fixed on the entrance-door side of living rooms	2s.	0	8	0
No: 4. ¾ in. ditto ditto ditto, 3 ft. 6 in. long, fixed in lobbies, with No. 3 iron hat and cloak pins screwed on to each	2s.	0	8	0
No. 24. Bow latches, fixing on internal doors	6d.	0	12	0
No. 4. 9 in barrel bolts, ditto on external doors	4d.	0	1	4
No. 4. 9 in rim locks, ditto ditto ditto	1s.	0	4	0
No. 1. 6 in dead ditto, ditto dust ditto	9d.	0	0	9

— continued on following page

Estimate — continued

	at	£	s.	d.
No. 4. Pairs ornamental hinge straps screwed on external doors with three screws each	4d.	0	1	4
No. 4.　Escutcheons ditto ditto	2d.	0	0	8
		£78	6	9

> NOTE: All Ironmongery not specially described, such as hinges, screws, nails, &c., must be provided and fixed by the Contractor.

SMITH AND FOUNDER

Cwt.	qrs.	lbs.		at	£	s.	d.
3	1	0	In No. 1. Cast iron girder, 12 ft. long 7½ in deep, with ¾ in. flange inside at bottom, to receive slate landing, top flange 2 in. wide, 1½ in. thick, projecting ½ in. on either side, with sunk holes for railing		1	12	0
3	2	0	In No. 1. Ditto ditto railing, 11 ft. 6 in. long and 3 ft. 3in. high	10s.	1	15	0
2	0	10	In No. 1. Cast iron railing, 7 ft. 6 in long ditto ditto	10s.	1	0	10
			No. 4. Ditto ditto springers, including one 6 in. coupling to each for floor and roof arches, built in external walls, &c., as per drawing, each 5 cwt. 3 qrs. 13 lbs.	52s.	10	8	0
			No. 4. Ditto ditto ditto, 8 ft. long, over small bed-rooms, each 1 cwt. 3 qrs. 13 lbs.	17s.	3	8	0
3	3	17	324 ft. run ¾ in. wrought iron tension rods with heads, couplings, and nutts, complete	28s.	5	9	4
			No. 1. Wrought iron suspension bar, 1½ in. by ½ in. to support upper winders of stairs, 19 in. long, turned at each end) No. 1. Ditto ditto, 12 in. long, ditto) No. 1. Ditto ditto, 9 in long, ditto)		0	2	0
			No 24. Iron casements, and No. 16 cross bars for windows, are included in joiner's work.				
					£23	15	2

FURNISHING IRONMONGER*

		at	£	s.	d.
No. 26.	Cast iron air bricks	9d.	0	19	6
No. 16.	Ditto internal ventilating valves, 12 in long	3s.	2	8	0
No. 16.	Ditto ditto ditto, 7 in. long	2s. 3d.	1	16	0

* This Ironmongery may be supplied according to agreement.

— continued on following page

Estimate – continued

		at	4	s.	d.
No. 12.	Cornice ditto	2s. 6d.	1	10	0
No. 4.	Box ventilators with dampers for safes	2s.	0	8	0
No. 4.	Cast iron dust doors, 10 in. by 8½ in.	7s. 6d.	1	10	0
No. 24.	4 in. bow latches, with brass furnitures	1s.	1	4	0
No. 4.	9 in. iron rim locks, with ditto and large knob	5s.	1	0	0
No. 4.	9 in. barrel bolts	9d.	0	3	0
No. 1.	6 in. dead lock	2s.	0	2	0
No. 4.	Pairs ornamental hinge straps	2s.	0	8	0
No. 4.	Escutcheons to key-holes	3d.	0	1	0
No. 4.	Nicholson's ranges, with oven and boiler fitted with brass tap	47s. 6d.	9	10	0
No. 4.	Bed-room stoves for 12 in. openings	17s.	3	8	0
No. 4.	Ditto ditto for 17 in. ditto	20s.	4	0	0
No. 2.	Scrapers included in Mason's work				

	£28	7	6

PLUMBER

lbs.					
24	4 lb. milled lead seatings to iron girder and springers	3½d.	0	7	0
Ft. in.					
39 0	Run 4 in. clear bore cast iron stack pipe, with heads, and junctions for four closets, including all straps, tacks, &c. fixed complete and made good to drains	1s. 6d.	2	18	6
28 0	Run 2 in lead waste pipe, and fixing to sinks, including six joints and all labour	2s.	2	16	0
30 0	Run ¾ in. iron gas pipe for service to sinks, including bends, elbows, couplings, &c., fixed complete	9d.	1	2	6
	No. 4. ½ in. brass bib cocks, with round water ways to sinks, fixed complete	5s.	1	0	0

No. 1. ¾ in. Dann's patent ball valve, and including 30 ft. run ¾ in. iron gas pipe for laying on the water to the cistern on roof, with bends, &c. complete — 33s. — 1 13 0

No. 1. Inch washer and waste, and including qbout 20 in. of lead pipe waste, with trumpet mouth, fixed in cistern, complete — 9s. — 0 9 0

No. 4. Sets of Dann's water-closet apparatus complete, with all necessary piping &c., and including Ridgway & Co.'s earthen pans fixed — 40s. — 8 0 0

	£18	6	0

– continued on following page

Estimate – continued

GLAZIER

Ft. in.				
154 8	Superficial good 21 oz. sheet glass properly bedded, and stopped in with putty	6d.	3 17 4	
32 8	Ditto ditto ¼ in. rough plate, ditto ditto ditto	1s.	1 12 8	
			£5 10 0	

PAINTER AND STAINER

Yds. ft. in.				
140 0	Run three oils red lead to cast iron girders and springers	)		
324 0	Run ditto ditto ditto to ¾ in. tension rods	)		
19 0	Run ditto ditto ditto iron railing, 3 ft. 3 in. high	)		
	No. 4. Dust doors, three oils, and finished stone colour	)		
	No. 26. Air bricks, ditto ditto ditto	)	2 16 0	
	No. 48. Ventilators, ditto ditto ditto	)		
	No. 2. Scrapers, ditto ditto ditto	)		
	No. 4. Plate racks, ditto ditto ditto	)		
208 0 0	Superficial * Wood Staining, as oak, and once varnish	6d.	5 4 0	
	No. 8. Three light window frames, 4 ft. 10 in. by 4 ft. 8 in., both sides, and including the window board and staff beads	1s. 6d.	0 12 0	
	No. 4. Two light ditto ditto, 4 ft. 8 in. by 3 ft. 4 in. ditto ditto ditto	1s. 4d.	0 5 4	
	No. 4. Two light ditto ditto, 3 ft. 4 in. by 2 ft. 7 in. ditto ditto ditto	1s. 3d.	0 5 0	
	No. 4. One light ditto ditto, 3 ft. 4 in. by 1 ft. 7 in. ditto ditto ditto	1s.	0 4 0	
			£9 6 4	

* If Oil Stain be used, the cost will be £3 9s. 1d.

SUMMARY OF THE FOREGOING WORKS

	£	s.	d.
Excavator and Bricklayer	206	11	9
Mason	20	19	11
Slater	28	10	0
Plasterer	39	1	2
Carpenter and Joiner	78	6	9
Smith and Founder	23	15	2
Furnishing Ironmonger	28	7	6
Plumber	18	6	0
Glazier	5	10	0
Painter and Stainer	9	6	4
	£458	14	7

*Reductions which may be made in the above amounts by the following
alterations, as described or referred to in the Specification*

	£	s.	d.
If the bed-rooms are divided according to the supplementary plan, one iron springer over the recess in each of the centre bed-rooms being dispensed with	5	1	6
If the springers for floor arches are partially brick in cement in lieu of stone to the central walls	2	8	0
Omitting 2 in. York slabs to fire-places where Portland cement is used	2	2	3
Hollow-brick window sills in lieu of tooled York	3	11	7
If cast iron enamelled sinks and other scullery fittings connected therewith are substituted for slate, as specified	4	0	0
If lime and ash floors, as described, be substituted for Portland cement on the upper story, allowing full 2 in. thickness over the crown of the arch, and 3 in. over the spandrils, levelled with concrete as provided, deduct 1s. 0d. per yard	4	15	0
If ditto ditto be substituted for tile or hollow brick on ground floor, deducting concrete, and allowing 1s. 6d. per yard for the lime and ash floor, with the substratum	8	14	2
Jamb bricks used for coping in lieu of Portland cement	4	0	0
If oil stain be used in lieu of stain and varnish	1	14	10

£36 7 4

£422 7 3

References for Chapter Five — *Philanthropic buildings and designs by Henry Roberts not directly connected with the Society for Improving the Condition of the Labouring Classes.*

1. Roberts, Henry, *The Improvement of the Dwellings of the Labouring Classes through the operation of Government Measures, by those of Public Bodies and Benevolent Associations, as well as Individual Efforts*, London, 1859, p. 11.

2. *Ibid*, p.12.
3. *Ibid.*, p. 12
4. *Ibid.*, p.15
5. *Ibid.*, p.15
6. *Ibid.*, p.18
7. *Ibid.*, p.20
8. *Ibid.*, p.21
9. *Ibid.*, p.21
10. *Ibid.*, p.25.

11. Sheppard, F. H. W. (ed.) *Survey of London*, Vol. XXVII. *Spitalfields and Mile End New Town*, London, 1957, p.275.

12. *Ibid.*
13. *Op. cit.*

14. *Ibid.*, p.275

15. *See* the *Survey of London*, Vol. XXVI, London, 1956, pp.34–6.

16. Roberts, Henry, *The Progress and Present Aspect of the Movement for Improving the Dwellings of the Labouring Classes*, London 1860, p.6.

17. *See* Vol. XXVII of the *Survey of London, op. cit.*, pp.273–5. *See also* Curl, James Stevens, 'An Indictment of Bad Planning', *Country Life*, 10 November 1977.

18. Roberts, Henry, *The Dwellings of the Labouring Classes*, etc., 1867 edition, p.139.

19. Roberts met Muller on several occasions, and refers to him in his publications. The two men were regular attenders at the various congresses of philanthropic organisations throughout Europe. *See* Muller, Emile and Cacheux, Emile. *Les Habitations Ouvrières en tous Pays*, Paris, 1889, for the details of housing in Europe. An earlier edition was published in 1878. *See also* Muller, Emile, *Habitations Ouvrières et Agricoles, Cités, Bains, Lavoirs, Sociétés Alimentaires, etc.*, Paris, 1856. Muller's work of 1889 contains the attribution to Roberts of the Albert Cottages at Mile End New Town.

20. Roberts, Henry, *The Dwellings of the Labouring Classes, etc., See also The Labourers' Friend*, June 1855, p. 85; and *The Builder*, Vol. XXX, 1872, p. 634.

21. Roberts, *The Improvement of the Dwellings of the Labouring Classes, etc.*, London, 1859, p.32.

22. *Ibid.*, p. 33.

23. Sheppard, F. H. W. (ed.), The *Survey of London*, Vol. XXXIX, London, 1977, pp.138–9.

24. The *Timber Trades Journal*, Annual Special Issue, January 1965, p.170. *See also* the Principal Probate Registry, Will of John Newson, 1873.

25. Roberts, Henry, *The Progress and Present Aspect of the Movement for Improving the Dwellings of the Labouring Classes*, London, 1861, pp. 10–11.

26. Mr. Peter Bezodis kindly provided information.

Appendix I to Chapter Five *(Referring to Roberts' scheme at Windsor)*

'A statement having been published of the cost of the above -described houses, which is based exclusively on the amounts given for each set or block of cottages in the *lowest* Tender, in order to prevent an erroneous conclusion being drawn therefrrom as to the relative cost of the several blocks of building, the following abstract is given of the *two lowest* Tenders, and the *average* amounts of the five Tenders made by the 31st May, 1852, in answer to Public advertisement.'

continued on following page

	Lowest Tender				Per tenement			Next Lowest Tender				Per tenement		
The centre block of houses for 8 families	£868	0	0	or	108	10	0	£775	13	9	or	96	19	3
Two pairs of double cottages for 4 families	420	0	0		105	0	0	476	3	2		119	0	9
Two blocks of houses for 8 families	834	0	0		104	5	0	863	17	6		107	19	8
Extra concrete to foundations, soft water and manure tanks, cesspools, and drains	118	5	0					127	10	0				
	£2,240	5	0					£2,243	4	5				

Average amounts of the five tenders

The centre block of houses for 8 families	£946	10	9	or	£118	6	4	per tenement
Two pairs of double cottages for 4 families	560	0	7		140	0	2	per tenement
Two blocks of houses for 8 families	1,077	11	6		134	14	0	per tenement
Extra concrete to foundations, soft water and manure tanks, cesspools and drains	125	16	8					
	£2,709	19	6					

'It ought, further, to be observed that, for the tenements in the centre block (which are arranged in flats on two stories), the extent of the frontage occupied, the relative cost of drainage, of water supply, of fencing, and of road-making, is less in proportion per tenement than to the self-contained houses.

'The highest weekly rents, including rates and taxes, which under ordinary circumstances ought to be expected for such tenements, are 3s. 6d. for those with two bedrooms, and 4s. 6d. for those with three bedrooms, in the centre block; 4s. for the two-bedroomed, and 5s. for the three-bedroomed tenements in the self-contained cottages. Higher charges than these might lead, in the three-bedroomed houses, to the very objectionable practice of taking in lodgers.

'In many places where building is less expensive than at Windsor, the rents would be remunerative at a lower rate'.

Appendix 2 to Chapter Five

Henry Roberts' list of recommendations relating to articles of importance in the construction and fitting up of dwellings for the labouring classes, with addresses.

'Messrs. Hertzlet & Broughton's REBATED TILES, are supplied from their works at Cliffe, near Wakefield, at 3d. each, and delivered at their Wharf, beneath the Adelphi Terrace, at 4d. each; they also supply to order, Staircase Steps, and other articles of Fire Clay.

'WINDOW SILLS, MULLIONS, and LABELS, with other plain and moulded articles in clay, of various colours, of a very superior quality, are supplied from the Holkham Works, Norfolk — Mr. Bolger, manager — and may be obtained at Blashfield's Wharf, Commercial Road, Lambeth.

'The best form of SOIL DRAIN is probably that shown in the margin' (this showed a half-round section, with fillets on which the cover could sit), ' which may be cleansed without any other removal than that of the upper tile, to which additional strength would be given by making it convex.

'The importance of obtaining a more effective, and at the same time, economical, arrangement for WATER CLOSETS, generally adapted to the dwellings of the labouring classes, than any now in use, has led the Board of Health to engage Messrs. Ridgway & Co., of the Staffordshire Potteries, to prepare a series of designs for improved Pans with Traps, Reservoirs, etc. The Author has also been in communication with them on this subject, and very shortly a list and description of the articles they have engaged to manufacture will be published, with prices and other directions. A strong and cheap washing basin, with reservoir for clean and receptacle for foul water, will also be supplied by the same parties, at a price which will, doubtless, insure its general adoption.

'Strong and well made ZINC QUARRY WINDOW LIGHTS may be obtained, in a quantity, at 18d. per foot superficial, exclusive of hinges and fastenings, of North, 121 London Road, Southwark. Suitable Fastenings at 9d. each, and Stays at 1s. each, may be obtained of Hart & Sons, Wych Street, Strand, who also manufacture, for 3s. each, Ventilators.

'IRON PUMPS, arranged for supplying the reservoir of the water-closet, as well as for common house use, may be obtained, at 35s. each, of Benjamin Fowler, Whitefriars Street, Fleet Street, who also supplies iron pipes and sinks. The same description of pump, with 6 feet of iron pipe, may be obtained, at 35s. each, of W. Williams, brick machine and agricultural implement maker, Bedford.

'The best COTTAGE RANGE brought under the notice of the Author is that manufactured by W. N. Nicholson, of Newark, to whom a prize was awarded by the Royal Agricultural Society of England, at the York meeting in 1848, for "the best and cheapest grate or stove for cottages, combining safety and economy of fuel, with effectual warmth and facility for cooking". The range, with oven and boiler, for a 3-feet 2-inch opening, is charged at 35s. without, and 41s. with a brass tap; other sizes in proportion. Bed-room stoves, with fire-brick backs, cast-iron chimney-piece and shelf, are supplied by the same manufacturer, at 8d. to 9d. per inch in width. One, 24 inches wide, a good bed-room size, costs 16s.

'For Lodging-Houses, IRON BEDSTEADS are recommended in preference to wood, those with patent joints, sold at the Bordsley Iron Works, Birmingham, and at No. 12, Panton Square, Piccadilly, London, are well made, and have the advantage of being easily taken to pieces; their price varies according to the value of iron; if on castors, and japanned dark green, 6 feet 4 inches long, and 2 feet 6 inches wide (the dimensions recommended), they have been sold at 15s. 6d. each, in quantities of not less than twelve; 4 feet 6 inches wide for the Superintendents', cost 23s. 6d. Between the mattress and iron laths a strong canvass bag, filled with cut straw, which may be easily changed, has been found to answer well'.

References for Chapter Six — *The Campaign to extend the Benefits of a Healthy Dwelling to the Labouring Population*

1. London, 1862.
2. Roberts, Henry, *The Essentials of a Healthy Dwelling, etc.*, London, 1862, p.3.
3. *Ibid.*   4. *Ibid.*, p.5.
5. *See* Curl, James Stevens, 'Taking the Waters in London I. Old Spas North of the Thames', *Country Life*, 2 December 1971; 'Taking the Waters in London II. In Search of Health and Pleasure. Old Spas South of the Thames', *Country Life*, 9 December 1971; 'Taking the Waters in London. Old Spas, Wells and Baths', *Country Life*, 11 November 1976; and 'Spas on the City's Fringes', *Country Life*, 18 November 1976. *See also* Curl, James Stevens, 'Spas and

pleasure gardens of London, from the seventeenth to the nineteenth centuries', *Garden History*, The *Journal* of the Garden History Society, Vol. VII, No. 2. Summer, 1979, pp.27–68.

6. *See* Curl, James Stevens, *The Victorian Celebration of Death*, Newton Abbot, 1972.
7. Roberts, *op. cit.*, p.6.
8. Roberts, *op. cit.*, p.7.
9. *Ibid.*, 1867 edition, p.35.
10. *Ibid.*, p.36.
11. Brewster, Sir David, 'Researches on Light'. Article in the *North British Review*, Vol. XXIX, 1858.
12. Roberts, *op. cit.*, p.44.
13. Roberts, Henry, *On the Extension of the Benefits of a Healthy Dwelling to the Labouring Population*, London, 1867, p.45.
14. *See* The *Survey of London*, Vol. XXXVII, London, 1973.
15. Roberts, *op. cit.*, p. 47.
16. *Ibid.*, p.47.   17. *Ibid.*, p. 50.
18. *See* Curl, James Stevens, 'A Victorian Model Town, Saltaire, Yorkshire', *Country Life*, 9 March 1972, and the same Author's *Victorian Architecture: its practical aspects*, Newton Abbot, 1973, pp.99–104.
19. Roberts, *op. cit.*, pp.50–1.
20. *Ibid.*, p.52.
21. Roberts, *passim.*
22. *Monitore Toscano*, 9 October 1854.
23. Roberts, *op. cit.*, p.54.

References for Chapter Seven – *Efforts on the Continent to Improve the Condition of the Labouring Classes.*

1. Roberts, Henry, *The Improvement of the Dwellings of the Labouring Classes through the operation of Government Measures by those of Public Bodies and Benevolent Associations, as well as Individual Efforts*, London, 1859, p.4.
2. Roberts, Henry, *On the Extension of the Benefits of a Healthy Dwelling to the Labouring Population*, A paper dated 20 January 1862, p. 56.
3. Papers in the Library of the *Société Industrielle de Mulhouse*.
4. Muller, Emile, *Habitations Ouvrières, etc.*, Paris, 1855–6.
5. Roberts, Henry, *On the Extension*, etc., *op. cit.*, p. 57, and *passim. See also* Véron, Eugène, *Les Institutions Ouvrières de Mulhouse et des Environs*, Paris, 1866, p. 275.
6. Baedeker, Karl, *The Rhine from Rotterdam to Constance*, Leipzig, 1900, p. 320. *See* Godin, J. B., *Solutions Sociales*, Paris, 1870. *See also* Engels, F., *The Housing Question*, London, 1942, p.58.
7. *The Labourers' Friend*, October 1866.
8. Roberts, *op. cit.*, footnote, p. 57.
9. *Ibid.*
10. *See* Curl, James Stevens, *European Cities and Society*, London, 1970, p.143.
11. *See* Rosenau, Helen, *The Ideal City. Its Architectural Evolution*, London, 1974, pp.144–50.
12. Curl, *op. cit.*, p.144.
13. Buber, M., *Paths in Utopia*, London, 1949. *See also* Mumford, Lewis, *The Story of Utopia*, London, 1923.
14. *See* Roberts on *The Essentials of a Healthy Dwelling*, *see* Bibliography.
15. Roberts, *op. cit.*, p. 58.
16. *Ibid.*

17. *See* the *Transactions* of the National Association for the Promotion of Social Science. *See also* Simons, Jules, *L'Ouvrier*, Paris, 1865.
18. *See* Roberts on *Efforts on the Continent* and the 1867 edition of his *The Dwellings of the Labouring Classes*, etc.
19. Roberts, *op. cit.*, p.59.
20. *Ibid.*, p.59.   21. *Ibid.*, p. 59.
22. Roberts, *The Improvement*, etc. (footnote 1), p.24.
23. Roberts, *passim*.
24. Roberts, *op. cit.*, p.61.
25. *See* Binns, J. A., A paper read at the Bradford meeting for the Promotion of Social Science in 1859, published in the *Transactions* of the National Association.
26. Roberts, *op. cit.*, p.64.
27. Quoted in Roberts, *op. cit.*, p. 65.
28. Pp. 583-620, 682-91.
29. Pp. 766-87, and 721.
30. *Transactions* of the National Association for the Promotion of Social Science, 1862, pp.774-80; 750-7; 807; 345.
31. *Transactions*, 1863, p.565.
32. *Ibid*, pp.675-9.   33. *Ibid.*, 1864, pp.433-6
34. *Ibid.*, 1865, pp.714-9; 459-462.
35. *See also* Oyon, A., *Le Familistère de Guise*, Paris, 1862.
36. Roberts, Henry, *Report on the Dwellings for the Working Classes, in connection with the International Exhibition in Paris, 1867*, London, 1868. Pamphlet in the R.I.B.A. British Architectural Library.
37. Battiscombe, Georgina, *Shaftesbury, A Biography of the Seventh Earl, 1801-1885*, London, 1974, p.302.
38. Minutes of the S.I.C.L.C.
39. 8 November 1852.
40. Battiscombe, *op. cit.*, p.139.
41. Florence, 1874.
42. *See* Bibliography and works by Muller.
43. *See* Bibliography Appendix.

References for Chapter Eight – *The Influence of Henry Roberts on Legislation concerning Working-Class Housing in Victorian Britain.*

1. *See* Bibliography.
2. In 1858, 1860, 1862, and 1864 particularly.
3. Especially 1862.
4. Roberts, Henry, Appendix to *On the Extension of The Benefits of a Healthy Dwelling to the Labouring Population* in the Edition of 1867, p. 67.
5. *Ibid.*   6. *Ibid.*, p.68.   7. *Ibid.*   8. *Ibid.*
9. Roberts, *passim*.
10. Roberts, *passim*.
11. By Dr. Letheby.
12. Roberts, *passim*.
13. Roberts, *op. cit.*, p. 69.
14. *Ibid.*   15. *Ibid.*, p.70.
16. Tarn, John Nelson, *Five Per Cent Philanthropy. An account of housing in urban areas between 1840 and 1914*, London and New York, 1973, p.51.

17. *Ibid.*
18. Wohl, Anthony S., *The Eternal Slum. Housing and Social Policy in Victorian London*, London, 1977, p.73.
19. *Ibid.*   20. *Ibid.*
21. 14 and 15 Victoria, Cap. XXVIII.
22. 14 and 15 Victoria, Cap. XXXIV.
23. 14 and 15 Victoria, Cap. XCI.
24. 18 and 19 Victoria, Cap. CXX.
25. 18 and 19 Victoria, Cap. CXXI.
26. 18 and 19 Victoria, Cap. CXXII.
27. 29 and 30 Victoria, Cap. XC.
28. *See* Bibliography.
29. Lambert, R., *Sir John Simon, 1816-1904*, London, 1963, pp.381, 383.
30. In *The Essentials of a Healthy Dwelling* and in other works.
31. Wohl, *op. cit.*, p.82.
32 18 and 19 Victoria, Cap. CXXXII.
33. 29 Victoria, Cap. XXVIII.
34. Wohl, *op. cit.*, p.82.
35. *See Hansard*, Third Series, CCXXII, 1875, pp.465-6.
36. Wohl, *op. cit.*, p. 84.
37. 31 and 32 Victoria, Cap. CXXX.
38. 37 and 38 Victoria, Cap. LIX.
39 *Op. cit.*, pp. 73-140.
40. 38 and 39 Victoria, Cap. XXXVI.
41. 42 and 43 Victoria, Cap. LXIII.
42. 45 and 46 Victoria, Cap. LIV.
43. 41 and 42 Victoria, Cap. XXXII.
44. 44 and 45 Victoria, Cap. CLXXXII.
45. 38 and 39 Victoria, Cap. LV.
46. Tarn, *op. cit.*, p. 83.
47. *Report of the Select Committee on Artizans' and Labourers' Dwellings*, 1882.
48. *Ibid.*   49. *Ibid.*
50. 45 and 46 Victoria, Cap. LIV.
51. 46 and 47 Victoria, Cap. XXXIV'
52. *On the Extension of the Benefits of a Healthy Dwelling to the Labouring Population*, London, 1867, p. 47.
53. The Author's italics.
54. Roberts, *op. cit.*, p.47.
55. *Ibid.*, p. 48.
56. Notably by Wohl, by Dyos and Wolff, and by Tarn. *See* Bibliography.
57. 48 and 49 Victoria, Cap. LXXI.
58. Curl, James Stevens, *European Cities and Society*, London, 1970.
59. 53 and 54 Victoria, Cap 70.

References for Chapter Nine – *A summing-up. The Importance of Roberts and an Evaluation of his Ideas and of his Architecture.*

1. *See* the Minutes of the S.I.C.L.C. for 5 April 1876.
2. Will of Henry Roberts, proved in London 7 June 1876 by the oaths of Catherine Roberts, Charles Gay Roberts, and Frederick Albert Roberts (both nephews of Henry). *See* Note 16 for Chapter One. *See also* Hare, Augustus J. C., *The Story of My Life*, London, 1900, IV, p. 467.
3. Information from her Tombstone in the *Cimitero degli Allori*, Florence, No. B. VII. 71.

4. *The Times*, 5 July 1916.   5. 1143.

6. The same address as that of Catherine Roberts (*ob.* 20 November 1905) who left Letters of Administration to her daughter. Her estate in England was £119 11s. 8d.

7. Frederick Albert Roberts, of Home Close, Grayswood, Haslemere, Surrey, Henry Roberts' nephew and Theodora Amélie's cousin, died at the age of 90 on 9 October 1938. Probate was granted at London on 11 November to Francis Hare Clayton, Charles Gordon Cooper, and Edmund Meacher. F. A. Roberts left £49,269 2s. 1d. The silver plate is not mentioned in the Will. F. A. Roberts married (in February 1881) Mary Parnell, daughter of Dr. Alfred Markwick, of London. He had married first a Cooper, but she died young. F. A. Roberts and his second wife, Mary Parnell Roberts, are buried on the north side of the Churchyard at Grayswood, Haslemere, Surrey. The main beneficiary of F. A. Roberts' Will, Francis Hare Clayton (24 April 1869--18 October 1956) was F. A. Roberts' solicitor, and was knighted in 1954, following his being awarded the O.B.E. in 1937. Francis Stephen Clayton was mentioned in the Will of Henry Roberts. The Clayton and Roberts families were close over two or three generations. The Claytons were solicitors. Sir Francis Hare Clayton was the senior partner in the firm of Clayton, Leach, Sims and Company of 18, Bedford Square, London. He was the son of Charles Houghton Clayton of Long Ditton, and of Lydia Mary, daughter of Thomas Hare. He married in 1906 Gertrude Adelaide, daughter of Sir Edmund Armstrong. Sir Francis Hare Clayton continued the family involvement in philanthropic works, for he joined the Committee of the Shaftesbury Homes and of the Arethusa Training Ship in 1894, becoming Deputy Chairman in 1918, and Chairman and Treasurer from 1926-1951. He is buried in Grayswood parish church-yard, near the grave of Frederick Albert and Mary Parnell Roberts. Sir Francis Hare Clayton compiled a history of the Clayton family, under the title of *The Claytons since 1800 A.D.*, which was published posthumously in 1959. There were several Claytons who were Evangelical clergymen associated with Captain Elliott and with the British and Foreign Sailors' Society. *See The Pilot, or Sailors' Magazine and Record of the Transactions of the British and Foreign Sailors' Society* for 1836 and 1846. The Claytons, like the Roberts family, had close associations with the Equitable Reversionary Interest Society.

8. For example in *National Evils and Practical Remedies*.

9. In *The Improvement of the Dwellings of the Labouring Classes through the Operation of Government Measures*, etc., London, 1859.

10. Minutes of the S.I.C.L.C.

11. Roberts, *op. cit.*, p.32 (footnote 14).

12. Tarn, John Nelson, *Five Per Cent Philanthropy. An account of housing in urban areas between 1840 and 1914*, Cambridge, 1973, p.43.

13. *Ibid.*   14. *Ibid.*   15. *Ibid.*, p.69.

16. *Ibid.* See also the *Journal* of the Society of Arts for 1864, pp.263, 472, and 489.

17. *The Artizans' and Labourers' Dwellings Act*, 31 and 32 Victoria, Cap. CXXX.

18. *See* Bibliography.

19. *Op. cit.*, pp. 67-81.

20. In *The Eternal Slum. Housing and Social Policy in Victorian London*, London, 1977.

21. In *London 1808-1870: The Infernal Wen*, London, 1971.

22. In *The Growth of Victorian London*, London, 1976.

23. *The Act for Consolidating and Amending the Acts relating to Public Health in England*, 38 and 39 Victoria, Cap. LV.

24. London, 1873.

25. 38 and 39 Victoria, Cap. XXXVI.

26. Hill, O., *Houses of the London Poor*, London, 1875, p.2.

27. Tarn, *op. cit*, p. 83.

28. 62 and 63 Victoria, Cap. XIV.

29. With the exception of Professor Tarn, who has given Roberts a just place in his *Five Per Cent Philanthropy*.

30. The italics are those of the present writer. The quotation is from the Preface of Roberts' 1867 edition of his *The Dwellings of the Labouring Classes*.

BIBLIOGRAPHY

Abercrombie, P., *The County of London Plan*, London, 1943.
—— *The Greater London Plan*, London, 1944.
Adkins, B., 'Concrete cottages selling', *Building News and Engineering*, 1867, p.74.
Adshead, S. D., *Liverpool Town Planning and Housing Exhibition*, Liverpool, 1914.
—— *Town Planning and Town Development*, London, 1923.
Akroyd, Edward, *Improved dwellings for the working classes*, London, 1862.
Alexander, M. S., *Memoir of Sarah Jane Isabella Wolff . . . eldest daughter of . . . M. S. Alexander . . . written by her father*, London, 1840.
Allen, J., *Healthy Houses*, London, 1885.
Alison, Archibald, *Observations on the Management of the Poor in Scotland and its Effects on the Health of Great Towns*, Edinburgh, 1840.
Allgemeine Bauzeitung, 'Arbeiterquartier in Mülhausen', 1857, p.244, pls. 160–4.
Andrimont, J. d', *Notice sur les installations ouvrières de la Société civile des Chargonnages du Hasard*, Liège, 1875.
Anonymous, *A Brief Inquiry into the Evils attendant upon the Present Method of Erecting, Purchasing and Renting Dwellings for the Industrial Classes, etc.*, London, 1851.
Anonymous, *Amélioration de la vie domestique de la classe ouvrière*, Paris, 1864.
Armytage, W. H. G., *Heavens Below: Utopian Experiments in England, 1560–1960*, London, 1961.
Ashpitel, A., *Town Dwellings: An Essay on the Erection of Fireproof Houses in Flats: A modification of the Scottish and Continental Systems*, London, 1855.
Austin, H., *An Instance of Faulty Arrangement of Dwellings and a Plan for its Improvement*, London, 1855.
Aveling, Rev. Thomas W., *Memorials of the Clayton Family*, London, 1867.
Avigdor, Ed. d', 'Arbeiterwohnungen in England'. *Zeitschrift des öster. Ingenieur und Architekten Vereins*, 1874, p.125.
—— *Arbeiter-Werkstätten in Paris*, Vienna, 1875.
Baedeker, Karl, *London and its Environs*, Leipzig, 1905.
Bagot, Jocelyn, *George Canning and his Friends*, London, 1909.
Baines, T., *Liverpool in 1859*, Liverpool, 1859.
Balgarnie, R., *Sir Titus Salt, Baronet: His Life and its Lessons*, London, 1877.
Balkowski, F., *Die zur Reform der Wohnungszustände in grossen Städten nothwendigen Massregeln*, Vienna, 1870.
Banfield, Frank, *The Great Landlords of London*, London, 1888.
Bardwell, W., *Healthy Homes and How to Make Them*, London, 1853.
—— *What a House should be versus Death in the House*, London, 1873.
Barmer Bau-Gesellschaft, *Wohnungen für Arbeiter*, Barmen, 1876.
Barnes, H., *The Slum: its Story and Solution*, London, 1931.
—— *Housing: The Facts and the Future*, London, 1923,
Barry, C., 'Metropolitan artisans and labourers dwellings association', *The Building News*, 1876, p.594.
Battiscombe, Georgina, *Shaftesbury. A Biography of the Seventh Earl, 1801–1885*, London, 1974.
Becker and Boring, *Wie Arbeiterwohnungen gut und gesund einzurichten zu erhalten sind*, Basel, 1859.
Beames, T., *The Rookeries of London: Past, Present and Prospective*, London, 1850.
Begg, James, *Report of the committee on houses for the working classes in connection with social morality to the General Assembly of the free church of Scotland*, Edinburgh, 1862.

Behr-Schmoldow, F. von, *Das Haus des Ländlichen Arbeiters*, Berlin, 1875.

Bellman, H., *The Building Society Movement*, London, 1929.

Benischek, I., 'Arbeiterhäuser in Böhmen', *Techn. Blätter.*, Prague, 1874, p. 73.

Bernard, C., *National and Peoples Bank in the United States of America. Cooperation as a business*, New York, 1887.

Besant, Sir Walter, *London in the Nineteenth Century*, London, 1909.

Best, G. F. A., *Shaftesbury*, London, 1964.

Böhmches, F., 'Arbeiterhäuser auf der Pariser Weltausstellung, 1867', *Allgemeine Bauzeitung*, 1868-9, p.156.

Booth, Charles, *Life and Labour of the People of London*, London, 1892.

Boring, *see* Becker.

Bosanquet, C. B. P., *London: Some Account of its Growth, Charitable Agencies and Wants*, London, 1868.

——— *The History and Mode of Operation of the Charity Organisation Society*, London, 1874.

Bosanquet, H., *Social Work in London 1869-1912: A History of the Charity Organisation Society*, London, 1914.

Bose, E., 'Des constructions rurales', *Gazette des Architectes et du Bâtiment*, 1874, pp.25, 33, 73, 81, 89.

Bourdin, Dr., *Du Progrès considéré particulièrement au point de vue du bien-être hygiènique des classes laborieuses*, 1865.

Bowie, J. (ed.), *Healthy Homes*, London, 1854.

Bowle, J., *Politics and Opinion in the Nineteenth Century*, London, 1954.

Bowley, M., *Housing and the State, 1919-1944*, London, 1945.

Bowmaker, E., *The Housing of the Working Classes*, London, 1895.

Brayley, E. W., Nightingale, Joseph, and Brewer, J. Norris, *London and Middlesex*, London, 1810-16.

Bready, J., *Lord Shaftesbury and Socio-Industrial Progress*, London, 1926.

Brett-James, N. G., *Mill Hill School 1807-1923*, Reigate, 1925.

——— *Mill Hill*, London and Glasgow, 1930.

Briggs, A., *The Age of Improvement*, London, 1959.

——— *Victorian Cities*, Harmondsworth, 1963.

Brown, Ford K., *Fathers of the Victorians*, Cambridge, 1961.

Buckingham, J. S., *National Evils and Practical Remedies with a plan of a Model Town*, London, 1849.

Builder, The, From 1843.

Building News, The, See especially Vol. XXXIII, 1877, p.522.

Bulteel, H., 'Artisans' dwellings, Plymouth', *The Building News*, 1883, p.126.

Burckhardt, Lucius, 'Imaginäre Besichtigung', *Bauwelt*, 7 January 1977.

Burgess, H. J., *Enterprise in Education. The story of the work of the Established Church in the education of the people prior to 1870*, London, 1958.

Burgess, J. H. M., *The Chronicles of Clapham*, London, 1929.

Burggrave, Dr., *Questions sociales. Amélioration de la vie domestique de la classe ouvrière*, Paris, 1864.

Burnett, John, *A Social History of Housing 1815-1970*, Newton Abbot, North Pomfret (VT), and Vancouver, 1978.

Cacheux, Emile, *See* Muller, Emile.

——— *Conférence relative aux logements d'ouvriers dans les grandes villes, faite au Congrès de l'Association française, tenu à Rouen*, Paris, 1883.

——— *L'Economiste pratique. Construction et organisation des crèches, salles d'asiles, hôtels pour célibataires, cuisines économiques, bains, lavoirs, cercles populaires, nourriceries, maternités, dispensaires, hôpitaux, hospices, asiles de nuit, postes de secours, habitations pour ouvriers et employés*, Paris, 1885.

——— *Etude sur les habitations ouvrières qui se trouvaient à l'exposition universelle de 1878*, Paris, 1879.

——— 'Habitations ouvrières', *Nouv. Annales de Construction*, 1882, p.103, pls. 31, 32.

——— 'Les habitations ouvrières', *Bulletin de la Société Industrielle de Rouen*, 1883, Vol. 12, p. 545.

Cacheux, Emile, *Journal d'Hygiène* for 1879. *See* especially 24 April, 23 June, and 13 November.
—— *Moyens pratique de remédier à la cherté des loyers des classes laborieuses dans Paris et aux environs*, Paris, 1879.
Caird, James, *English Agriculture in 1850 and 1851*, London, 1852.
Chadwick, E., *Commentaries on the Report of the Royal Commission on Metropolitan Sewage Discharge, and on the Combined and Separate Systems of Town Drainage*, London, 1885.
—— *The Health of Nations*, London, 1887.
Chadwick, Owen, *The Victorian Church*, London, 1966 and 1970.
Chambers, W., *The Sanitary Movement*, London, 1850.
—— *Industrial Investment and Associations*, London, 1851.
—— *Improved Dwellings for the Humbler and Other Classes, based on the Scottish Dwelling House System*, London, 1855.
Chancellor, F., 'Labourer's cottage in Essex', *The Building News*, 1874, p.488.
Chapman, Stanley D. (ed.), *The History of Working-Class Housing: A Symposium*, Newton Abbot, 1971.
Chapron, L., 'Maisons ouvrières', *Gazette des architectes et du bâtiment*, 1868-9, p.251.
Charity Organisation Society, The, *Report of the Special Dwellings Committee*, London, 1873 and 1881.
Charpignon, Dr., *Conseils d'hygiène aux ouvriers des villes et aux habitants des campagnes*, Paris, 1856.
Christian Observer, The, 'Pauperism and Cottage Allotments', Vol. 32, 1832, pp.574, 842.
Checkland, S. G., *The Gladstones*, London, 1971.
—— *The Rise of Industrial Society in England, 1815-1885*, London, 1964.
Child, G.-W., 'Dwelling-Houses of the Poor and the Sanitary Legislation', *The Contemporary Review*, Vol. 32, 1866, p.297.
Clapham Antiquarian Society, *Clapham and the Clapham Sect*, London, 1927.
Clark, George, *Les habitations des classes ouvrières en France. Nouveau système de logements garnis pour célibataires à Paris*, Paris, 1854.
Clark, G. K., *The Making of Victorian England*, London, 1962.
Clarke, Charles, 'Dwellings for the industrial classes at Hoxton', *The Builder*, 1880, p.50.
Clarke, J. J., *The Housing Problem, its History, Growth, Legislation and Procedure*, London, 1920.
Clarkson, Thomas, *History of the Abolition of the Slave Trade*, London, 1807.
Claux, Vincent de, 'Petits logements parisiens', *Bulletin des Annales d'hygiène publique et de médicine légale*, 1883, third series, Book IX, No. 6.
Clayton, Sir Francis Hare, *The Claytons since 1800 A.D.*, London 1959.
Cleary, E. J., *The Building Society Movement*, London, 1965.
Cobbe, F. P., 'Schools and dwellings of the poor', *Fraser's Magazine*, Vol. 73, 1865, p.143.
Cochrane, C., *How to Improve the Homes of the Poor*, London, 1849.
Cole, G. D. H., *The Life of Robert Owen*, London, 1930.
—— *The Common People 1746-1946*, London, 1949.
Contemporary Review, The, From 1866.
Cooney, E. W., 'The Origins of the Victorian Master-Builders', *Economic History Review*, 1955, pp.167-76.;
Corey, M. W. M., *From Rabbi to Bishop: the biography of M. S. Alexander*, London, 1956.
Dauby, Fr. and Jacquet, L., *Projet de construction de maisons à deux étages et sur rez-de-chaussée renfermant des logements à bon marché*, Paris, 1884.
Danset, S., *See* Scrive brothers.
Davison, T. R., *Port Sunlight, A Record of Artistic and Pictorial Aspect*, London, 1916.
Degrand and Faucher, *Les habitations ouvrières à l'Exposition universelle de 1867 à Paris. Collection des rapports du jury*, Paris, 1867.
Détain, G., 'Les habitations ouvrières', *Revue générale de l'architecture*, 1867, pp.158, 219.
Dewsnup, E. R., *The Housing Problem in England: its Statistics, Legislation and Policy*, Manchester, 1907.
Dickens, Charles, Several novels include descriptions of working-class housing and life. *See* especially *Hard Times* (1854), *Oliver Twist* (1838-9), and *Dombey and Son* (1846-8).

Disraeli, Benjamin, *Sybil, or The Two Nations*, London, 1845.

— *Tancred, or The New Crusade*, London, 1847.

Ducpétiaux, Dr., *Rapport sur un projet d'association pour la construction d'habitations ouvrières à Bruxelles*, Brussels, 1857.

Dollfus, Jean, *Note sur les cités ouvrières de Mulhouse. Brochure avec plan, extraite de compte rendu du congrès de Francfort-sur-Mein*, 1857.

Duffield, H. G., *The Stranger's Guide to Manchester*, Manchester, 1850.

Dutton, R., *The Victorian Home*, London, 1954.

Dyos, H. J., *Victorian Suburb, A Study of the Growth of Camberwell*, Leicester, 1961.

— 'The Slums of Victorian London' in *Victorian Studies*, XI, September 1967.

— 'Railways and Housing in Victorian London' in *Journal of Transport History*, 1955.

— and Wolff, Michael (eds.), *The Victorian City*, London, 1973.

Eassie, W., *Healthy Homes. A handbook to the history, defects, and remedies of drainage, etc.*, London, 1872.

— *Sanitary Arrangements for Dwellings*, London, 1874.

Edwards, P., *London Street Improvements*, London, 1898.

Eisenbahnzeitung, 'Arbeiterwohnungen zu Friedrichshafen', 1857, p.29.

Eissen, M., 'Colonie ouvrière des mines dehouille de Bandeisel', *Nouvelles Annales de construction*, 1870, p.25.

Elmes, James, and Shepherd, Thos. H., *Metropolitan Improvements: or London in the Nineteenth Century: Being a Series of Views, of the New and Most interesting Objects, in the British Metropolis & its Vicinity: from Original drawings by Thos. H. Shepherd. With Historical, Topographical & Critical Illustrations, by James Elmes, M.R.I.A.*, London, 1827-31.

Emerson, George Rose, *London, How the Great City Grew*, London, 1862.

Emmich, W., 'Wohnhäuser der Berliner gemeinnützigen Baugesellschaft', *Zeitschrift für Bauwesen*, 1851, p.146, pls, 25 and 26.

Engels, F., *The Condition of the Working Class in England in 1844*, Leipzig, 1845. A modern annotated edition by W. O. Henderson and W. H. Chaloner, of 1958 is probably the best working copy.

Esmann, A., 'Arbeiterwohnhaus', *Baugewerks Zeitung*, 1876, p.60.

Esteulle, E., *Historique de la fondation de l'organisation et du fonctionnement de l'Union Foncière, fondée à Reims, sur le modèle des Building Societies anglaises, pour favoriser l'acquisition de la propriété*, London, 1877.

Everett, J., *Panorama of Manchester*, Manchester, 1834.

Fabri, M., *Die Wohnungsnoth der Arbeiter in den Fabrikstädten*, Elberfeld, 1862.

Faligau, E., 'L'amélioration des logements ouvriers et l'initiative privée en Angleterre', *Union économique*, July 1886.

Feierabend, *See* Hirschberg.

Ferrand, Stanislas, *Les maisons de grand rapport et les loyers à bon marché*, Paris, 1871.

Finer, S. E., *The Life and Times of Sir Edwin Chadwick*, London, 1952.

Fitzgerald, Percy, *London City Suburbs*, London, 1893.

Flattich, W. von, 'Wohnhäuser für Arbeiter', *Zeitschrift des öst. Ingenieur und Architektenvereins*, 1866, p.124.

Fletcher, B., *Model Houses for the Industrial Classes*, London, 1871.

Foerster, L., 'Entwurf für Arbeiterwohnungen in Wien', *Allgemeine Bauzeitung*, 1849, p.119, pl.263.

Fonteret, A. L., *Hygiène physique et morale de l'ouvrier dans les grandes villes et général et dans la ville de Lyon en particulier*, Paris, 1858.

Forster, E. M., *Marianne Thornton*, London, 1956.

Foucher de Careil, Comte, *Les habitations ouvrières*, Paris, 1868.

Fraser, P. A., *On some of the Causes which at present retard the Moral and Intellectual Progress of the Working Classes*, London, 1857.

Friedlander, D. and Roshier, R. J., 'Study of Internal Migration in England and Wales', *Population Studies*, Vol. 19, 1965-6.

Fuisseaux, E. N., *Questions ouvrières*, Paris, 1864.

Fuisseaux, E. N., *Des Habitations ouvrières*, Brussels, 1864.

Gaebler, Dr., 'Wohnhäuser der berliner gemeinnützigen Baugesellschaft', *Zeitschrift für Bauwesen*, 1867, p.327.

Galton, D., *Observations on the Construction of Healthy Dwellings*, London, 1880.

Gatliffe, C., *Practical Suggestions on Improved Dwellings for the Industrious Classes*, London, 1854.

—— *On Improved Dwellings and their Beneficial Effect on Health and Morals, and Suggestions for their Extension*, London, 1875.

Gauldie, Enid, *Cruel Habitations: A History of Working-Class Housing, 1780-1918*, London, 1974.

Gavin, H., *Sanitary Ramblings*, London, 1848.

—— *The Habitations of the Working Classes*, London, 1851.

—— *The Unhealthiness of London and the Necessity of Remedial Measures*, London, 1847.

George, M. Dorothy, *London Life in the XVIII Century*, London, 1925.

George, W. L., *Labour and Housing at Port Sunlight*, London, 1909.

Gibbons, D., *The Metropolitan Building Act, 1844*, London, 1844.

—— *The Metropolitan Building Act, 1855*, London, 1855.

Gilbert, W., 'Dwelling houses of the London poor', *Good Works*, Vol. 13, 1872, p.458.

Girdlestone, C., *Letters on the Unhealthy Condition of the Lower Class of Dwellings, especially in Large Towns*, London, 1854.

Glen, A., *Glen's Law of Public Health and Local Government*, London, 1858.

Gloag, John, *The Englishman's Castle*, London, 1944.

Goldie, I., *Housing and Slum Clearance in London*, London, 1934.

Godin, J.-B., *Solutions sociales. Organisation, fonctionnement, plans d'exécution et vue d'ensemble du familistère de Guise*, Paris, 1871.

Godwin, G., *London Shadows*, London, 1854.

—— *Town Swamps and Social Bridges*, London, 1859.

—— *Another Blow for Life*, London, 1864.

Gomme, Sir George Lawrence, *London in the Reign of Victoria, 1837-1897*, London, 1898.

Goltz, R. von der, *Die Gross-städte in ihrer Wohnungsnoth und die durchgreifende Abhülfe*, Leipzig, 1874.

—— *Ländliche Arbeiterwohnungen*, Königsberg and Tilsit, 1864.

Goodwin, M., *Nineteenth Century Opinion*, London, 1951.

Gosset, A., 'Cité ouvrière de l'usine de l'Espérance', *Encyclopédie d'architecture*, 1879, p.86.

—— *La construction hygiènique des logements Collectifs*, Reims, 1888.

Gould, E. R. L., *See* Wight, Carroll, D.

Grandpierre, Henri, *Les logements à bon marché. Etude sur les discussions du Conseil municipal, projet de propositions*, Paris, 1884.

Gray, B. K., *Philanthropy and the State*, London, 1908.

Groves, J. W., *Old Clapham*, London, 1887.

Hammond, J. L. & B., *The Age of the Chartists*, London, 1930.

——, —— *The Bleak Age*, London, 1947.

——, —— *The Town Labourer 1760-1832*, London, 1917.

Hansen, P. Ch., 'Ueber die Arbeiter wohnungen in Dänemark', *Vierteljahrsschrift für Volkswirtschaft und Kulturg.*, 1879.

Hares, T., *Thoughts on the Dwellings of the People, Charitable Estates, Improvements and Local Government of the Metropolis*, London, 1862.

Hashick, P. H., *Cheap Dwellings*, London, 1906.

Hasse, C., *Die Wohnungsverhältnisse der ärmern Volksklassen in Leipzig*, Leipzig, 1886.

Haussonville, Comte d', *Misère et Remèdes. Misère à Paris*, Paris, 1886.

Hennell, Michael, *John Venn and the Clapham Sect*, London, 1958.

Henrez, P., 'Maisons ouvrières de Varangeville-Dombasle', *Nouv. Annales de construction*, 1880, p.150.

Hill, O., *Homes of the London Poor*, London, 1875.

—— *Letters on Housing*, London, 1933.

Hill, W. T., *Octavia Hill: Pioneer of the National Trust and Housing Reformer*, London, 1956.

Hirschberg, Rh. and Feierabend, Oskar, *Die Wohnhäuser der Bau- und Spargenossenschaft*, Munich, 1875.

Hitchcock, Henry-Russell, *Early Victorian Architecture in Britain*, New Haven and London, 1954.

Hitchen, W. E., *Surrey at the Opening of the XXth Century*, Brighton, 1907.

Hobhouse, Hermione, *Thomas Cubitt, Master Builder*, London, 1971.

Hodder, E., *The Life and Works of the Seventh Earl of Shaftesbury*, London, 1888.

Hoffmann, C. W., *Die Wohnungen der Arbeiter und der Armen*, Berlin, 1852.

Hole, Charles, *The Early History of the Church Missionary Society*, London, 1896.

Hole, J., *The Homes of the Working Classes with Suggestions for their Improvement*, London, 1866.

Holekamp, I., 'Arbeiterkolonie Leinhausen', *Baugewerks Zeitung*, 1880, p.596.

Hoole, E., 'South Lambeth dwellings, Lambeth Road', *The Building News*, 1879, p.796.

Hornemann, Dr. E., *Cités ouvrières en Danemarck*, Copenhagen, 1876.

Hoskin, W., *A Guide to the Proper Regulation of Buildings in Towns, as a means of promoting and securing the Health, Comfort and Safety of the Inhabitants*, London, 1848.

Houssoullier, Charles, 'Habitations ouvrières en Angleterre', *Gazette des Architectes et du bâtiment*, 1875, p.21.

Howse, Ernest Marshall, *Saints in Politics. The Clapham Sect and the Growth of Freedom*, London, 1952.

Huber, V. A., *Reisebrief aus Belgien, Frankreich und England*, Hamburg, 1855.

——— *Die Wohnungsnoth der kleinen Leute in grossen Städten*, Leipzig, 1857.

Ingestre, Viscount, *Meliora, or Better Times to Come*, London, 1852.

——— *Social Evils, their Causes and their Cures*, London, 1853.

Inglis, K. S., *Churches and the working Classes in Victorian England*, London, 1963.

Jacquet, L., *See* Dauby, Fr.

Jenkins, E., *See* Stewart, A. P.

Jephson, H., *The Sanitary Evolution of London*, London, 1907.

Jonas, Stephen, *Cité de Mulhouse*, Paris, 1853.

Jones, G. Stedman, *Outcast London*, London, 1971.

Jones, R. Tudor, *Congregationalism in England 1662–1962*, London, 1962.

Judge, M., *Sanitary Arrangements of Dwelling Houses*, London, 1884.

Kay, James Phillips, *The Moral and Physical Condition of the Working Classes Employed in the Cotton Manufacture in Manchester*, London, 1832.

Kellett, J. R., *The Impact of Railways on Victorian Cities*, London, 1969.

Kendall, J., 'Labourers' Cottages', *The Builder*, 1865, p.393.

Kent, Nathaniel, *Hints to Gentlemen of Landed Property*, London, 1775.

Klasen, Ludwig, *Arbeiterwohnhäuser*, Leipzig, 1872.

——— *Die Arbeiter Wohnhäuser in ihrer baulichen Anlage und Ausführung Sowie die Anlage von Arbeiter-Colonien*, Leipzig, 1879.

Knight, Charles (ed.), *London*, London, 1841.

Knutsford, Lady, *Zachary Macaulay*, London, 1900.

Kolz, K., 'Entwurf zu einem Arbeiterhause', *Deutsche Bauzeitung*, 1881, p.192.

——— 'Arbeiterhäuser aus Beton', *Deutsche Bauzeitung*, 1882, p.524.

——— 'Arbeiterhäuser bei Lübeck', *Deutsche Bauzeitung*, 1883, p.197.

Kverndal, Roald, *The Origin and Nature of Nordic Missions to Seamen*, Bergen, 1978.

Labourers' Friend Magazine, The, 1834–1884.

Laing, S., *National Distress: Its Causes and Remedies*, London, 1844.

Lascelles, W. H., *But and Ben, or Workman's House*, London, 1878.

Laspeyres, G., *Der Einfluss der Wohnung auf Sittlichkeit*, Berlin, 1869.

Lavollée, M., 'Rapport à la Société d'Encouragement pour l'Industrie nationale sur les habitations Ouvrières', *Bulletin* of the Société, 1882.

Lavollée, René, *Les classes ouvrières en Europe*, Paris, 1884.

Lebon, Dr. F., *Des habitations ouvrières de Nivelles*, Nivelles, 1871.

Leclerc Imprimerie, *Cités ouvrières de Bolbec et Cités ouvrières du Havre*, Le Havre, 1878.

Leclere, I., *Compte rendu de l'enquête officielle faite sur les habitations ouvrières de la province de Liège*, Liège, 1887.

Leeds, W. H., The supplement to Britton and Pugin's *Public Buildings in London*, London, 1838.

Le Rousseau, Julien, *Projet d'éstablissement d'un quartier mixte et libre pour 10,000 âmes*, Paris, 1864.

Lewis, C. L., *Dr. Southwood Smith*, London, 1898.

Lewis, R. A., *Edwin Chadwick and the Public Health Movement, 1832-1854*, London, 1952.

Liddle, J., *Sanitary Report (Supplement), Whitechapel*, London, 1842.

Loftie, W. J., *A History of London*, London, 1883.

London County Council, *The Survey of London*, Various volumes, but especially Vol. XXVI.

—— *The Housing Question in London 1855-1900*, London, 1900.

—— *Housing of the Working Classes in London, 1855-1912*, London, 1913.

Loransky, A., *Aperçu sur les institutions subsidiaires pour les ouvriers attachés aux éstablissements métallurgiques en Russie*, St Petersburg, 1876.

Loudon, John Claudius, *Encyclopaedia of Cottage, Farm, and Villa Architecture*, London, 1833.

Love, L. B., *The Handbook of Manchester*, Manchester, 1842.

Macaulay, H., 'Dwellings for the industrial classes', *The Builder*, 1875, p.347.

Madre, Cte de, *Des ouvriers et des moyens d'améliorer leurs conditions dans les villes*, Paris, 1863.

Manega, C., *Die Anlage von Arbeiterwohnungen*, Weimar, 1871.

Marriott, W. T., *Some Real Wants and Some Legitimate Claims of the Working Classes*, London, 1860.

Marsilio (ed.), *Proceedings* of the Convegno Internazionale di Storia Urbanistica, Lucca, 7-11 September 1977.

Martens, G., 'Arbeiterhäuser auf Marton Hall', *Architekt. Skizzenbuch*, Berlin, 1884, pl.3.

Maurice, C. Edmund, *Life of Octavia Hill as told in her letters*, London, 1964.

Mayhew, H., *London Labour and the London Poor*, London, 1851.

Meacham, Standish, *Henry Thornton of Clapham*, London, 1964.

Meakin, B., *Model Factories and Villages: Ideal Conditions of Labour and Housing*, London, 1905.

Mearns, W. C., *The Bitter Cry of Outcast London: An Inquiry into the Condition of the Abject Poor*, London, 1883.

Menzies, G. K., *The Story of the Royal Society of Arts*, London, n.d.

Metcalf, Priscilla, *The Halls of the Fishmongers' Company. An Architectural History of a Riverside Site*, London and Chichester, 1977.

Meyer, Ferdinand, 'Les logements d'ouvriers', *Nouvelle Revue*, 18 May 1883.

Millington, F. H., *The Housing of the Poor*, London, 1891.

Mognier, G., *Les institutions ouvrières de la Suisse, rédigé à la demande de la commission centrale de la Confédération Suisse pour l'Exposition Universelle de Paris*, Paris, 1867.

Mowat, C. L., *The Charity Organisation Society, 1869-1913*, London, 1961.

Mühlhauser Arbeiterviertel, Das, *Das Mühlhauser Arbeiterviertel seine Badeanstakten und Waschküchen* Mulhouse, 1891.

Muller, Emile, *Habitations Ouvrières et Agricoles, Cités, Bains, Lavoirs, Sociétés Alimentaires*, Paris, 1856.

——, and Cacheux, Emile, *Les Habitations Ouvrières en tous Pays. Situation en 1878. Avenir*, Paris, 1879.

——, ——, Another edition of the above of 1889.

Muyden, G. Van, 'Les habitations ouvrières'. *Bibliothèque universelle et Revue Suisse*, December 1886.

Narjoux, Félix, *Les logements à bon marché, ce qu'ils sont, ce qu'ils doivent être*, Paris, 1883.

National Association for the Promotion of Social Science, *Transactions*, 1858-70.

Needleman, L., *The Economics of Housing*, London, 1965.

New Monthly Magazine, The, 1821-81.

Norton, G., *Victorian London*, London, 1969.

Olsen, Donald J., *The Growth of Victorian London*, London, 1976.

—— *Town Planning in London. The Eighteenth and Nineteenth Centuries*, New Haven, 1964.

Owen, D., *English Philanthropy, 1660–1960*, London, 1965.

Owen, John, *History of the British and Foreign Bible Society*, London, 1816.

Parker, F., *George Peabody, 1795–1869*, Nashville, 1955.

Parkes, E. A., *Public Health*, London, 1876.

Parsons, J., *Housing by Voluntary Enterprises*, London, 1903.

Patterson, C. B., *Angela Burdett Coutts and the Victorians*, London, 1953.

Paul, Dr., *Rapport sur les habitations ouvrières exposées à Bruxelles en 1876*, Brussels, 1877.

Pearson, C. (ed.), *Proceedings of a Public Meeting held at the London Tavern*, London, 1854.

Penot, A., *Les cités ouvrières de Mulhouse et du département du Haut-Rhin*, Mulhouse and Paris, 1867.

Plasman, M. de, *Des cités ouvrières et du projet de leur établissement à Paris*, Paris, 1881.

Platt, Sam E., *Building Societies. Not as they are but as they should be*, London, 1877.

Plon, E. & Cie., *Visite à l'usine de Noisiel*, Paris, 1878.

Plume, R., 'Artisans' and Labourers' dwellings at Hornsey', *The Builder*, 1883, p.880.

Pollock, John, *Wilberforce*, London, 1977.

Poulain, C., 'Rapport sur les cités ouvrières', *Bulletin de la Société industrielle de Reims*, Reims, 1866.

Price, J., *Homes of the Poor*, London, 1874.

Price, S., *Building Societies, Their Origin and History*, London, 1958.

Printzsköld, Dr. O., *Rapport sur l'hygiène, le sauvetage et la condition des classes ouvrières en Suède*, Stockholm, 1876.

Puteaux, Projet, *Construction de maisons à petits logements le long du boulevard extérieur*, Paris, 1848.

Quarterly Review, The, From 1809.

Quennell, C. H. B., *Modern Suburban Housing*, London, 1906.

Quickley, H., *Housing and Slum Clearance in London*, London, 1934.

Rabaud, Camille, *La cité ouvrière de Mazamet. Appel à l'opinion les logements des pauvres*, Paris 1867.

Raffalovich, Arthur, *Le logement de l'ouvrier et du Pauvre*, Paris, 1887.

Raoux, Edward, *La Cité des familles*, Lausanne, 1876.

——— *Le familistère de Guise ou le Palais Social*, Paris, 1872.

Rasmussen, Steen Eiler, *London: the Unique City*, London, 1937.

Rathke, P., 'Arbeiterwohnhaus für vier Familien in Dobritz', *Baugew. Zeitung.*, 1880, p.259.

Rawlinson, Robert, *Lectures, Reports, Letters and Papers on Sanitary Questions*, London, 1876.

Reichardt, Dr. Erwin, *Die Grundzüge der Arbeiterwohnungsfrage*, Berlin, 1885.

Reid, H. G., *Every man his own landlord*, London, 1880.

Rendle, W., *London Vestries and their Sanitary Work*, London, 1865.

Revett, Nicholas, *See* Stuart, James.

Richardson, B. W., *Hygeia: A City of Health*, London, 1876.

——— *The Health of Nations. A Review of the Works of Edwin Chadwick*, London, 1887.

Robbins, Michael, *Middlesex*, London, 1953.

Roberts, D., *Victorian Origins of the British Welfare State*, New Haven, 1960.

Roberts, Henry, *Proposed People's Palace and Gardens for the Northern and Midland Counties, to Employ Factory Operatives*, London and Manchester, 1863. This pamphlet, dated 1 July 1863, has been attributed to Henry Roberts, F.S.A. There is no evidence to suggest that Henry Roberts and Henry Roberts, F.S.A., were one and the same person.

Roberts, Henry, F.S.A., 'Arbeiterwohnungen in England', *Allgemeine Bauzeitung*, 1850, p.152, pls.329–333.

——— *The circulation of a pure and instructive literature, adapted to the capacities and means of the labouring population*, London, 1862. Reprinted from the complete *Proceedings* of the *Congrès International de Bienfaisance, 1862*.

——— *Conseils aux personnes de la classe ouvrière pour l'amélioration et la bonne tenue de leurs demeures, etc.*, Neuchâtel, 1856.

——— *Consigli ai braccianti per migliorare le loro case*, Rome, 1873.

Roberts, Henry, F.S.A., *De la condition physique des classes ouvrières résultant de l'état de leurs habitations et des heureux effets des améliorations sanitaires récemment adoptées en Angleterre ... Traduit de l'anglais*, Paris, 1855. Another edition was published in Lausanne in 1856.

—— *The Dwellings of the Labouring Classes, their arrangement and construction, &c.*, London, 1850, with subsequent editions. The 1867 revised edition was also published in a French translation.

—— *Des Habitations des Classes ouvrières ... Traduit et publié par ordre du Président de la République*, Paris, 1850.

—— *Efforts on the Continent for improving the Dwellings of the Labouring Classes*, Florence, 1874.

—— *The Essentials of a Healthy Dwelling, and the extension of its benefits to the Labouring Population*, London, 1862.

—— *Healthy Dwellings, and prevailing sanitary defects in the homes of the working classes*, A lecture published in a tract by the Ladies' Sanitary Association, London, 1859.

—— *Home Reform, or, What the working classes may do to improve their dwellings*, London, 1852.

—— *The improvement of the dwellings of the labouring classes through the operation of government measures, &c.*, London, 1859.

—— *Lodging Houses for unmarried workmen or labourers*, London, c. 1860.

—— *Model Houses for Four Families erected in Hyde Park at the Industrial Exhibition of 1851*, London, c. 1860.

—— *Das Musterhaus für Arbeiterfamilien von Henry Roberts. Aus dem Englischen übersetzt von Busse*, Potsdam, 1852.

—— *On Hollow Brickwork*, London, 1851.

—— *The Physical Condition of the Labouring Classes, resulting from the State of their dwellings*, London, 1866.

—— *Plans issued by the Society for Improving the Condition of the Labouring Classes*, by Henry Roberts, Hony. Archt.

—— *Plans for a pair of labourers' cottages Nos. 1-7*, London, c. 1860.

—— *The progress and present aspect of the movement for improving the dwellings of the labouring classes*. A report made to the National Association for the Promotion of Social Science. Reprinted from the *Transactions*.

—— *La réforme domestique, ou conseils aux personnes de la classe ouvrière pour l'amélioration et la bonne tenue de leurs demeures*, Neuchâtel, 1856.

—— *Report on the Proceedings of the Congrès International de Bienfaisance & on the Association Internationale de Bienfaisance*, London, 1859.

—— *Windsor Royal Society's model houses for eight families, Nos. 1-3*, London, c. 1860.

Roberts, William, *Memoirs of the Life and Correspondence of Mrs. Hannah More*, London, 1834.

Roi, J. F. A. de le, *Michael Solomon Alexander der erste evangelische Bischof in Jerusalem*, Gütersloh, 1897.

Roshier, R. J., *See* Friedlander, D.

Royal College of Physicians, *A Memorial on the Condition of the Poor in London*, London, 1874.

Royal Institute of British Architects, *Transactions*, From 1835.

Runge, L., 'Wohnhäuser für vier Arbeiterfamilien in London', *Zeitschrift für Bauwesen*, 1852, p.48, pl.14.

Ruprecht, Dr. Wilch, *Die Wohnungen der arbeitenden Klassen in London*, Göttingen, 1885.

Rusch, H., 'Arbeiterwohnhaus mit Holzleistengeflecht', *Baugewerks Zeitung*, 1883, p.401.

Sailors' Magazine, The, Various years, but notably 1846-50.

Sala, George Augustus, *Gaslight and Daylight*, London, 1859.

Saulnier, D., 'Maison pour habitations d'ouvriers à Noisiel', *Encyclopédie d'architecture*, 1875, p.110.

Sax, E. *Die Wohnungszustände der arbeitenden Klassen und ihre Reform*, Vienna, 1869.

Schmölcke, D., 'Diezweckmässige Anlage das Arbeiterwohnhausen', *Wochenblatt für Arch. und Ing.*, Berlin, 1883, p.458.

—— *Das Wohnhaus des Arbeiters*, Bonn, 1885.

Scott, Sir George Gilbert, *Personal and Professional Recollections* (edited by G. Gilbert Scott), London, 1879.

Scratchley, Arthur, *A special treatise of building and land societies*, London, 1875.

Scrive Brothers, and Danset, S., *Habitations Ouvrières*, Lille, 1851.

Scrope, G. P., *Suggested Legislation, with a View to the Improvement of the Dwellings of the Poor*, London, 1849.

Sharp, Reginald R., *London and the Kingdom*, London, 1894–5.

Shaw, W. A., *Manchester Old and New*, London, 1896.

Shepherd, Thos. H., *See*, Elmes, James.

Sheppard, Francis, *London, 1808–1870: The Infernal Wen*, London, 1971.

Simon, Sir John, *Public Health Reports*, London, 1887.

Simonin, Louis, *Les cités ouvrières de houilleurs dans les mines du centre français*, Paris, 1867.

—— *Les cités ouvrières des mineurs*, Paris, 1867,

Smalley, G., *The Life of Sir Sydney H. Waterlow, Bart.*, London, 1909.

Smirke, S., *Suggestions for the Improvement of the Western Parts of London*, London, 1834.

Smith, A. E., *Norbiton Church 1842–1942: The Story of 100 years*, n.d.

Smith, Frank, *The Life and Work of Sir James Kay-Shuttleworth*, London, 1923.

Smith, John Thomas, *An Antiquarian Ramble in the Streets of London*, London, 1846.

Smith, Roger, 'Early Victorian Household Structure', *International Review of Social History*, Vol. 15, 1970.

Smith, S., *Results of Sanitary Improvements Illustrated by the Operation of the Metropolitan Societies*, London, 1854.

Smith, T. Roger, and White, W. H., 'Model Dwellings for the Rich', *The Architect*, Vol. XV, 1876.

Society for Bettering the Condition of the Poor, *Reports*, 1798 *et seq.*

Society for the encouragement of arts, manufactures and commerce, *Journal* of the, From 1852.

Society for Improving the Condition of the Labouring Classes, The Minutes of the Society now in the possession of the Peabody Trust.

Solly, H., *Industrial Villages, a Remedy for Crowded Towns and Deserted Fields*, London, 1884.

—— *Rehousing of the Industrial Classes, or Village Communities v. Town Rookeries*, London, 1884.

Spencer, Edward, *Homes of the Working Classes in Dublin*, London, 1884.

Spetzler, D., 'Wohngebäude für verheirathete und unverheirathete Arbeiter des Bochumer Bergbau-Vereins, *Zeitschrift für Baukunde*, 1879, p.537.

Steiner, Maximilian, *Ueber die Errichtung von Arbeiterwohnungen in Wien*, Vienna, 1884.

Stephen, Sir James, *Essays in Ecclesiastical Biography*, London, 1860.

Stewart, A. P. and Jenkins, E., *The Medical and Legal Aspects of Sanitary Reform*, Leicester, 1969.

Stewart, Cecil, *A Prospect of Cities*, London, 1952.

Strange, R., *Lodging Houses Acts*, London, 1851.

Strickland, C. W., *On Cottage Design*, London, 1864.

Stuart, James, and Revett, Nicholas, *The Antiquities of Athens*, London, 1762–1830, Five volumes.

Studnitz, E. von, *Nordamerikanische Arbeiterwohnungen*, Leipzig, 1879.

Stumpt, Wilhelm, *Die Arbeiterwohnungen des Bochumer Vereins für Bergbau and Guss-stahlfabrikation*, Bochum, 1876.

Sutcliffe, Anthony (ed.), *Multi-Storey Living. The British Working-Class Experience*, London, 1974.

—— 'Working-Class Housing in Nineteenth Century Britain: A Review of Recent Research', *Society for the Study of Labour History*, Bulletin 24, Spring 1972.

Sykes, J. F. J., *Public Health and Housing*, London, 1901.

Tait, A. C., *The Spiritual Wants of the Metropolis and its Suburbs*, London, 1863.

Tarn, J. N., *Working-Class Housing in 19th-century Britain*, Architectural Association Paper Number 7, London, 1971.

Tarn, John Nelson, *Five Per Cent Philanthropy. An account of housing in urban areas between 1840 and 1914*, Cambridge, 1973.

Teale, T. Pridgin, *Dangers to Health*, London, 1879.

—— *Dangers au point de vue sanitaire des maisons mal construites*, Paris, 1882.

Teignmouth, Charles Shore, Second Lord, *Reminiscences of Many Years*, London, 1878.

Thompson, E. P., *The Making of the English Working Class*, London, 1963.

Thornbury, Walter, *Old and New London*, London, 1873.

Timbs, John, *Curiosities of London*, London, 1855.

Timms, Duncan, *The Urban Mosaic*, Cambridge, 1971.

Tollet, C., *Mémoire présenté au congrès international d'hygiène de Paris en 1878, sur les logements collectifs, hôpitaux, casernes, etc.*, Paris, 1878.

Town Planning Review, The, From 1910.

Tremenheere, G. B., *Dwellings of the Labouring Classes in the Metropolis*, London, 1856.

Turner, R. E., *James Silk Buckingham, A Social Biography*, London, 1934.

Vanderlinden, Edouard, *Etude, sur l'amélioration des habitations ouvrières et sur l'organisation du domicile de secours en Belgique*, Brussels, 1875.

Varnhagen, O., 'Ueber Arbeiterwohnungen', *Centralblatt der Bauverw.*, Berlin, 1881, p.133.

Véron, Eugène, *Les Institutions Ouvrières de Mulhouse et des Environs*, Paris, 1866.

Victorian Studies, Since 1957.

Vivian, H., *Co-partnership in Housing in its Health Relationship*, London, 1908.

Vleminckx, Dr. V., *Rapport au ministre de l'Intérieur belge, sur la construction des habitations destinés à la classe ouvrière*, Brussels, 1887.

Weale, John (ed.), *London Exhibited in 1851*.

Weber, Adna Ferrin, *The Growth of Cities in the Nineteenth Century*, New York, 1899.

Weber, Max, *L'éthique protestante et l'esprit du capitalisme*, Paris, 1964.

Welch, Charles, *A Modern History of the City of London*, London, 1896.

Wheatley, Henry B., *London Past and Present*, London, 1891.

White, J., *Better homes for working-men*, New York, 1885.

White, W. H., *See* Smith, T. Roger.

Whitley, W. T., *The Baptists of London 1612–1928*, London, n.d.

Wiebenson, Dora, *Sources of Greek Revival Architecture*, London, 1969.

Wight, Carroll D. and Gould, E. R. L., *The Housing of the Working People*, Washington, 1895.

Williams, R., *London Rookeries and Colliers Slums*, London, 1893.

Willmott, P., *See* Young, M.

Wintzingerode-Knorr, Levin, Freiherr von, *Die deutschen Arbeiterhäuser, ein Betrag zur Lösung der Vagabondenfrage*, Halle a/S., 1885.

Wiseman, Cardinal, *An Appeal to the Reason and Good Feeling of the English People on the Subject of the Catholic Hierarchy*, London, 1850.

Wiss, P., *Ueber die Wohnungsnoth in Deutschland*, Berlin, 1872.

Wist, J., 'Arbeiterwohnhaus auf der Wiener Weltausstellung, 1873', *Zeitschrift des österr. Ingenieur und Architekten Vereins*, 1874, p.186. *See also* the same journal for 1875, p.293, and 1877, p.206.

Wist, Jean, *Les habitations ouvrières a l'Exposition universelle de 1873, à Vienne*, Vienna, 1877.

Wohl, Anthony S., *The Eternal Slum. Housing and Social Policy in Victorian London*, London, 1977.

Wolff, *See* Dyos.

Wolff, M. P., *Die Ernährung der arbeitenden Klassen*, Berlin, 1885.

Woodward, E. L., *The Age of Reform, 1815–70*, London, 1962.

Worthington, T. L., *Dwellings of the People*, London, 1893.

Wrigley, Edmund, *How to manage building associations*, Philadelphia, 1876. *See also* the *Directory and handbook of building and freehold societies*, London, 1876.

—— *The Working man's way to wealth. A practical treatise on building associations*, Philadelphia, 1874.

Wylson, J., *Remarks on Workmen's Houses in Town Districts*, London, n.d.

Young, G. M., *Early Victorian England*, London, 1934.

—— *Victorian England, Portrait of an Age*, London, 1953.

Young, M. with Willmott, P., *Family and Kinship in East London*, London, 1957.

BIBLIOGRAPHY APPENDIX

Various articles and papers relevant to Roberts and to aspects of his work arranged chronologically. Where no author is given, the work named is not signed. Most items in this appendix are pamphlets, or articles in journals.

1832   1. 'Pauperism and cottage allotments', *Christian Observer*, London, Vol. 32, pp.574, 842.
1837   2. 'Arbeiterquartier in Mühlhausen', *Allgemeine Bauzeitung*, p.244 (pls.160–4).
1838   3. *Projet d'association financière pour l'amélioration des habitations et l'assainissement des quartiers habités par la classe ouvrière de Bruxelles*, Brussels, 1846.
1847   4. 'Wohnungen der Arbeiter', *Rombergs Zeitschrift für prakt. Baukunst*, p.287.
1850   5. Parisius, C., 'Ueber Arbeiterwohnungen', *Der Arbeiterfreund*.
       6. *Statuten und Fundamentalschriften der berliner gemeinnützigen Baugesellschaft*, Berlin, 1850.
1858   7. 'Arbeiterhäuser des Kohlenwerkes in Brandeisl', *Allgemeine Bauzeitung*, p.86 (pls.176–7).
       8. 'Dwelling houses of London Poor', *London Quarterly Review*, Vol. 9, p.459.
1860   9. 'Ueber Wohnungen für Arbeiterfamilien mit Rücksicht auf Heizung und Ventilation', *Zeitschrift für Bauhandwerk*, p.193.
1861 10. 'Arbeiterstadt in Mülhausen', *Rombergs Zeitschrift für praktische Baukunst*, p.213.
      11. 'Wohnungsverhältnisse der arbeitenden Klassen in England', *ibid.*, p.141.
      12. 'Arbeiterhäuser in Frankreich', *Scientific American*, N.S., Vol. V, p.86.
1862 13. 'On healthy and well-constructed dwellings for the working classes', *The Builder*, pp.904 and 925.
      14. Eyton, M., 'Workers' housing in Hull', *The Builder*, p.569.
      15. 'Bauernhäuser in Westfalen und Holstein', *Zeitschrift für Bauhandwerk*, p.157.
1863 16. Stapleton, J., 'Working-class housing. An esquisse', *The Builder*, p.131.
      17. 'Buildings for workers. Reckoning the costs', *The Engineer*, Vol. 16, p.110.
      18. 'On working-class housing', *Civil Engineering*, p.33.
      19. Kestner, K., 'Die Arbeiterstadt zu Mühlhausen in Elsass', *Hannover Bauzeitung*, p.463.
      20. Felber, P., 'Arbeiterwohnungen', *Zeitschrift für Bauhandwerk*, p.156.
      21. Darbishire, H. A., 'Housing for the poor', *Civ. Engineering*, p.368.
1864 22. 'On workers' dwellings', *The Builder*, p. 421.
      23. Birch, W., 'Labourers' cottages', *The Builder*, p.952 (pl.).
      24. 'Workers' dwellings', *Civ. Engineering*, p.149.
      25. Kestner, K., 'Die Arbeiterstadt zu Mülhausen in Elsass', *Bayerisches Kunst und Gewerbeblatt*, p.307.
      26. 'Competition for labourers' cottages', *Civ. Engineering*, p.168.
      27. Felber, P., 'Arbeitercasernen', *Zeitschrift für Bauhandwerk*, p.77.
      28. Denton, W., 'The economy of agricultural cottages', *Civ. Engineering*, pp.170, 201.
      29. Sonnenmann, K., 'Bericht für den deutschen Arbeiterkongress', *Ueber die Arbeiterwohnungen*, Frankfurt-am-Main, 1864.
      30. *Statistics of dwellings improvements in the metropolis*, London, 1864.
1865 31. Klette, von, 'Die Wohnung und die Wohnungsnoth', *Zeitschrift für Bauhandwerk*, pp.13, 30, 48.
      32. Japy, P., 'Habitations ouvrières', *Génie industriel*, Vol. 29, p.125;
      33. *Peabody Gift to the poor of London. Rapport des commissaires chargés d'appliquer la donation de 150000 L. st. faite par Peabody pour créer à Londres l'œuvre la plus utile pour améliorer le sort des classes laborieuses*, London, 1865.
      34. Penot, A., 'Les cités ouvrières du Haut-Rhin', *Bulletin de la Société industrielle de Mulhouse*, p.385.

1865 35. 'Dwellings and food of laboring classes', *Christian Remembrancer*, Vol. 50, p. 15.
      36. *Der Arbeiterfreund. Zeitschrift des Centralvereins für das Wohl der arbeitenden Klassen.* Contains several articles on the dwellings of the labouring classes by M. M. Braemer.
      37. *Mittheilungen des preussischen Centralvereins für das Wohl der arbeitenden Klassen.* Berlin, 1865.
1866 38. 'Workmen's cottages at Llandaff, near Cardiff', *The Builder*, p.885.
      39. 'Labourers' dwellings, West Hill Park, Halifax', *Civ. Engineering*, pp.1 and 55.
      40. 'Dwelling-Houses of the Poor', *Chambers' Edinburgh Journal*, Vol. 43, p.252.
1867 41. 'Wohnhäuser für niedere Eisenbahnbedienstete', *Zeitschrift für Bauwesen*, Berlin, p.175 (pls.25–8).
      42. 'Wohnhäuser für niedere Eisenbahnbeamte', *Erbkams Zeitschrift*, p.175.
      43. 'Die Arbeiterstadt von Mülhausen', *Wochenblatt Architekt*, V, p.116.
      44. 'Housing for the poor in towns', *Civ. Engineering*, p.35.
      45. 'Arbeiterwohnungen', *Deutsche Bauzeitung*, pp.249, 257.
      46. 'Die Arbeiterhäuser auf der Ausstellung zu Paris 1867', *Ann. d. Ldw. in d. Kgl. preuss. St.*, pp.336, 348.
1868 47. Detaing, P., 'Les habitations ouvrières', *Revue générale de l'architecture*, pp.64, 110, 209 (pls. 11 and 51).
      48. 'Arbeiter-Quartier in Kuchen', *Deutsche Bauzeitung*, pp.299, 307 (6 engravings).
      49. 'Arbeiterwohnungen', *Deutsche Bauzeitung*, p.13.
      50. 'Arbeiterwohnungen in Riga', *Notizblatt des technischen Vereins zu Riga*, pp.35, 145.
      51. Helberg, K., 'Ueber Arbeiterwohnungen', *Wochenblatt des Architektenvereins*, p.13.
      52. Klesse, O., 'Zur Frage der Arbeiterwohnungen', *Zeitschrift für Bauhandwerk*, p. 54.
      53. Regis de Curel, 'Habitations ouvrières pour l'Egypte', *Annales du Génie civil*, p.475.
      54. Reiter, P., 'Das Quartier für Angestellte und Arbeiter in Nieder-Töss bei Winterthur', *Schweizerische polytechnische Zeitschrift*, p.59.
      55. 'Dwelling Houses for Artisans at Mulhouse', *Saint James's Magazine*, Vol. 22, p.109.
      56. *Description de la cité ouvrière de MM. Staub et Cie, de Kuchen et des institutions qui s'y rattachent*, Stuttgart, 1868.
1869 57. 'Arbeiterwohnungen in Riga', *Notizblatt des technischen Vereins zu Riga*, p.82.
      58. Burden, J., 'Islington Workhouse', *The Builder*, pp.464, 467.
      59. 'On dwellings for the working classes', *The Engineer*, Vol. 27, p.223.
      60. 'Das Staubsche Arbeiterquartier in Kuchen (Württemberg)', *Zeitschrift des Vereins deutscher Ingenieure*, p.329.
      61. Hilbig, K., 'Arbeiterwohnungen der Sprot'schen Stiftung in Riga', *Notizblatt des technischen Vereins zu Riga*, p.82 (pls. 10 and 11).
      62. Staub, E., 'Les cités ouvrières', *Nouv. Ann. de construction*, p.100.
      63. Flattich, W. von, 'Ueber de Arbeiterhäuser der österr. Südbahngesellschaft in Marburg und Meidling (Auszug eines Vortrags)', *Zeitschrift des österr. Ingenieur-Vereins*, p. 260.
      64. Bour, E., 'Les maisons ouvrières à l'Exposition de'Amsterdam', *Annuaire industriel*, p.692.
      65. 'Artisans' Dwelling-Houses', *British Quarterly Review*, Vol. 51, p.343.
      66. *Maisons ouvrières construites par le bureau de bienfaisance d'Anvers*, Antwerp, 1869.
      67. Articles by M. Senftleben in *Der Arbeiterfreund. Zeitschrift des Centralvereins für das Wohl der arbeitenden Klassen.*
1870 68. Oppermann, A. 'Maison de garde simple des chemins de fer de Portugal', *Nouvelles Annales de construction*, p.75, (pl. 35).
      69. Detaing, E., 'Habitations ouvrières', *Revue générale de l'architecture*, 1870–1, pp.66, 110, 214, 260 (pls. 18 and 19).
      70. 'Arbeiterwohnungen', *Notizblatt des technischen Vereins zu Riga*, p.7.
      71. 'Dwellings for the poor, Chequer Alley, St Luke's, Middlesex', *The Builder*, p.141.
      72. Szafarkiewicz, F., 'Grundzüge (nebst Kostenanschlag) für die Herstellung von Arbeiterwohnungen bei Ziegel und Kalkwerken', *Notizblatt des deutschen Vereins der Ziegelf*, p.64.
      73. Rinecker, K., 'Stewart's Hotel Für Arbeiterinnen in New-York', *Zeitschrift des Bayer. Architekten und Ingenieur Vereins*, p.9.

1870 74. 'Ueber die neuen Nicoll'schen Patent Musterhäuser für Arbeiter', *Zeitschrift für Bauhandwerk*, p.78.

75. 'On cottages for miners and agricultural labourers', *Mechanics Magazine*, N.S., Vol. 24, p.164.

76. 'Labourers' cottages designed by the "Central Cottage Improvement Society"', *Engineering*, Vol. 30, p.259.

77. Stolp, P., 'Die Wohnungsfrage', *Berliner städtische Jahrbuch*, 1870.

1871 78. Bürkner, K., 'Arbeiter Familienhaus und Œfen für Arbeiterwohnungen ausgeführt in der Neumark', *Deutsche Bauzeitung*, p.222 (5 engravings).

79. 'Arbeiterwohnungen in Riga', *Notizblatt des technischen Vereins zu Riga*, p.7.

80. 'Arbeiter Colonie in Görz', *Rombergs Zeitschrift für prakt. Bauhandwerk*, p.161.

81. Fletcher, J., 'Model dwellings for the industrial classes', *The Builder*, p.860 (engravings).

82. Jahns, F., 'Ueber die Ausführung der Arbeiterhäuser in England', *Zeitschrift des Vereins deutscher Ingenieure*, p.285.

83. Stallard, J., 'On the economical construction of workmen's dwellings and especially in reference to improving the health and habits of the class', *The Builder*, p.343.

84. Chapman, S., 'Improved dwellings for the very poor', *The Builder*, p.841.

85. Walford, Edward, 'Workingmen's dwelling-houses', *Old and New London*, Vol. 4, p.488.

86. 'Cottage Building in Norway', *Engineering Magazine, Vol. 6, p.591.*

87. Dollfus-Mieg, 'Sur les maisons d'ouvriers construites à Dornach', *Bulletin de la Société industrielle de Mulhouse*, p.288.

88. Vuillemin, G., *Enquête sur les habitations, les écoles et le degré d'instruction de la population ouvrière des mines de houille des bassins du Nord et du Pas-de-Calais*, Paris, 1871.

89. 'Ueber Arbeiterhäuser von Beton', *Deutsch. Ing. Zeitschrift.*, p.83.

90. 'Arbeiterhäuser von Beton', *Baugewerb. Zeitschrift.*, p.105.

91. Lette, E., *Die Wohnungsfrage*, Berlin, 1871.

1872 92. Rebolledo, C., *Casas para obreros. Viuda é hijos de Galiano.*

93. Willebrand, K., 'Arbeiterwohnungen zu Rabensteinfeld', *Deutsche Bauzeitung*, pp.33, 37 (2 engravings).

94. 'Cottages for laboring classes', *Scientific American*, N.S., Vol. 26, p.84.

95. Hoffmann, H., 'Arbeiterwohnungen für zwei Familien; Anschlags Extrakt', *N.V.Ziegelf.*, pp.316, 320.

96. Bruch, M., 'Wohnungsnoth und Hülfe', *Städtische Jahrbuch für Volkswirthsch. und Statistik.*, Berlin, 1872.

97. Engel, K., 'Die Wohnungsnoth', *Zeitschrift der preussischen Statistik Bureaux.*

1873 98. 'Labourers' cottages', *Iron*, Vol. 1, pp.432, 464, 496, 520, 560, 585, 617, 649, 680, 712, 745; Vol. 2, p. 9.

99. 'Arbeiterhäuser', *Zeitschrift für Bauhandwerk*, pp.152, 163, 180.

100. 'Arbeiterhäuser (Nach Hagen's Theorie gewoelbter, feuersicherer Bauten)', *Grothe Polytechnische Zeitschrift*, p.462.

101. Dittmar, O., 'Ueber Arbeiterwohnungen', *Zeitschrift des Vereins deutscher Ingenieure*, p.525.

102. Hemming, W., 'Iron dwelling houses at the Vienna Exhibition 1873', *Engineering*, Vol. 116, p.410.

103. Engel, K., *Die moderne Wohnungsnoth. Signatur, Ursachen und Abhülfe*, Leipzig, 1873.

1874 104. Morlok., 'Colonie für die Niederbediensteten der k. würtemberg. Berkehrsanstalten', *Allgemeine Bauzeitung*, p.78 (pls.79–89).

105. 'Arbeiterwohnungen', *Deutsche Bauzeitung*, p. 343.

106. *Die Arbeiterhäuser in Böhmen. Herausgegeben vom deutschen polytechnischen Vereine in Böhmen* (Abstracts from *Technische Blätter*), Prague, 1874.

1876 107. 'Französiches Arbeiterhaus für zwei Familien', *Baugewerks Zeitung*, Berlin, p.280 (2 engravings).

108. *Die Einrichtungen zum Besten der Arbeiter auf den Bergwerken Preussens*, Berlin, 1875-6.

109. *Wohlfahrtseinrichtungen der F. Krupp'schen Guss-stahlfabrik zu Essen, zum Besten ihrer Arbeiter*, Essen, 1876.

110. Knudsen, J., *Exposé statistique des institutions et sociétés danoises ayant pour l'améliora-tion des classes ouvrières et peu aisées*, Copenhagen, 1876.
111. 'The rural labourer in his model home', *The Labourers' Friend*, No. CCLII.
1877 112. 'Double cottage for labourers', *The Building News*, p.438 (2 plates).
113. 'Houses of the poor in towns', *Cornhill Magazine*, Vol. 36, p.74.
114. 'Labourers' cottages', *The Building News*, pp.144, 168 (2 plates).
115. *Improved dwellings for the labouring classes*, New York, 1877.
116. *Mémoires couronnés à la suite du concours institué par la ville de Genève sur la question des petits logements*, Geneva, 1877.
1878 117. 'Arbeiterhäuser in Mülhausen', *Baugewerks Zeitung*, pp.150 and 627 (4 engravings).
118. Lemaitre, M., 'Maisons ouvrières du Havre', *Nouvelles Annales de la construction*, p.148 (pl. 42).
119. Sorieul, E., 'Maisons ouvrières de Bolbec', *Nouvelles Annales de la construction*, p.161 (pls. 43 and 44).
120. 'Cercle d'ouvriers dit "Cercle Franklin du Havre"', *Nouvelles Annales de la construction*, p.147.
1879 121. 'Arbeiterhäuser in Dänemark', *Baugewerks Zeitung*, pp.3 and 16 (12 engravings).
122. Schwering, K., 'Arbeiter Colonie des Werkstättenbahnhofes in Leinhausen', *Zeitschrift des Architkten und Ingr. Vereins Hannover*, p.23 (pl. 767).
123. Cacheux and Brulé, 'Habitations ouvrières à Paris', *Nouvelles Annales de la construction*, p.133 (pl. 38).
124. Varinet, M., 'Type des maisons ouvrières de Gaulier, près Sedan', *Nouvelles Annales de la construction*, p. 6 (pl. 4).
125. 'Separate dwellings. Lodgings for artisans and labourers', *The Builder*, p.405 (plates).
126. 'Selection of Building Cities', *American Architect*, Vol. 7, p.214.
1880 127. 'Arbeiterwohnungen nach dem Cottage System', *Deutsche Bauzeitung*, pp.388, 428, 450.
128. Lavy, E., 'Cité ouvrière d'Epernay', *Nouv. Annales de Construction*, p.34 (pl. 11).
129. Cacheux, E., *l'Architecte*, Sixth Year, Nos. 49-52.
130. Cacheux, E., *Rapport fait à la Société internationale des études pratiques d'économie sociale, sur la question des habitations ouvrières. Discussion à laquelle ont pris part MM. Delaire, A. Burat, M. Gaussen, C. Lavollée, E. Cheyson. Bulletin de la Société d'Economie Sociale*, Vol. VII.
131. Cacheux, E., *Rapport à la Société des Ingénieurs Civils sur les habitations ouvrières exposées en 1878. Brochure avec plans*, Paris, 1880.
132. Publications of the Birkbeck Building Society. Offices: Southampton Buildings, Chancery Lane, London.
133. Cacheux, E., *Rapport sur les habitations ouvrières construites boulevard Murat, à Paris, fait au Congrès de l'association française pour l'avancement des sciences, tenu à Reims. Discussion à laquelle ont pris part MM. Le Carpentier, Yves Guyot, Félix Prunoy.*
1881 134. 'Sur les habitations ouvrières', *Economiste français*, 24 August 1881.
135. 'Arbeiterwohnungen', *Wochenblatt für Arch. und Ing.*, Berlin, p.75.
136. 'Entwürfe prämirter Arbeiterhäuser', *Rombergs Zeitschrift*, p.336 (pl. 33).
137. Hoole, E., 'South Lambeth dwellings, Lambeth Road', *The Builder*, p.572 (2 plates).
138. 'Arbeiterwohnhaus in St-Petersburg', *Wochenblatt für Arch. und Ing.*, Berlin, p.469.
139. *Economiste français*, 27 August. 'Rapport à l'Assemblée générale des actionnaires de la Société anonyme des habitations ouvrières de Passy-Auteuil'.
1882 140. Tidy, W. 'The dwellings of the poor', *The illustrated Carpenter and Builder*, Vol. 11, p.278.
141. Tidy, W., *Sanitary Engineering*, Vol. VII, p.133.
142. 'Les habitations ouvrières', *Société d'encouragement*, Vol. 81, p.481.
143. 'Les habitations ouvrières à Paris', *Moniteur industriel* (Belgian), Vol. 9, p.272.
144. 'Double cottage', *The Manufacturer and Builder*, Vol. 14, p.213.
145. 'Prize labourers' cottages', *The illustrated Carpenter and Builder*, Vol. 10, p.386.
146. 'Specification of cottages', *Builder and Woodworker*, Vol. 18, p.121.
147. 'Artisans' and labourers' dwellings', *Carpenter and Builder*, Vol. 11, pp.2 and 49.

148. 'Cottages Mutual Improvement Society', *Builder and Woodworker*, Vol. 18, p.42.

149. Société anonyme des habitations ouvrières de Passy-Auteuil. *Rapport du jury chargé de juger le concours pour l'adoption du meilleur type d'habitations ouvrières. Brochure avec plans,* Paris, 1882.

1883 150. Dyson, J., 'Separate dwellings for small families', *The Building News*, p.338.

151. Ongh, H., 'Artisans cottages', *The Building News*, p.357.

152. 'Labourers dwellings', *Scientific American Supplement*, pp.6617.

153. Commission administrative chargée de l'étude des questions relatives à la création des logements à bon marché pour la population ouvrière de Paris. *Brochure contenant: 1° les rapports de M. le Directeur des travaux de Paris, de M. Bartet, ingénieur en chef; — 2° les arrêtés préfectoraux instituant la commission et nommant les membres; — 3° les propositions et pétitions adressées au conseil. — Institution de la Commission: Rapport de M. Directeur des Travaux de Paris: Rapport de M. l'Ingénieur en chef Bartet; Arrêté préfectoral instituant la Commission (29 janvier 1883); Arrêté préfectoral nommant deux nouveaux membres (19 février 1883); Propositions et pétitions adressées au Conseil municipal et à l'Administration.*

154. Manier, M., *Expropriation au profit de la ville de Paris du sol compris dans l'enceinte fortifiée, en indemnisant les propriétaires au moyen d'obligations communales hypothécaires amortissables,* Paris, 1883.

155. Républicains communalistes du XIVe arrondissement. *Pétition demandant la mise à l'ordre du jour de la proposition précédente.*

156. Fiaux, E., *Construction par la ville de Paris de maisons sur les terrains de la zone militaire y compris les fortifications de l'enceinte continue, qui seraient démolies.*

157. Decamp, M., *Démolition de l'enceinte fortifiée et création d'un boulevard circulaire sur son emplacement.*

158. Plainchamp, C., *Remplacement du mur d'enceinte de Paris par une nouvelle limite plus étendue, création d'une nouvelle ligne de boulevards extérieurs, et vente des terrains avec obligation de ne construire que des maisons d'un modèle déterminé et, au besoin, fixation d'un maximum des loyers par étage et par quartier. Etablissement d'un chemin de fer métropolitain.*

159. Le Rouge, E., *Construction, par la Ville, de maisons de trois étages, sur les terrains qui longent les fortifications ,,intramuros'', au moyen des ressources provenant: 1° d'un emprunt de 300 Millions: — 2° d'un impôt de 2 francs par tête sur toute personne qui vient à Paris d'une distance de plus de 25 kilomètres.*

160. Caisse Centrale Populaire. *Note remise à la Commission administrative des logements à bon marché pour développer la proposition de se charger de la construction d'habitations ouvrières valant cent cinquante millions de francs.*

161. Villard, J. *Rapport présenté au Conseil municipal de Paris sur: 1° une proposition de M. Manier tendant à l'expropriation au profit de la ville de Paris du sol compris dans son enceinte fortifiée; — 2° diverses pétitions relatives aux mesures à prendre pour arriver à l'abaissement du prix des loyers.*

162. Cabourneau, E. *Brochure avec plans développant une proposition de construire des maisons à petits logements sur 760000 mètres de terrain situé dans Paris.*

163. Amouroux, J. *Rapport annexé au procès-verbal de la séance du 13 décembre sur diverses propositions relatives à la construction des logements à bon marché faites par M. E. Hamel: MM. Vauthier et Ball; M. Manier; M. Cattiaux; la Caisse Centrale populaire; M. Le Rouge; M. Minder; M. Terrier; M. Harouard; M. Yverneau; M. Joly; M. Cabourneau; MM. Rolland et Plaisant; M. Dodel; M. Cheon; M. Potier, etc.*

164. Commission administrative des logements à bon marché: *Mémoire de M. le Préfet de la Seine au Conseil municipal contenant: Project de convention entre la Ville de Paris et le Crédit Foncier de France; le projet de loi approuvant cette convention et le rapport présenté au Conseil municipal par M. Gamard sur le projet de la convention à intervenir entre l'Etat et le Crédit Foncier. — Procès-verbaux des séances de la Commission administrative 24-27-31 mars et 3 avril 1883.*

165. 'Arbeiterwohnungen in England, Frankreich und Deutschland', *Gesundheit*, Vol. 8, p.9.

166. Balmer, P., 'Gesunde und billige Wohnungen für Arbeiter', *Baugewerksblatt*, Vol. 2, p.358.
167. Gosselin, E., 'Les habitations économiques', *Bulletin de la Société industrielle de Rouen*, Vol. 10, p.480.
168. 'Labourers' and artisans' dwellings', *Carpenter*, Vol. 13, p.290.
169. Sevin and Lattner, 'Wohnhäuser für je eine Arbeiterfamilie', *Baugewerksblatt*, Vol. 2, p.17.
170. 'Arbeiterwohnhäuser', *Wochenblatt für Architekt und Ingenieur*, Vol. 5, p.458.
171. 'Dwellings for the poor in large cities', *Plumber and Sanitary Engineering*, Vol. 8, p.583.
172. 'Artisans' dwellings', *Carpenter*, Vol. 13, p.355.
173. 'Habitations ouvrières à La Roche', *Annales industrielles*, Vol. 15, p.500.
174. 'Artisan dwellings, Whitechapel', *The Builder*, Vol. 45, p.516.
175. 'Logements ouvriers, Plymouth', *Semaine des constructeurs*, Vol. 8, p.148.
176. 'Artisans estates, Hornsey', *The Builder*, Vol. 47, p.880.
177. 'Americanische Arbeiterwohnungen', *Baugew. Zeit.*, Vol. 15, p.156.
178. 'Arbeiterwohnhaus', *Baugewerks Zeitung*, Vol. 15, p.401.
179. 'Maison pour cité ouvrière', *Annales industrielles*, Vol. 15, pp.2, 437.
180. 'Arbeiterhäuser des Bochumer Vereins', *Ann. für Gew. und Bauwesen.*, Vol. 12, p.241.
181. 'Dwellings for the working classes', *The Builder*, Vol. 44, p.616.
182. Reygeal, F., *Rapport présenté au Conseil municipal de Paris, au nom de la commission des logements à bon marché, sur diverses propositions relatives à la construction de petites maisons.*
183. *Bulletin municipal officiel de la ville de Paris.* Discussion de la convention relative à la construction de petits logements, à intervenir entre la ville et le Crédit Foncier. Séances des 14 et 20 juin.
184. Conseil municipal de Paris. *Propositions de MM. Gamard et Réty au sujet de l'établissement de logements à bon marché*, 16 April 1883.
1884 185. 'Arbeiterwohnungen', *Gesundheit*, Vol. 9, pp.276, 337, 356.
186. Les logements insalubres et les logements à bon marché', *Semaine des constructeurs*, Vol. 8, p.328.
187. Botrel, E., 'Habitations ouvrières', *Bulletin de la Société industrielle de Rouen*, Vol. 12, p.675.
188. Napias, C., 'Les habitations ouvrières', *Annales industrielles*, Vol. 16, p.651.
189. Reed, J., 'Dwelling for 1,500 dollars', *American Agriculture*, Vol. 43, p.357.
190. The Improved Dwellings Company Limited. *Special report of the directors upon the work accomplished during twenty one years.*
191. 'Gesetze für Arbeiterwohnungen in England', *Gesundheit*, Vol. 9, pp.309, 324.
192. Schwering, W., 'Arbeiter Colonie Leinhausen bei Hannover', *Zeitschrift des Architecten und Ingenieur-Vereins Hannover*, Vol. 30, p.556.
193. 'Arbeiterwohnhäuser', *Deutsches Baugewerks Bl.*, Vol. 3, p.773.
194. 'Artisans' and labourers' dwellings', *The Builder*, Vol. 46, pp.192, 249.
195. 'Les logements à bon marché', *Gazette des architectes*, Vol. 20, p.241.
196. Hoole, E., 'Dwellings of the poor in large towns', *Journal of Arts*, Vol. 32, p.1023.
197. Tischler, W., 'Doppelwohngebäude auf den Stadterweiterungsgrunden Wien', *Försters Bauzeitung*, Vol. 49, p.103.
198. 'Artisan's dwellings Birmingham', *The Illustrated Carpenter and Builder*, Vol. 14, pp.145, 193.
199. 'Dwellings of the poor', *Sanitary Engineering*, Vol. 8, p.385.
200. 'The housing of the poor', *The Builder*, Vol. 46, p.735.
201. 'Suburban cottages', *Builder and Woodworker*, Vol. 20, pp.84, 93.
202. 'Chalets doubles Felixstow', *Gazettes des architectes*, Vol. 20, p.305.
203. 'Maison de garde', *Gazette des architectes*, Vol. 20, p.77.
204. Conseil municipal de Paris. *Rapport présenté par M. Cernesson au nom de la commission spéciale des logements à bon marché, sur des propositions tendant à la construction directe par la ville.*
205. 'Health in the dwelling. Dwellings for the poor'. Sanitary construction of houses. Promotion of social science, 1884. *Conférences faites à l'exposition d'hygiène de Londres.*
1885 206. Masson, L. and Martin, Dr. A.-J., *Les maisons salubres et insalubres a l'Exposition internationale d'hygiène de Londres.* Paris, 1885.

207. Schloss, E., *The homes of the poor*, London, 1885.
208. The Royal Commission of the Housing of the Working Classes. Four large volumes containing the evidence of persons called before the Commission of Inquiry, and the complete transcript of the evidence, London, 1885.
209. Conseil municipal de Paris. *Rapport présenté par M. Dreyfus au nom de la Commission des logements à bon marché sur un projet de construction de quatre maisons types renfermant des logements à bon marché.*
210. Cacheux, Emile, *Etat en l'an 1885 des habitations ouvrières parisiennes.*
211. Bureau de bienfaisance de Nivelles. *Moyen pratique de faciliter aux classes laborieuses l'accès du capital et de la propriété*, Nivelles, 1885.
212. Wolff, M. P., *Die Ernährung der arbeitenden Klassen. Ein Plan für Gründung öffentlicher Küchen, von M.P.W. kgl. preus. Hauptmann. Aus dem Deutschen vom verfasser bearbeitete Ausgabe. Mit einer Vorrede von Prof. Dr J. König, in Minster i. W., und einem Plan*, Berlin 1885.
1886 213. 'L'enquête sur la condition des petits logements en France et à l'étranger', *Union économique*, April and May 1886.
214. *Annuaire de législation étrangère publié par la Société de législation comparée*, A. Cotillon et Cie, rue Soufflot, Paris.
215. Westgarth prize essays on the street realignment reconstruction and sanitation of central London and of the rehousing of the poorer classes 1886.
216. Mansion House Council on the Dwellings of the people, *Report 1885–1886*, London.
217. *Die Wohnungsnoth der ärmeren Klassen in den deutschen Gross-städten.* Two volumes published by the *Verein für Social Politik* dealing with Hamburg, Frankfurt, Strasbourg, Bochum, Chemnitz, Osnabrück, Krefeld, Dortmund, Essen, Berlin, Elberfeld, Breslau, Leipzig, London, Paris, and France. Leipzig, 1886.
218. *Verhandlungen der Generalversammlung des Vereins für Social Politik 24–25 September*, Leipzig, 1886.
1887 219. Wiss, E., 'La disette de logements pour les classes pauvres de la population dans les grandes villes', *Vierteljahrsschrift für Volksw.*, No. 1.
220. Monmartin, E., 'Les logements à bon marché', *Soleil*, Supplement of 6 October 1887.
221. Cheysson, E., *La question des habitations ouvrières en France et à l'étranger. La situation actuelle. Ses dangers. Ses remèdes. Conference faite à l'exposition d'hygiène de la caserne Lobau*, Paris, 1887.
222. Delaire, A., 'Les logements d'ouvriers et le devoir des classes dirigeantes', *Contemporain*, Lyon, 1887.
223. Engels, F., *Zur Wohnungsfrage*, Social demokratische Bibliothek., Zürich, 1887.
224. Volumes of the senatorial inquiry in America dealing with the relationships between capital and labour. *Foreign office report*, No. 43.
225. *Building Association and Home Journal*, 529, Commerce Street, Philadelphia.
226. Conseil supérieur d'hygiène publique (Belgium). *Enquête sur les habitations ouvrières*, Brussels, 1887.
227. *Zeitschrift des öst. Ingenieur und Architektenvereines*, Nos. 42 and 43. *Die Arbeiterwohnhäuser und Bezirke (Favoriten) in Wien*, Vienna, 1887.
228. Conseils d'hygiène et Commissions des logements insalubres. *Rapports sur leurs travaux*, Paris, 1887.
229. Meissner, Aloïs, Extrait du *Bulletin de la Société des Ingénieurs et Architectes Hongrois*, Budapest, 1887.
230. Rémaury, L., *Articles sur les habitations Ouvrières Publiés dans le Génie Civil*, Paris, 1887.
1888 231. Régis Faure, *De habitations ouvrières et d'un devoir social*, Clermont-Ferrand, 1888.
232. Cacheux, Emile, 'Une cité sanitaire modèle', *Bulletin de la Société de Médecine publique.*

INDEX

by *Helen Baz*

Note: numbers in italics refer to Text figures

LIST OF SUBSCRIBERS

Elizabeth Ahern
James Annandale
Architectural Association Library
John Ashdown
Dr. Eileen E. Blackstock
John Blackstock
Brian Blackwood, FRIBA, FRTPI,
	FSA Scot
Dr T. S. Brindley
Peter A. T. Burman
L. D. Butler
Dr. Jur Otto C. Carlsson
Canon Clifford Carver
Howard Colvin
Hazel Conway
Brian Cook
Mrs. E. M. Cuningham
Hubert J. C. Cuningham
John McK. Curl
Mrs. Sarah Curl
Rev. Geoffrey Curtis
Miss H. Drew
Rt. Hon. The Lord Dunleath, TD,
	DL
Edinburgh University Library
G. D. C. and M. C. Evans
Miss K. E. Fraser
Ian Clifford Frerichs
David Gibson
Andor Gomme
Lord Greenwood of Rossendale

R. H. Hayward
Hermione Hobhouse
Hans Juergen Hollerbaum
Donald W. Insall & Associates
Institute of Advanced Architectu-
	ral Studies, University of York
The Irish Architectural Archive
Professor R. Ian Jack
Penelope Jessel
Pamela Pomerance Johnson
Stephan Jonas
John Radcliffe Jones
Juliet Jones
Kenneth Kettle
Pat Kirkham
H. R. C. Leadbetter
Gilbert Lewis
E. G. M. Leycester-Roxby
Helen I. Logan
R. C. Lowe
L. H. H. Luithlen
R. C. McKinney
Roland McKinney
Robert McKinstry
Graham McNicol
Noel Mander MBE, FSA
Stephen Marks, FSA
Irene Matthews
Geoffrey Middleton
Dr. Mervyn Miller
Michael Morris

Stefan Muthesius
Northern Ireland Housing
	Executive Library
Richard W. Patterson
John Physick, FSA
Grant Pitches
Dolly Potter
Hermione Preedy
Hans Reye
W. N. B. Richardson
Rowan P. M. Roenisch
John Sambrook
Harold Sanders
Prof. M. Shinomiya
Dr. C. R. Sladden
Alan Spencer
Gavin Stamp
J. J. Stanton
Mary B. W. Stewart
Tower Hamlets Library
Mr. & Mrs. G. L' E. Turner
University of Keele
The University of London Library
Merlin Unwin
Mrs. A. Vigar
Mrs. P. G. Walker
Prof. Chas. R. Whitfield
Walter Wiemer
Peter Willis
Mr. and Mrs. Hal Wilson
B. Zumthor